NO ONE'S SON

TEWODROS FEKADU

Leapfrog Press
Fredonia, NY

Published in 2012 in the United States by
Leapfrog Press LLC
PO Box 505
Fredonia, NY 14063
www.leapfrogpress.com

Distributed in the United States by
Consortium Book Sales and Distribution
St. Paul, Minnesota 55114
www.cbsd.com

First Edition

Library of Congress Cataloging-in-Publication Data

Fekadu, Tewodros.
  No one's son / Tewodros Fekadu. – 1st ed.
    p. cm. – (A leapsci book leapfrog science and history)
  Includes bibliographical references.
  ISBN 978-1-935248-26-2 (alk. paper)
  1. Fekadu, Tewodros. 2. Eritrean-Ethiopian War, 1998—Refugees–
Biography. 3. Refugees–Ethiopia–Biography. 4. Refugees–Australia–
Biography. 5. Ethiopia–Biography. 6. Australia–Biography. I. Title.
  DT388.35.F45 2012
  963.507'2–dc23
  [B]

                          2012004956

Printed in the United States of America

To Anita,

If love is a miracle
then you are mine.

Author's Note

There is no universally recognised system for transliterating Ethiopian and Eritrean languages into the English alphabet. I have chosen forms which are simple and familiar in current usage and which approximate local pronunciation. The glossary includes terms in Amharic, Tigrinya and other language references in the book.

Some names have been changed in the interests of certain people, but all events and circumstances have been adequately researched. The appendix includes a comprehensive list of prominent people and their relationships to me.

Contents

Book One: The Quest

Book Two: Far Horizons

FOREWORD

I was born into an Australia obscenely proud of its imposed, fully imported monoculturism. The indigenous population had suffered killings, exploitation, assimilation and sundry forms of paternalism and were, in 1939, being largely ignored. This deadly combination of practice and policy meant that few white kids like myself had ever met an Aborigine. For us, black Australians seemed as fanciful and fictitious as bunyips. And the White Australia policy—a sort of tariff barrier against human beings—was there to protect us from the African, the Chinese, the Japanese, and the Indian. Our Christian country also walled out anyone from Jesus' Middle East. We would not welcome Jews, Muslims, Hindus, or other pagan faiths. Protestant Australia wasn't very happy with its Irish Catholics.

In the playground at East Kew State, post-war refugees were disparaged as "reffos" and on the receiving end of chants to "go back to your own country."

And sixty-five years later, decades after the embarrassed dismantling of the White Australia policy, the same chants can be heard again. No need for a Pauline Hanson or One Nation. The prejudice, justified by "national security" (as was White Australia), comes loud and clear from pundits, shock jocks and conservative politicians in mainstream parties—in venomous response to a few hundred sad, desperate people coming over the horizon in battered boats.

Even so, the claim is made for a transcendent form of tolerance as Australia's defining attribute. And we had, for a while, celebrated cultural diversity—provided it didn't challenge the comfort zone of what one immigration minister called "the core culture."

Were I religiously inclined, I'd go down on my knees to thank the Gods (all of them) for the racial mixture I was persuaded to deplore as a child. This country, which had done its ethnic cleansing in advance, was enriched beyond measure—culturally as well as economically—by the millions of refugees who arrived here after World War II. A society that remained claustrophobic for generations—an amazing achievement, given the vastness of its real estate—came alive. We achieved a rare degree of ethnic and religious complexity without much "blood on the wattle."

And for me, one of the great examples of the gift of the refugee came when I met Tewodros Fekadu in Brisbane a few years back—during the previous battle with the demons of White Australian bigotry surrounding Tampa, Siev X and the "Pacific Solution." We spoke briefly of his story—clearly one of epic dimensions—and Teddy told me he was writing a biography about his life of exclusion, rejection and war. I murmured some encouragement but didn't expect to hear from him again. And if a manuscript did arrive in the letterbox it seemed unreasonable to expect a major achievement.

Yet No One's Son is exactly that. As fine a piece of writing as you're likely to read from any Australian author, it comes from the sort of person Australia has spent much of its history trying to exclude. I must be careful not to lapse into the sort of inspirational jargon that tends to accompany stories like Teddy's—Oprah Winfry-ish references to human suffering, personal triumph, the sort of words about struggle, survival and the power of love that cover the covers of inspirational bestsellers—but this is one book for which such clichés are not only appropriate, but essential.

Teddy's young life spans continents, cultures, ancient and urgent conflicts. We are doubly fortunate that he has the gifts to describe them so vividly—and that this remarkable man has chosen a somewhat reluctant Australia to be his refuge. We need to welcome refugees like Tewodros Fekadu. Not just to help them, but to help us.

Phillip Adams is a notably awarded and prolific broadcaster, writer and filmmaker. He also has many board memberships connected with the arts, film, university, the environment, and special interests.

Map of Ethiopia & Eritrea

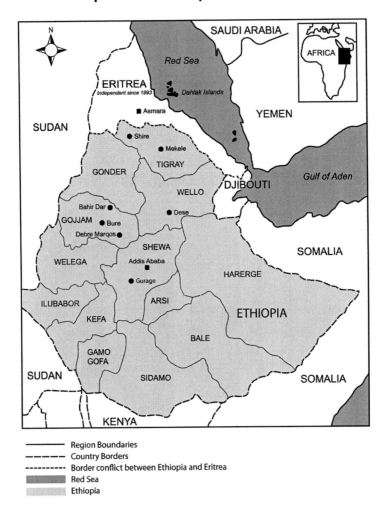

At the time of writing, tensions between Ethiopia and Eritrea had eased slightly. However, the border remains closed and there is no way to travel directly between the two countries (including air travel). There is also a 25km deep demilitarised zone which runs the entire length of the internationally recognised border between the two countries. The border is yet to be officially demarcated.

The Fekadu Family Tree

Father's side   Mother's Side

Reda - m - Melesu   Gezahegne - m - Zenebech

(my great-grandfather
was killed fighting for
the Italians during the
Tripoli war)

(my great-grandmother,
Ge-ge)

5 children   5 children

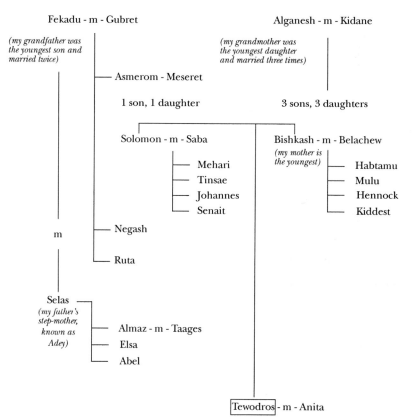

Fekadu - m - Gubret   Alganesh - m - Kidane

(my grandfather was
the youngest son and
married twice)

(my grandmother was
the youngest daughter
and married three times)

— Asmerom - Meseret

1 son, 1 daughter   3 sons, 3 daughters

— Solomon - m - Saba   Bishkash - m - Belachew

(my mother is
the youngest)

— Mehari   — Habtamu
— Tinsae   — Mulu
— Johannes   — Hennock
— Senait   — Kiddest

m   — Negash

— Ruta

Selas —
(my father's
step-mother,
known as
Adey)

— Almaz - m - Taages
— Elsa
— Abel

Tewodros - m - Anita

m = married

INTRODUCTION

Death feared him for he had the heart of a lion.[1]

When someone mentions Africa, people of the Western world tend to think of a homogenous land, people and culture that are distant from their own in so many ways. Typically coming to the fore are iconic images of drums, famine, troubled politics, or the lions of the Serengeti plains.

The heart of Africa is so much more.

The many nations that make up its core and history have their own diverse heritage, which was thriving long before the Australian continent became the treasure that colonial empires desired.

My Africa is Ethiopia. This land has gained renown as the birthplace of the human race. Elevated on the Horn of Africa, Ethiopia claims a noble lineage going all the way back to the Queen of Sheba and King Solomon. Smaller nations on every side have frequently aspired to partake of its greatness. And in their turn, superpowers undermined its stability to serve their own remote needs.

I entered a tumultuous world where nobility, pride and beliefs

---

1. Arabian proverb.

were thrown into chaos. The family became the only safe haven, yet this too could be torn apart by the terrors of war.

I come from the streets: from rejection, violence and betrayal. Denied the refuge of family, I struggled like a lion in the wilderness. I sought freedom abroad, in Egypt and Japan, only to be imprisoned by bureaucracy. In a practical sense, the triumph of surviving all this is in coming to Australia. The real triumph is in not becoming bitter or corrupt, but emerging still in love with life.

At times, I have been the voice of change for those whose humanity has been crushed. The need to belong, to survive, to be free—all drove me beyond hardship to seek the life of my dreams. I rejoice in celebrating my culture. I empathise with all who have suffered loss, wherever they may be. Yet it is my African heart, this heart of a lion, that brought me to the true freedom of love.

Through these pages, as you walk with me on my journey, I invite you to discover yourself through your own dreams. Seek them. Embrace them. Live them. In knowing ourselves, we can give to others. In giving to others, we make the world a better place.

Follow your heart. May you have the courage of a lion all your days.

BOOK ONE

THE QUEST

*It seemed there were angels and devils everywhere.
I wondered on which side I would finally land.*

1

WHAT'S IN A NAME?

My Africa has stretched my heart in all ways but one. And that one needed a miracle, which was a long time in coming.

Would a child of the devil have coped better with the life I'd been dealt? Some named me Satan's child. Others told me that life's challenges are determined by God's will. If there are gods of irony, they must have been greatly entertained by the mad twists of fate I've endured.

This is not a romantic tale, yet here is romance. This is not a heroic saga, but within these pages is the heroism of human spirit. Through fragility and defiance, from despair to laughter, it is not so much about me as about the universal quest for truth, for freedom and for love.

Like all good stories, mine begins in a distant, exotic land. . . .

The rainy season had transformed the otherwise barren landscape into lush colour. A muddy trail led from the main road and forged the arduous slippery climb up to the shadow of the mountain, in the highlands of Eritrea. I wrestled the jeep through the grime, occasionally catching on the black rock beneath.

Small stone huts hugged the incline. Faces peeped shyly from the doorways, as these dignified reclusive people wondered over the stranger entering their land.

After parking, I gathered the camera equipment necessary for my interviews. The village children giggled coyly from a distance, then cheekily shuffled each other forward to dare ask who I was. Their curiosity quickly overcame all else and, after checking me over, they all wanted to welcome me—into this home, and this, and this.

I had travelled halfway around the world to return to the place of my birth. I was hoping to clarify the secrets that cloaked my early years. Trekking far up into this remote region, I sought out the only remaining relatives who could offer some clues to what had eluded me for so long.

An old man emerged from his home, with his family clustering respectfully behind him. His movements were sparing, though not weak. Here was a strange blend of pride and humility that came from knowing he was part of the land and that the land was part of his people. He greeted me with the traditional kisses on each cheek. "At last, Tewodros, you have come," he said.

Even though I'd grown up here, I now sought to make my peace with a culture for which religion, tradition and superstition are the mainstays of society. Encompassing these is the strongest of all: family. Anything falling outside these firm parameters is condemned.

Family is everything. It gives you identity. Your father's name is the invaluable link to your quality of life because people connect with you and judge you on your lineage.

Naming traditions are very particular, since all one's connections are revealed and judged from the initial introduction. There are no surnames. The child is given a proper name (often representing a beneficial quality or, as in my case, a great leader). This is followed by the father's first name and then *his* father's, to complete the title. So, my full name is Tewodros (after an emperor) Solomon (my father's first name) Fekadu (his father's first name).

To lose your name is to die forever. Yet even death is preferable to being cast out. As an outcast, I knew that first hand.

As an illegitimate child, I was no one's son. My father would not shelter me nor give me his name. I needed to understand why, so I must look to *his* father and his father's father in trying to find the heart of the man I had feared but never really known.

I held the sword in my hands. The old man had passed it to me reverently, carefully, almost reluctantly. Since it was handed down to the eldest in each generation, he was its current guardian.

It was a sword of war. The rust marks along its surface mirrored the blood it must have spilt long ago. But it no longer represented death. It was a symbol of loyalty and family pride.

Under the Italian regime on the Horn of Africa during WWI, my great grandfather, Reda Woldegergish, had been conscripted into the army. Equipped with this sword and a knife (which has also been passed down), he had to march away from his homeland, wife and children.

Reda was killed on a Libyan battlefield. He died because of politics, but he fought because of honour.

I was born into a world of war; not the same war that killed Reda, but Africa's longest civil war.[1] I arrived in the midst of the Eritreans' quest for independence from Ethiopia. Their fierce commitment to this goal precipitated a devastating violence that spanned three decades. With an Eritrean father and an Ethiopian mother, my butt cheeks were firmly planted on either side of the border. War would snatch at me wherever I ventured in this land. For my whole life, I strove to escape—and finally succeeded. Miracles do happen.

---

1. Eritrean War of Independence, 1961–1991.

Looking at the blade's jaded surface, I saw not a weapon but a sword of truth. Perhaps this symbol of honour that drew our family together could cut through the swathe of past confusion and finally help me to forgive the ravager of my mother's youth, the thief of *my* honour, the traitor of all that his grandfather had so valiantly died for.

The metal felt warm. Was I getting closer to the answers?

The old man, the sword-bearer, was Reda's eldest son. Seeing my awed expression, he grew excited to share more about his ancestry. Mine, too. He turned and called into the house. There was much scraping and shuffling and, finally, a large, worn, crudely fashioned chair made by Reda's own strong hands was delivered from the dark interior. It was handled with such care that one might think it was the Ark of the Covenant.

If the strength of a man is in what he makes then here was the evidence. Sturdy legs held firm on the hard barren ground, and the armrests spread wide to support the chair's occupant in the seat of woven skin. With the glint of an emperor in his eyes, the old man sat, as only he had the right to do. Then the stories began to pour out.

His words were seeds that sprouted new family roots in my heart. He could have given me no greater gift.

Great-grandfather Reda became a deacon with the Orthodox Church and was known for his beautiful chanting voice. Even though he sang like an angel, he was also immensely strong. He was a man of the people, his feet firmly planted in the earth he ploughed, his principles as straight as the sword in my hands. It is said the ground crunched under him as he walked, signalling to everyone: *He's coming!*

Folk tell me that Reda often disagreed with the local judge. If my experience with village politics is anything to go by, corruption probably paved the way to the courthouse. I'm proud to think that Reda was a noble man, standing up against such things. In fact,

What's in a Name?

Reda was the descendent of Ras Meron, a noble from the region of Gondar. (*Ras* means duke.)

Long before Reda, another of the duke's descendents, Ras Tesfasion, broke with tradition surrounding inheritance. In those grand bygone days, the eldest son inherited everything material, including land. The other family members inherited blessings—as powerful in their hearts and minds as any possession.

Tesfasion observed the constant civil unrest in Ethiopia (which included Eritrea at the time). Instead of giving his possessions to one son and blessings to the rest of his children, he divided his lands and blessings equally among his progeny, hoping this would keep his children loyal to each other.

But even the best-intended plans can be torn asunder by the many-headed beast of politics. Alliances shifted. The land was lost. And the family fled as villages burned behind them. It wasn't until generations later when Reda's son Fekadu reclaimed the land that we were able to recover our heritage in more than name only.

But I go too quickly. If the pieces are to make sense, I must look at each in its turn.

Although strong and noble, great-grandfather Reda was not powerful enough to resist conscription under colonial rule. He was not alone. He and his friends marched together as men of principle who would not shirk their responsibility, even a forced one.

So, on foreign soil, Reda held the rear guard, defending the line while his friends retreated. It seemed that all of the enemy lay dead but, as Reda made his way back, one of the Libyan soldiers sat up and shot him from behind. A friend who witnessed his death retrieved his body and chanted a poem for Reda's spirit and bravery, singing his name to the heavens. This friend returned to Reda's pregnant wife and four children, giving them the gifts of Reda's sword and knife.

Not long after Reda's death, his fifth child was born: my grandfather, Fekadu. His name means "God's permission." Like me, he would grow up fatherless, but he would be inspired by stories of his father's greatness. I'm sure this made fatherhood all the more important to him when he finally had his own family.

While his siblings remained farmers, Fekadu joined the police force in Eritrea, by then under British military administration. During the year, he and his wife, Gubret, and their expanding family lived in the police camp on the outskirts of Asmara, Eritrea's capital city. They also owned arable land in the countryside and, every summer, they joined the farmers who leased it to help harvest the crops.

The income from farming complemented Fekadu's government subsidies and food rations. He and Gubret sacrificed much and invested everything to secure a better future for their children.

Fekadu was a strict, yet devoted, father. He loved having the children around him. If he returned late from work, he would wake them to sit with him while he ate his supper. He escorted them to and from school every day and watched over them as they did their homework every night. He believed that education was the only means of improving one's standard of living and enlarging one's horizons.

According to the family, he used to say, "I don't want my children to be like me." I suppose he meant that he didn't want them to be poor or to struggle through life.

When his children were still young, Fekadu was rewarded for his police work with a parcel of land in upper Asmara. There, he built a house and was finally able to move his family out of the police camp.

Longing to regain his true roots, he also strove to reclaim Ras Tesfasion's property in the Eritrean highlands. Though the age of dukes had passed (for us), Fekadu took possession of some of that long-lost land.

There, he built a house which still stands today, although sadly it is neglected. He intended that none of the family would ever feel displaced or homeless again.

At that time, Fekadu had four children: three boys and a girl. They all grew up in Asmara, attending school there until the completion of Year Twelve. At that time, university education was only available in Ethiopia. So eventually they had to relocate to pursue their career studies.

Asmerom, the eldest, became a doctor specialising in tropical diseases. The next son, Negash, excelled at school. Consequently, he was sequestered into the Haile Selassie Military Academy. After some years, he was awarded a scholarship and went to Germany to study engineering. My father, Solomon, was the second youngest, born in 1946. He, too, became a doctor—a brilliant doctor, I'm told. After gaining experience in various positions around the countryside, he was promoted to lecture in anatomy at the Addis Ababa University. He also partnered in running a private clinic. The girl, Ruta, remained in Eritrea and became a nurse.

What a great legacy they gained from a man who started with nothing. If only it had extended to me.

But in those early years, Fekadu's dedication could not ward off tragedy. Gubret passed away when the children were still quite young. I wonder if that was the first deep wound that changed my father (only eight years old at the time) into a man who needed to strike out at life.

Fekadu was challenged to raise the four children alone. Relatives arranged a marriage as a well-intended solution. His young bride, Selas, had to step into his world and his ways, but I understand that she loved him dearly and, out of principle if nothing else, I'm sure he was dedicated to her as part of his family. She bore him three more children: two girls and a boy. This was not an unusually large family, but I imagine it was hard on motherless Solomon, who now had to grow up quickly with the arrival of younger siblings.

This gave me another clue to understanding him. I desperately needed to qualify his brutal treatment of me, but then—maybe he was just a bastard, after all.

Through Fekadu's efforts, Selas's three children also had successful lives. The eldest girl, Almaz, went into banking and still lives in Asmara. Her sister, Elsa, married and moved to America, as did Abel, the youngest son.

One of my ambitions on this return journey was to consolidate a positive adult relationship with each member of my African family. My childhood encounters with them had been either brief moments of pity, extended episodes of scorn, or complete denial—all because Solomon would not acknowledge me as his son.

Whether that came from pride or shame, the result was the same.

Fekadu hadn't struggled to educate his children so they would become arrogant; he wanted them to learn, to be inspired so they could make better choices. What would *he* have said or done to set things right? Sadly, I'll never know. He suffered through a long battle with liver disease and passed away, aged only 58, just a few months before I was born. He was completely unaware of my imminent arrival.

His first brood of children were all adults by then, but Selas still had her three living at home, aged 18, 15 and 12. As the eldest, Almaz took it upon herself to run things with the efficiency of a successful banker-in-training.

Perhaps I speak out of turn, but from my experience she saw life as opportunities for profit, rejecting anything that remotely smacked of loss. That included me.

Tidy house, cold heart.

As a child, I might be forgiven for seeing monsters where there were none but, even now as I returned to Eritrea as an adult, I was at the mercy of her domineering ways. She was furious to find that I was writing a book—this book—about my life. She rallied the family to convince me that I must stop. Why? Because it was not honourable! She was confident that she could have me thrown in prison if I didn't comply. No phone call. No lawyer. Just a dark cell, underground and out of sight, somewhere in the countryside. And in Eritrea, such disappearances were frequent enough for me to be afraid.

Her reaction justified my fearful childhood memories of all the mistreatment I'd suffered. As I sat before this "high council" who craved my silence, I knew how urgent it was to speak out. There were truths that needed to be told. Their actions came from fear. Well . . . fear and ego. The only other emotion I know that can cause blind extreme behaviour is love—and there was certainly none of that.

Still, I didn't want to judge or blame them: I wanted to understand them. I had hoped to build a bridge of new connectedness, but if the bridge was cut from the other side, what more could I do?

Reda's sword meant something to them. Fekadu's devotion had improved their quality of life. Surely, my quest for truth was as worthy of respect.

Before this confrontation occurred, I'd already sought out Fekadu's oldest brother and listened to his stories. They *did* fill me with pride. I *do* come from great men. He said Reda was a hero, Fekadu was a champion and now I had returned to be the strong one for the family. "At last," he said, "someone can pass on these stories."

I don't know what he really expected me to do but, if I could, I would free us from the ongoing pain of Solomon's lies.

After our long afternoon, rich with memories and feelings, the old man rose to bid me farewell. And like those fathers of olden days, he gave me his blessing.

I was deeply moved by these people of the highlands who live so simply, yet share everything. Compared to most, they have nothing. Looking back through their lineage, they believe they are connected to good and noble people. This is their strength.

Back in the city at my relative's house, where the family gathered to grill me on my intentions, I woke every morning and looked across the room at a large framed photograph of Solomon. Even though he'd been dead for some years, he was still an imposing figure in their lives.

My confusion over him endured. How could I make sense of it all?

Perhaps it *wasn't* enough to try to find my father through his father. Our proud superstitious tribal natures had been determinedly set long ago, since the days of the most famous Solomon in history. The dynasty of Ethiopia's emperors began with him and so, it seemed, must I.

King Solomon's wisdom was famed even as far south as the realm of Sheba.[2] Curious to meet this wise ruler, Sheba's queen embarked on a diplomatic visit to Israel. Different tales describe her impressive wealth and her own keen mind; and, of course, she is personified as a great beauty.

It is written that she was so enthralled with King Solomon's philosophy that she adopted his religion. Likewise, King Solomon was impressed with her, though he had less spiritual intentions. They satisfied each other intellectually, but physically she still refused him.

On the final night of her visit, the king arranged a lavish banquet and encouraged her to partake of spicy food and energetic dancing. Once more, he propositioned her unsuccessfully. She demanded that he not force her to acquiesce. He agreed on the condition that she took nothing from his palace without his permission.

After much festivity, the queen grew thirsty and reached for some water. Immediately, Solomon claimed his right to her bed, since she had sipped without asking.

Legend insists on their epic love and, like all great fables, this holds naïve appeal. Stripped of its charm, the tale is more sinister: he forced himself upon her, fathering a son who would grow up without him.

2. At that time, Sheba was made up of parts of Yemen, Eritrea and Ethiopia.

What's in a Name?

The Queen of Sheba returned to her kingdom and gave birth near the lands of my ancestors. Her son, Menelik I, was originally named "Son of the Wise"[3] and became the first Jewish emperor of Ethiopia. Reputedly, he returned to Jerusalem as an adult to receive his father's blessing.

King Solomon commissioned a replica of the Ark of the Covenant as a gift for Menelik's accession to Sheba's throne. It is recorded that devious companions swapped the copy for the genuine Ark and brought it to Ethiopia where supposedly it remains to this day, hidden in the ancient town of Aksum.

The Abyssinian Empire grew up around Aksum. Menelik's rule founded the Imperial House of Ethiopia—the Solomonic dynasty—which would rule for almost 3000 years, with few interruptions, until Emperor Haile Selassie was ousted in 1974. Its beginnings are immortalised in the *Kebra Nagast* (*Glory of Kings*)—an ancient tome of historically based stories that continue to inspire the nation.

So, there is the *origin* of our national pride, which continued to swell as the realm prospered. At its height, the empire rivalled those of Rome, China and Persia. New values emerged with the conversion to Christianity in the fourth century. Additional influences came with early Muslims who were fleeing persecution. They sought and received peaceful co-existence among us; a situation unique even today.

Though the empire empowered us, we were still rivalling as strong-minded independent ethnic groups, each loyal to our own. Our identity was further refined by the man who envisioned one nation instead of a land constantly torn among warring tribes. Destined for greatness, Tewodros II[4] fought his way to the throne after being an outcast. When he was still a boy, his wealthy father died not long after divorcing his mother. Ambitious relatives sought to divide the deceased man's fortune among themselves, so they

---

3. Ebna la-Hakim.
4. Crowned in 1855.

13

expelled his son from the family and denied his claims to the inheritance.

Though centuries distanced me from him, such betrayal echoed *my* rejection.

Tewodros II's defiance unified Ethiopia. True to his passionate spirit, he died on his own terms. Under attack from the British army, this fierce emperor took his own life rather than surrender to the enemy. His name has since become synonymous with determined fighters who refuse to yield to the will of others or be defeated on another's terms.

Even as a boy I sought courage in tales of the past. I found remarkable similarities between my life and my namesakes', King Solomon and Tewodros II. But my personal pride was somewhat clouded. The Solomon in my life was not a king, though many considered him a great man. Despite that, he tricked my mother, betraying her innocence, and I too would grow up fatherless.

Everyone expected that with such an impressive name, life would unfold well. Yet my father's name was *my* curse. I was *his* shame.

There was a savage appeal in Tewodros II's defiance that rescued me. Such a quality would endanger my life as often as not. War snapped at my heels as I travelled across the land that he'd conquered. (I'm still amazed that I survived.) Sometimes searching, sometimes chased, I was always yearning for a life of peace.

One of Ethiopia's great writers[5] believed the country's name to mean "Land of Higher Peace." It is a place of profound beauty, diversity and legendary history. In fierce contrast to that, there have been centuries of internal fighting between arrogant warlords, tribal uprisings, as well as long-term impact incurred from foreign invasions. This higher peace comes at great cost, and it is still not fully realised.

---

5. Late Ethiopian scholar and poet laureate, Tsegaye Gebre-Medhin (1936–2006).

What's in a Name?

As the quality of life frays, we hold ever harder to tradition. We hope for relief; we endure darkness for that brighter day; we practise all that gives a sense of comfort or stability—for that might be all we have left.

Despite its staunch safeguards, tradition can be blind. Like a knife, it can unequivocally cut away anything that doesn't conform, not the least a pregnant girl or a fatherless child.

In my early years, I lived on hope: that my Africa would not abandon me; that home would reach out and cradle me. Surely my family would protect me . . . wouldn't they?

Much occurred to wear that hope away and large parts of me with it. Now, all these years later, I was hoping for a benevolent welcome back. Instead, I almost fell victim to Aunt Almaz's malicious plans to cut me down and silence me forever.

I was of this land. It was hard to get to and (evidently) harder to leave. The family's rejection was an even heavier blow, this time. Regret tore through me when I realised that I could never return.

Families: are they blessings or to be cursed? After all, what's in a name if there is no truth in the heart?

Safely back in Australia, I've been carefully putting the pieces of my life together. If the whole is greater than its parts, then I must look at all the parts before I can become whole. It is time to understand my mother, Bishkash, for *a home without a mother is a desert.*[6] And I have been thirsty for so long.

---

6. Eritrean proverb.

2

BISHKASH THE GREAT

Bishkash was beautiful. Her long hair, unusually straight and soft, framed her smoky almond-shaped eyes. Proud cheek bones curved out under two precise perfectly sculpted scars on each temple, the result of an age-old medical practice to prevent eye disease. Unlike other girls her age, she moved with certainty and a deep sense of purpose.

These qualities were seen as assets that could ensure lifelong security for her whole family, who hoped she would draw the attention of an ambitious honourable man, and marry well.

Bishkash lived in the northern highlands of Ethiopia in the village of Slehleka. Here, in the region of Tigray, the ancient Christian kingdom of Aksum had thrived in bygone days. As with a shiny coin that is passed repeatedly between many hands, the radiance of those grand days had worn to a dull glimmer. Greatness was long since a cosy memory: still inspiring from a distance, though untended and overgrown like the crumbling ruins of the past.

The heavy-weight conflicts of the Second World War had settled a decade before. Instead of fighting (in a foreign army), people of this remote mountain region could devote themselves to family, farming and prayer.

In those times, village life was simple. The day's toil provided food. The nights brought safety from the savage wilderness that stretched between the clusters of homes making up the village communities. People assured themselves and each other of the rhythm of life through pious habits and enduring folklore. These covered every known possibility for peace of mind. The rest was in God's hands.

Sometimes, though, no matter how many prayers are said, no matter how many curses are spat out to keep evil at bay, a demon can disguise itself as a blessing and snatch away life's goodness faster than a hyena on the hunt.

But let's linger a moment in better times, before we must face that dark truth.

Bishkash grew up listening to her grandmother, Zenebech, recount endless stories about the privileged lives of her ancestors in Tigray; family lines that could be traced all the way back through the great Solomonic dynasty. For generations, her ancestors had owned vast tracts of land until Emperor Menelik II[1] rose to power.

Menelik was from the southern Amhara tribe, a rival of the northern Tigrayans. He had successfully diminished the power of the Tigrayan elite (including Zenebech's family) by confiscating family-owned land and redistributing it among the State, the Church and tribal leaders.

Zenebech described the further erosion of her family's wealth under subsequent government regimes. Each story reflected her heartache at seeing "mountains and mountains" slip from her family's control.

Diminished landholdings resulted in declining social status for Zenebech's family. To counter this, her father built a church in

---

1. Ruled 1889–1913.

honour of his ancestors. Secluded high in the mountains away from thieves, it was a place of sanctuary for the local villagers (and is still in use today).

This act generated enormous loyalty and respect among the people, especially when he delivered a *tabot*[2] from the region of Gondar, under the close guard of soldiers. His deeds restored dignity to the family despite their dwindling wealth, and Zenebech could still hold her head high as she walked around the village.

After her father's death, Zenebech inherited part of his land. Settling there, she married a baron, raised a family and maintained the privileged habits of her elite status where possible.

When Zenebech was widowed, she moved to a nearby village to be closer to her married daughter, Alganesh, who was struggling financially to raise her children (three boys and three girls). After Alganesh's husband died, the burden became too much, so Zenebech informally adopted 2-year-old Bishkash.

I wandered the streets of my mother's childhood, trying to recapture that cherished beginning. When you are loved, the world seems brighter. Danger is merely bad dreams and superstition. A child's nature is to be curious, not suspicious; to trust, rather than doubt.

People say I have my mother's eyes. Could I see what she had seen? At her age, would I have walked blindly, trustingly, onto the path of treachery?

Zenebech was strict and urged Bishkash to be industrious in her studies. Given the changing times she'd witnessed, this ageing woman realised that education, rather than marriage, was the only way for her granddaughter to escape the shackles of poverty that lay ahead. She expected the girl to be clever and resilient, to be

---

2. A replica of the Ark of the Covenant kept in the inner sanctuary of every Orthodox church.

respectful, obedient and, most importantly, suspicious.

Suspicion is a guard against evil in a slippery world where it is too easy to fall into disgrace: a door should never be opened without first knowing who stands on the other side; a ride should never be accepted from a stranger; one should never venture out after dark—especially if one is a girl. Disaster is always on the prowl and when a girl is not suspicious it strikes her down, bringing disgrace to the entire family.

Chastity was a virtue and a commodity. Virginity was an expectation for marriage. A young woman might be blessed with beauty and bestowed with a willingness to obey. She would celebrate her selection as the bride of someone deemed worthy or successful enough by the family elders. Impurity brought stigma and mortification not only to the girl, but to all her relatives. The man's superior place was rarely questioned; it was always the woman or the Devil (or both) who were to blame.

No one dared to defy this. Any occurrence that fell outside our ways was harshly condemned. Once a person was cursed with rejection, disaster had struck.

Bishkash was a sensible girl and obediently followed her grandmother's guidance. She was studious, motivated and determined, and had earned the nickname "Bishkash the Great" at school. Zenebech was proud of her granddaughter and knew she would do well in life and care for her in her old age.

From their early years, children are instilled with the knowledge of this forthcoming responsibility. The older generation treat them as an investment in the future. All is done for them, given to them, that they may be grateful caretakers as adults. The poorer people are, the more fiercely this knowledge is delivered. The fear of dying old, impoverished and alone overwhelms any sensitivity towards a child's fragility in a harsh world. All focus is on following tradition now and ensuring security in the future.

Even though their living conditions were no longer aristocratic,

Bishkash never felt burdened by that future obligation. Her grandmother gave her dignity and she anticipated providing well, when the time came. She had reached her fourteenth year and was full of wonderful expectation for all that lay ahead.

The village of Slehleka had a new resident. After studying hard at university, Solomon Fekadu was the ambitious young man appointed as the new health officer at the Mekane Yesus Mission Hospital. This was an impressive beginning to a career that would continue to prosper.

His workplace shared a fence with the Mission school, and so Bishkash's beauty did not go unnoticed. Every day, he watched this bright young girl blossoming into womanhood.

If the young doctor had followed the ways of tradition, this tale might have had a very different ending. Unfortunately, while his professional life was about to flourish, his move to the village unleashed darker deeds and signalled the beginnings of an untoward private life.

I wish I could look at him with my mother's eyes and see his regret. I want to remove the mask from his dark face and feel compassion for someone who was tormented by the shadow of shame dogging his steps. But his truth has passed with him, and my efforts to find honour can only come from the remaining fragments uncovered here.

At the end of grade eight, Bishkash moved to the nearby town of Mekele to continue her studies. There she lived with her older cousin, Egegayhu, but pined for the companionship of her grandmother.

Zenebech offered comfort from afar. Whenever the opportunity arose, she sent care packages containing food and money through visiting family and friends.

Back in Slehleka, the young health officer had noticed the girl's absence. She no longer appeared in the schoolyard. He didn't know her name or connections, so he began enquiring into her whereabouts using the very efficient Ethiopian "message bank."

This system could source or transmit information from any street corner through every eager ear along the way to far destinations. In the absence of modern technology such as telephones, it was considered the most efficient way of getting and sending news and, to this day, it's still a cornerstone of our culture.

So, following threads of gossip, Solomon soon discovered the girl's name and the details of her family.

Mekele was a sizeable town; big enough to offer Bishkash and Egegayhu a sense of the wider world, but not so big that it daunted them. The townsfolk upheld sturdy suburban rituals that imbued life with rhythm and security. Markets jostled everyone awake with their lively chatter. The enticing aroma of brewing coffee reminded everyone it was time to gather. People greeted each other politely or called one another aside to share the latest news.

Coffee has its origins in Ethiopia. From there it spread to Arabia, where it was cultivated and distributed further, finally to become a household beverage worldwide.

How do you like your cup of java? In my homeland, coffee is prepared in such a way that the senses are enticed at every stage. The experience anchors one in belonging, in sharing, in tradition.

The green coffee beans are roasted over hot coals. A tall coffee pot filled with water is set on the coals while the darkened beans are crushed into a coarse powder. This is spooned into the heating water. Small cups are set out. While waiting for the brew, everyone discusses local happenings and gives opinions on everybody's business but their own (with the best of intentions, of course). The cups are filled and passed around, the rich flavour warming the mood. Three times, the cups are passed. Not until then is the ceremony complete.

Bishkash and Egegayhu rented a single room. Though basic, it adequately served the needs of two students. The girls did their

No One's Son

best to brighten their home with decorative wall hangings and floor coverings. Just inside the door, they had organised a cooking space, with a small pantry shelf. Although their budget was slim, they were sure to have coffee on hand. It just wouldn't do if visitors arrived and there was nothing to brew.

Delighted at their independence, Bishkash and Egegayhu enjoyed the shared responsibilities of cooking and cleaning. Egegayhu encouraged her shy roommate to talk of her dreams and to keep striving towards her goals.

The future looked plump with possibility.

Early one evening, Bishkash was tidying up after dinner when there was a knock at the door.

"*Men ika?*"[3] she asked (suspiciously), not opening the door until she knew who stood behind it.

"It's Afwerke," a familiar voice replied. "Grandmother has sent you a parcel, Bishkash! Open the door."

She recognised that it was her cousin. Afwerke often stopped by with something from Zenebech. She swung the door wide open, only to reveal that Afwerke was empty-handed.

He saw her confusion and reassured her. "We have to go and fetch the parcel. Why don't you get something warm to put on and I'll wait for you in the car," he suggested.

Egegayhu hadn't noticed the visitor. She'd been sitting on her bed, absorbed in study. As Bishkash swirled her *netela*[4] around her shoulders, Egegayhu looked up and saw the door hanging ajar. "Surely, you're not going out," she cautioned.

"Grandma has sent a parcel," Bishkash chirped. "I'm going with Cousin Afwerke to collect it."

"But it's getting dark. Wait till tomorrow, then I can come with you."

3. Who is it? (Tigrinya)
4. A hand-woven cotton shawl. (Amharic)

22

"Afwerke is with me. I'll be fine. See you soon." She flitted out the door before anything more could be said.

Egegayhu was concerned, but Bishkash was a prudent girl *and* she was with family. Of course, she'd be all right.

Approaching the idling Land Rover, Bishkash baulked on seeing a stranger in the driver's seat. Still, tradition said that a friend of Afwerke's was a friend of hers, so she stepped forward, trusting that all was as it should be.

The last light of day silhouetted folk on their way home from the markets, driving their donkeys and goats before them. Conflicting with the peaceful village rhythm, the vehicle sped along the narrow streets, dodging livestock and smothering all with the dust in its wake. The neighbourhood dogs were barking loudly, almost as if they were warning Bishkash. Trusting in Afwerke's company, she pressed into the back seat and closed her eyes to imagine lovely surprises from Zenebech.

I always assumed that my parents had some kind of relationship because I never heard my mother speak ill of my father. It is only in recent years that I learned of this horrid night.

My mother has related only small snippets, over time. Our cultural shyness makes it difficult to talk openly about such things. I appreciate her vulnerability, but in trying to piece together my own life, I had to know how it began.

Finally, I summoned the courage to ask her, hoping she would be as courageous in answering. I think fear must have shut her down because she struggles for cohesive memories of those stolen hours. They still snap at her like vicious shadows: the tyres on the gravel . . . the slam of the door . . . the cold snatching at her legs.

All she can say is that at some point, Afwerke was no longer in the car. It was unacceptable for her, as a girl, to speak out. She could not ask why she was left alone with a stranger—or where they were.

She has always been a demure woman. When I ask her what

happened next, her words falter, her hands twist in knots in her lap.

It was an unfamiliar neighbourhood, far from her little haven with Egegayhu. The stranger said nothing. Not until he stopped the car and came around to her door did she recognise him as the health officer from Slehleka.

She doesn't remember screaming as he dragged her into a near-by house, only her shoes scuffing the dirt as she tried to resist, and his big hands gripping her arms.

How could this be happening? Hadn't she studied hard? Wasn't she respectful and obedient? Bad things don't happen to good people. They just don't!

Oh, but they do.

In that moment, the darkness was complete (in more ways than one).

I see the tendons in her neck tense. She looks down at her hands, at the floor on one side of her feet, and then on the other. She briefly flicks her gaze up at me, and down again.

Perched on the edge of the sofa, she looks so tiny and frail. I'm deeply moved at the incredible shock that must have swallowed her up, all those years ago. Bishkash—no longer bouncing on her grandmother's knee, no longer just the beautiful young schoolgirl whom everyone admired.

For all their guarded ways and dire warnings, people in Ethiopia never discussed sex. They felt it was enough to practise piety and suspicion, without being clear on details.

Bishkash had no understanding of her situation. There would be no parcel from Grandmother that night.

Naturally, I wanted the whole truth, so I sought out those who might know more. Sadly, Afwerke had passed away, but family members recollect discussing the event with him. Apparently, he knew the young doctor by reputation and might have anticipated that a betrothal was forthcoming. After all, this man was the perfect suitor: he had a respectable job and earned a decent salary. Bishkash would have a good life and want for nothing.

I found out that Solomon had borrowed his brother Asmerom's car. No one knows whose house it was, only that it was far from where Bishkash lived.

Egegayhu told me that Bishkash was gone for four hours, and when she returned she was wrapped up tightly in her *netela* and went straight to bed, not able to speak.

As calmly as possible, I asked my mother to continue.

"I remember the dogs," she says haltingly. "Their barks were so loud, so vicious. I don't know how long he kept me. It might have been days, weeks or even a month. I don't know. The dogs kept barking."

She smiles a little, and says she'd much rather talk about my naughtiness.

Nauseous. Confused. Stunned. Those hands bundled her brusquely back into the Land Rover, and the man drove like he had a date with the Devil. No words were exchanged. As if she was an unwanted parcel, he dumped her at her door. Crumpled and stamped with disgrace, she felt completely hollow.

If not for me, that might have been true.

There is no stronger medicine than determination, though it's usually bitter and it's never a cure-all. Bishkash was determined to forget. She was determined to better herself. If somehow she'd done something to deserve such degradation, she was determined it would never happen again.

She told no one of the incident. The horror of it dulled, but the humility weighed heavily on her conscience. Why hadn't she listened to Egegayhu? What would Zenebech say? Why, why, oh why hadn't she been suspicious?

Over the following weeks, she focused on her studies, but it was soon apparent to those around her that something was terribly wrong. Egegayhu was concerned about Bishkash's lack of energy, and when she overheard my mother vomiting one morning, she decided to seek advice from their landlady.

The landlady was a short round-bellied older woman. She was considered wise, though was also known to be highly superstitious. Given that, she suspected evil spirits were the cause of my mother's illness. She felt they needed to identify the curse that was responsible, so she came to speak with the girls after school that day.

The landlady quickly closed the door behind my mother and paced uncomfortably within the room. "Bishkash, we fear that you may have been given the *budha*."[5]

The *budha* and other wayward spirits are believed to invade the human body, or even just part of the body (for example your big toe), either through a curse that someone has cast or through the spirit's own will and determination.

The intangible world is considered as important as the material world by many Ethiopians, and is often used to bring reason to inexplicable circumstances such as a change in somebody's character, a misfortune, a mysterious illness, or even a death.

The landlady herself claimed to be possessed by a coffee-loving spirit (how convenient). At various times during the day, she *had* to perform a coffee ceremony and drink enough coffee to satisfy the spirit. Failing to do so left her unable to control her moods or behaviour, and her yelling often rattled the walls—not very dignified, but forgivable if it was due to evil spirits.

Bishkash never felt comfortable with these concepts, given her Orthodox Christian upbringing. To her, such things were nonsense. But the seriousness of the landlady's tone of voice frightened her.

Egegayhu snatched quick glances at Bishkash, who was staring at the floor. The landlady's pacing continued, her skirt swishing sibilantly.

"Who has cursed you? Eh?" the landlady barked nervously. "Have

---

5. Evil spirit, thought to possess. (Amharic)

you upset someone at school? What about the old lady next door?"

Then the swishing stopped.

"Bishkash, tomorrow we are taking you to see—" Wary of eaves-droppers, the landlady paused to peer through a small window. "We're taking you to see a well-respected old man," she whispered. "He is a *merigata*[6]—you know—a medicine man."

My mother had heard school friends discussing the *merigata*, who claim to be gifted in the extraction of *budha* from the human body through direct oral communication. The communication flows be-tween the *merigata* and the spirit via the mouth of the inflicted per-son, whereby the *merigata* can persuade the spirit to leave the body. Visiting a *merigata* was rarely spoken of, although everybody knew of them and many had visited one for themselves or with a relative at some time during their lives.

Bishkash refused. After a long discussion, a compromise was reached when the landlady coaxed her to ask the local Orthodox Christian priest for a blessing.

So the next day, with Egegayhu and the landlady hovering be-hind her, Bishkash sat meekly before an elderly priest. His small frame was cloaked in a long white shawl, and a white turban-like hat rested neatly on his elongated head. "So," he looked at her in-tently, "what seems to be the problem?"

"*Aboykeshie.*"[7] The landlady couldn't contain her concern. "Our Bishkash hasn't been herself lately. She has an upset stomach and seems so moody."

Egegayhu giggled nervously.

The priest ignored them and asked Bishkash, "When did this all begin?"

The landlady jumped in, "About a month ago."

Bishkash, hands clenched, couldn't force her gaze from her lap.

The priest patted his cheek and nodded thoughtfully. "Bishkash,

6. Head of God. (Amharic)
7. Father. Term of reverence for a priest. (Tigrinya)

explain to me exactly what happened?"

She couldn't do that! Instead she described how she'd been feeling.

The priest leaned back and pondered her words.

The landlady, prickly with impatience, decided to prompt him. "*Aboykeshie*, the family feels that she may have been given the . . . the uh . . . well, you know . . . *budha*." Her eyes darted around. Would God's wrath descend on her for speaking of such things in His house?

The priest spat out in disgust, "*Budha?* Rubbish! There is no such thing! You villagers and all your silly beliefs!" He shook his head in dismay.

The landlady couldn't be stopped. She rattled out her explanation in a fearful rasp. "We feel that her body may have been invaded by evil spirits. That she's been cursed. That's really why we are here. We're hoping you can rid her of them."

Adjusting his slight body on the small three-legged wooden stool, the priest flicked his long white tasselled shawl over his shoulder, as if flicking away his rising temper. "I cannot cure this young girl of the *budha* of which you speak. You are a guest in God's house now and I ask that you show some respect and *stop speaking such nonsense!*"

The landlady shrank back, hiding her face behind her *netela*. If she'd upset God, she didn't want him to be able to identify her.

The old priest stood up and left the room, soon returning with a small basin of holy water and a large exquisitely ornate silver cross. He sat across from my mother. "Close your eyes," he commanded. "God protect you and help you through this time of difficulty. May He take care of you and restore your health and vitality," he murmured.

Bishkash felt sprinkles of cold water trickle from the top of her head, down through her tightly woven braids, onto her forehead and over her closed eyes. She tried not to flinch as the priest continued to shower her with water and then press the cross to her forehead.

"Bishkash, open your eyes," he said.

"How do you feel?" the landlady wheezed from behind her shawl.

"I'm . . . not . . . sure," Bishkash offered, wiping the water away with her *netela*, which had been draped around her shoulders. She felt no different, but didn't want to upset anyone.

"My child," said the priest, "go home and rest. If your health continues to fail, I suggest you go and visit a doctor—a real doctor—not one of those medicine men." He patted her on the head.

She bent forward and humbly took the priest's wrinkled hand, kissed it, then touched her forehead to it; a process she repeated three times to show him respect and gratitude. Egegayhu and the landlady followed suit.

This sign of reverence was customary. On meeting a priest, normally a handshake is sufficient, but many people kiss the right hand of the priest in deference to his connection with heaven. Bowing low, you kiss the priest's hand and then touch it to your forehead before kissing it again. Obviously, the more help you need, the more kissing there is.

When Bishkash's health failed to show any improvement, Grandmother Zenebech came. She made the girl's favourite *doro wet*.[8] Then she spent the evening rubbing my mother's upset stomach (and me), massaging with the palms of her hands like a baker kneading dough. As a child, Bishkash was hardly sick a day, so her grandmother feared that something was horribly wrong.

Her illness persisted. Bishkash had heard older women in the village talk of pregnancy. Gradually, she realised that her belly was expanding. As her belly swelled, so did her anguish. Anguish became despair when she could no longer deny that disaster (uncompromising devastating disaster) was fast approaching.

8. Spicy chicken curry. (Amharic)

Bishkash knew of women who were cursed or disowned by the family, cast out alone into the glares of disgusted villagers and a life of poverty. Although she didn't know anyone personally (because good girls don't know "people like that"), she'd heard of unmarried pregnant girls committing suicide because they were unable to cope with the public humiliation suffered by the family. Death was preferable to dishonour.

Why is it that we don't think anything terrible will happen to us—until it does? Bad things only happen to others—or to people who deserve it. And even when disaster strikes, we try to stack it away . . . pretend that it isn't so . . . ignore it until it crushes all denial and sucks us dry of solutions. In a society that is too polite, where etiquette is favoured over ethics, how can we not falter under wavering towers of self-deceit?

I wish for my mother's sake that she'd been given more than traditional teachings and vague explanations. We cannot protect ourselves from something if we cannot identify it. When honour is more important than knowledge, the ignorant walk a hazardous path.

Bishkash wrapped her skirts tighter, held her books closer, dropped her gaze lower and pretended that a magical solution would appear to take away this impending doom. There was no one she could seek advice from because everyone would shun her.

Just keep walking. Keep wishing. Keep quiet.

On the way home from school one day, Egegayhu ran up behind her. "Bishkash, you walk so quickly. I've been trying to catch you!" She grabbed her cousin's arm and brought her to a halt.

Bishkash shook her off. She didn't want to stop. It was hot. She had a headache. And she had to get home to hide herself away.

"Bishkash, everyone at school is talking about you," Egegayhu began.

My mother blankly returned her gaze.

Egegayhu's lips barely moved, but the words leaked out in a hoarse whisper, "They're saying you are *pregnant*."

The accusation hung in the humid air. It might as well have been painted across the sky which, unable to bear its weight, seemed to crash down upon Bishkash.

"Well, what would they know?" Bishkash retorted. "They don't know. They—" She spun away and paced towards home even faster. Shocked by the schoolyard gossip, she wanted to run—and keep running far from this cruel fate.

Egegayhu caught up with her. "Bishkash, I must admit, I've been wondering, too."

My mother halted, her throat tight with truth, her eyes wells of sorrow. A tear rolled down her cheek. "I think . . . they might be right. Look at my stomach!" Her hands rounded over the bulging belly that was woefully constricted within her tightly wrapped skirt.

Egegayhu stared. "But I don't understand. Who? When? You're Bishkash the Great. This can't happen to you!" Then she remembered. "That night Afwerke came to our house? You haven't been the same since then. Is that when . . . it happened?" her voice quavered.

"I try to forget it. I couldn't stop him. I—" Bishkash sobbed now, shaking from the remembered horror.

"Was it Afwerke? May God send him directly to Hell!" Egegayhu spat out, disgusted with their relative.

"No, no, not Cousin Afwerke." My mother choked back her tears. "The—health—officer!"

"What health officer?" Egegayhu was confused.

"From Slehleka. I recognised his face. He worked at the hospital next to my old school."

"I don't understand. Why did he come here? Why you?"

Bishkash moaned, wiping her cheeks repeatedly, trying to stop the rush of tears. "I don't know. I'd never even spoken to him before. I'm just a schoolgirl. I just want to do my studies."

Abruptly, their surroundings came into focus. They were standing in the street, engaged in a very public display of emotions (in itself a most unacceptable act for girls or women). Some villagers were inquisitively watching from under the awning of a nearby corner store. Egegayhu grabbed my mother and ushered her home.

The following day, accompanied by Egegayhu and their landlady, Bishkash again found herself sitting in front of a strange man. This time he was a doctor, a real one, as the priest had instructed. He was a balding man with a thick grey moustache. Unable to meet his gaze, Bishkash focused on the coarse hairs over his lip which rose towards his nostrils in time with his heavy breathing. He sat behind a desk and peered intently at the test results. His upper lip began twitching.

"What are you? Fourteen? Fifteen?" He tilted his head and peered over his glasses at Bishkash.

"Fourteen, I think," she replied timidly. Birthdays were not a celebrated occasion and there was no official record of her birth.

Silence. More deep breathing. The doctor shook his head in disapproval. "Well, the test confirms your suspicions: you are, in fact, pregnant." He leaned back, clearly unimpressed.

The landlady shrieked, "*Eway! Eway!*[9] Why are you making me hear such horrible things?" and raised her hands to her head, rocking back and forth in her chair. Without saying another word, the doctor signalled for them to leave. Stiff with shock, they departed.

They stood in the street. Nobody spoke.

My mother felt a vicious chill spread through her. Would the earth swallow her up now? Would torrential rains pour down, dissolving her belly, her being, her shame, leaving nothing but a pool of regret? No such kindness for her. The world as she knew it was spinning away to be replaced by one of scorn and repulsion. Tradition made it so.

The landlady was spitting on the pavement. Cursing and spitting.

---

9. Oh Lord! Oh Lord! (Tigrinya)

Egegayhu was crying.

Bishkash straightened her back, pushed her palms against her forehead and pressed a mask of acceptance down over her face. As her hands dropped to her sides, her innocence fell. No longer Bishkash the Great, she was now Bishkash the Damned. In that instant, she knew she would have to leave Tigray.

So, when an Eritrean man forced his "superiority" on his young Ethiopian conquest, everyone had an opinion, all yielding the same result: I must be a child spawned of evil.

Some argued that the spirit world was to blame for the pregnancy. Others simply believed that Bishkash's misfortune came because she hadn't said enough prayers to the right saint. Either way, they all agreed it was the devil's work. Be damned!

My mother became an outcast. No respectable man would dare marry her. My beginning ended her promising future.

This knowledge solved a big part of the puzzle for me. It explained much about my parents' chaotic relationships with me. Within the bounds of our traditional expectations, it explained why the extended family were never able to show me the same care that Solomon received from Fekadu, or Bishkash from Zenebech.

These answers challenged me as much as the confusion that prompted my search for the truth. All I could do was to keep following my mother's footsteps to find the path that finally set me free.

3

SUBURBAN NOMADS

Everywhere you go in Ethiopia, there is evidence of a spicy history. Standing before remnants of the ancient Aksumite Empire or some marvellous edifice from more recent history, you become swept up by the flavours and influences that have pervaded the country over time.

This land's potential was always alluring to foreigners (whose interests were hardly welcome and barely tolerated). Waves of political change brought extremes in government, each creating different kinds of havoc. The intensity of those changes was so convoluted and tragic that it's challenging to describe. Perhaps if politics was like a game of soccer it might have made more sense.

In my Africa, the diverse range of players has included various dominant tribes, emperors, European colonists, rebels, communists, and equally ambitious Americans. The goal for each was the same: power. The ball in play was most often Eritrea, which hugs the coastline north of Ethiopia and looks across the sea to Saudi Arabia.

Let's consider Britain as the self-appointed referee, since many interventions (or lack thereof) were decided by her governments—with *no* bias towards her own gains, of course.

The colonial game kicked off late in the nineteenth century, with the Italians winning the toss. Keen to score points ahead of other European countries, the Italians spread their team across more and more of the field. By 1890, they had annexed enough of the Horn of Africa, including Eritrea, to call it "The Kingdom of Italy."

The defending team, Ethiopia, forced and won a penalty in the city of Adwa, in 1896. The Italians withdrew to Eritrea, with a warning from the British referee.

The home crowd was ecstatic. The world arena viewed Ethiopia with new respect as the first African nation to claim independence from colonisation.

The Italians took time out. They regrouped, building team morale by introducing some home comforts: cafés, familiar architecture, finished roads, and a decent infrastructure. Many of the locals appreciated the developments, yet they were continually demoted to C-grade conditions under white supremacy. Various foreigners jostled from the sidelines, waiting for an opportunity to claim the field.

During World War I, the Italians were fairly confident that they could make a comeback, although the British allowed play to advantage the defending team.

Mussolini led a strong midfield back into the match in World War II. It looked like a tiebreaker until the Ethiopians made a tactical switch by calling in the Allied forces. Finally, the Italians were sent off for good.

It should have been game over—but the British referees substituted themselves as the competing team.

The new kids on the block, USA and their USSR rivals, were scouting for talent and tried buying out players from Ethiopia and Eritrea.

By this time, the Eritreans were sick of being kicked around.

No One's Son

After the war, they petitioned the international committee, and were awarded their own team. For a short time, the competition was a draw. But in 1961, Ethiopia was booked for the unsporting behaviour of attempting to annex all of Eritrea.

The game went into extra time for the next thirty years, with plenty of penalty shots from both sides. In 1974, in a radical move to grab victory over imperialists *and* rebels, Ethiopia changed captains. The ousted Emperor Selassie was replaced by the dictator Mengistu.

Drastic weather conditions had already swept through Mengistu's field, causing recurring famine. Many of the team's supporters lost their spirit. Certainly there was no incentive for victory under Mengistu's cruel regime. (Anyone refusing to "play" was shot.)

In a series of tactical moves, Eritrea's underdog team finally scored independence. It really was game over this time.

Since then, there have been many attempts at a re-match. Instead of retiring on their win, the Eritreans tried to extend the field. But the lines have been redrawn so many times that the teams just keep dribbling the power back and forth. Injuries and mortal loss of players have stacked up in the millions. And, without a referee, it looks like the goalkeeper is the Devil himself and every ball is a foul.

There's been an ongoing cacophony of booing and hissing from the sidelines. Nobody has seemed interested in buying tickets anymore, except scalpers and a few loyal fans.

This was the rough-and-ready crowd that would swallow up Bishkash. This was the arena into which I was born.

One month before giving birth, my mother made final preparations for heading north over the border to Eritrea. A dangerous war seemed far less threatening than falling under the fire of public scorn. This destination was considered sufficiently distant to spare immediate family members any humiliation. Bishkash anticipated

36

staying with Egegayhu's sister, Nigisti. There, she could give birth in seclusion, and come to terms with her new status in life.

Egegayhu was to continue her studies in the village of Adigrat, so the two girls travelled that far together by bus. The stopover to deliver and collect passengers was brief. Egegayhu lifted her bags from the rack, ready to sidle along the aisle. Her cousin hunched down in her seat, dreading the unchaperoned journey ahead.

Egegayhu leaned close. "Bishkash, your baby will be beautiful. I just know it. My sister, Nigisti, can't resist babies. And I'll come and see you during school break. It'll be fine. You'll see."

My mother sat quietly. Egegayhu gently kissed away the tears on each cheek. Then she was gone.

The vehicle continued through the stony mountains to Eritrea. Overcrowding didn't lessen Bishkash's desolate state. She had never travelled far from the villages of her childhood. The craggy mountains seemed to leer over her, peering at her shame, dwarfing the rickety bus which faltered along the narrow winding track.

It was the beginning of the wet season and a muggy afternoon storm was gathering. Dust that churned up from the road seeped through cracks in the windows and clung to Bishkash.

Swirling thoughts of doubt tumbled over in her mind. Sleepless nights had not produced clearer options. How was she, an unmarried 15-year-old expectant mother, to support herself in a strange city?

Her concerns increased as she became acutely aware of soldiers, armed with machine guns, perched on rocky outcrops like eagles eyeing their prey. The violent struggle for Eritrean independence was well-established. Traffic across the border was monitored suspiciously.

The bus crawled on.

The rough terrain jolted the passengers mercilessly. It took all of Bishkash's determination to keep her swollen body on the narrow seat. She swallowed back nausea from the stench of her travelling companions' musty clothes and bodies. Yet all journeys come to an end and, some twelve hours after setting off, the bus spluttered and jerked its way into the city of Asmara, Eritrea's capital.

If busy passersby had stopped to look, they would have seen a girl's face pressed up against the smeared bus window as she strained for a first impression of her new temporary home. Her eyes widened when she saw a sophisticated city with a strong European ambience imbued by the previous Italian occupation. Asmara was much bigger than anything Bishkash had experienced before, but (as Egegayhu had described) it was beautiful. Immaculate streets were lined with palm trees. Elegantly dressed women strolled along the footpaths. Neatly groomed men in Italian-style suits sipped *macchiato* from petite cups and ate spaghetti in exotically named restaurants, like *Bar Vittoria* and *Pasticceria Modern*. So cosmopolitan. So vibrant. For Bishkash, it certainly lived up to its nickname *Piccolo Roma*,[1] as it was known throughout the region.

By the time the bus reached the city centre, darkness had descended, bringing rain with it. Bishkash went in search of Nigisti's house. Eritreans share a language similar to that of the Tigrayan people, so it wasn't long before Bishkash was able to find her way to Aba Shawl, the area where Nigisti lived.

This vibrant market district was in the heart of the city, not far from the bus terminal. At night, the streets came to life as local residents socialised. On every corner, people were beginning to gather, despite the weather. Bishkash stood in the shadows, on the edge of the square. Here among the elite hustle and bustle, and the subculture of prostitutes and beggars, she was meant to find sanctuary.

Nigisti managed a *suwa*[2] business. She had converted the front room of her house into a small bar, a popular venue with the locals. Bishkash had never been in such a place. As she peeked through the entrance, her senses were assaulted by the circus of activity

---

1. Little Rome. (Italian)
2. Home-brewed barley beer. (Tigrinya)

within. Patrons jostled in groups on narrow wooden benches that hugged three of the walls. In the centre of the room, there was a table neatly lined with glasses. Heavy tentacles of incense smoke spiralled upwards. The floor had been sprinkled with water, then covered with straw, to contain the dust. And in one corner, a woman sat performing the traditional coffee ceremony.

Lively discussions swayed the heads of drunken customers whose eyes were already bloodshot from swigging too much *suwa*. Rowdy voices. Pungent smells. Staring strangers. The sensitive girl couldn't free her grip from the door frame for fear of collapsing.

Egegayhu's sister, Nigisti, was touring the room, refilling glasses. She had a plump round face and pouting lips. Her hair was wrapped high on her head with a red scarf. Noticing the timid form in the dim entrance, she bustled over.

Her smile shone through the murky atmosphere. "*Ben venuto,*"[3] she greeted in Italian, as was the custom in Asmara.

"*Selam,*"[4] my mother mumbled.

"You made it! I've been expecting you." Nigisti leaned in to greet Bishkash with traditional kisses, cheek to cheek to cheek. "Come," she said, and led my mother beyond the bar, into the cramped abode which she shared with her husband. "Here, you are with family, Bishkash," she said.

When it is offered, such loyalty is sublime.

Paving the way for Bishkash, Egegayhu's message had omitted the reason for her trip, only mentioning that she needed somewhere to stay. Over the following days, Nigisti became increasingly concerned for her cousin's well-being as she observed her odd eating habits. While having coffee at a neighbour's, Nigisti revealed some details.

"I'm worried that my cousin may be ill," she mentioned between sips of the dark brew. "She barely eats anything I prepare."

3. Welcome. (Italian)
4. Hello. (Tigrinya)

"Well, maybe that's just your cooking!" the neighbour teased as she added some ground ginger to a second serving.

"No, really . . . she often says, 'I can't swallow the *injera*[5] or 'It hurts my throat to eat this.' How can anyone *not* swallow *injera*? It's so soft."

Her neighbour nodded and passed Nigisti another round. "A friend of mine used to make similar complaints. You know what was wrong with her? She was pregnant!"

Nigisti's grip slipped, spilling coffee on her *gabi.*[6] Her hands shook as she retrieved the cup from the dirt floor.

The neighbour continued, "Haven't you noticed the clothing she wears? What young girl wears such bulky clothes at her age? Don't you think that's strange?"

"Yes." Nigisti paused, realising her neighbour had a point. *"Eway! Eway!"* she moaned, pulling her *gabi* up over her head and across her face, not wanting to hear anymore.

That night, Nigisti confronted my mother. Although Bishkash hadn't spoken to Nigisti about the pregnancy, she assumed Egegay-hu had told her. Now she feared expulsion, but Nigisti remained supportive (after recovering from her initial shock) and actually looked forward to my arrival.

So, there in Nigisti's house, when the heavens cleared for a bright September afternoon in 1971, I took my first breath, filling my lungs with the taste of freedom—a flavour that would afterwards elude me until adulthood.

Somewhere in the distance, sounds bounced off tin roofs like firecrackers at a festival—only it was gunfire. No welcome for me, but a warning of harsh times ahead.

In an attempt to save my doomed soul, Bishkash had me baptised in a quaint Orthodox church. Throughout the ceremony, the *keshie*[7] looked on while I wiggled, squirmed and squawked in my

---

5. A flat pancake-like bread made from the Ethiopian grain *teff*. (Amharic)
6. A handmade cotton cloth wrapped around the body for warmth. (Amharic)
7. Coptic priest. (Tigrinya)

mother's arms. I hollered as I was lifted in and out of the basin of Holy Water three times (once for each entity of the Holy Trinity). I put up such a fight that the *keshie* suggested naming me "Tewodros," for my defiance.

The holy man anointed my forehead, chin and inner wrists with oil, and carefully placed a drop in my mouth. He raised a large cross over me, blessed a loaf of freshly baked *ambasha*[8] to be shared among family, and then tied a *metab*[9] around my neck; this had been customary ever since Saint Peter's baptismal ceremonies in the River Jordan. It is said that Saint Peter cut string from his prayer shawl and tied it around the newly baptised person's neck. I would wear my *metab* for most of my childhood.

"You must call this boy Tewodros," the *keshie* again urged Bishkash, as they both observed my determined little fingers tugging at the cord.

He must have foreseen my personality or, in giving me such a title, had ultimately determined my future. My name was written in the book of God. Cursed or not, fated or not, my quest had begun.

Despite the circumstances, Nigisti arranged a small celebration in recognition of my birth. She shared a slaughtered sheep among a gathering of surprised family and friends. Outweighing their shock, everyone was incredulous over my enormous size in contrast with Bishkash's slender frame. Instead of cooing endearing affection, the visitors gawked at me lying on the bed.

My mother tells me she didn't mind; though she *was* relieved that I had a straight nose. When *Ge-ge*[10] Zenebech learned of my birth, she feared that her rigorous massage during Bishkash's early pregnancy may have damaged my nose in the womb. Knowing her concern, it was the first thing my mother checked. She was pleased

8. Spiced bread served on special occasions. (Tigrinya)
9. Small leather cross on a cord. (Amharic)
10. Term of endearment for great grandmother. (African)

to report that Ge-ge's great-grandson had no facial deformities!

My arrival prompted fury from Bishkash's extended family, targeting one man: Solomon. When they all learned of the events that led to my birth, the motives behind Solomon's actions became a hotly debated topic. Two schools of thought emerged from these discussions.

Proponents of the first school claimed to have heard rumours that Solomon had visited Zenebech some weeks before he abducted Bishkash. Supposedly, he declared his love for my mother and asked for a blessing on the marriage. Zenebech had expected her granddaughter's beauty to draw suitors. However, after a brief discussion, she decided that Solomon was unacceptable. You see, he was Protestant. As an Orthodox Christian, Zenebech objected to marriage outside her religion. Therefore, she refused him.

No doubt, Solomon would have been humiliated by the rejection. It's been suggested that he sexually assaulted my mother to punish her family. What better vengeance than a constant reminder of himself: *me?*

While this theory is plausible, nobody ever thought to ask Zenebech for confirmation, so the truth went with her to the grave.

The second conjecture qualifies the attack as a malicious act of tribal vengeance. The tension and mutual dislike between the neighbouring Eritreans and Tigrayans was well known. It was not uncommon for men of one tribe to molest women from the other. If my mother had come from the same ethnic group as my father, I'm told he would've been killed for his actions. But as she was an outsider, there would be no retribution.

Bishkash believed the latter explanation. She'd never spoken a word to Solomon before that fateful visit, so she couldn't understand why he would have wanted to marry her.

I'm not convinced either way. Both theories have merit.

Adding salt to the family's already painful wounds, Solomon denied he was my father. Several relatives tried to meet with him to claim compensation, but he managed to evade them. On the few occasions when he was cornered, he was distant, vague and unrepentant.

Some family members were so incensed that they were unable to mention his name without spitting on the ground. He might have shirked responsibility in tangible terms, but spiritually he could not escape their ire. From first light of morning until well after the sun disappeared from the African sky, they cursed him. Cries reverberated onto the street, such as, "God, punish Solomon for his sins! May he go directly to Hell!" Other imperatives were ground out through gritted teeth, including, "Hyenas: eat him!" or "Car: hit him!"

Three weeks after my birth, Bishkash decided it was time to move. Nigisti's husband was a poorly paid driver and, although Nigisti did a roaring trade, the *suwa* business delivered little profit. They never complained. What they lacked in money they made up in heart. But we had burdened them long enough.

Leaving Nigisti's house, we moved in with Mebrat, another cousin. Although married with children, she was in a better financial position to help us. She was a colourful woman, as feisty as they come. Influenced heavily by the pervading Italian culture, she dressed like a European woman and even argued as robustly as an Italian mama. She was also one of my father's more vocal critics and insisted that we stay with her.

News of "that baby" spread quickly to Slehleka (where Solomon was still residing). An elderly Eritrean man, who worked as a guard at the hospital, worried about the young health officer's deviant deeds.

Members of the older generation are held in high esteem and often step in to mediate others' domestic problems. Some people might think this is just interfering, but overall it provides cultural strength, particularly in the villages.

The distressed guard approached Solomon and persuaded him

to make amends. For *where there is no shame, there is no honour.*[11]

Solomon complied. He was an Eritrean living in a Tigrayan village, and the locals had heard the rumours. Was he safe from their condemnation? Probably not.

After meeting with my father, the old man travelled to Asmara, bringing news of Solomon's imminent arrival. Bishkash wasn't surprised by the old man's intervention, though she was astonished at how far he'd travelled to give her the message.

When would he come? How would he behave? Still really just a girl, Bishkash swayed under fearful memories and the anxiety of having to face her attacker.

Not long after the old man's visit, she received a second caller: the culprit himself. Arriving late at night and unannounced, a tall elegant young man stood in the doorway. On appearance, it was hard to believe that such a dashing fellow could have done something so atrocious, but his behaviour and attitude towards Bishkash soon revealed otherwise. Unapologetic and arrogant, he demanded to see the baby everyone *claimed* was his.

Amazing herself, Bishkash (usually timid and obedient) spoke with provocative directness. She firmly stated her right to his support, and then itemised a small list of necessities for their baby.

Solomon fumed. "Where is his birth certificate?" he demanded as he stormed around the room, snatching up pieces of paper from a table. Then he rushed at her. "Where is it?"

She faltered. His height, his shouting and those big hands waving in her face almost shattered her resolve. Almost. She walked to the bed in the corner, lifted the mattress and pulled out the certificate. Solomon grabbed it and dragged his fingers across the print in frenzy. Three words were in indelible ink: *his* name as the father.

He fell silent.

Did he think I was a figment of everyone's imagination—that his anger was more convincing than my existence?

---

11. Ethiopian proverb.

Bishkash gingerly retrieved the certificate from him and replaced it under the mattress.

Until that moment, Solomon's denials had seemed reckless and immature, but then he did something remarkable: he called to a friend who was waiting outside. My father explained to Bishkash that she could contact this man, Meles, should she need anything. He promised to return soon himself, with baby clothes and money.

Such a promise and such preparation suggest integrity. I want to believe that he was an honourable man who realised he had made a terrible mistake. I know what it is to make mistakes, to make desperate choices. But my mistakes *were* out of desperation, and if I could reverse any of them—all of them—I would.

By acknowledging me, he would have redeemed himself. I want to reverse time to that moment and tell him how much *I* would honour *him* as my father and—yes—that I would forgive him. Is that desperate, too?

Although distressed, my mother's relatives offered us some dignity. Conversely, Solomon's family were still completely ignorant of my existence and the precursory events.

Meles was supposed to deliver monthly payments on behalf of Solomon—which never came. During the next year, Meles visited us regularly, watching our conditions worsen without the promised support. Finally, he came to Bishkash in a distressed state, no longer willing to be a part of such neglect.

"*While the wound stays hidden, the cure will hide,*"[12] he explained. "I will speak to Solomon's family."

"But—I—" Bishkash hesitated.

"Someone must be accountable," asserted Meles.

"Yes. Of course. You are right," Bishkash conceded.

And, of course, he was.

He went directly to Solomon's stepmother, Selas. Her goodness

---

12. Eritrean proverb.

prevailed over her shock and she assured Meles that she would discuss the issue with Solomon's oldest brother, Asmerom. He had become the official head of the family after Fekadu's death. Asmerom was an upright man who commanded respect. He was sure to resolve things.

The rest of the family struggled to accept the situation. They flared with denials and counter-accusations, but not Asmerom. He was deeply disappointed, though not surprised. "It's just like him," he huffed. Clearing a path through everyone's volatile emotions, he confronted his brother to determine the truth.

Reluctantly, Solomon admitted his crime. By law, he (or his family by default) was required to provide support for five years. But it was Asmerom who sent us 30 *birr*[13] each month, for the designated time. Even that small amount made a difference.

Asmerom's wife, Meseret, sympathised with Bishkash and visited from time to time with baby clothes and food parcels. Her marriage to Asmerom had met with disapproval from the outset because she was from the Amhara tribe. Even complete strangers had strong opinions about the union and didn't hesitate to share them with her—frequently.

Grandmother Selas was not limited by others' opinions. She consoled us in her gentle graceful ways. She combed her house for simple essential items, and brought something with her each time she came to visit.

My mother graciously received these attentions. With no real education, Bishkash couldn't find work, so our survival hinged on the generosity of others. In the face of strong condemnation arising from traditional views, these acts of kindness were noble.

My early memories are rich with love and nurturing from Selas— "Adey,"[14] I called her. If I hadn't known that joy, I would never have

---

13. US$6.00 (approximately). Birr is the Ethiopian currency.
14. Term of endearment for grandmother. (Tigrinya)

understood what I was searching for in later years.

Adey still lived in the house Fekadu had built. She welcomed us as frequent guests. In material terms, she wasn't able to provide more than the occasional meal, but my mother valued her much-needed words of comfort, and I adored being enfolded in her tender embrace.

As promised, Egegayhu came to visit. She accompanied my mother and me to Adey's house one afternoon. Adey served *geat*,[15] and the girls reminisced about carefree days. Nurtured by such attention, Bishkash was able to put her worries aside, even if only for a few hours.

She tells me now that those first years of motherhood were the most difficult of her life. We lived like suburban nomads, shifting back and forth between relatives' houses, anxious about burdening anyone for too long. We slept on dirt floors, or a sofa if we were lucky. On such a paltry income, my mother struggled to keep me nourished. It wasn't unusual for her to go without food for days in order to feed me.

Several times, Adey urged Bishkash to move closer, and even offered to raise me once I was weened. But Adey's neighbourhood was too expensive, and Bishkash feared losing her relatives' support base, so she declined. (I'm guessing she was also trying to salvage what little pride she had left. Despite the circumstances being thrust upon her, she was determined to fulfil her responsibility rather than hand me over.)

Bishkash was worn down from the humiliation of continual begging. So, in our third and final year in Asmara, she used Asmerom's monthly allowance to rent a room. This small step towards independence was meant to stabilise our lives.

Not long after we relocated, Solomon arranged to see us for the second time. Cousin Mebrat offered to host the meeting at her house. She wanted to be sure of a successful outcome and would

---

15. Barley or wheat porridge, often served with spiced butter and sauce. (Tigrinya)

not be daunted by "the scoundrel." When Mebrat learned that Solomon had arrived empty-handed, her rage rattled the roof. She shouted at him hysterically, until my mother could no longer cope.

Bishkash pleaded with her to leave the room. Mebrat composed herself, gave my father a chilling glare and stepped out, but remained within earshot.

After a few moments of tense silence, Solomon howled, "Why are you trying to ruin my life?"

Bishkash went numb. Maybe Mebrat's anger was justified. But my mother hated quarrelling and refused to respond. Besides, what could she say? She hadn't asked to be kidnapped and abused. Barely more than a child herself, she was ill-prepared to raise one. In retrospect, she realised that she should have been more cautious but, in the end, this mess was all his doing.

"Answer me!" he demanded. Hearing his raised voice, Mebrat burst back into the room.

Her seething anger resurfaced. "Get out of my house. Now!" she shouted. "I will not have you come here insulting Bishkash when you are the one at fault. *You* have ruined *her* life—and you ruined your own. Now *GET OUT!*" Her tendons strained, her voice was hoarse, she choked out, "May you burn in Hell!" and spat on the ground as he retreated.

In upholding traditional values, people prayed hard and cursed even harder, condemning what was unacceptable. But when one person, one brutal act, had caused so much harm, not a thousand customs or curses or words of comfort could set things right.

Bishkash had never seen Mebrat so upset. Anxious for her cousin, Bishkash didn't know what to do. Should she rush after my father? Could she beg for his help? Casting all etiquette aside, was there *anything* she could do to save everyone from further anguish?

The front door swung closed. She never saw Solomon again.

Political and social chaos ravaged the country. This was not a game of power play. It was savagery in broad brutal strokes. With no singular front, guerrilla fighters launched multiple surprise attacks which, in turn, drew retaliation. Everyone was caught in the crossfire. People struggled as cruelty heaped upon cruelty, and despair smothered hope on both sides of the border.

It was 1973. Emperor Haile Selassie was about to lose his reign. He no longer had the political acumen to maintain influence overseas. Advancing senility left him slow to respond effectively. His ministers floundered under faltering leadership.

Separate episodes of famine had widespread impact. Selassie's ministers had not alerted him of the crisis, choosing instead to direct diminishing resources to the long-term war.

When Selassie discovered the severity of the situation, he immediately visited the affected regions and declared a state of emergency. Efforts to keep news of the catastrophe from international media failed. The pride of the nation was put aside as camps were established and foreign aid was embraced. Fighting continued, nevertheless.

The region of Welo was struck hard by famine. This was close to Bishkash's homeland of Tigray. My mother worried constantly about the well-being of her family, in particular Zenebech. There'd been no word from her for some time. Bishkash desperately wanted to return to Tigray, but there were battlefields on both sides of the border. Any attempt at crossing, particularly with a toddler in tow, was unthinkable.

Soon the war crept from the outskirts of Asmara into the suburbs. Peaceful streets became battlegrounds. The non-Eritrean residents of Piccolo Roma, fearing for their lives, fled the city.

Two years after my birth, all major Eritrean towns and highways had fallen under imperial control. The sight of soldiers on the street was unnerving, and whenever battle was too close for comfort, my mother would huddle with me under the bed until the ear-piercing noise of gunfire subsided.

On one particular day, our room shuddered from fighting in a nearby street. The vibration came through the ground and shook us to the foundations of our hearts. Bishkash bundled me up and scurried for the sanctuary of the local church. Hugging buildings and dashing across streets, she burst through the chapel doors to an astounding sight: hundreds of terrified people crammed onto narrow pews, frantically wailing to God for salvation. Fearful of their hysteria, my mother backed away. Smothering her tears on my neck, she ran all the way to Mebrat's house for comfort.

Despite the trauma that ricocheted across their lives, my mother's family rarely let Solomon get far from their thoughts, and their anger towards him never diminished. In fact, the tension caused by the political situation fuelled their hatred, not the least because he was from a different tribe. Daily, they cursed him. Frequently, their distress led to arguments and more grief. On one occasion, my uncle announced his intention to kill my father; on another, he vandalised Solomon's car.

This undulating fracas was our life until 1974. Almost three years after my birth, Selassie was deposed by a military coup and the legendary 3000-year rule of the Solomonic dynasty came to an abrupt end. The last Ethiopian emperor was shuttled from his palace in a Volkswagen Beetle.

As news of his downfall spread, the future of the Horn became uncertain. There was no opposing political party to direct the power. The people were at the mercy of the Dergue: self-installed rebel idealists with communistic vision.

Stability was nowhere. Soldiers were everywhere.

Bishkash knew it was time to leave Eritrea.Pining for the comfort of home, she wondered if the harshness of war would outweigh her shame among her real family. Could one person's suffering diminish if it was surrounded by the suffering of many more? Would she find higher peace in the highlands of Tigray?

Following her heart, she packed our bag of toil and looked to the mountains in hope.

4

THE LITTLE DEVIL

Even before dawn crept tentatively down the foothills, my mother strapped me with cotton cloth to her skeletal frame and we joined the exodus snaking its way south to Tigray.

Land mines peppered the roads. The charred remains of bombed bridges left villages disconnected, with no mainstream thoroughfare between the two countries. The 250km bus trip Bishkash had planned to her homeland was halted at the border. From there, she was forced to continue on foot; barefoot in fact, since she couldn't afford shoes.

With me bundled on her back, Bishkash began the arduous trek over the rugged mountains. Increasing dread kept pace with her footfalls. She came across concealed camps of soldiers in the highlands. The terrain she crossed was scarred by recent battles and she had to sidestep abandoned military equipment. Gunfire growled persistently around us and echoed through the valleys below.

War is not just a battle for power: it is an all-consuming chaos. No one is safe—not the wealthy, nor the earnest, nor the innocent. In times of peace, when you hear of trouble elsewhere, you might feel distant sympathy. Everyone can roll their eyes over statistics and poor politics, but those who haven't lived it cannot comprehend the real tragedy. Think what it is to trudge in the worn tracks of hope that *tomorrow* this madness will cease, only to have a string of tomorrows multiply into weeks, months and years.

Despite her youth, Bishkash was malnourished and frail. Shouldering an energetic 3-year-old, she was unable to carry enough food to sustain us for the entire journey. Instead, she relied on the generosity of strangers we met along the way.

My mother had little more than a few sips of water to keep her going and my boisterousness strained her already limited energy. I refused to keep still on her back no matter how tightly she strapped me to her. As often as she threw a cloth over our heads to protect us from dust and harsh sunlight I would pull it away, curious to see this new passing world. The more she tried, the more determined I was to poke my head back out into the open.

She walked all day and most nights, stopping from time to time at farmers' houses along the way to beg for something to eat and a place to rest. After the recent famine, families were struggling to feed their own let alone the child of a stranger, but we were usually permitted to rest outside the houses until Bishkash could summon the strength to press on.

With each passing hour, her footfalls grew heavier, yet she continued to walk, losing count of time. It took others up to two weeks to complete the journey. So many lives were torn that had once been simple and safe. The only encouragement one traveller could offer another was that they were not alone.

When we finally arrived in Slehleka, Bishkash was in a terrible state. Her shoeless feet were cut and swollen. Starvation, dehydration and sleep deprivation had all taken their toll.

People say it takes a crisis to bring out our best. I don't really know if that's true when the crisis is not a single event but has become a constant condition of life. Sometimes, all we can do is put one foot in front of the other and just keep going.

Considering the debilitating challenges thrust on her, I am amazed at my mother's resilience. Perhaps her inner strength had a subtle influence on my own determination to succeed against the odds later in life. If so, I will always be grateful.

I'm told that Bishkash's fortitude came from family pride in their heritage. Yet, believing she was of a noble people, it was all the harder for her to face reality. There was no practical wisdom to aid her now, just dusty genealogy. One thought drew her on: the comfort of Zenebech. It was all she had left.

The marathon journey was meant to rescue us from the trials we'd faced so far, for *what one hopes for is always better than what one has*,[1] but Bishkash was distressed to learn that Zenebech was facing her own challenges. The region had been ravaged by famine. Zenebech's son has been killed in the war and the family wealth had dwindled further, leaving her devastated. She had free-fallen from the last remnants of privilege and now struggled to adjust to an impoverished life. Thus, Zenebech was unable to offer my mother any long-term assistance, but allowed us to stay with her until other arrangements could be made.

After three months, Great-grandmother asked one of her nephews if he could take us in. Unable to refuse the request of an elderly relative, he agreed. Shortly afterwards, he was transferred to Aksum for work. So, determined to keep a roof our heads, he took us to his daughter, Brinesh, who lived nearby in Shire.

"I can no longer keep my promise to Zenebech," the nephew explained. "I need you to take care of this family for me."

Brinesh kindly agreed.

Though we'd tumbled from one transient state to another, family loyalty cushioned us from utter despair, for a while longer at least.

Tribal allegiance is an age-old strength in my country, though some

---

1. Ethiopian proverb.

may argue otherwise. There are numerous ethnic groups, each tremendously loyal to their own. Anyone of the same bloodline, even a stranger, is welcomed like a long-lost brother when entering the tribal region.

In the past, such links ensured survival. But with emerging political systems, some regions thrived while others suffered, depending on the ruling tribe's preference for its own.

By the time Emperor Selassie was dethroned in 1974, Tigray had become the poorest and least developed region in Ethiopia. The ongoing economic struggle, compounded by decades of recurring famine, heightened the people's dissatisfaction. The Tigrayan peasants were further alienated by the new regime's labour and land policies, which restructured all holdings into national farms.

In 1975, a group of university students launched the Tigrayan People's Liberation Front.[2] Initially, they formed clandestine cells among the discontented populace, inspiring a grassroots revolution. Retaliation from the ruling Dergue was fierce.

We had one thing in common with the TPLF: their home base was also ours—Shire. So Bishkash had literally walked out of one war and straight into the heart of another. It wasn't long before battles between the TPLF and the Dergue moved from the outskirts of the village to the main streets of Shire and we were once again surrounded by the sights, sounds and putrid smells of war.

As a young child in Shire (I was about four at the time), I rarely felt safe. Fear accompanied me everywhere like an overbearing friend. There was no escaping it. When I look back at my childhood photo, I can see it lurking there. The vivid sensation of constant severe insecurity still jars me with nightmares.

Like voracious monsters, tanks incessantly rumbled through the streets. Outbursts of nearby gunfire startled me. Barely suppressed terror on the adult's faces kept me on edge. For a small boy with no

2. TPLF.

other experience, the world seemed a sinister place.

As I huddled behind closed doors, listening to battles passing by, I could never imagine that children in other parts of the world might be watching afternoon television or going to soccer training; their dinner would never be scant; at night, they could snuggle under freshly laundered linen, gazing up at posters of their heroes on the wall. All I knew was the constant threat of bullet holes in mine.

I have no memory of my mother ever attempting to allay my fears. She never clasped me in her arms for comfort or whispered that everything would be all right. I can't say that Bishkash didn't love me, but I always felt she was more like my caretaker. I suspect she was so consumed with her own personal struggle for survival that she overlooked my emotional needs. Even as young as five, I understood that I didn't have a father, so in my mind there was an equal chance that I didn't have a real mother.

I had to cope alone. In the surrounding uncertainty, she never provided me with any routine, so I was left to wander the streets. The unpredictability of each moment gave me little sense of belonging.

There was one exception though, one place where the worries of my world disappeared: when I was cradled in the velvet-smooth embrace of Ge-ge Zenebech. My mother and I visited her regularly, and I treasure fond memories of the times I spent with her.

Once, while scouting for adventure some distance from her house, I came across some farmers cutting *teff*.[3] Golden piles of the harvest rose before me like an emperor's treasure trove. No sooner had I crawled to the top of a mountain of grain, when I heard Ge-ge calling me from the house, "Tewodros? Where are you my son? Are you okay? Please, my son, come home."

Her voice was music to my ears, and the only one I obeyed. When she spoke, I listened. When she called me, I came running.

---

3. An Ethiopian grain. (Amharic)

Bishkash and Cousin Brinesh would shake their heads in disbelief. They always struggled to keep me out of mischief, yet saw me following my great-grandmother's orders without question.

My mother began to regret following the priest's advice in naming me. Defiant to the core, I rebelled against authority and refused discipline. Brinesh sometimes wondered why the saints had burdened my mother with such an ungovernable son. Worse still, Bishkash herself worried that I actually was the son of the Devil.

My uncontrollable behaviour continued day-in day-out, though it was Brinesh who suffered most. I regret this because my antics were never aimed at her. I was crying out for attention from my mother, but as I became conscious of her coldness towards me, I started to resent her. My rebellion flared in wicked ways.

Brinesh's husband wore fine neatly pressed shirts, with pearly buttons. When I realised that the buttons were perfect for using in games with my friends, I couldn't resist them. I was secretly proud of possessing a rusty old razorblade and I often used it to painstakingly slice off the buttons, one by one, being careful not to slip and cut the shirt. Understandably, Brinesh was not happy, especially when her husband was preparing for a business trip and discovered that not a single button remained on any of his shirts.

To avoid discovery (and subsequent punishment), I became quite inventive at concealing my implement. Anywhere outside the house was too risky, as some other kid would probably find it. Inside the house was the women's domain where no private hoard was left undisturbed. So, after much trial and error, I found two places that I considered safe enough to avoid detection. The first was inside my shoes. Here my treasure was easy to access and was with me all day long (should I happen to chance upon a shirt with buttons still intact), and it was not an obvious hiding place to the adults. Sometimes I didn't wear shoes. On such occasions, I carefully wrapped the blade in paper and placed it between my buttocks. *Wah-ha!* I was so pleased with myself the first time Brinesh turned the house upside down looking for the mysterious slicer, when all along it was planted securely between my cheeks.

As well as the masterly button-ectomy, my favourite operation was performed on the rope of the village well. I'd gleefully make seesaw cuts through the coarse fibres until the hoisting wheel spun out the ends of the rope and the bucket hurtled into the depths with a satisfying splash. This made it impossible for the families of the village to get their water, and it cost Brinesh a hefty three *birr*[4] to fix each time.

My capriciousness troubled more than the adults. Brinesh's daughters still tease me over one incident. Their father had arrived home from a trip, bringing dresses for them but nothing for me. Feeling excluded, I was incensed whenever I saw the girls wearing their outfits.

An opportunity for revenge came one day when they were flouncing about in their fine clothes. We were outside when I happened to notice a freshly dug deep hole, which workmen had prepared for an electricity pole. I told the girls I wanted to play a new game and asked them to stand in the hole.

Unquestioningly, they did.

I started covering them with dirt and was about halfway through my mission when an elderly man passed by. He began shouting, "*Ata, baallaga!*[5] Stop it!" (The older villagers considered themselves the watchdogs of the community.) He threw his hands in the air and said, "May the Devil come and take you!" He glanced around and shouted to the neighbours, "Come and see what Bishkash's naughty boy is doing this time!"

Quickly, I became the focus of quite a crowd. It wasn't wise to stay a moment longer, so I made myself scarce before punishment (or the Devil) could snatch me.

---

4. US$0.60 (approximately).
5. You misbehaving child! (Amharic)

The Little Devil

Religion is an intrinsic part of Ethiopian life. Some people pray for hours each day. The Orthodox priest always carries a sizeable crucifix in his chest pocket. Whenever he is out walking, people approach him and ask to kiss the cross. Patiently, he presents it for their veneration.

Whenever people pass by churches, they stop and kiss the ground or the wall in front of the church and say a prayer. Usually they pray for their lives to improve. Even when motoring past, people bow their heads and make a sign of the cross.

It is also common to see religious symbols as body art. When Bishkash was a child, her right hand was tattooed with an Orthodox cross. Brinesh has a similar tattoo, though more prominent, in the centre of her forehead.

People from my culture bargain with God and his diverse multitude of saints: *Please, God, if you do this for me, I will make that prayer. . . .* This tradition even reflects the old superstitions of animal sacrifices made to various nature spirits for good fortune. A minority of the population still adheres to those old customs.

Although people are devoutly religious, the traditional superstitions maintain a strong underlying influence in everyone's thinking. One might expect that there would be a conflict between these two belief systems, but the motivation for each is the same: fear. In the old ways, you fear that the Devil will get you; in the expressions of Coptic belief, you fear that God will punish you.

Parents give their children three things: food, clothing, and the fear of God. A child means security for the parents (and grandparents), who dread the time when they can no longer provide for themselves. This future responsibility might seem burdensome, but it gives the child a sense of worth, of belonging, of deserving.

If you adhere to your family's wishes, they will praise you: *may you have good health; may you be rich; may you have a long and happy life.* But such blessings are generally the language of the wealthy.

On the other hand, a child who disrespects his elders in any way is cursed severely. The *argeman*[6] understand first hand the importance of this cycle and generously heap curses upon their future providers.

In a society where fear is inherent, a curse is a powerful thing.

Children of the poorer castes have no choice but to work for the family from an early age. They are anxious about being expelled from the family (the only form of security and safety they know). Parents intimidate and often reject young ones who misbehave. These outcasts become street kids. Shunned by all, they face a terrible struggle for survival.

As the generations roll on, those who have been reared on threats and curses in turn deliver threats. Yet nothing diminishes the fear, and the negative cycle continues.

Without fully understanding it, I was hovering precariously close to becoming an outcast. But what does a small child understand of such harsh truths? I trusted in my *metab* to protect me and recklessly pursued every invitation from life to be curious, inventive and one step beyond the reach of reproach.

If there was mischief to be had, I could find it. When Brinesh's maid spent hours preparing curry, then served it up only to discover that the meat had vanished, I was the culprit (with a sated belly). If a single shoe disappeared just as someone was about to go out, the finger was always pointed at me—quite rightly, of course.

Did any of this bring the motherly attention I craved? Sadly, no.

Despite my waywardness, I'd like to think that I occasionally did my part in contributing to the house. My friends and I would go out to the fields and sit on the raised bed-like platforms positioned for watching over the tall crops (such as corn). We kept a sentinel eye on any birds or animals that might come foraging. Our preferred weapons for defending the harvest were slingshots made from a forked branch and some old tyre-tubing. Sometimes our shots were

6. Tribal elders. (Amharic)

accurate and powerful enough to slay the thief. Like proud hunters, we returned home and displayed our kill. If it was deemed edible, it would be plucked or skinned and served up for dinner.

Our culture's foundations are embedded in the sense of community. The communal consciousness means you are part of a large, single entity. The wellness of the whole is crucial to the wellness of the individuals, not the reverse.

Given that the motivation for each day is to provide food, this becomes the focal point. Every morning, the villagers gather at someone's house for the coffee ceremony. The people attune themselves as a group to the success of the day, and then go to it. The next morning, someone else will be the host, all the problems will be solved and all the good things celebrated. That's tradition.

Skipping its merry way through all the differences of ethnicity, language and religion, there is one element that pervades all aspects of life and dissolves all barriers: rhythm. The drum is always calling. It is all around you and its magic grows within you from infancy. The drum is in church, at weddings and festivals; even in the street. Its rhythm is never lonely, as it inspires music and song. People dance and sing and freely express themselves. All cares fade as everyone comes together in this basic, life-affirming pastime.

I remember when Ge-ge took me to a wedding. During the ceremony when everyone's attention was on the bride and groom, I bowled up to the groom and challenged him, "Excuse me, mister, but you have to leave because *I* am going to marry the bride, so just be on your way now."

Embarrassed by my interruption, Zenebech hurriedly covered my mouth while I tried wriggling free to continue shouting my intentions to the world.

I wonder if I felt so displaced from my perceived lack of love that I thought creating my own family would make things right. Or perhaps I really was a naughty little devil.

61

I had become expert at disappearing when the occasion demanded. Only once did these vanishing antics actually cause any concern for Bishkash and Brinesh. I was about seven years old when I somehow ended up 30km away at Ge-ge's place, shoeless and thirsty. I can't remember how or why I did it, only that I was so angry with my mother that I wanted to be far away from her. Whatever saints still had faith in me must have guided my steps past land mines, hidden me from soldiers and kept me below any lines of fire. I'd never ventured that far alone in the past, and I don't think Bishkash had even noticed my absence until a message from Ge-ge informed her of my expedition.

I was escorted home to Shire by a relative who decided to take the shorter route through the mountains. On the way, we came across a group of TPLF soldiers sitting on rocks, cleaning their guns. They looked up as we timidly passed by and one of them shouted, "Hey—boy! You have to fight with us and win this war!"

Although I was used to seeing the soldiers on the streets, none had ever spoken to me before and I was quite intimidated. My disappearing tricks ceased from that moment.

You might think that school was the best place for such a scallywag to learn some discipline, but I was still too small.

At the time, starting school was not based on age but on physical development. It was generally accepted that a child's level of hand-to-eye co-ordination determined his or her ability to concentrate and process information. Until the limbs had grown enough, co-ordination was supposedly insufficient for successful learning. Quite simply, until the child could reach over his head and touch his opposite ear, he wasn't ready for school.

I was underdeveloped in this respect, so my early lessons came from the street. It was there that I discovered the importance of networking. Without connections you were likely to be teased, beaten up or even have your buttons stolen!

The Little Devil

Although I had friends, they weren't always around when most needed, so I quickly learned to protect myself by mastering the art of talking—not just any kind of talking (because that could get me into trouble too), but talking with confidence—like a tough guy— like I wasn't afraid of anyone. I observed the older boys and mimicked their gestures, their speech and their attitude. I used words and phrases that I didn't fully understand. Having a smart mouth brought me respect. Nobody dared tease me.

But it was a façade. On the inside, I was still a scared little boy.

Street life was often disrupted by the sound of gunfire and explosions, which sent the children (including tough-talkers like me) scurrying home. The safest place was under the bed. At times, bullets would hit Brinesh's house, piercing the walls and sending puffs of dust into the air. Every day, I cautiously stepped out to find shops and buildings scarred from the lead rain of the day before. Many houses in the area were dotted with black tar, which filled the bullet holes, keeping the real rain out.

One afternoon, I was playing with my friend Alula, near the hospital not far from Brinesh's house. Alula and I met up each day and ventured around the village (looking for mischief). Sometimes we played soccer with the other boys; other times we threw rocks at stray dogs or built things from rubbish we found on the roadside. On this particular afternoon, we were sitting in the dust trying to make new slingshots from some recently discarded rubber.

While we were experimenting with the best way to attach the rubber to the branch, a commotion erupted nearby. The yelling didn't sound like a neighbours' dispute. It must have been soldiers. Alula and I ran to see what was happening. The shouting intensified as we snuck closer. When we reached the corner, we cautiously edged our heads around to see three men standing against the hospital's stone wall.

Through a gap in the fence beside us, I spied a lady, crouching in her garden. She was frantically signalling for us to leave. She had pulled her scarf over her head and tightly across her face, as if that would block her senses from what was about to happen.

I looked back at the wall. The three men had raised their hands, as ordered by the surrounding soldiers. Then, one soldier took aim and pulled the trigger—three times. My ears screamed with the echoing shots. Three corpses now slumped at the foot of the wall in pools of blood.

The image poured in through my widened eyes, filling me with heavy horror. I couldn't breathe, couldn't blink, couldn't move— until the fearful weight hit my feet and I raced for the sanctuary of home, with Alula as my shadow.

Later, we made a pact, by spitting on the ground and stomping our feet, never to tell anyone what we had witnessed that day. It wasn't the last time I heard gunshots from the direction of the hospital wall, but I didn't dare venture there again.

With an increasing number of such spontaneous executions, even in a remote place like Shire, we were beginning to feel an uncompromising terror. The latest surge of counteraction from government troops lodged a new kind of fear in our bellies. Anyone whose blink even looked like it was ideologically opposed to the communist regime had their eyes closed forever.

I was too young to understand politics, but I understood blood and death and horror.

We stayed with Brinesh until I was six years old. Despite all the trouble I'd caused, she didn't want us to leave. My mother was grateful, but felt that we must move on, again.

Bishkash yearned to be independent. She had resumed her school studies at the Year Ten level, hoping this would lead to better options for our future. She wanted to have a place of her own where she could raise me and focus on her studies.

By this time, the monthly contributions from Asmerom had stopped. Somehow, my mother managed to pay the rent on a one-room unit in the same neighbourhood as Brinesh. At 0.5 *birr* per month, the cost was only half of what it would have been under Selassie's rule. The room was small and cramped, but good enough for the two of us, and we weren't far from Brinesh's house and her continuing care.

A shift in house meant a shift in awareness as I became conscious of my impoverished world. The stark reality of my mother's financial situation became painfully apparent with the shrinking size of the meals. Ingredients were carefully rationed and portions were limited to about half of what I'd been getting at Brinesh's house.

I relished each mouthful all the more. But I was like a ravenous hyena if there was a threat of having to share the meal with an unexpected visitor—and usually that visitor was Brinesh. Too often, I went to bed still famished. I learned that a guest at mealtime was not good. On one occasion, my defensive eating nearly cost me my life.

It was early evening. I'd just returned from playing outside and sat down on the dirt floor at the small table where my mother had served up *doro wet.*

Throughout the day, the appetising scent of curry had drifted from the small pot on the stove out into the streets, wooing keen grumbles from my belly. A curry containing meat was a rarity because it was so expensive.

As I salivated over my soon-to-be-filled plate, footsteps neared the front door. I sucked in a defensive breath, almost choking on my tongue. Soldiers? No. Thieves? Of course not. A guest for dinner? Most likely!

I looked to the heavens. Even though I had no idea who "the Lord" was, I'd often heard my mother asking Him for help. It seemed that He could resolve almost any unfavourable situation. *Please, Lord,* my thoughts raced, *whoever is at the front door, send them away until dinner is—*

"Hello?" Brinesh's voice interrupted. "Bishkash? Tewodros? Is anyone at home?"

I kept silent and signalled for my mother to do the same, but instead she walked over and opened the door. As the women greeted one another, my mind was racing. I had only two options: share the food with Brinesh and go to bed hungry, or eat as much as I could before she could sit down. Based on experience, I decided on the latter.

I tore off a piece of *injera*, soaked it in the sauce of the *doro wet*, then wrapped it around the biggest piece of chicken I could find on the plate and shoved the whole lot directly into my small mouth. My cheeks expanded to maximum capacity and my jaw could hardly move. I put my hand to my mouth and squeezed my lips shut to keep the contents from spilling out onto the table.

At that point, my mother turned and started to lead Brinesh to the table. Desperately wanting to get one more mouthful in before they sat down, I decided to swallow this one whole, because chewing first wasn't filling my belly. As I pushed the wad of food to the back of my mouth, the spices burned my throat. I began coughing and spluttering, occasionally releasing a half-chewed missile. Unable to breathe, I gulped, trying desperately to snatch a pocket of air.

The women were baffled. Brinesh's forehead pressed into furrowed wrinkles that swallowed up her tattooed cross. I don't remember anyone's panic but my own, which I tried to hold back along with the precious mouthful.

After almost choking to death, I finally surrendered and spat everything out onto a tissue my mother held before me. My greed had wasted the very food I'd so desperately wanted. So you could say that I lived to starve another day.

Since arriving in Shire, Bishkash had been busy trying to re-establish her life and move with dignity into the adult world. Brinesh's father, who was a judge, had urged my mother to sue my father for financial assistance. In October 1978, the court case was announced in the local paper.

The Little Devil

File No: 113/70

The plaintiff, Miss Bishkash Kidane, is suing the defendant, Doctor Solomon Fekadu. The matter is to be heard on 9 November, 1978. The defendant should come on the date specified otherwise the court will review the case based on documentation submitted by the plaintiff. The matter will be decided by the court based on that documentation.

Stamp: Shire District Court

My father failed to attend any of the hearings and so my mother eventually gave up. (I've recently learned that Solomon was furthering his medical qualifications at Addis Ababa University and therefore would have been extremely protective of his reputation in those circles.)

Around this time, the flawed foundations of my existence crumbled further. Bishkash began a relationship with Belachew, a classmate of hers. He was from the region of Gojjam in west Ethiopia, home to the Amhara tribe. He was a short stocky man with a round face and a moustache that made him look several years older than his real age.

I can't recall meeting Belachew for the first time, but much to my chagrin he soon became a regular part of our lives. Prior to this, I'd been the only man in my mother's life—even if her attention was either functional or fleeting. I disliked my rival from the very beginning.

In reaction to Belachew's arrival, my behaviour regressed significantly; something I sensed myself, even though I was only seven years old. I was constantly frustrated, lashing out at everything and everyone. I noticed how Bishkash looked at Belachew adoringly and tended to his every need. I was resentful and jealous of the attention she gave him, so I made their contact as difficult as I could.

My rage often drove me outside into the rain. I slathered my body with mud, ignoring their calls for me to come back inside. At night when they went to bed together or when she made him breakfast in the mornings, I left the house, collected a handful of rocks and threw them at their bedroom wall or on the roof. During this time, I felt more abandoned than ever.

Tired of my antics, Bishkash decided it was time for punishment. One day, she called me to the outside kitchen. Without any explanation, she calmly tied my hands behind my back, just as I'd seen the people at the markets tie up a sheep's legs. Still silent, she covered my face with a sticky paste of *beso*[7] and sugar. Then she dragged me outside into the sunlight where I had to stand and endure flies and other insects crawling over my face. My mother knew how much I hated *beso* and thought this would be the ultimate punishment.

I whinged and cried and begged her to release me while throwing my head backwards and forwards, trying to get the sticky paste to fall from my face. Eventually, exhausted, I surrendered. Not until I apologised for my behaviour did Bishkash untie my hands. I couldn't wash my face fast enough.

After completing their Year Ten studies, Bishkash and Belachew became engaged. Upon hearing the news, Brinesh teased, "How can you truly love an Amhara? He's so short!"

My mother steadfastly replied, "But, Brinesh—love has no eyes!"

In reality, I think Bishkash was probably relieved to find a good man who was prepared to marry her after all she'd been through. Although I wasn't conscious of it at the time, Belachew was softly spoken and treated her well, which is more than she and her family could have hoped for just a few years before.

In the political and social climate of the time, it was also much safer for her to be married. The Dergue soldiers had earned a reputation for raping unmarried women.

---

7. Barley. (Amharic)

Already familiar with such an ordeal and its lifelong consequences, Bishkash was willing to do almost anything to prevent it from happening again. And she was not alone; many women at this time married only for the security it provided.

Like my mother, Belachew didn't have a lot of money. He started work at Shire Hospital as a nurse's aide. Although he didn't live with us, he supported us as best he could on a modest income. In the meantime, Bishkash was struggling to pay the rent, so she found a cheaper place for us to live until they married.

There were many singular experiences that signalled change in my life at this time. Two of them had a lasting impact.

First, I discovered milk, straight from the cow. Every morning, Bishkash sent me to the neighbour's house to collect a bottle of fresh warm milk. I took my time, stopping where I pleased to chat with friends on the street.

On the way home, my empty stomach would coax me to plunder the frothy milk. As if watching someone else, I saw my arm raise the bottle to my mouth, and then felt myself guzzling half of its delicious contents. Believe me, it was out of my control: irresistible the first day, delicious the next, habit from then on. I cleverly disguised my theft (or so I thought) by stopping at another neighbour's house and asking for some water with which I secretly topped up the milk bottle.

My mother always complained that the milk was thin and tasteless, but she continued to send me for it and I continued to water it down. Then one day when she and some neighbours were having coffee, one of them asked her why I wanted water every morning. Of course Bishkash realised that it wasn't an ailing cow but a wicked boy who had produced the watery milk.

The next morning, I went on my errand as usual, but the moment I asked the neighbour for water, Bishkash and the others came running triumphantly from their houses.

I stood with the half-empty bottle in my hand and looked at my mother in shock. I couldn't believe she had outsmarted *me*, her street-wise son. As her laughter mingled with the others', I thought there'd be no punishment, but her smile dropped as she walked over to me. She bent and pinched me hard on the inner thigh, twisting my skin until tears welled up in my eyes.

The pain was brief, but my craving for milk has remained. Even now, fresh milk is one of my favourite drinks and the taste transports me back to those carefree mornings.

The second notable experience came when my mother began to share her love of English with me. It was the first time she showed any real interest in my development and I savoured every moment. I had no idea what English was, except that it sounded strange; and even less of an idea that, decades later, it would lead me to freedom and the love of my life.

Each night in our shared bed, we would lie head to foot while she went through simple words such as *hair, nose,* and *eye,* repeating them over and over until they were firmly embedded in my memory. I couldn't understand the importance of learning the strange-sounding words, but I looked forward to my nightly lessons because it was the only time she spent with me.

When Bishkash married Belachew, we moved to yet another house; this time with him. It was newer and larger than our previous place, but I quickly found that "newer" didn't necessarily equate with better.

The walls of the house were made from a coarse mixture of grass, mud and cow manure plied onto a wooden frame and lined on the inside with newspaper. I can still remember that awful stench. Not even the strong smell of *etan*[8] and roasting coffee could hide it.

Like all the houses in the village, its floor was dirt, and there was no electricity. Our only source of light in the evenings was a gas lamp.

---

8. Frankincense. (Amharic, Tigrinya)

In 1979, my mother had a baby boy called Habtamu. His arrival diverted the little attention I had from Bishkash. And a bigger family meant even less food. Meat was no longer even a luxury: it was an exclusion.

Occasionally, extended family members would enquire about our situation. A visit from my mother's cousin, Bisrat, heralded another radical change for me. She was disturbed to see how we lived. Even by Ethiopian standards, our impoverished lives were extreme. Distressed at the sight of my malnourished body, Bisrat offered to take me in, but Bishkash refused. Then Bisrat suggested she could arrange for me to live with Solomon or one of his relatives.

Curses were still routinely heaped upon my father. By now I had an idea of the Lord, and I had a healthy fear of the Devil. But the grimaces and sour whispers associated with "that evil snake-on-two-legs sin-bringing bastard" had me thinking there were worse monsters yet; though I didn't know it meant *him*.

My mother could see that our situation was worsening each day, especially now with the new baby. She and her husband struggled to put food on the table and keep a roof over our heads. She wasn't in a position to take proper care of her children and knew that I would be better off with Bisrat or even (God save me) with Solomon's family, despite the fact that Eritrea was in as much political and social turmoil as Tigray.

After seizing control in Ethiopia, the Dergue naively believed that the Eritrean insurgents fighting for independence would lay down their arms once the imperial regime was overthrown. How wrong they were. The struggle became the most important political challenge the Dergue would face since taking full power. During our time in Shire, the new leader, Colonel Mengistu Haile Mariam, ordered the arrest and mass slaughter of so-called enemies of the revolution, including Tigrayans and Eritreans. This sinister period of Ethiopian history became known as the Red Terror. The Dergue even proudly brandished signs in the capital, which read

"Let Red Terror be Intensified."

Everyone looked sideways at their neighbours. No one knew what might get them killed, much less how to endure.

So, Bishkash was in a quandary: either I could remain with her where my health would continue to suffer or she could send me to live with my father's family, who were financially better off, though their lives were constantly buffeted by the ongoing civil war.

If I'd known what plans were being laid for me, I would have run to Ge-ge Zenebech, fear giving me winged feet. For worse than the terror of war is to discover that you are the son of Satan, and into his den you will be inevitably drawn.

5

'TWIXT HEAVEN AND HELL

A mighty warrior leads a cavalcade across his domain. The dust clouds cannot dim his glory. From horizon to horizon, he knows no fear . . . I wish.

I was eight years old (well, almost nine, but still just a kid—tiny and terrorised). I woke in the dark, sensing that something had changed. Faint patters of doom quivered through me. With wide-eyed apprehension, I watched my mother place a few possessions in a small plastic bag. She moved quietly, efficiently, and did not look me in the eye.

She gave me a piece of bread and a glass of milk. Perhaps, if I didn't consume them, I could hold off what was about to happen (whatever it was). Hunger first, heroics later. I gobbled them up.

My mother took me by the hand where I had just wiped my milky lips. The chill air sharpened my fear as we stepped out into the yawning day, on an unscheduled excursion.

Bishkash walked brusquely. She didn't speak. Maybe we were quietly racing away from Belachew and the baby. Maybe my mother

73

realised that living in a house made of shit was just as foolish as *I* thought it was and we would travel together to find a new home, just the two of us. The crunch of her shoes on the gravel was echoed by my shuffling to keep up.

Noises reached out to us through the dark. The bestial baritone rumble of a truck convoy throbbed in the town centre: soldiers' trucks. Obediently lined up and poised for a journey, they pointed north.

Smoky black exhaust entwined with clouds of dust from the frenzy of the jostling crowd. People were thrusting an assortment of life's possessions onto the end truck's tray, desperately trying to clamber aboard, squeezing out a space for themselves, and bickering over who'd been there first. Bags of clothing, pots and pans, mattresses, and even chickens were being thrown backwards and forwards until they were absorbed into the conglomeration. They looked like a writhing, multiheaded monster skulking in the dark, hiding from whatever dread they were escaping. The smoke enveloped them in slow circles while they raced and pressed and hunched before becoming desperately still.

Untouched by the chaos, market vendors filed past with their donkeys and sheep, bringing the dawn with them. *They* were not leaving. They would start this day like any other, eyes straight ahead. Do what you know and keep doing it. God will take care of the rest.

The driver's assistant barked an alert of imminent departure. A deep roar from the truck shuddered through my feet. Bishkash brushed her lips on my forehead, lifted me with my small bag into the belly of the beast and mouthed goodbye under the din.

A relative, already seated, held me firmly as I lurched back, realising what had happened. She was *not* coming with me.

"Ma-ma! Please, please let me stay with you!" I managed to grab and hold tightly to her *gabi*. She unclenched my fingers and used the corner of it to wipe away the tears streaming down my cheeks.

"Tewodros, behave yourself."

"I will. *I will.* I'll behave myself here *with you*, I—I'll take care of Habtamu. And be nice to Belachew. Please, *Moth*—!"

"Adey Selas is expecting you. You will be much happier where you are going." She spoke sternly now, stepping back, watching hands drag me into the depths of the truck as I reached for the unreachable.

They pushed me into a squat. I landed on a chicken which shrieked in protest. My cries burst forth, too. Screaming, crying, begging, I called for my mother to take me back. Was she crying? Were her big eyes taking their last look at me?

As the truck moved off, my vision flooded. My mother's face disappeared into the crowd and eventually into the distance. I didn't know when or where I would see her again.

No amount of wishing could instil the heart of a warrior in me.

The bleak sky capped the world in numbness. I felt nothing, yet all of me ached. I was hollow, yet bursting. The wind bit through my thin clothes and whipped across my face. Exhaust fumes and dust spewed up into the open back where we all huddled. Everyone drew shawls or pulled sweaters over their noses and mouths against the filthy air. All eyes remained closed, shutting out the grit.

The sounds and sights of war and violence were familiar to me (though one never gets used to that), but these people had always gathered together for coffee or shared what they had, reminding each other that life goes on. They bewildered me now—shrunken, afraid and closed. I was in deep shock over being sent away, but these fearful faces frightened me more. I couldn't comprehend how living could suck the life out of you.

Careful not to stumble on another wretched chicken, I clambered over people and their possessions to the front where I could snuggle against the truck cabin to gain some relief from the winds. I pushed my face up to the glass window and peered at the road beyond.

75

We were trailing after several military jeeps. They were equipped with machine guns and carried armed Dergue soldiers, who drove in advance in case TPLF guerrilla fighters decided to attack. A few jeeps also followed closely behind.

The convoy scaled the rugged terrain that Bishkash and I had traversed only a few years earlier. Our journey, then, had been to trudge doggedly onward. Now, the trip was punctuated with abrupt halts, each one thrusting the stowaways forward and squashing me against the cabin. Wary soldiers stared ahead or up into the hillsides. The rush of stillness would hover around us, then explode with gunfire—not every time, but often enough. Any nearby shepherds would dive behind rock cover while their animals scampered madly in all directions, their braying echoing after them. My fellow passengers clutched desperately at their rosary beads, violently whispering every prayer they knew to every saint they could remember. The air was thick with terror. I tried to bury my head, my mind and my heart down between my arms for the duration of the crossing.

At times, we were suspended in apprehension. Minutes whispered by. Boots barely shuffled on the gravel as soldiers tensed for action. Involuntary curiosity drew my gaze hypnotically up out of my private cave to stare at the same nothing that absorbed them.

I peeked through the front window where I could see soldiers cautiously stepping over the road in zigzag sweeps. Their strange movements confused me. This truck, this island of petrified people amid the sea of uncertainty, was now my whole world. I struggled to see some logic, some stability that reassured me there was a way through this. Later, I learned that the soldiers stopped whenever they suspected there were landmines on the road ahead.

We eventually made it safely to Asmara, the city of my birth. So much had happened there in the first third of my short life, but I recalled none of it. As I was lifted from the engorged truck, it was like being born again, only this time there was no mother to hold me.

Asmara is home to around half a million people, approximately one-eighth of the Eritrean population. There are nine distinct ethnic groups, and roughly one-third of these are nomadic or semi-nomadic. Tigrinya is the national language although, for a period in the 1950s, Emperor Haile Selassie attempted to impose Amharic as the language of non-choice. As a consequence, the latter is still widely spoken throughout the country. Arabic is common along the coast and the Sudanese border. Elsewhere, the language is determined by the dominant ethnic group of the area.

I was too exhausted just then to appreciate the surroundings, but I couldn't help noticing how clean everything was: the city, the people, the air . . . everything seemed to shine somehow. All that I'd known before was so worn and dull and tired. As time went on, I came to observe that Eritreans lived far more modern and wealthier lives than Ethiopians. Then, at least.

The Italian influence had favourably flavoured the atmosphere. It was evident in the architecture, food, fashion, and even the language. People were comfortable incorporating basic Italian words into their conversations.

There were patisseries and spaghetti restaurants. Going out for coffee and cake was somehow more festive and exciting than the traditional coffee ceremony at someone's house, particularly for the younger people.

Whereas Emperor Selassie had endured the Eritreans' struggle for independence, Mengistu sought dominance by force. This decisive action only inspired Eritreans to fight all the more fiercely for their goal.

By the time I arrived in Asmara in 1980, the Dergue regime had increased its military presence throughout the region. Relatives who lived there later noted that the period from 1978 to 1982 was the worst. Tigrinya was banned again during that time and dissidents of the revolution were hanged in public. Their mutilated bodies were piled high and left to rot on street corners.

Eritrean insurgents continued to counterattack, often so desperate to win the battle that they deployed disabled soldiers in the front line, a sure death sentence for most because they were used as a shield for the able-bodied men behind them. Even those with an arm missing were paired up with another amputee to work together, one pulling the trigger while the other fed bullets into the machine gun. This was a shocking contrast to Eritrean elegance in times of peace.

And here I was in the midst of it.

The dark shame of being my father's child was a mystery to me. I had no idea who he was or where he was, just that somehow, because of him, I was cursed. I didn't know if he would claim me or if I would be abandoned—or which would be worse.

Uncertainty is like churning gravel in the belly.

From the truck, I was whisked away to Cousin Bisrat's house where I remained for about a month. Bishkash had intended for me to live with Adey Selas, but Bisrat wanted to fatten me up before sending me on to my grandmother. In those weeks preceding Christmas, I was constantly offered food—I'd never known such a consistent luxury. Bisrat watched over me, encouraging me to talk and play—and eat. Although my mother was never far from my thoughts, I settled in reasonably well and enjoyed the company of Bisrat's grandchildren. Still, I missed my friends from Shire and wished especially that Alula could be with me.

As in Shire, games in Asmara were left up to our imaginations with whatever piece of junk we found. More often, though, activities were passed down from one kid to another, like privileged knowledge. When you spent enough time on the streets, you earned your place.

The most popular game in Asmara back then was racing a bicycle wheel or a car tyre down a hill. The city was filled with bicycles. Rusty old wheels were often lying about in side streets or rubbish areas. The hilly terrain was perfect for this game. With no shortage of slopes to race down, we were entertained for hours.

Sometimes, we spent the entire day walking around the city trying to find the steepest slope. When satisfied with our choice, we lined up across the crest with our wheel frames standing upright beside us. We were not children of war, playing with scrap because there was nothing else: we were proud and unified, skilled in the art of wheel-spinning. Admired by wheel-less onlookers, we were ready to sprint to glory. With one of the younger followers chosen as referee, we tensed, waiting for his command.

"Ready, set, go!"

We raced the wheels down the hill, chasing but never outpacing them as they spun to the depths. Victory was claimed by the one who could catch his wheel. The outcome was almost always the same: a pile of ragged dolls with skinned knees and bloodied noses lying higgledy-piggledy below. I don't recall anyone ever succeeding, but the thrill of achieving something that no one else had done was just too great to resist, so we would continue to race over and over, until our battered legs could carry us no more.

When we weren't racing, the wheels were like our mascots. They accompanied us everywhere and often got us into plenty of trouble. Neighbours complained as we propelled them around the streets, knocking over their parked bicycles, their children or sometimes their shop stands.

There are some common impressions of Africa that hold true: it *is* wild at heart. There may not be lions roaming the streets, but hyenas can sniff out opportunities from human carelessness. Their insidious presence had prompted a notably common structural feature from village to city: walls. Not only were homes surrounded by walls, but most people had a dog in their compound, which they never restrained.

As wild children of the streets, we roamed with a sense of freedom and daring. Occasionally, our swagger turned to a sprint as we raced to escape the bite of defensive dogs. Wah! I wasn't always fast enough.

I'd been living with Bisrat for some time and was just feeling comfortable, but change was at hand once more. Previously in Asmara, my mother and I had lived with Bisrat's daughter, Mebrat. By now, she thought her mother had done enough to help me and that it was time for me to move on. Mebrat had never been shy about making her thoughts known and could be very persuasive.

It was about midmorning when Mebrat came out onto the street and called me back to the house. She told me to pack up my belongings. Then we walked to the main road, and hailed a taxi.

"Mebrat, where are we going?" I asked cautiously, as we rode away. The past weeks had been like a blanket of security over my grief at being shunned. Now, tiny doubts peeked out.

"You're going to live with your grandmother," she said, looking out at the streets that rushed by. "But, don't worry. She doesn't live far, so you can visit us anytime."

Something must be wrong with me. Why else would people keep sending me away? I knew I was naughty, but no worse than many of the children I played with. Perhaps my mother was right—maybe I was the Devil's son.

The taxi entered the hilltop area of Maitemenai and continued along the main road, which had smaller streets branching off down the hill, back towards the city. We turned into one of these and descended about halfway when the taxi came to halt. I sat for a moment and looked around. All of the houses were enclosed by high fences, far more impressive than those downtown. Each house had a solid gate for a car to enter and, within that gate, there was a smaller grill about the size of a doorway through which the owners or visitors came and went.

Every fence looked exactly the same, only varying in colour. Adey's was cream. Mebrat knocked loudly on the metal gate. The door soon squeaked open to reveal a tall lady, who was renting one of Adey's two front rooms. She told Mebrat that Adey was not at home.

Mebrat then turned to me, "Tewodros, I'm sorry, but I have to leave."

I am a cave, forever echoing those words.

"This is your grandmother's house and you must wait here until she returns." As she spoke, she pointed to the front entrance where I was to remain. "Your grandmother should be home soon. If you need anything, knock on that door. Understand?" She cradled my chin, making sure that I was taking in each word.

Family—this fortress of identity—had no place for me. Like *the son of the Nile who thirsts for water*,[1] I had family all around me, yet none for myself.

I did not yammer or protest. I sat on the designated step. Overwhelmed by loneliness, I could not stop slow swollen tears welling from my heart and rolling down my cheeks. I struggled to breathe, my chest heaving under this new burden of grief.

"I will come back soon and visit you, okay?"

I couldn't respond. The inside of my body felt dry, like a piece of *injera* that had been left uncovered in the hot sun.

Mebrat must have felt guilty. She soon returned with a *beles*[2] in one hand and one *birr* in the other. *Beles* is a fruit loved by all Eritreans but, as I was new to the region, it had little significance for me. Her gifts were like matches to someone drowning; the gesture more for her comfort than mine.

In those desperate earlier days, when Bishkash had packed up and crossed the mountains looking for stability, she hadn't said goodbye to Adey Selas. I don't know why—shame, most likely. One day, Adey arrived for a regular visit to find everything intact: the bed,

1. Ethiopian proverb.
2. Cactus fruit; a sweet, spiky fruit that turns red when ripe. (Tigrinya)

the wash basin, all the miniature comforts of our little existence still in place, as if we'd just popped out on an errand. She tried to find us for months afterwards. No one had news. In the strife of war, anything could have happened.

Sometime after that, Bishkash had sent Adey a letter asking if money could be delivered to her in Shire. Of course, Adey complied, but their contact dissipated with distance and time, until not even money was a link.

I wonder if, during the following years of increasing chaos, I became a dim memory of the past for Adey, as she had become for me.

I sat, quietly sobbing, inside the gated compound entrance. For a child, five minutes of waiting is interminable. I was there for hours.

At last, a lady approached. She was dressed flawlessly in brilliant white, so bright that I had to squint as she entered the yard. The small sack of food in her arms rustled as she paused and inspected me.

She had one of the warmest faces I've ever seen and reminded me of Ge-ge Zenebech.

"Young boy?" she approached me. "What are you doing on my doorstep?" Just then, the tenant poked her head out and offered an explanation.

Adey marvelled, "Tewodros? Is that you?"

"Yes, I'm Tewodros," I replied meekly, unsure of how Adey would react to my presence. I was a toddler the last time we'd met.

She dropped the sack and swept me into a comforting embrace. Her clothes smelled of sweet perfume. I could feel her warm skin and her beating heart. She pulled me even closer. Enveloped in white, with my face buried in her round stomach, I struggled to breathe.

"How could I forget these beautiful soft curls and long eyelashes?" She rescued me from the folds of cloth and cupped my cheeks between her soft hands. Her smile gleamed with two silver teeth, one on each side of her mouth. I was forced to squint again as the sun was reflected directly into my eyes.

Adey opened her front door and guided me into the house. I'd never been inside such a sturdy structure before. It was rendered brick. All the furniture glistened and gleamed.

Till now, dust had been such an insidious part of my life. It puffed up from the unsealed roads and the grassless surrounds; it wafted in through every crevice and crack; it descended upon every surface like tired air breathing out.

Adey's home was a shiny new world.

She led me down the hallway and pointed to a spare bed in her room. "My son, this will be your bed while you are with me," she said.

I'd never had my own bed before, let alone one of such beauty. Each metal post was ornately decorated and sculpted, resembling the shape of the tops of Muslim mosques. It was painted white, with gold tips. The smooth finish felt sleek under my curious fingers. Viewing the rest of the room, I noted no bullet holes in the walls and it didn't reek of manure. I'd walked into a palace! My heart thrummed a rhythm of joy.

I looked on as Adey carefully unpacked my plastic bag of belongings and placed the things on *her* bedside table. She was making space for *me*. As each thing was laid out, it was like a validation: You belong here.

Without warning, loud footsteps stomped down the hallway towards us. An immaculately dressed young lady burst into the room, took one look at me and thrust out her arm as if to keep my (evil) presence at bay.

Snapping out of my short-lived bliss, I couldn't help but notice her perfectly manicured long blood-red nails shoved directly in my face.

"What is *he* doing here?" she demanded of Adey.

"This is Tewodros—Solomon's son," my grandmother replied as

she stood behind me, gently squeezing my shoulders.

"I know who he is! I want to know WHY he is HERE?" she yelled, her dark face reddening like her nail polish.

Okay, so she knew who I was, but who was she? And why was she so angered over me? (Had news of my naughtiness already travelled?) I gulped hard as she continued to rant. She removed the shawl from around her shoulders and threw it onto the bed, as if reclaiming ownership of what was to be mine. "He should be with his mother! This is not *your* problem, mother," she screeched.

"Almaz, please calm down. I didn't know Tewodros was coming to stay, but he is my grandson. What am I supposed to do? Turn him out on the streets so the hyenas can eat him?" My grandmother's hands trembled on my shoulders as she spoke. "Or should I send him to the EPLF headquarters to become a child soldier? Would that satisfy you?" she challenged softly.

Like the Big Bad Wolf, Almaz huffed and puffed and then stormed from the house, disappearing through the front gates. By then, I'd worked out that the angry lady was Adey's daughter and therefore my aunt. I was petrified when I realised she lived with Adey—with me—if this was my new home (who knew for how long).

It seemed there were angels and devils everywhere. I wondered on which side I would finally land.

I was nine years old when I first attended school and, until then, I had absolutely no understanding of structure, rules or how to follow a routine. For much of my young life, I was shunned by adults, and only got a modicum of attention for the basic essentials (*Come in/Eat/Get out*) or received the full force of someone's focus when I was in trouble. I was used to doing things in my own time (and mostly getting away with it) and struggled with the concept of being told what to do, and how and when to do it. Now, I was compelled to belong. A small rebel in a new world of domination, I marched daily to battle.

By this time, the Dergue had consolidated its communist philosophy into the mainstays of life's routines. On the first day of school, each student was given a textbook with Mengistu's picture, large and imposing, on the opening page. Every morning, we would sing the national anthem. The aptitude for conforming, not only to teachers but to a greater authority, was reinforced in all our learning. And, of course, we all wore uniforms. We were the young seeds that would become abundant with the Dergue's vision of one people, one state. It was so different from traditional trust in God. This was a brutal definition of a successful society that was to be carved into our mentality.

From a child's perspective, adults carry some secret knowledge of life. They've grown tall, a testament to their survival acumen; they control things, demonstrating that they have skills of a kind; and when they decide on something, they make it happen. A child either fits into their plans, or is seen at fault. There is no middle ground.

Children *always* showed respect for adults, particularly their parents and grandparents. We would stand when they entered a room, help them to carry things and address them politely using their appropriate titles. It was part of traditional belonging.

Respecting teachers was no different, except that they had no family obligation to us. They seemed to exploit their position of power over us, often speaking rudely, taunting or embarrassing us. They would call me (or any one of us) up in front of the class and ask a question about something way beyond my knowledge, leaving me to return to my seat under the mocking laughter of classmates (who were only relieved it wasn't their turn).

Punishment was a standard part of the curriculum and the teachers delivered it without exception. Students who lived remotely could walk for two to three hours to get to school, but if they were even five minutes late, they were punished. Childhood harboured many fears.

A strange dichotomy emerged for me. Living with Adey, I found an environment that rescued me from one kind of fear (of rejection) and delivered me into another (of punishment). This new dread dwelt in my belly. It weakened my legs. It made my hands shake.

Most often, the teachers automatically assumed we had already done something wrong or we were about to. Yelling was the preferred method of communication.

When someone is yelling at you, you are scared through and through. The brain shuts down. You panic. You can't think of what is required or why you are being yelled at in the first place. Sometimes, I peed myself from fear.

I was often late for school, since I was in no hurry to go under the hammer of conformity. My tardy appearance would invariably prompt a torrent of fury and derision from the teacher. If I was going to be punished anyway, then I might as well miss as much school as possible. Right? So I would dawdle along, kidding myself that I was fascinated by the lizard on the wall or slowed by the pebble in my shoe. Really, I was quaking inside at another impending confrontation.

Adults' faces can be quite funny when they're angry (though you shudder all the while). Their eyes bulge. The tendons in their necks strain. They puff up and their voices sound like raked pebbles. They ask you questions and then answer for you. They tower over you. They curse you. Their words don't really matter. It all comes down to the same thing: you are bad, bad, bad. *Now get out of my sight!*

I spent a lot of time on my knees outside the classroom door.

Then, of course, there was the whip—made from a bull's penis. It hung in full view of the class, within easy reach of a teacher just itching to give us another "lesson." What with the bruises on my knees and the welts from the whip, I learned a lot about compliance, if not school lessons.

Making friends was also challenging. Although I spoke Tigrinya, the dialect in Asmara was slightly different from that used in Tigray. My classmates constantly singled me out for being strange, poked fun at my use of words and funny accent, and called me *agame*.[3] I felt uncomfortable and awkward at school. I was out of my depth, and counted down the minutes until I could return to the street.

Socialising on the street was now limited to after school and weekends, but I soon found a group of neighbourhood children to play with each day. We were all keen to play soccer, but equipment was not readily available. Soccer balls, for instance, were difficult to come by, so we learned how to make our own—another skill passed down from one streetwise kid to another.

We used sponge and cloth, preferably with a silky texture, torn into long thin strips. The sponge formed the centre of the ball, which was carefully wrapped in several layers of cloth and stitched together with a needle and thread. Each kid meticulously stitched his own ball, paying careful attention to colour and design.

When deluxe scrap items were nowhere to be found, the only option was socks. We would gather a mountain of old socks, choose the largest, and keep stuffing it with the others until it resembled a decent-sized sphere.

Soccer boots or any kind of sports shoes were also a rarity and most children, including me, played in Congo shoes, which were plastic sandals favoured by soldiers and available quite cheaply almost anywhere. Many even played barefoot.

Every day after school I rushed home, threw my school bag on the bed, changed into some old clothes, and ran out onto the street to play soccer. Everyone brought along his own handcrafted balls. These were compared and scrutinised before a decision was made by consensus as to which ball was the best. Having your ball chosen for play gained you status. Although my ball wasn't always the favourite, I was very proud of those I made. I paid attention to detail

---

3. Outsider. Refers to a village in Tigray, but is used as an insult. (Tigrinya)

and, without a doubt, mine were always the best-stitched and lasted long after others had fallen apart.

Once a ball had been selected and teams were formed, it was time to set the goals—not for the game, but for money. We each placed bets of between five and ten cents on which team we thought would win. Ultimately, of course, each team member expected their own to be the champions.

At the end of the game, the winning team collected payment from the losing team and divided it up among themselves, according to how much each had outlaid. This phase of the afternoon was the most dangerous, as many of the losers resented handing over their money; including me. It took all my cunning to get even a few coins and I was never happy to let go of something that was painfully acquired.

I had discovered that Adey kept a jar of coins in the top cabinet of her glassware cupboard and occasionally, when she wasn't home, I would sneak into the kitchen and take some small change. The wolf-lady Almaz found me more than once with my hand in the bounty and always growled her displeasure at such scavenging. Each time she caught me, she pinched me hard on the inner thigh, creating a bruise and leaving me in tears.

Some nights, after she'd punished me, I sobbed long and hard, but my endless whimpering only infuriated her further.

Way past bedtime, she would enter my room in a huff (and a puff to blow my door down) and close the door so Adey would not hear. She seemed to leap across the room in her billowing night robe and land beside my bed in one bound. Rapping me on the head with her knuckles, she'd hiss, "BE QUIET! You dreadful boy! Shush or I'll send you to your drunken father!"

She'd push her face down close to mine, breathing directly into my ear, "And you know what he will do? That drunk will beat you all day and night, and then he will kill you! Is that what you want?"

Secretly, I'd parcelled away the larger-than-life horror of my father and instead created the idea of a good man, and slotted him into it. Those venomous family curses scared me, for sure, but I took them more as a direct hit, adding to my feeling that I was bad and unwanted. Now, all the singular criticisms of him, all the jibes and tense whispers started to piece themselves together into a jagged image of a truly scary man. My aunt described him as cruel, wicked and rotten to the core. And if he was *her* brother, I started to think it could be possible.

She continually taunted me with the possibility of meeting him. Was he a man or a demon? Like a wild dog savaging a rag to tatters, fear flung me every which way.

Red-clawed Aunt Almaz still hadn't figured out how to make me compliant to her will, and her threats and punishment only upset me further, increasing her frustration. Many a night she returned three or four times to my bed, heckling me to be silent. Her shadow monster on the wall kept eating me up and spitting me out.

As time passed, I became less inclined to steal soccer money from Adey and resorted to another kind of theft. I got coins from elderly neighbours, friends to Adey. "Excuse me," I asked politely, "but Adey was wondering if she could borrow ten cents from you?" Since my grandmother was quite respected in the area, the answer was always, "Yes." Somehow Aunt Almaz managed to find out about this too and the punishment resumed.

Other children were acquiring their gambling money in a similar manner. When bets were being paid, fights often broke out over whose money it really was.

The first time I saw a fight in Asmara was particularly frightening. I hadn't been exposed to Eritrean-style fighting before and was shocked to see two boys using their *testa*[4] instead of their fists to strike each other. Eritrean men actually have a thicker brow bone, which lends itself to this type of fighting. I looked on partly in awe

4. Heads. (Tigrinya)

and partly in disgust. Like two charging bulls locking horns, they fearlessly smashed their heads together. The sound was sickening and was often accompanied by blood spatter. No one seemed too disturbed by this as it was the common way for locals to settle their disagreements. I later observed this unique practice being carried out after soccer games, in bar brawls and even at the markets, between stall owners and their customers.

While money was a source of tension among the soccer players, there was also trouble between street gangs, making it almost impossible for one of our members to walk safely through another group's territory without being accompanied by an adult.

Each area had its own gang of kids, who ambled along together or played soccer. Strangers were immediately identified and the dominating gang would hurl rocks at the intruder.

If I wanted to go somewhere that lay beyond another group's territory, I walked the long way around to avoid being stoned.

The leader of each gang was usually the strongest, and his presence sent the younger kids running in all directions to escape a beating. Even in the middle of a soccer game, if a leader started walking down the street, everyone would instantly disappear. Like a cartoon western, doors slammed, the street emptied and the ball would still be rolling to a stop; a fine trophy for the leader's collection. When someone got beaten up by the leader, the only retaliation was to go home and cry to the family. Magically, doors would swing open and angry family members would demand to know what was going on. There'd be a rush of accusations, a swift re-alliance of accomplices and then everybody would tromp down the street to confront the leader's family.

It was scary, exciting and sometimes delightfully rewarding. Even small children could occasionally score a victory.

On one particular afternoon, Adey took me to visit Mebrat. I hid behind my grandmother's long flowing cotton dress, desperately trying to disguise myself and escape the attention of the local kids. As we walked up the street, a rock sailed through the air and struck me on the back of the head. Luckily it was thrown from a distance and had lost considerable force by the time it hit my skull. It startled me, and I winced all the same. Adey stopped abruptly. Pulling her shawl back to show her displeased face, she peered around for the culprit. She scanned the other children slowly from left to right and then right to left, looking for an obvious suspect.

Like a baby bird under attack, I relished her protection. I didn't have to worry, if only for a short time.

The children were wily, however, and smiled innocently at Adey as she met each gaze. She gave them all one last scornful look, then placed her shawl-covered arm around me like a sheltering wing and we continued walking. But when I snuck a cautious look back, they were making throat-cutting gestures. I was relieved when we finally got to the main road and could continue safely to Mebrat's house.

Maybe this secretive world of the streets was our way of processing the violence of the war around us. Through it all, family was the ultimate safe haven.

I hadn't seen Mebrat since she'd left me sitting in the entrance of Adey's house with a *beles* in one hand one *birr* in the other. My memory of her was tarnished by the trauma of that day, but this time her warm welcome soothed me and I forgave her.

As she set about making coffee for Adey, they discussed my progress. I was rarely privy to adult conversation as I was usually sent outside, but this time I was permitted to stay. I was shocked to hear my grandmother speak so frankly in front of me.

"Not long after Tewodros was born here in Asmara, I begged Bishkash to let me take care of him," my grandmother said, shaking her head in disappointment. "But she refused, instead taking him to Tigray, spoiling him and letting him to do whatever he pleased.

As they say, *the cow is only as good as the pasture in which it grazes*."[5] She spoke as if I was invisible, but I listened intently when she continued. "And now when he is nothing but trouble, she sends him back and expects me to look after him!" Adey shook her head and sipped her coffee.

"It sounds like Tewodros has been disturbing you," Mebrat sympathised. She shot me one of those looks that implies universal disapproval for troublesome behaviour. I pretended not to notice.

"Well, I don't think he's any worse than other children these days, but Almaz thinks he's a bad seed." My grandmother sighed.

I rolled my eyes.

She went on, "She's always punishing the poor boy. It breaks my heart to see him suffer."

Mebrat put down the *jebena*.[6] "What do you mean?"

Adey reached over and lifted the leg of my shorts to reveal a purplish bruise the size of a clenched fist.

"*Eway! Eway!*" Mebrat gasped at the sight of my wounded leg, "Adey, you can't allow her to do this. You must put an end to it at once!"

Adey nodded. "If only Fekadu was still alive. He was a generous old soul and would see to it that his grandson was taken care of." Her eyes glistened tearfully.

We concluded our visit early in the evening and I felt encouraged that at least Mebrat was prepared to speak up in my defence— and maybe Grandpa Fekadu was watching over me from above. I returned home with a sense of confidence I'd never known before; a confidence about to be shattered with the resounding blow of my end-of-year school results.

I was still struggling with the school system and this was painfully evident on my report card. It was the first one I'd ever received, so

---

5. Ethiopian proverb.
6. Coffee pot. (Amharic)

I was looking forward to having a record of achievement, only it wasn't the shining result I'd hoped for. Maybe if I'd scored points for kneeling. . . .

As I opened the card, my eyes raced over the paper. I was still learning to read and struggled to understand the jumbled letters. I looked up at my teacher.

"Tewodros, you failed your first year," he scoffed and signalled for the next student in line to step forward.

I dammed up fierce tears of regret. I didn't want to be a failure. I didn't want to disappoint my lovely Adey.

On the way home, I was tempted to destroy the report card. I didn't want to show Adey, as it only confirmed the negative things Aunt Almaz had said about me all along. I knew Adey would be upset, but I couldn't lie to her.

She was waiting for me. I handed her the report, my eyes pleading for patience. She looked at it briefly and said nothing.

Thankfully, my second year in Asmara began on an upbeat. Imagine my delight when I heard that wolf-lady Almaz had graduated from her studies, was engaged to be married *and* would be moving out of Adey's house. In a flurry of elation, I pranced through the rooms and punched the air excitedly. I couldn't wait to say, "Good riddance!" I checked her room each day after school, expecting her belongings to disappear.

I couldn't imagine what kind of person would want to marry such a fearsome woman. I wondered if the man really knew what she was like. Maybe she'd been sweet to him until now, but I was sure it wouldn't be long before she snapped savagely at him. I only hoped that he didn't send her back to Adey's when she did.

Oh, blissful day. At last, Aunt Almaz moved out.

My relationship with Adey flourished. She seemed much more relaxed, and freely expressed her love for me without worrying about insinuating comments from her daughter.

With the devil-woman out of the house, I was more angelic. Can you believe it? Sometimes, I would press my hands together and whisper *thank you* to the heavens that she was gone, swiftly following with *please, please, please let me be an angel for Adey*. This gave me a glow all over which lasted—ooh—until the next irresistible opportunity for mischief arose . . . but I'm sure my good intentions were genuine.

Adey often took me out on excursions after that. Once, we travelled by horse and carriage to her home town for an annual festival held at the local church. At other times, we attended weddings (although I was excluded from Aunt Almaz's).

Those occasions were magical. There was always fresh, fragrant straw on the floor and the air was layered with drum rhythms, perfume and the intoxicating aromas of festive food. Children ate last, often getting the leftovers from other people's plates. The cake was always delicious—usually from an Italian recipe.

I enjoyed spending time with Adey immensely. We were good friends and I lapped up all the attention she showered on me. She seemed as delighted as I was for our next adventure.

It was also a good year for me at school. I'd settled in, made friends and was no longer taunted as the *agame*. To my relief (and secret wish to deserve grandmother's pride), I achieved good grades. Pleased with my progress, Adey prepared *tamot*[7] every afternoon at five. This could be freshly baked *kitcha*[8] served with tomato and onion sauce or *injera* soaked in a special creamy butter. Even now when I think of it, my mouth waters.

One year older (and certainly faster), my gang of friends assumed a more confident swagger, as we graduated into the groups of bigger boys. Our impromptu escapades were coloured with the kind of freedom that only childhood can deliver.

7. Afternoon snack. (Tigrinya)
8. Thin bread made from wheat; a staple food in Eritrea. (Tigrinya)

Whenever there was a big soccer game, we would walk all the way to the stadium and try to find a hole in the fence to peek through. Spying our favourite players, we would call out their names. "Look, there's Korerit, and there's Fuji!" Afterwards, we waited around outside until the crowds spilled onto the street. They'd be at fever pitch and we eavesdropped for the score and the game highlights.

Sometimes we'd catch a bus up to the higher city outskirts. Like emperors of past eons, we would sit atop the mountain, gazing down over the city and beyond.

There's something about a horizon that reaches into your heart and stretches it far into the distance. I felt drawn to something I had not yet even imagined. I strained to see, to feel, to know what dreams lay beyond the setting sun. One day.

So, life was as good as it could be. I felt loved for the first time. I wasn't hungry. I had friends and, despite the intensifying war, I felt hopeful. Hints of a much greater adventure dangled before me, though I could never have recognised them at the time. One of these was discovering movies. I saw my first film in Asmara. It was a Chuck Norris martial arts movie with all the action and drama a boy could desire. My mind boggled.

Horizons beckoned.

Whenever Aunt Almaz dropped by to visit Adey, I reverted to my disappearing trick. Usually I walked up to the main road, the long way of course (avoiding enemy gangs), to hang out with some friends at the local shops.

Whenever we saw merchants pushing their carts along, we would offer to help in the hope of getting a small reward. Sometimes, we pushed the cart for miles, only to receive a caramel toffee. But a treat is a treat and all the better to savour if there's sweat in your mouth.

Sucking on the sweet candy, I had no idea that my aunt was busy trying to offload me elsewhere. On numerous occasions, she'd asked Solomon to provide Adey with financial support but, in the ten long years since my birth, he remained in denial. His advice: Send him back to his mother!

Aunt Almaz began searching long and hard for Bishkash. The civil war was raging between the Dergue and the TPLF in Shire, making communication erratic at best. With no news of my mother, Aunt Almaz's grim determination to be rid of me left only one option. She decided it was time for me to live with my drunken father.

Angels and devils, horizons and hideaways. . . . Was life beckoning me on or about to close the door and throw away the key?

6

PRINCE OR PAUPER?

The lion is a symbol of Ethiopian pride. Our legends tell that the lion was born dead and then received the breath of life from the lioness. This powerful statement of resurrection has been embraced by emperors and commoners alike.

Tewodros II surrounded himself with lions. They wandered his palace grounds, and he even took them into battle. Selassie favoured them as pets as well as icons. Ethiopia's capital is bedecked with statues, images and titles that allude to their courageous, untameable grandeur.

In nature, lions are fiercely loyal to their families—their pride. Drawn by this, rejected young members become nomads, constantly searching for acceptance and security in that harsh world.

With the life I knew now dead, I longed for resurrection and the comfort of a family. Could I make my father proud? Would I finally belong somewhere? I would soon find out.

Aunt Almaz's efficient planning put me on a plane, but it wasn't quite the adventure of my dreams. Streaming sunshine pulsed through a magnificent sky. It should have felt like heaven, but I was bound for Addis Ababa and the hell gates that would yawn reluctantly wide enough to swallow me whole.

Aunt Almaz had arranged for her brother-in-law, Tariku, to escort me on the journey. I'd been polite, respectful, quiet—all the things required of a good travelling companion, though my angelic behaviour was really an attempt to avert my mind from our final destination.

Echoes of wolf-lady's hiss in my ears conjured irrepressible images. "Son of a king, you'd like to think. But "S" stands for Satan, not Solomon!"

Did his frizzy black hair cleverly hide stumpy horns? And at the base of his spine, was there a long tail coiled and concealed in his trousers? For all the cursing and spitting that had regularly punctuated my existence, I'd never seen a real live devil.

I looked up at Tariku, clutching my midriff. "*Kebdey hamimea!*"[1] I groaned. He reached over and cradled one of my sweaty hands. What could he say to a child no one wanted? Denied by one parent, banished by another, I closed my eyes and wished I could just keep flying. But after a brief hour in the air, the plane began its descent.

The capital city nestles in the heart of the Ethiopia. Throughout history, every new leader chose his own point of power, so there was no enduring ruling centre until 1886 when Empress Taytu, wife of Menelik II, chose the site. It was the perfect political hub, with the added benefits of pleasing weather and gentle terrain. The Empress named the future city *Addis Ababa*, meaning "New Flower," after the steam patterns rising from hot springs in the area. Taytu had great influence throughout her husband's reign and the city, extending beyond her husband's vision, has become Africa's capital, hosting the Organisation of African Unity (now titled the African Union) and the UNECA.[2]

---

1. I feel sick in the stomach! (Tigrinya)
2. United Nations Economic Commission for Africa.

Prince or Pauper?

Addis Ababa is recognised as both a city and a state. Having expanded outwards from the emperor's palace, it has a population of around 2.8 million, predominantly consisting of Christian and Muslim communities. Within these, there are as many as 80 different ethnic groups, each with its own unique language.

As we flew over the city, I failed to see steam rising from the ground since I was distracted by the suburban sprawl extending out across the plains. From the air, it looked much bigger than Asmara and I was to discover that it was markedly different.

This city is a melting pot of cultures. Although it has a strong American feel, there are two areas that have their own distinct identities yet, amazingly, sit right next to each other.

The wilder of the two is Merkato, the main business hub not only of Addis Ababa, but of all of Ethiopia. Perched high on a hill overlooking the city, the area is abuzz with traditional merchants and modern hawkers who buy, trade or sell anything from livestock and grains to fabrics and technological gadgets.

Insidious to Merkarto is a squirming conglomeration of pickpockets, street kids and horn-blasting taxi drivers jostling competitively with barefoot cart-pushing vendors. All swarm to the higher ground of Merkato in the early hours of the morning and remain there until late at night, harassing shoppers, tourists and anyone else who ventures onto those streets.

The second distinctive area, quieter and more refined, is Piassa. It has a strong European ambience, much like Asmara. Narrow streets are hugged by cosy cafés and restaurants where visitors can relish a brief interlude from the mayhem of Merkato.

Like a crazy two-sided *carnivale*[3] mask, both of these environments would reflect my double life in days to come; one honing my survival skills, the other inspiring dreams of finer things, each stripping me of my naïveté.

Tariku and I had no time to take in the sights. The chilly air

---

3. Carnival. (Italian)

chased us relentlessly forward—a kind man leading a frightened boy. We caught a taxi, made a quick stop at Asmerom's office (he now lived in Addis) and then headed for the inevitable endpoint of our trip.

It was mid-afternoon as our vehicle approached the towering edifice of the Black Lion Hospital.[4] Opened in 1968, it became a teaching hospital, marking an important development in the modernisation of Ethiopia.

Tariku leaned forward, "This is where your father works, Tewodros," he announced. "He's a doctor, a very smart man. I'm sure he'll take good care of you," he reassured me.

I was confused. His certainty belied my aunt's description. Benefactor or beast: it would determine my life.

The taxi departed swiftly, leaving us before the huge metal gates of the hospital. (What did I tell you? Just like hell gates!) Two guards emerged from a small corrugated iron hut near the entrance.

"What can we do for you?" one of them asked Tariku, as the other inspected us intently.

"*Selam.* We are looking for Doctor Solomon Fekadu. He teaches anatomy," Tariku replied.

"Do you have an appointment?" the guard asked suspiciously.

"No, but this young man is Doctor Solomon's son." He patted me on the shoulder. "He needs to see his father."

The guards nodded at each other and permitted us to enter the grounds. They gave us directions to the opposite side of the building where the medical university was located.

Once inside, we walked along a cold wide corridor until we found a white-coated young man with a clipboard and notes in one hand and some kind of medical instrument in the other. Tariku asked him for directions to my father's office.

The young man invited us to sit while he went to check on

4. "Black Lion" refers to the anti-fascist movement in Ethiopia during the Italian occupation.

Solomon's whereabouts. *The doctor no longer worked here*, I hoped he would say, or *No such fellow existed*. But he soon returned, explaining, "Yes, he's here until four-thirty. He will exit through those doors, so if you take a seat over there you should catch him before he leaves."

"Thank you very much for your help." Tariku nodded in appreciation.

We sat.

Okay, this is it, I thought as my bilious belly threatened mutiny.

We waited.

The hard plastic chairs seemed to harden time; it passed so slowly. I shifted from one side of my bony buttocks to the other and swung my legs back and forth, ready to stand (ready to flee). The hallway echoed with footsteps coming and going. Not his. Not yet.

We waited some more.

The young doctor, so caring and polite, returned on several occasions to update us on my father's whereabouts.

Can you believe it? Despite my tension, I'd almost fallen asleep when the doors burst open and a tall dark-skinned man in a stylish suit strode confidently into the waiting room, followed closely by a beautiful younger lady. The helpful young doctor appeared from a doorway and directed the couple's attention to Tariku.

"Doctor Solomon, I'm Tariku, brother-in-law to your sister Almaz."

I gulped. My mouth went dry and my tongue felt swollen to twice its size. I gulped again and stared hard at this mystery man. He'd been so different in my mind. He was actually much taller, a lot darker and—to my relief—there were no horns!

"Tariku? How are you? I didn't know you were in Addis. What brings you my way?" he enquired and walked towards the exit, signalling for Tariku to follow.

I cautiously tagged along.

"This is your son: Tewodros. Almaz has sent him to live with you."

As Tariku spoke, he gently pushed me towards Solomon.

Abruptly immobile, Solomon squinted at me, then whipped his eyes away. "I. Do. Not," his emphatic tone slammed the words home, "have a son. Called *Tewodros*. Do you understand? He's *not* mine. I don't know what you're talking about. All right? I. Am. Not. His father!"

Shocked at this outburst, Tariku quietly replied, "Perhaps you shouldn't say such things in front of the boy."

"Well, he is not my boy! I told you. Now, step aside. We're leaving." Solomon turned to his wife, Saba, and gestured for her to get in the car.

In the deep crevasses of my soul, I hoped he was right, that I wasn't his son and that Tariku would take me with him back to my grandmother's house. Instead, Solomon's wife stepped forward, took my hand and turned to her husband. "It's too late to say such things. Just come home!" she snapped while opening the car door and ushering me in.

I really didn't want to get into the car, but it all happened so quickly.

On the way, we dropped Tariku at his hotel. As he exited the car, I hollered uncontrollably. "Please don't leave me!" I grasped his shirt sleeve. "Please!"

"It's all right, Tewodros," he whispered. "If it doesn't work out with your father, you can come and live with me. But you have to try this first, okay?"

No, it's not okay, I was desperate to tell him. Instead I released his sleeve, kicked the back of the passenger's seat (just once) and let fat forlorn tears roll down my cheeks. I continued to cry all the way to my father's house, making no effort to stop. When I needed it most, defiance had left me.

Doctor Solomon lived in an area of the city known as Baqlo Bet, which translates (appropriately) to mean "Mule's House." I have no idea why this area had such a name because, contrary to the images it conjures up, Baqlo Bet is actually one of the more exclusive areas of the city and my father's house was certainly testimony to this.

The car pulled up at the front gates, the horn honked and within seconds an elderly man opened for us to enter. He closed the gates behind us and returned to the darkness. The headlights illuminated the front yard as we drove on, revealing a grand European-style house more incredible than anything I'd ever seen. White windows were set in tall walls of rendered brick, painted pale yellow. The façade was softened by green shrubs and trees planted across the front. I thought my grandmother's place was a palace, but this! For a second, I almost felt excited.

I swiped off the tears to make way for astonishment and followed Solomon and his wife, Saba, inside. I was asked to sit in the lounge room while they went behind closed doors. Clutching my small bag to my chest, I was straining to hear the discussion on the other side of the wall when four young children (three boys and a girl) came bounding into the room.

This was another shock. I had no idea they existed and, judging by the looks on their faces, my presence was just as big a surprise for them.

The oldest boy, Mehari, was the first to break the awkward silence. "*Selam*," he greeted.

I remained mute.

One of them pointed to my puffy face and giggled. The others joined in and then started talking at me in Amharic (the national language of Ethiopia), which was very different from the two dialects of Tigrinya I'd learned so far.

My blank expression stirred them into further fits of giggles and taunts. As they ran around the room laughing and pointing at me, I burst into tears once again, prompting more scornful merriment.

Not until the room had descended into chaos did the two adults return. I sensed a shift in my father's attitude towards me. While

Saba calmed the children, he came to talk with me. "Tewodros, why don't the two of us go for a drive so I can show you the city?" he said, taking my hand and lulling me into pliability.

I tentatively followed him out to the car. I didn't have a good first impression of him. I wished his wife was joining us. She looked so kind.

Setting off on our drive, we headed back towards the city. Our first stop was at an ice-cream shop in the area of Addis called Mexico. "Tewodros, do you like ice-cream?" he asked.

I sat in silence with my arms folded firmly against my chest.

"Come, let's get out of the car and have something to eat, no?" he invited. I refused to move. The anxiety and humiliation of the day now pushed me into the familiar corner where defiance was my last stand.

A few children were sitting on the front step of the shop, licking melted ice-cream off their hands as it dribbled down from their cones. My father left me alone and entered the building. The shop was painted bright green, a colour that reminded me of the mountains in Tigray. Why wasn't I *there?*

I was still in lock-down mode when he emerged with an ice-cream for me. This was a luxury. Given my previous efforts to earn a caramel, imagine how much more I would have done even for a lick of ice-cream. He handed me the treat through the car window. I tossed it straight back out onto the ground and re-crossed my arms.

The children stopped their licking and laughed at me.

"You little— What are you doing?" my father demanded.

We were at loggerheads: my defiance versus his anger. If only I could have demonstrated my frustration *and* kept the ice-cream. Needless to say, this was the first and last time it was ever offered to me.

He recovered his composure as he resumed his seat behind the wheel. "So you don't want ice-cream? What about milk? You like that? Every boy likes milk," he said as he reversed back onto the street and drove towards the city centre.

Our next stop was a café. He parked directly in front and wound down the window. After a few minutes, a waitress came to take our order. I asked for warm milk. My father ordered a beer.

As we drank, he turned to me. "Tewodros, if you're a good boy, you can study and become a doctor like me. If you study hard, you might be good enough to go to England or America to live. What do you think of that?"

I'd never heard of England or America. Were they southern regions of Ethiopia? All I heard was: away, away, far away.

His outright rejection of me at the hospital still stung. I soothed myself with slow sips of milk. My reticence contrasted with his enthusiasm as he downed his beer and ordered another.

Just then, a friend of his parked beside us. I was surprised when Solomon proudly introduced me as his son. Did I hear that right? My head had been so full of the Aunt Almaz's horror stories. I didn't like her. I didn't want to believe her. A tiny shimmer of hope stirred in my heart.

Three beers later, my father's affections seemed to have grown. He decided to give me a guided tour of the city on the way home. "That's Government House," he said, as we passed a large building. "The president works over there," he continued when we drove through the area known as Arat Kilo, the hub of government and education. "And that big building, can you see it? That's Addis Ababa University," he crowed. "That's where I studied medicine, Tewodros! And if you behave, one day you can study there too!"

Earnestly wishing to be filled with wonder, I strained to see the buildings he described, but all was darkness and shadows.

We returned to his house several hours later. My mood had mellowed considerably. He hadn't beaten me, eaten me or transformed himself into a monster. This tall, proud man was my father. I was his son. I began to believe that I was safe at last.

Solomon's wife, Saba, did her best to welcome me and give me a feeling of belonging. She oversaw a tenuous truce between her children and me, and I exerted my all to show her my appreciation.

Now that I was ensconced in the lap of luxury, my clothes were a betraying eyesore. I'd always worn secondhand things while living with Adey. Worse than that, imagine my embarrassment when Aunt Almaz altered some of her own clothing to fit me, in order to save her mother money. (Maybe her plan was to shame me into running away.) She took needle and thread to brightly coloured flared pants. Sides were taken in. Bottoms were chopped off. She made them so tight that I had to hold my breath to get them on, so high that they reached well above my rib cage and so long that they covered my shoes. Puffs of dust rose up around my ankles as I walked along. She always altered them in the same way, no matter how much I complained.

A beacon for bad fashion (that people could see coming from a mile away), I was endlessly mocked. The amalgamated jeers described me as a cross-dressing Elvis clown! *Who was this El-vis?* I used to think and *why would he want to dress like a girl?*

Within days of my big city arrival, Saba insisted that Solomon take me shopping for some clothes—something I'd never, ever done before. Owning new clothes seemed, well, princely! What an appropriate (royal) outing for father and son.

I chose a pair of dark denim jeans, a silky blue jacket which reminded me of a navy officer's uniform and a pair of black leather shoes. They smelled so good, so clean; it was wonderful to have something that wasn't already tainted by other people's odours. I was ecstatic, dancing around the shop gleefully waving my choices about. The shop owner probably thought I was crazy!

My delight was soon dampened by Solomon's refusal to part with his money. Saba, the true heroine of this expedition, oversaw the transaction. Without her support, I'm sure his wallet would have remained fat and my wardrobe shameful.

Arriving home, I didn't have time to consider his behaviour or what it really meant since I was asked to don my new outfit for a dinner invitation. Saba's brother, Robel, had invited the whole family—including me. There wasn't room for all of us in my father's small Mazda (that should have given me a clue), so we children were waiting on the front porch where Robel came to collect us in his shiny, cherry-red Opel. He worked as a steward for Ethiopian Airlines, a very glamorous job at the time. I'd never felt so special: new clothes, cool car and one happy family. I though I was in Heaven.

From the moment we arrived at Uncle Robel's house until well into the evening, my father was never without a glass of alcohol in his hand. In his drunken state, I could hear him telling everyone about the week's events and how I was now living with his family. I didn't want to play with the other children. Instead, I just wanted to listen, to believe that there was truth in every word he uttered when he proudly referred to me as his son. I wanted to beat my expanding chest like a baboon. By the end of the night, I was beaming with confidence I'd never known.

I should be made of rubber. Then I could keep bouncing back after each drastic change in my life. My newfound ease was incredibly short-lived. The clothes were not purchased for the dinner, as I'd thought, but in preparation for my departure. My father had already arranged to send me to the city of Dese, northeast of Addis, where I would attend a mission school—for *orphans*! What a lie.

Lies become twisted versions of credibility when enough people perpetrate them. In Ethiopia, where a man's life quality depends on his fellows' esteem, half-truths masquerade as complete. The man will never behave (or admit to behaving) unworthily. Public pride is his strength. Public approval determines his success. This has nothing to do with the truth. How could it? Yet, anyone who cannot uphold this pretence is fiercely judged.

Solomon was a proud man. Everything in his life demonstrated this: he had a beautiful wife, clever children and a luxury home. Everyone spoke highly of him. And I'm sure he deserved their admiration in many ways.

Was he a good doctor? Yes, he was. But this was professional pride, not his personal truth. Hidden from the world was his alcoholism and the occasional violence towards his wife. And then, of course, there was the product of his unworthy behaviour that would not become untrue, no matter how much he wished it.

I represented his public disgrace—a threat to his family and therefore the potential demise of all that a proud honourable Eritrean man required.

I wanted his love, so that I could be proud. He wanted me gone, so that he could be proud. The tug-o-war of our desires was destined to keep us apart for as long as he lived. There would be no give and take, no honest reconnection to value each other as a decent father and an honourable son—as good men.

My father's lies shudder through our family still. We live in heavy cowardly shadows.

Ironically enough, it was through his good reputation that Solomon was able to offload me to the orphanage. Before settling in Addis Ababa, he had lived in the Welo region, not far from Dese. As the only doctor in the vicinity, he was required to work as a general practitioner and a surgeon, thus further developing his skills. Despite bouts of all-night drinking, he always turned up for work on time and became so widely respected that people used to travel even from as far as Yemen to receive medical treatment from him.

At the time, the Catholic Church was the only organisation in the area with a car, which doubled as an ambulance to taxi the sick and injured to Doctor Solomon's surgery. Over time, he formed friendships with the priests, in particular Father Tesfaldete. They had stayed in contact over the years and now this priest was head of the Church and its mission in Dese. Father Tesfaldete agreed to take me in for 30 *birr*[5] a month. On my father's salary this would have been easily affordable but, according to church accounts, he attempted to negotiate the price down to 15 *birr*. Eventually it was agreed that he would pay 25 *birr* a month.

So at the age of 11, Solomon's son for less than a week, I was taken to the Franciscan Church seminary in Addis Ababa where I spent the night in preparation for my trip to Dese. This constant shuffling through life kept me dizzy. It seemed I only just gained my balance in one situation before I was tossed into another. When the angels were first expelled from heaven, they descended into hell. Thrust into the presence of this man I'd dreaded for so long, only to be swiftly ejected again, I didn't know if I was falling up or down.

Early in the morning, I was woken by an aging priest and dropped at the Merkato bus terminal with an older man, my chaperone for the trip. He introduced himself as Tesfaye. He'd been in Addis Ababa for medical treatment and was returning to the Dese mission where he was a servant at the church.

Dese is one of the largest cities in the country. It lies north of the capital on the paved Addis Ababa-Asmara highway. In 1882, Emperor Johannes IV was on a camping trip in the vicinity and was awestruck by a comet blazing across the night sky. He decided to found a city where he stood, naming it Dese, which means "my joy" in English.

Yet the city has not entirely lived up to its name over the years, as it lies at the centre of the Welo region, which scarcely endures severe recurring famine and drought.

This region was the straw that broke the starving camel's back under the final emperor, Selassie. Because of Ethiopia's public shame and his inability to solve the crisis, he was overthrown. His

5. US$5.00 (approximately).

successor, Mengistu, forced everyone into submission "for their own good." But his iron will was no match for the extremes of nature. Now, Solomon had banished me to the Welo region, which was cracking under the worst famine yet.

The long, dusty journey north reflected my own personal drought, only instead of having a desperate need for water, I was thirsty for love.

The trip took about eight hours, so it was mid-afternoon by the time the bus zigzagged from the foot of the mountains to the valley where Dese was situated. Peering ahead from the outskirts, I noticed that the city seemed pinched and thin, jammed into a narrow passage between two ridges.

The highway continued right through the city centre, which was lined with various small businesses including a bank and a petrol station. Small roads threaded off the arterial thoroughfare leading behind the shops to residential areas.

"We have great singers and dancers here," Tesfaye noted, as we journeyed through the city. "Very good ones, very good," he almost whispered to himself.

What's to sing about? I wondered, straining to imagine a future that was less than grim.

When we reached the northernmost point of the city, he signalled for the driver to stop. I looked around in search of something that might resemble a mission.

"Tewodros, we have to walk from here," Tesfaye said, bending down to adjust the ragged shoes on his feet. The soles were barely attached, so he'd wrapped the shoelaces around his feet and then tied them off neatly at the top, just like a boxed Italian Christmas cake that I'd seen at Adey's house.

As he moved off, I noticed his leg had a tourniquet wrapped around it just below the knee. This injury must have prompted his visit to Addis Ababa. His body jerked violently from side to side as he walked. Even so, he soon outpaced me.

"Tewodros!" he called out from a considerable distance ahead. "We need to make it to the top of that hill before it gets dark. Grab your bag and let's go!" He dusted off a long stick that he could use for support on the climb.

His silhouette diminished. His stumbling gate mocked my own weariness and disbelief at landing in the middle of nowhere. Dragging my bag up the incline was less of a burden than dragging my heart.

The sun hadn't long set when we walked through the large blue-painted metal gates at the entrance to the mission. I squinted to look around the grounds before complete darkness set in. Directly before me, there was a huddle of small offices. To my right, an old church made of stone presided over an open grassy field. (Grass—not dust!) Opposite this was a large old European-style house which, I later learned, accommodated the sisters (nuns) and the girls at the mission. Everywhere was ghostly quiet, without a soul in sight.

"It's prayer time," Tesfaye explained, as if reading my mind.

We entered one of the buildings adjoining the church: the boys' quarters. I was presented to Emanuel, a layperson at the mission, who explained that one of his duties was to help the children settle in. He gave me bed linen, a towel and a pair of pyjamas (my first ever).

Emanuel led me outside along a grey-tiled veranda that over-looked a grassy courtyard. There were several doors leading off the veranda; the first was the kitchen (I could smell dinner), the next the dining hall and, after that, the sleeping quarters. We headed for that last door. Inside, I found a large rectangular-shaped room where the two longest walls were lined with bunk beds. I'd never seen a bunk bed before and the novelty intrigued me. Emanuel pointed to one of the upper beds and said it was mine. I got to sleep on top! After stowing my bag, I climbed up and down the metal ladder, and up again, testing the bed each time.

"Be careful, young man. You're not a monkey, you know."

Emanuel seemed to enjoy my curiosity. The guided tour around the mission continued through the grounds and finished back in the kitchen.

The staff members were busy with final dinner preparations. Emanuel introduced me to them as Doctor Solomon's son. Shocked gasps rose like steam.

A lady stopped stirring a big pot of curry. "What is the son of Doctor Solomon doing here?"

Emanuel tilted his head, uncertain how to reply.

"Well then, boy," she adjusted her tone, "your father is a great man. We are very pleased to have you staying with us."

After leaving the kitchen, I asked Emanuel why my presence surprised her.

"You see, Tewodros, this place is usually for children who have no parents or for those from very poor families who are unable to care for their children." He paused to gauge my reaction. "Your father is a highly respected doctor in these parts. That lady thought—well—there must be a good reason why you've come to stay with us. *Baqqa*."[6] Emanuel walked off into the dining hall and waited there for me to follow.

The doctor's son? *The doctor's son!* Like a punishing rhythm, those words would continue to beat me down wherever I went. The expectations of that title were great, as if people were waiting to be impressed. But a title is not a life, and a boy in need is a boy in need, no matter who has named or rejected him.

Dinner was served. Despite the long day, I'd lost my appetite. I just stared at the plate.

As the tables were cleared, Emanuel brought me a glass of fresh milk. I remembered those carefree mornings, long ago, fetching milk for my mother. My hand trembled as I took the glass. A tide of grief swelled in my throat. Mother . . . Adey . . . somebody: *find me—love me!* I sipped the milk, swallowing back the tears. I didn't

---

6. That's all. (Amharic)

want the others to see me cry. Solomon's children had already taught me to hide that truth.

After dinner, the priests came in to deliver messages to the children. Then, they acknowledged my presence and officially welcomed me to the mission.

Routine swallowed time.

Mornings at the mission ran like clockwork. At sunrise, we awoke to the insistent clang of a bell. We dressed, had breakfast, did our chores and went to school.

The school was part of the mission, though positioned further up the hill. We trudged up a tyre-tracked lane and passed through a set of gates which defined where the mission grounds ended and the schoolyard began.

Each morning before class, we obediently lined up outside and sang the national anthem (like good communist children) while a flag was hoisted to oversee our day. No longer bearing the imperial Lion of Judah, the naked strips of colour hung limply in a barren sky. Each evening, we said prayers (like good Christian children).

There were about 30 students on the mission, but the school grounds jostled like a city market when children from the surrounding areas came to attend classes.

I spent the most time with the other mission boys, avoiding interaction with many of the day students, mainly because we weren't allowed to leave the grounds to socialise with them. Our insular world was quite unlike theirs. They returned home to their families each afternoon. This didn't make our lives bad, just different. I'd been used to playing out on the streets after school and venturing wherever my heart desired, but at the mission I was bound by fences.

After school, we were free to choose our activities until evening prayer. Dinner rounded off the routine for the day. During those hours, some children wisely studied while others, like me, played soccer on the field in front of the church.

In comparison to my street games with homemade soccer balls, a grassy field and a real ball were incomprehensible luxuries, especially considering the surrounding poverty. Just like the street gang friction, there was rivalry between the mission teams. So, with only one ball, luxury became necessity.

The older boys who'd been at the mission longest asserted their authority and bullied the younger ones. They pushed and shoved and played hard against us, thumping our heads with their fists whenever we tried to get the ball from them. They were downright mean. The cruelty on the soccer field continued off the field.

Like many of the younger boys, I was beaten up on a daily basis. I incurred such punishment by refusing to do petty jobs for the older boys: their morning chores, polishing their shoes or running their messages. Each night, I went to bed with a new bruise or a fresh cut.

Nothing a good night's sleep wouldn't fix? If only. Some of the long-term residents had become particularly adept at pitching random objects in any direction, making a precision landing on someone's head. Shoes were a particular favourite. When the lights went out, projectiles became invisible and the day's assault of raw fists morphed into nights of stealth bombers. The top bunk was no place for sleep.

As the new kid, I had "target" written all over me. Surviving the street gang violence of Asmara taught me that alerting adults was futile and would most likely cause more vengeance (and projectiles) to rain down on me.

Although we attended prayer every afternoon before dinner and were each given our own set of rosary beads, I had no understanding of what religion really was or to which God I was supposedly offering up my prayers. Apart from my Christian Orthodox baptism, I'd only been dragged to church by Adey Selas for special occasions such as Easter and New Year. This Catholic mission took for granted that I had prior knowledge of its rituals. In my naiveté, I thought it must be something others were born with. Not needing another reminder of my evil nature, I attempted to fake my way into God's good opinion.

Hoping my commitment would outweigh my ignorance, I boldly imitated the other children. When the bell rang in the morning, I followed them to the dining hall. While the flag was being hoisted, I stood erect and patriotically mouthed mumbo-jumbo. Likewise in church, I stood, kneeled and said prayer words by rote.

It all seemed to be working relatively well until the Holy Communion of my first Sunday Mass. It looked like the priest was handing out food, so I joined the others filing from the pews. Reaching the front, I stepped before the priest, mouth open as reverently as the boy beside me, when my collar was yanked back, pulling me out of the line. Amid stern frowns and much finger-waving, the front row of brothers glared at me. Worse than the walk of shame back down the aisle were the sniggers and sideways glances from the other children who were now fired up for more extra-curricular target practice.

In Bible class the following week, the brother explained to everyone (although he was looking directly at me) that only those who had studied the sacrament of Holy Communion were allowed to receive the body of Christ. When I learned that it was Christ's body (what?) on offer and not some delicious snack, I felt relief more than loss.

For the most part, I remained completely baffled about religion and the teachings of Jesus. Each day, the priests reminded us to *Love one another as Jesus has loved you* or *Do unto others as you would have them do unto you.* Outside, I saw these same priests kicking and hitting children or even fighting with other adults.

One episode still sticks vividly in my memory. It was early evening. The school's politics teacher came to the mission to ask for a key. For whatever reason, he did this on a regular basis. His communistic approach conflicted with the priests' strong religious beliefs but, under Mengistu's reign, the teacher had the upper hand. Despite the constant underlying tension, the priests always gave him the key. Not this day, though. Father Tesfaldete flatly refused.

They were standing on the veranda, near the kitchen. Within minutes, their verbal battle became physical as the priest and the teacher began shoving each other and throwing punches. I ran with some other children to get a closer look. *Wah!* Father Tesfaldete was giving as good as he got.

At one point during the fight, he lost his glasses. Unable to see, he broke free and tried to dodge past the open-mouthed children, up the kitchen steps. He just made it to the top when the teacher tackled him from behind. They tumbled backwards down the stairs, thudding onto the ground right beside us. Instead of shrieking with fright, we cheered for Father Tesfaldete. "Beat him, father, beat him," we shouted in chorus. "To your left, father, now punch higher," we cried as he blindly struggled to aim. We cringed each time he took a blow.

When Father Tesfaldete regained his footing, somehow he'd scooped up a lump of wood and proceeded to swing it wildly about. We scattered as he hit a pole instead of his sparring partner. The teacher made a hasty exit, leaving Father Tesfaldete collapsed on the bottom step with the wood in one hand and his head in the other. In response to a formal complaint, the local council commandeered the lump of wood as evidence but, as far as I know, no charges were ever laid.

Suffering through the various battlefronts during the week, I longed for weekends. There were fewer children and less chores, which was a relief, but I experienced real joy for the first time by caring for another.

Each mission child was required to rear a calf. I named my calf Taytu, after the former empress. As soon as my history teacher had described the gracious woman, I knew that was the name for my little beauty. My calf was soft, brown and white, with big droopy brown eyes and the longest eyelashes. To me, she was just like a princess. More importantly, she was always there for me. It felt so good to be needed, to be relied on, even if it was only by an animal.

Taytu became my oasis of goodness. I used to sneak into the barn to escape the bullying, to be alone or when I was just plain bored. I enjoyed cleaning her pen, giving her fresh feed (which I sometimes stole from the other calves!) and rubbing her soft coat.

I confided in her, describing all my fears and loneliness. I shared my dreams with her, too—about becoming a soccer star; not for the money, but to have adoring fans and to be special. This was my best kept secret, so I told her she should feel lucky to be the only other one in the world to know it. It was a pure, bright friendship that armoured me against the harsh mission life.

Not love, nor dreams, nor devotion can stop some things from happening.

My Taytu died.

Death was something that happened because of war or age. It happened to other people. Not me. Hadn't I lost enough already? Did God hate me so much that he took away the only thing I could love? I saw Tesfaye dragging Taytu's limp body out of the barn. In that moment, all those whispered dreams became scooped out husks, their echoes dim and empty of meaning.

The immediate assumption was that I was to blame. There was no sympathy for me, no mourning for Taytu. People die every day; what was an animal's death in comparison? My distress was exacerbated by jibes from the other children who teased me for neglecting her. If only they knew.

In all, I spent one year of desperate loneliness at the Dese mission. There, the priests taught me to live with precision and order. I learned to accept that many things were out of my hands and to focus on what I could control.

The discipline of routine, the small thrill of pride that comes from completing tasks responsibly, gave me fortitude. Our cleanliness was meant to reflect our godliness (since all we did was intended for God). I wasn't overwhelmed with religious belief for *a cat may go to a monastery, but she still remains a cat.*[7] Yet the discipline began to define my character in a way that, till then, had only been haphazard combinations of defiance and longing.

Everyone has dealt with challenges. Everyone must reach a point at which he feels *from here, I can move forward . . . at least I know what I can do from here.* Somehow, the random dice rolls of my life never rested for long. After gaining strength from taking this one step forward, I was pushed two steps back.

My father's payments to the mission for my board and tuition had dwindled down to nothing by the end of the year. As a result, my time in Dese was about to end, although not without a bang.

Father Tesfaldete suddenly departed (probably due to his fight with the teacher). He was replaced by Brother Mengestabe, a stern fellow who awakened the fear of God with every gesture. He'd been the director of the school and now that he was also the head of the mission, I saw him more often.

One day after classes, I was sitting on the Church steps when one of older boys headed in my direction. I sensed an imminent beating and, as none of my friends were in sight, I jumped up and ran to the priests' office to seek protection, assuming they would sort it out.

I never felt comfortable around Brother Mengestabe, so I was hoping to meet one of the other priests. But there he was at his desk, when I burst in. He flashed me an agitated look. "What?" he shouted at me.

After nervously pouring out my woes about the beatings, he

7. Ethiopian proverb.

removed his reading glasses and threw them on the desk. He stood, walked outside and called the accused boy into the office.

Feeling relieved and gloating slightly, I relished the look of terror on the older boy's face as I sat and waited for the Brother Mengestabe to reprimand him.

"Boys," he said matter-of-factly as he rummaged around behind his desk. "Stand up!"

Did I hear correctly? Was that plural: b-o-y-s? Cautiously, I stood beside the other boy.

"Hold out your hands," the priest demanded. I looked at him in disbelief. Maybe I'd misunderstood. I was still coming to grips with Amharic. I gawped at the boy next to me, who robotically raised his hands, palms facing the ceiling.

"Tewodros, YOU TOO!" Brother Mengestabe barked.

This was the perfect time to regret that I'd chosen endless afternoons of dodging gang harassment over long hours of study and piety.

He walked around the desk to tower over us. His presence was like a magnet and my fingers quivered out into the air before him. From the corner of my eye, I could see a long snake-like object.

He adjusted our stiff arms to a satisfactory height and then, without warning, unleashed the snake. I closed my eyes just in time, pulling my head back like a tortoise, so that I wouldn't lose my nose. At precisely the same moment, the other boy and I screamed, our palms shockingly welted from the blow. Not satisfied with one lashing, the priest gave us another, just to be sure we'd learned our lesson. Exactly what *he* thought we were gaining, I don't know, but I learned never to trust anyone again, not even a priest.

The whipping and the betrayal were enough to endure, but of course the other boy wanted revenge. No sooner had we made our way out of the priests' office when he turned on me, dragged me out of view and kicked and punched me enough to render me immobile for hours.

Without payment for my keep, Brother Mengestabe must expel me. Maybe *that* was the lesson: I didn't belong. As swift as his striking whip, he sent me back to Addis Ababa to live with Doctor Solomon.

This time, I knew for sure: I was descending, and it was a long way to fall.

7

MIXED BLESSINGS

Night. From the outskirts of the city, you might hear the hyenas cackle as they roamed the surrounding hills. On the jumbled streets, the rush of the day morphed into a dark world of predators of another kind. From behind closed doors, secrets snuck out. Adult longings came alive. This was no place for children.

I hated nighttime the most at my father's house and this night was no different. I heard him stumble drunkenly down the hallway to my bedroom.

"Te-ros!" he attempted to call my name beyond the closed door. I buried my face deep under the covers.

"Te-ros!" he repeated. "Wake up!"

He began thumping heavily on the wood. I held my breath and pretended I was invisible.

Thump, thump.

Am I really here . . . or is it just Aunt Almaz's taunts yelling in my imagination?

Thump.

What if I could fly? Yes, flying would be good! I could take off

121

through the window and fly to mother. "Look, mother," I'd say, "I've become an ange—"

Thump—

"You in there!"

Bang, bang.

"I need beer!" he growled. "Don't you—" *thump* "play games with me—" *bang, bang, BANG.* "I know you're awake."

I boldly (fearfully) peeped out from under the covers and watched the strip of his swaying shadow under the door.

"*Anchi gered!*[1] Tell that boy to go get me some beer," he demanded. "It's all he's good for. *Ye materrba leg.*"[2] He lurched back down the hallway to the lounge room where I heard him fall into his armchair. Not long after, the maid carefully slid my door open and whispered that I should run the errand for my father. She handed me some change, and I reluctantly slipped on my Congo sandals and snuck out through the side door.

In the distance, stray dogs howled as they gathered in packs and descended on the neighbourhood for nighttime foraging. With my eyes wide, searchlights of fear, I tiptoed carefully along the street, scouring the landscape for anything that might fancy *me* as a midnight snack.

The first time my father sent me on a beer run, I had knocked on almost every shop door in the area, calling to the owners who lived out the back. Eventually, I found an old man who was prepared to make a few extra *birr*. I decided to go straight back to him, this time.

"Hello?" I rattled the aluminium shutter on the shop window. "Hello? Old man, are you there?" I rattled the shutter again, much louder. "Please sell me some beer; otherwise my father will kill me." (How close to the truth might that be?)

"You noisy child, have you no respect?" a neighbour shouted.

---

1. Hey maid! (Amharic)
2. Useless boy. (Amharic)

Intent on my mission, I continued to clamour. I could see a crack of light through the window in the back room, so I knew he wasn't asleep. "Please, mister, I beg you. I can't go home without beer."

Eventually, the old man emerged at the side door. "You again?" He looked at me disapprovingly.

"Yes. Sorry, mister." I was relieved that he'd come out before the neighbours did.

He looked up and down the street, put his hands on his hips and stretched his back. "Very well. You want the same as last time?"

I nodded and handed him the money. He went inside and returned with two large warm bottles of beer. "Now, you're not going to disturb me again tonight, are you?" he queried.

I shook my head, hoping this would be true, but Solomon's supplies often needed replenishing more than once during the night.

"Your father should be ashamed sending you out at all hours," the old man sympathised. He cleared his throat and spat on the ground near my foot, before returning inside.

Lugging my cargo, I headed back. I hated nighttime at my father's house.

I wasn't doomed to be a midnight runner indefinitely. The resourceful Doctor Solomon soon found another Catholic-run mission in which to hide the seed of his past; south this time, in the Gurage region.

Only in recent years have I learned of the circumstances that would send me several hundred kilometres from the capital. Father Dalloi, the director of Gurage's mission school, was summoned along with his assistant, Father Daniel, to an urgent meeting at my father's house. After preliminary politeness, the two priests tensed.

My father leaned in. "I'm . . . uh . . . I need help," he began, uncharacteristically nervous. "There's this boy. Not my wife's child. He's m—my son with another woman."

The priests rocked back (*because evil is contagious, you know*).

Father Dalloi looked at Solomon. "If you wish to come to confession, I'm sure that God will forgive—"

"No, it's not that, *Abbata*.[3] You see, recently this boy, Tewodros, was sent to live with me, but my wife is unhappy about the arrangement. His presence has caused great tension between us," my father lied.

"Perhaps we can talk with Saba," Father Daniel suggested.

"No, no, no. That's not appropriate."

"Well, what exactly do you think we can do?" Father Daniel was confused about the point of the meeting.

"Please, *Abbate*, I have a good job and manage all I can with patients and teaching, but I'm not prepared to jeopardise my marriage any longer. I need you to find somewhere for this boy to live."

The priests nodded at each other. Perhaps he was right; after all, money wasn't a problem for this family. If they could help the good doctor save his marriage, it might be for the best.

On such short notice, it was difficult to find a mission willing to take on another child. So they both agreed that Father Dalloi's mission in Gurage would be the most appropriate. First, they'd have to seek approval from Father Thomas (head of the mission) before any final decisions could be made.

My father urged them to do whatever they could to convince Father Thomas to take me in.

The priests drove home in silence. Father Dalloi told me later that he couldn't comprehend the news. He'd known Doctor Solomon for some years and had a close relationship with the family. At the time, he was unaware that I'd already been at the Dese mission. He tells me now that if he'd known the true nature of my circumstances he could have made more suitable arrangements, since a mission was no place for the son of Doctor Solomon.

Despite its presumptions, that title left me to scavenge for the good will of others. He might as well have been dead to me, for *it is*

3. Father; term of reverence for a priest. (Amharic)

better to be the cub of a live jackal than of a dead lion.[4]

Father Thomas quickly granted permission for me to attend the Gurage mission and, within a few short days, Solomon had deposited me at the Franciscan church, just like last time when he sent me to Dese. He'd arranged for a visiting Gurage priest to collect me.

I lay in the church that night, relieved that there would be no drunken shadow looming over me. Old whispers of a curse hung like cobwebs in my memory. I'd once asked Bishkash about it, dreading the burden of a doomed life.

"Nonsense," she scoffed. "That's just superstition. Besides," she added, "the *meqseft*[5] only lasts for four generations, and you are the fifth."

I wondered if my ancestors were bad at counting.

The Gurage priest and I travelled by Land Rover throughout the next day. As we approached our destination, the dusk sky was brilliant pink and orange, silhouetting the hilly terrain.

"That's where the locals live. Funny houses, aren't they?" the priest chuckled, as he pointed to the small round thatched-roof huts that dotted the countryside. Each was neatly constructed and fenced in with whittled tree branches. Closely laced together, the poles held the residents' animals within the yard boundaries and kept others out. I'd seen this type of fencing before, but never so orderly. From a distance, it looked like a magical miniature world.

"How do they build them?" I asked.

"With a lot of effort, my son, a lot of effort," he reflected. "The Gurage people are very hardworking."

A group of children were shepherding their animals home, beside the road. The priest slammed on the brakes and swerved to avoid a goat that had sauntered out in front of us. The children turned and waved. Some of their heads were shaved except for a long plait at the base of their skulls. Laughing, they shooed the herd on.

---

4. Ethiopian proverb.
5. A curse, calamity or catastrophe. (Amharic)

"Tewodros," the priest grinned at me, "I think you'll have a great time here. Nice people. Friendly. And funny!"

Funny haircuts, funny houses, funny people. I was tickled by the faint hope of a new life.

Gurageland is located approximately 240 kilometres southwest of Addis Ababa. It is a lush hilly region where the rhythm of agriculture dominates the locals' lives. *Enste*[6] is their main staple crop, as well as coffee and *chat*.[7] The lively Gurage people are well-known throughout Ethiopia for their flamboyant society and interesting dialect.

It was the rainy season. We parted curtain after curtain of late afternoon showers as we traversed the terraced hills. Finally, we slipped and bumped up the narrow road that led to the mission.

The darkness of night had arrived with us. As the Land Rover reached the top of the driveway, the headlights lit up a number of small buildings and a stone church. It was like, yet not like, Dese.

Until this point, I had no clear idea of my destination. I'd been left at the church in Addis without explanation. And I didn't have the voice for questions. I wasn't upset that Solomon had sent me away. I was actually relieved not to live with him any longer. But I felt suspended over an abyss of uncertainty. No home, no family, no friends. Would this next place swallow me up and spit me out, too?

A tall boy, not much older than me, approached the car and greeted us. First, he bowed, lifting the priest's hand to his lips and forehead. Then, he introduced himself to me as Tebeka and ushered us under the veranda, out of the wet.

"I'm a former student here. Now I help around the mission," he said proudly. "Come. I'll show you around!"

His friendliness washed over me like the cleansing rain. After we

---

6. False banana plant. (Amharic)
7. A mildly intoxicating chewable leaf; common in Ethiopia, but illegal in Eritrea. (Amharic)

delivered the priest's belongings to his room, Tebeka led me on a guided tour. We giggled, darting from building to building to keep ourselves dry.

Unlike Dese, this was a boys-only mission. A small number of boys lived on the mission grounds with the priests, while the majority of day students came from the surrounding villages and farmland.

There were five priests living there. Each of them was responsible for different parishes in the area, except for the mission's Italian founder, Father Gabriel. He was too old to work. The sisters were responsible for his well-being during the final years of his long life.

The sisters had their own building. In addition to caring for the old priest, their duties extended to fulfilling requests from the other priests and managing the medical clinic located at the driveway entrance.

Tebeka had explained all this by the time we had walked over to the church. Light seeped from the closed entrance. Tebeka listened intently, then reached up and opened one of the large heavy timber doors. A priest was walking down the aisle towards us while others remained in the pews, deep in prayer.

"I'm sorry, *Abba*,[8] if we interrupted you," Tebeka said.

"You're never an interruption," the dark-skinned priest said. "I've finished my prayers and was leaving anyway." He had such kind eyes (and huge lips). He seemed much friendlier and more relaxed than the priests I'd encountered at Dese.

The priest guided us outside and then turned his attention to me. "Young Tewodros. You've arrived!" He rubbed my cheek. "You're early, but it's good you're here." He smiled. "You must be hungry, no?"

I nodded.

"Tebeka, why don't you get him something to eat and show him to his room?"

"Yes, *Abba*," Tebeka replied, respectfully.

8. Father; shortened term of reverence for a priest. (Amharic)

"Now, Tewodros, school doesn't start for a few weeks yet, so there are no other children here, but Tebeka will take care of you. All right?"

Again, I nodded and was led across to the dining room.

"That's *Abba* Thomas," Tebeka explained.

I looked at him blankly.

"He's the head of this mission. He rides a motorbike and plays soccer with us after school and on weekends! Such a nice priest."

I giggled—a priest riding a motorbike? I couldn't imagine it.

As it turned out, I didn't have to wait very long to see this playful priest in action because the very next evening, while I was sitting under a tree with Tebeka, a rebellious engine rumbled up through the valley. Birds dispersed. Dogs barked. The peace enveloping the village vanished.

The old guard ran towards the mission gates and opened them expectantly. Tebeka nudged me in the ribs and pointed. Within seconds, Father Thomas came tearing up the driveway on his motorbike, in a spray of rocks and grit. Then, in a flashy sweep, he skidded to a standstill just beside us.

I ducked into my t-shirt, away from the churning dust. It seemed irreverent for a priest to have such fun. I peeked out to see him dismount, brush off his hands and walk towards the church, waving for us to follow. He was about to deliver a sermon. I looked across at Tebeka and smiled. I'd only known the *fear* of God before. If Father Thomas could show me a god that loved play and light-heartedness, then maybe this was the place for me.

Hallelujah to that!

Occasionally over the following weeks other children arrived, so that by the time the new school year commenced there were six of us in total. Our group expanded dramatically with the influx of day students, many of whom had to walk for miles to attend.

The school was located on a plateau, across the road from the medical clinic. Two rectangular buildings housed the classrooms. Fences extended from them to form the boundaries of the playing field.

On our first official day of lessons my father's friend, Father Dalloi, was introduced to us as School Director. On the veranda in front of the classrooms, he'd set up a temporary office to register new students. Like stray cubs yearning for acceptance, we clambered excitedly around his shaky old desk. He pointed to us one by one, asking for names, ages and current school level.

I proudly told him that I'd completed Grade Two and should definitely go into the next level. He looked me up and down and scribbled my name *on the Grade Three list.* This was my first taste of having power over my destiny. What a thrill!

Lessons were conducted in Amharic, but in the playground the children reverted to the local dialect of Guraginya. From experience, I thought that the key to being part of a group was to master the local language. Since my arrival, I'd been listening intently for as many words and expressions as possible. With Tebeka's help, I picked up the basics of Guraginya quite quickly. This would be my fourth language so far.

Unfortunately, language alone wasn't enough to escape the wrath of the local children. Once more I struggled to belong. As the only Tigrayan-Eritrean among the predominantly Gurage group, I often had the words *"ante anjebegna"*[9] echoing after me. Some children were even bold enough to spit in my face. I wasn't afraid to fight anyone. Since the beatings at Dese Mission, I'd vowed never to be bullied again. My tough-talking skills from the days of street-gang soccer meant I could scare off my provokers with words rather than fists.

On a recent trip back to Ethiopia, I met Tebeka and asked him about all that teasing. He told me very matter-of-factly, "Tewodros, when you arrived, you dressed like a stuck-up city boy and played

9. "You are stuck up." (Amharic)

soccer like you thought you were the son of Pele!"[10]

He was probably right. Although the irony was that new clothes had become the wrapping, and I was always the package being sent away.

Just as in the previous mission, chores such as gardening and cleaning were a daily activity. The difference was my version of hard work compared to that of the Gurage people. They were well-known for their diligent attitude and entrepreneurial skills and, even at a young age, the Gurage children energetically carried out their tasks. My dawdling approach drew more teasing. Work for work's sake never appealed to me.

When the priests were satisfied that we'd completed our chores, Father Thomas coached us in soccer.

Like music, soccer unifies people. There's a bond that goes beyond language. Everyone is linked through the ball. It passes between players like a pulse, lifting them out of their separate existence into a sense of play.

Father Thomas loved soccer as much as he loved "his" children and some of my happiest memories come from this time—running around on an open field with him and the mission boys. I couldn't connect with the other children through language or work ethic, but I excelled at this game and gradually won their approval.

I often dreamed that I was kicking a goal in front of an ecstatic crowd. They'd chant my name. The breeze would ruffle my hair as I leaped through the air with my teammates. How wonderful that would be.

On top of this, a new delight arrived in three colours. Our team was supplied with uniforms from Italy (some distant land—I had no idea where) and we were able to compete in the local soccer league competition. Thanks to regular meals and consistent training (which were often not available to the children of other teams),

---

10. Nickname for Brazilian soccer player voted "Athlete of the Century"; real name: Edison Arantes do Nascimento.

we won most of our games.

In Gurage, we were free. Far enough from the hot zones of civil war, we never saw soldiers or felt the terror of those ongoing conditions. We could venture as far and wide around the village as our curiosity took us. We weren't confined by boundaries and could visit day students at their homes, if we pleased. We could even stay the night with them if we asked for Father Thomas's permission, which he almost always granted. I loved the Gurage mission and wished that my wretched father had sent me there first.

When your need for food, shelter and clothing is fulfilled—not just temporarily or infrequently—then you have time to believe in something. When you begin to know generosity, you start to believe in God.

Sister Jimma taught "Morals and Ethics" and was undoubtedly one of my favourite teachers. She was small in stature, but huge in heart. Everything she did was with passion and zest, whether it was saying her daily prayers or pruning her roses in the convent gardens. She loved life, and we loved her. Thanks to the quality she inspired in us, belief became a profound experience, the highlight of which was receiving my First Holy Communion.

From the commencement of the school year, Sister Jimma had been busily preparing our class for this momentous day. The five chosen candidates had to pass a test on the Seven Sacraments, the Hail Mary prayer, the Ten Commandments, passages from the Bible, and anything else considered essential knowledge for a good Catholic boy. I was always the first to raise my hand to answer her questions. The little devil was emulating goodness (most of the time, anyway).

As the anticipated event approached, visitors distributed gifts among us. These included rosary beads, pictures of Jesus and Mary and (much sought after) glow-in-the-dark statues. We were showered with attention and could say or do no wrong. I felt the hand of God reaching out to me, inviting me to know that life could shine.

On the day itself, we scrubbed ourselves to angelic standards. We each dressed in a crisp new shirt, new pants and shiny new shoes—all the way from Italy. I was very impressed with the Italian-made clothing: the elegant cloth, the fine stitching. It was my first conscious appreciation of something well-made. I promised myself that when I became a famous soccer star, I would only wear clothes from Italy. (I'm happy to say that, although I'm still waiting for my World Cup soccer jersey, the rest of my wardrobe is quite elegant.)

The ceremony started at midnight. There was no electricity at the mission (at that stage), so the old stone church was lit entirely by candlelight. It looked magical, like another world. I wondered how Heaven compared to that.

We filed down the aisle to the front of the church where certain pews had been decorated in white cloth and reserved for us. The congregation all smiled adoringly at us. I felt indescribably good.

During the Mass, I exuberantly recited all the prayers and said "Amen" in all the right places, almost lifting out of my shoes with excitement. I realised my foolishness at the Dese mission when I thought everyone else was getting a treat. Well, they were, but now I understood its significance and was eager to taste the small white crisp bread that I'd previously been denied.

When the time came for us to receive Communion, we neatly filed down the aisle and waited patiently in turn. I wanted the moment to be sublime, and for Sister Jimma to be proud of me. The priest placed the bread reverently on my tongue. I closed my mouth, but the wafer wedged up behind my teeth, gagging me. The priest looked unimpressed. From the front row, Sister Jimma stifled laughter in her hymn book.

After Mass, we were escorted into the dining hall where a feast had been prepared. This was the perfect end to a perfect night. I went to bed in the early hours of the morning feeling completely at peace.

Little by little, my confidence grew. I started to trust again—in people, in devotion—in life.

Achieving First Communion brought special privileges. It meant we could assist the maids and priests with the enviable task of making the Communion bread. A special batter was prepared and poured into a hot mould of small circles. After carefully cooking each batch, we cut out the circles with a specific tool. There were always offcuts, which we nibbled gleefully while working for God.

With a full load of freshly baked Holy bread, we'd follow the priests to the church and help set up for the ceremony. On occasion, I snuck a few sips of wine. It wasn't as pleasant as milk, but since it was supposedly sacred, I thought it might enhance my goodness. I always wiped the goblet carefully, just in case I'd left any traces of naughtiness behind.

Except for the wildlife and the village huts, there was nothing in Gurage; not even a restaurant. All that existed was under the Church's control, but that only included the mission, the school and the medical clinic.

Without electricity, the village fell into darkness after sundown. Only small flickering candlelight could be seen inside the huts. We had a generator at the mission, which often left us in the dark due to mechanical issues. (Maybe it was possessed.)

Aside from the occasional wedding or religious event, there was little to do.

One weekend, the priests decided to show us the magic of movies. They dragged the generator across to the school and converted a classroom into a cinema. People walked for hours to attend.

After my Chuck Norris viewing in Asmara, I anticipated larger-than-life action. I was clueless about the diverse magical world of storytelling through moving images.

Tebeka and I arrived early and watched the priests set up the old projector. Instead of a screen, they used a chalkboard, testing the flickering black-and-white images for focus before the big show.

When the classroom was full, the priests hushed everyone and announced Charlie Chaplin—completely unknown to us. Imagine a room full of dark faces, raucously laughing at the antics of that quirky little moustached man. Some of the viewers closely inspected the projector, thinking he was in the lens.

Hilarity exhausted us, yet we begged for a replay as soon as the reel spun out. But, like all children who must go to school the next day, we had to pack up and get to bed.

As the year progressed, I helped Father Dalloi establish electricity around the mission. We connected wiring down to the medical clinic and, as required, to other areas of the village. I thrived on his attention and the importance of my role. The other children and I had also been helping him renovate the old seminary on the mission grounds. It had been closed for several years and was about to re-open. He gave us a sense of achievement.

At the end of the school year, Father Dalloi was transferred. I was devastated. I couldn't imagine the mission without him.

He was replaced by two new priests: Father Tekle (who took over Father Dalloi's old parish) and Father Franco (who took over as School Director); the latter managed to destroy my blossoming trust in one fell swoop.

Trouble began when one of my classmates, Mohammed, told me that he'd seen Father Franco committing a sin against God: passionately kissing one of the maids. This was scandalous. Sister Jimma's class taught me that God would definitely disapprove. A priest would never—! Just thinking about it felt sinful. I didn't want to believe it so I put it out of my mind.

One day after school, Mohammed and I got into a fight, not for the first time. It started off as a verbal spat, but quickly deteriorated into a physical brawl. Mohammed charged, grappling one of my legs, half-tackling me. As I hopped about, frantically trying to keep my balance, I thumped his back while he worked at throwing me down. After several seconds of tussling, he managed to lift my other leg, thudding us both to the ground.

Losing the fight was nothing compared to the shock of being winded for the first time (though I didn't understand it was as simple as that). My chest heaved futilely. I struggled to breathe, to no avail. It's strange how the mind can race in stress and fear. I wondered if this was what Taytu experienced in her last moments of consciousness. I hoped she hadn't suffered like this. *She deserved to go in peace,* I thought with my presumed dying breath.

Slowly my muscles relaxed and I sucked in some air. I wanted revenge. Beating Mohammed was not a sure thing. Name-calling would only provoke more violence. I needed something powerful, something so surprising that he would think twice before attacking me again. Then I saw Father Franco walking up the driveway and remembered what Mohammed had told me a few days before.

I was sure that a boy who spoke of such sinfulness would be punished, not realising that I would be doing exactly that. I never paused to consider Father Franco's reaction. I'd hardly uttered the dreadful tale when the priest grabbed me by the shirt and dragged me back to our sleeping quarters. On the way, he rounded up Mohammed.

"Pull down your pants," he screeched. He was clearly enraged; his nostrils flared in heavy breathing and his forehead bubbled with sticky beads of perspiration.

Mohammed obediently pulled down his pants. Too terrified for defiance, I did the same. Standing behind us, Father Franco told us to bend forward and place our hands on the bed. I recognised the shape of things to come—the long slender shape of a hose length. *Holy Mary, what was I thinking?!*

Mohammed began to sob.

Whoosh! The hose swiftly descended, making a cracking noise as it hit bare skin. Mohammed screamed. I slammed my hands over my ears and tightly hunched my bottom away from the priest.

"PUT YOUR HANDS ON THE BED!" Father Franco yelled.

Mohammed continued to holler. Tears flowed freely down my cheeks. How quickly events had turned. With hands rigid on the bed end, I clenched my eyes and mouth shut, determined not to let the priest get any satisfaction from his punishment. When the hose cracked across my bottom, it was with such force that I felt sliced in half. My eyes flew open expecting to see my legs no longer attached to my body.

"Now get out of here, you stupid boys!" Father Franco screamed. Howling, holding our hands to our welted bottoms, we both stumbled towards the door with our pants still around our ankles. We spent the next two days bed-ridden, as it was too painful to walk.

From this, I learned that one person's truth could be another person's nightmare. *Thou shalt not lie*[11] never explained that detail.

Mohammed and I bonded through our suffering and our united front against Father Franco. We recovered just in time for the *Meskel*[12] festival, held in September; the most important annual celebration in the region. The festival runs for eight days, and celebrates the finding of the cross on which Jesus was crucified. It also marks the end of the rainy season and the return of the sun. Each day is given a special name and is symbolised by the eating of a special part of a sacrificial ox—a practice which is believed to renew the fertility of women and crops.

There was always an air of excitement leading up to the festive season, much like Christmas in Western countries. It was a time for families to gather and migrant workers to return to their homelands. Gifts were exchanged and an array of special food was prepared.

---

11. Eight Commandment, according to Roman Catholic teaching.
12. Meskel means "cross" in Ge'ez (the classic language of Ethiopia).

Mixed Blessings

During my first *Meskel* festival, I became interested in dancing. The lively upbeat music wove irresistibly around me until my tapping feet carried me into the swaying crowd. There were pipes, harmonicas, and of course the drums.

The villagers gathered and danced in their own distinct style. With their palms together in a prayer-like pose, they vigorously moved their hands backwards and forwards from their chest while kicking out their legs in time with the music. My friends and I copied their exuberant movements. It was so much fun joking with the village children as we danced (and danced and danced)!

During the festive season, the boys at the mission returned to their family homes in nearby villages to enjoy the celebrations together. As the only "orphaned" boy, I visited my friends' houses. The sisters had made me a small cotton sack in which I packed a towel and a change of clothes. Like a little nomad, I migrated from house to house each night and even stayed at the maids' houses to celebrate with their families.

For once, having no family didn't feel like a famine of the heart.

Adventure beckoned. My village friends and I always pursued it. We'd go bathing or skim rocks in a nearby stream. In those interludes, we were carefree and wild at heart. Even so, fear was always lurking at the edges of our innocence.

The local people believed in possession. There was an *ebd*[13] living nearby whom the priests said had too many devils in him; there simply weren't enough blessings to save him. If I saw him, I'd run past with my mouth snapped shut, so that his demons wouldn't pass into me.

Too often after my escapades, I had to scurry home before sunset, whispering to every saint to protect me. The *agante*[14] come out at night, you know.

13. Crazy man. (Amharic)
14. Devils. (Amharic)

Even though many of the festivities were conducted on the church grounds, my friends and I wandered around the countryside to take part in some of the smaller activities. One evening, we cut across a small valley on the way to a local wedding. Thoughts of food and dancing were interrupted by yelling from the bushes. Two white-cloaked elders emerged at the far side of the stream we were crossing.

"STOP!" one of them shouted. "Stay back!"

We halted, thigh-deep in water.

"*Seytan*[15] is over there!" the other man cautioned.

We looked at them in disbelief. They weren't joking.

"Boys, it's best you take another route," one of them said, as they passed us and continued into the distance.

The fear of the Devil had been drilled into us so deeply that none of us was prepared to take another step in that direction. Mouths dry, hearts pounding, we cautiously retraced our steps, scouring the landscape for anything that might resemble *Seytan*.

I wonder now what it really was that they didn't want us to witness. The adult world has murky corners that a child shouldn't see, whether they are superstitions, immoral behaviour or the monster that lurks in a bottle of alcohol. Such fleeting moments of terror reminded me that I was a boy with a dark past and an uncertain future.

The hills around Gurage were not only haunted by Satan, but also crawling with wild animals, the most notorious of which was the hyena.

I pestered the priests to go for a night drive to the market areas, where hyenas scavenged for scraps remaining from the day's trade. Most often, my requests were flatly denied, but occasionally one of the priests would squeeze us into the back of the Land Rover and

---

15. Satan. (Amharic, Tigrinya)

we launched our safari in the dark.

We bumped down the rocky track, breathless with excitement. Without fail, the market area would be full of yipping. The lights of the vehicle flashed over luminous eyes and ferocious teeth as the beasts raised their heads to the approaching sound.

Sensing danger, they fled.

Inside the car, we would chant "Chase them, *Abba*! Chase them!" If the priest was up for it, he would follow closely behind as they ran towards the outskirts of town. Then our chants would turn to "Hit them! Run the hyenas over, *Abba*!" But, of course, our driver never obliged.

Facing wickedness is easy enough in a carload of laughing friends.

The year's end was speeding after me on inescapable wheels of change. It was time to face *my* Satan again.

8

THE NOT-SO-PRODIGAL SON

My heart was a harrowing marketplace where thoughts and feelings were traded like perishable commodities in each new situation. All this time, I'd kept my mother standing in the dusty corner of that early morning long ago, regretting my departure and waiting for my return.

Even a boy can sense the hollowness of such secret yearning. I knew (yet could never accept) that there was more between us now than just distance and time.

Life at the mission had equipped me with a set of values and beliefs. The priests and sisters taught goodness. They expected integrity. These were my new tools with which to navigate the world. I had more clarity and stability than the dreams of a frightened boy, but the heart is ever hopeful and I still pined for the soothing shores of love and acceptance.

Annual school holidays meant returning to my father's house for two arduous months. It didn't matter what I'd achieved throughout the year or how confident I'd become, his presence reduced me to confusion and dread.

Night.

I knew how things went. I was about twelve years old, and asleep, when drunken Solomon started pounding on my door. Assuming he wanted drinking supplies, I dragged myself out of bed and faced him. Ignoring him was pointless. One way or another, he forced me to comply.

"Te-ros!" he slurred. His eyes were bloodshot. He reeked of cigarettes. "Come with me." He prodded me down the hall to the lounge room where Saba was watching television. "Si'down," he said, plopping into his armchair. "There's some'ing I need to tell you."

What could he concoct this time? I sat (at a safe distance) and silently watched him try to project a semblance of sobriety.

"You know . . . Te-ros, I hate t' be the one to tell you this . . . but," he burped, "I'm not really your father."

Every cell tingled. Could it be true? I *was* different from his other children. Was that why he didn't care for me? It was the best possible news. My heart raced. I could be free from this life—from him.

"I'm actually doing your real father a favour," he mumbled.

"Solomon, don't be ridiculous," Saba interrupted.

"*Suk beli!*[1] He needs to know the *truth!*" he spat the words back at her, then spun back to me. "Now, where was I . . . yesss . . . your father . . . he's a brave young man . . . fighting in th' mountains f' our freedom," he boasted.

I stared blankly at him.

"He is a soldier, Te-ros, a soldier!"

I looked at Saba, who only shook her head in disgust. Solomon ignored her and continued. "In fact, he's been gone for so long . . . he might even be dead, sooo—really, Te-ros, I am doing you a big favour . . . big." His hand shot forward on the last word, punctuating the air just in front of me.

1. Shut up! (Tigrinya).

"Leave him alone!" Saba snapped. "Tewodros, darling, it's best you forget what this fool has told you and go back to bed."

Back in my room, I spent the next few hours wide awake. As much as I wanted to believe him, what reason did I have? Surely Saba would have told me otherwise. Was I Solomon's son, or the son of a stranger, or no one's son at all?

I became the invisible child, trying to fit in, exerting my best manners and behaviour, looking for signs that the barriers had fallen.

Daytime brought relief since Solomon worked long hours, but my life's education expanded in unpredictable ways in the company of my two younger stepbrothers. Sneaking under the watchful pictures of saints adorning the house, Mehari and Tinsae were less than angelic in their activities. Proud of being the doctor's sons, they delighted in shocking me with "operations" on unsuspecting frogs and snakes. With gruesome glee, they dissected such creatures, pulling out strings of intestines and pretending to eat them.

Snakes were generally feared. Knowing this, the boys schemed to ambush passers-by, with dramatic results. There was a certain tree with branches that curved very much like a resting snake. Mehari broke off a decent-sized branch while Tinsae pried glowing eyes from the saints' pictures inside the house. These were glued to one end of the branch, which was then placed strategically near the footpath. A string on the other end looped back behind the bushes where the boys could spy on the street. It was wickedness in waiting.

Someone would approach, unsuspecting. At just the right moment, the string was pulled, the "snake" lurched and each pedestrian would run screaming and flapping their arms, praying for salvation.

The boys giggled mischievously, as they reset the trap for the next victim.

Mischief has such great appeal, but the naughty boy within me didn't dare join in. The fear of my father was greater than my desire to cause a little havoc. Not without justification. One day I saw him punish his boys for more hooligan behaviour. They had scraped together some pie-sized mud packs, deposited their own brown-coloured waste in them and made "poo grenades"; the perfect ammunition for launching at the neighbour's side wall. When Solomon found out (this time he didn't immediately think *I* was the culprit), he whipped their behinds, emphasising that they were *doctor's* sons. Apparently, because of that, they should have known better.

Tension seemed to ease as days went by, but it would reappear harshly, without warning. I remember the family was preparing for an outing to a famous hot spring resort called Sodera. Assuming by now that I was part of the family, I prepared to join them. Everyone was wearing their best clothes. I only had one good outfit. As I emerged from the house and walked towards the car, my father lunged at me.

"What do you think you're doing?" he sneered.

"You said we were going on a family outing." My knees started to quiver.

"That's right. *We* are. You are *not* part of the family, so get back inside and take those clothes off before you ruin them!"

I felt so ashamed. His (other) children saw it all. Saba was standing behind Solomon and appeared upset, but said nothing. I made it to the top step of the veranda, where I crumpled into a whimpering heap.

He'd loaded everyone into the car and shouted from the window, "You should know better. Don't make me teach you this lesson again!"

I didn't see how his sons should know better for *being* doctor's sons and somehow *I* should know better than being *with* doctor's sons.

If I couldn't win his favour, then perhaps I could connect with the rest of the family. Over time, I had collected about twenty sets of rosary beads, pictures of saints and small badges from my time at the mission; some were even from my First Holy Communion celebration.

This was a common hobby for children my age. Whenever we met a priest or a nun, we begged them to give us some token to add to our collection. The gilt-edged holy cards were palm-sized, with European art depicting different saints. Mary was my favourite. She became a young mother unexpectedly (like mine) and she raised Jesus to be a good boy. I always wanted a mother like that.

These cards and beads were my most precious possessions. I brought my small but growing collection to my father's house during school holidays and gave them to his wife and children, thinking it would be a noble gesture.

When he returned from work later that evening, the children excitedly showed him what I'd given them. He reacted in fury, calling me a thief and a liar. He told the children that I'd stolen them and couldn't be trusted.

Crushed, I finally realised the devil he really was.

Since first meeting him at the hospital, I'd battled against the storm of his resentment, trying to find ways to land my tiny raft of hope in safety. But he always raged on. I had to stay on guard now. Just get through the rest of the holidays and get (the hell) out of there.

The New Year meant new life for me. The mission was my salvation. Every twelve months, I would return: the not-so-prodigal son—to endure the purgatory of his company once more.

After one such holiday interlude (I was about thirteen), I was packing my things for the new school year. Solomon and I were already in the car but, spontaneously, he decided to check my bags.

During my visit, I'd been given some of the other children's old toys to play with. I had decided to pack them for entertainment at the mission. I don't even remember what they were; just that no one else wanted them.

When Solomon rummaged through my bag and discovered these things, his mood was fierce. He wrenched the passenger door wide, dragged me out onto the ground and began hitting and kicking me, cursing me through his clenched teeth.

I compacted into a ball of hatred. In my mind, I screamed, "ENOUGH!" Such violence. Such selfishness. He was a grown man beating a child. What was he so afraid of that he needed to thump me out of existence? He was a doctor—a healer. What was the point of all that education if he was really just a monster?

In adulthood, my search for truth and peace has inspired me to seek deeper understanding of him. His portrait is complex, and not without merit.

Solomon was not just a good doctor: he was great. He took on the kind of medicine that traditional beliefs shied away from, though all saw it as necessary to promoting better health. His students praised him as a patient and thorough teacher. His children felt loved, despite his violent outbursts. (Yet today they wrestle with uncertainty over this.) His associates knew him to be a drunk, a liar and a scrooge, but he never let his off-duty vices jeopardise his work.

What terrible thing might have happened to make him so full of fury? I cannot be the only dark secret he was trying to drown in alcohol. What other demons terrorised him in the fragile recesses of his mind?

I'm not trying to justify his actions. I want to find some humanity in him, some way to forgiveness. No matter what we've been through, I think there comes a point in life when we can choose integrity and not be a product of our past. He obviously didn't. No wonder he couldn't face me—the constant reminder that no matter how great he became in the eyes of others, he would always be the coward who robbed a young girl and her son of a decent life.

As I lay there on the ground, taking blow after blow, *my* rage made me stronger: I would never be like him. I would never ask for his help. I never wanted to see him again.

I returned to the mission for my final year of primary school and was faced with more bad news. Father Thomas had been transferred and was replaced by a very stern priest called Father Tesfamariam. Soon after his arrival, Father Franco and Father Tekle also left. Without any replacements, Father Tesfamariam was in control of the school, the mission and one of the parishes.

The atmosphere changed under the heavy hand of the new priest. He was a traditional cleric who kept his distance, refused to play soccer with us and was not receptive to jokes. My time at the Gurage mission became less and less enjoyable.

At the end of the year, I managed to score above average grades and was looking forward to attending senior school with everyone else. The mission didn't run a high school, but graduating students usually continued their studies at the local government high school. Father Tesfamariam called for me one day, after receiving my school report. I was justifiably pleased over my results and thought he was going to congratulate me.

"Tewodros, I need to talk to you about your future." His stern tone held no compliments. "As you and I both know, your father is not just any doctor, but one making a good living. He can well afford to pay for your education." He stopped to clear his throat.

Throat-clearing is never a good sign in a conversation.

"And based on that knowledge, I have decided you will not be sent on to the government school with the other children." He gathered up the papers before him, and began organising them into piles.

The pages clack-clacked onto the hard wooden desk.

I saw his hands moving and knew that they were hands. I could feel my feet tensing in my shoes and knew that they were my feet. But I couldn't find my voice. My eyes flicked around the familiar room, looking for understanding.

"You don't belong to the Church, Tewodros. You are not our responsibility."

Clack, clack.

"Do you understand? You cannot stay."

My words came all at once. "But *Abba*, please! I *can't* go back to *him*!"

"You must. I'm sorry. There are other children who need our help more than you."

"If I can't go to school, then can I stay here and study to become a priest?" I'd try anything to avoid further contact with my father.

The priest shook his head.

"Please *Abba*, you can ask Sister Jimma. She knows what a good student I am and how I believe in God!"

"Stop working yourself up, child!" he snapped. "I told you no. That's firm. There's nothing you can do to convince me otherwise. This mission has taken care of you long enough. Your father is a doctor, after all!"

What did that really mean?!

Father Tesfamariam's chilling conclusion sent me racing in search of Sister Jimma. I found her rummaging in the garden.

"My star pupil! How are you, my friend?" she asked. "I'm all out of rosary beads, so I hope that's not the reason for your visit!" she joked.

"I—need to talk—with you," I begged, choking on distress.

Her instant concern calmed me a little. "Of course. Let's take a walk."

After dusting off the dirt and leaves from her clothes, she put her arm reassuringly around my shoulders. We walked through the convent grounds and I explained my dilemma. She suggested we go and talk with Father Tesfamariam together.

Bolstered by Sister Jimma's presence, I approached the presbytery.

Father Tesfamariam was talking with a guest on the veranda. The visitor was Ms. Aida, a plump Italian lady, who often stopped by with gifts from Italy for the priests and sisters.

Sister Jimma and I waited patiently. After a while, Ms. Aida noticed us hovering in the background.

"Is everything all right, Sister?" Ms. Aida called out to us.

"No, everything is not all right." Sister Jimma didn't hesitate for a second. "Young Tewodros has been told that he cannot continue his schooling here and will have to return to his father."

"His *doctor* father," Father Tesfamariam added.

"But you know he doesn't get along with him. It doesn't matter what his occupation is."

"It does matter because he can afford to pay for this child. The Church doesn't need to carry any unnecessary burdens," he interrupted.

Ms. Aida listened patiently while the other two continued to debate responsibility for my care. Then she enquired as to the whereabouts of my mother.

"I think she might be in Asmara," I said.

Sister Jimma added, "Yes. We've helped Tewodros send several letters to her but, to date, there's been no response."

The adults continued to talk over my head. I watched my fate being tossed from one side to another and back again as they determined the best course of action. After much discussion, it was agreed that I should return to Addis Ababa and begin searching for my mother, to live with her, if possible. Ms. Aida offered to take me to Holy Saviour Church in the capital, where she knew an Italian priest who might assist me.

Within just a few days, I was leaving the mission nestled deep in the pristine mountains of Gurage. This precious pocket of paradise was the place I'd felt most at home. How quickly it seemed to vanish behind us as Ms. Aida drove me towards the shanties of the capital city.

The wheels of change rolled on.

9

VELVET GLOVE, IRON FIST

What is it that turns a boy into a man? Diverse cultures mark the reaching of maturity in different ways, all of which celebrate a boy's new place among peers.

Ethiopian tradition doesn't place emphasis on specific dates, unless they are religious, so birthdays are fleetingly noted, if at all. I used to count my years in surviving rather than fulfilling possibilities, and felt regret at the loss of so much time. I wasn't even certain of my exact birth date, just my approximate age. Even so, I was expected to have achieved particular skills and knowledge within an age time frame and to act with certain awareness and responsibility.

Not yet a man, though no longer a boy, I had no real education or skills, and my hitherto rite of passage extended from dodging bullets to a secluded life in a church orphanage—not exactly executive material. I had no solid ground of my own on which to make my stand. I had to trust in the solutions offered by the adults around me.

We don't want him. His father won't keep him. His mother should take him.

I don't know what I really thought would happen when I found my mother. I was too much of a child to think beyond that, but everyone else seemed confident that being with her was right and good, and they expected (as did I) that my troubles would end with her.

Despite all these good intentions, I was being cast out once more. This was not a fairy tale with a happy ending. This was to be another journey of desperation and would result in the most challenging conditions yet.

For a lion in the wilderness, belonging is the difference between life and death. The search goes on and the heart *is* a lonely hunter.

"Tewodros, this is Padre[1] Roberto." Ms. Aida spoke Italian when introducing me to the old priest.

We were in his office at Holy Saviour Church in Addis Ababa. Padre Roberto stood up and acknowledged us both with a kiss on each cheek. He was a rotund man of diminutive height, dressed in a simple brown robe of the Franciscan order. His eyes twinkled through little round reading glasses. There was a small cap on his balding head, but what hair he lacked on top certainly contrasted with his generous beard. This was wiry, grey and so long that it touched the desk in front of him when he sat back down. I was mesmerised as his beard made scratching noises on the desk each time he spoke.

Padre Roberto and Ms. Aida continued conversing in Italian. Amid strange words and beard-waving, there wasn't much I could follow. He was the first white priest I'd ever seen and I wondered if he could speak Amharic.

They talked in depth for some time. *Scratch.* Murmur. *Scratch, scratch.* Finally, Padre Roberto turned to me and said (in Amharic— yes!), "It seems you are in a bit of pickle, my child, but we will help you find your mother so that you don't have to worry any longer, *va bene?*"[2]

---

1. Father. (Italian)
2. Okay. (Italian)

I nodded.

Ms. Aida stood up and handed him some money to help with my transportation. *"In bocca al lupo,"*[3] she said, as she left the office.

That afternoon, Padre Roberto invited me to sit with him in the church garden, while we considered my options. He already had some facts from Ms. Aida, but he wanted to know more about my family and with whom I had the strongest connections.

As he patiently listened, encouraging me to talk in chatty descriptions rather than nervous monosyllables, he occasionally reached into the front pocket of his robe and withdrew a slim silver case. It was round, just like him. He flicked open a small hole on the side and poured a tiny mound of fine brown powder into the hollow between his thumb and forefinger. This he snorted stiffly into his flared nostrils, leaving little hints of dust on his nose and in his beard.

I was fascinated.

He kept listening, nodding and sniffing, as I told more of my strange tale. He agreed that my grandmother might know of Bishkash's whereabouts, so he suggested starting in Asmara. Perhaps (I was hoping) my mother was already there.

It took almost one month to organise the details of my trip. Padre Roberto took care of everything: he made sure I had enough money to put a roof over my head and some food in my belly; he sent me on an errand to Gurage to get special identification documents that would allow me to travel; and (naturally) he encouraged me to come to church.

I visited him often. I felt that we'd become good friends. I even grew cheeky enough to brush the snuff powder from his beard. With that twinkle in his eye, he constantly reassured me that all would be well.

Finally, equipped with a plane ticket for Asmara, I went to see Padre to collect the belongings he'd stored for me. He was usually

---

3. Good luck. (Italian)

busy so I went early, before he left for Mass.

I was knocking on his window when I noticed some men down the street struggling with a cow. They were most likely intending to slaughter it for the approaching Easter celebrations. The cow was lying on its back with its four legs stuck up in the air (like my poor Taytu). Maybe it was morbid curiosity that drew me closer or perhaps I was trying to be a man, among men. Either way, I stepped in to help.

I grabbed one of the cow's hind legs. With an almighty kick, its hoof struck me full in the face, and I was knocked backwards onto the ground. Morning turned to night as galaxies filled my vision. I could taste blood, and feverishly felt all over my face to make sure bits weren't missing. The men failed to notice. They were dodging danger themselves as the cow continued to protest.

If being a man meant taking life on the chin, then I'd hold onto my childhood for as long as I could.

Shaken, and besmirched from the dusty street, I wobbled back to Padre Roberto's window and knocked again, though a little feebler than before. This time, he emerged, and took one amazed look at me. Watching a priest laughing uncontrollably was disconcerting. They are normally so contained and serious.

He pointed at my swollen mouth. "Tewodros! You have lips like a camel!" he wheezed. "And as red as a baboon's bottom!"

My face hurt so much that I couldn't laugh with him, even if I'd wanted to, but his playful honest reaction eased my shock and embarrassment.

He put his hand up to his chest and tried to control his breathing. "You know, Tewodros, when the Bible says 'turn the other cheek', it's not literal," he gently teased. "Come in, my son, we need to finish preparing your belongings for the trip."

While he packed a bag for me, I washed out my mouth and regained some composure. It was unusual to be allowed into a priest's room, so I wasted no time in looking around this secret world.

"Padre, I think I need this!" I exclaimed, pointing to an un-opened bar of soap sitting on his sink. "Oh, and those t-shirts would be very nice, too! Are they Italian-made?"

"Yes, yes," he said. "Anything else, my child?" He joked.

"Now that you ask, I need it all!" I ran around his room excitedly. I was going on an adventure and my mother would be waiting at its end.

"I think that cow might have damaged your brain."

I ignored his quips and continued collecting items.

"Tewodros, just look at your bag. If I put another thing in here, the plane won't get off the ground and everyone will be very upset with me."

We both sat down on his bed and this time I laughed with him.

Later that afternoon, when the thrust of the plane's engines pressed me heavily back in the seat, I remembered Padre Roberto's words. *Is my bag holding us down? There's no way this lumbering metal shell will lift off,* I worried, while the plane chugged down the run-way. My previous airplane experience had been weighted with a different kind of fear when I'd flown towards my father. Now, I was flying away. The magic of that would have given me wings, even if the plane could not. As it thrust upward, defying gravity (much to my relief), I was defying the fate of a cursed past.

My quest for a new life had begun.

I was 10 years old when I left Eritrea and now, taller though per-haps no wiser, I was returning. It had been just over four years, but it felt longer. So much had happened since then.

Using money from Padre Roberto, I took a taxi from the airport and asked the driver to take me to the Coca Cola factory in Maite-menai; this was always the landmark I used to find my way home when I lived with Adey. Once at the factory, I easily remembered the way and guided the taxi driver to the front gates of my grand-mother's house.

Just like that first time when Mebrat had left me there, my grandmother was not at home. The tenants in the front room of her house told me she was visiting wolf-lady—I mean, Aunt Almaz—who lived a few streets away. I was relieved when they went to tell Adey that she had a visitor. Brave as I was about my quest, I wavered at facing my aunt so soon.

Eventually they returned with my grandmother in tow. She looked at me in disbelief, standing there on her front step. The incident from my early childhood was being played out again, only this time I was smiling instead of crying.

"Tewodros? How are you my son?" She opened her arms and pulled me into her big soft bosom, then kissed the top of my head. She was wearing the same sweet-smelling perfume and I inhaled it deeply—the scent of comfort. She took a step back to get a full view of me. "My son! Look at how you've grown!" She smiled and hugged me again.

We went inside and had *shai*[4] together and caught up on the events since we'd been apart. She was shocked to learn that I'd been sent to two different missions because she'd been told I was attending a good school somewhere in Addis Ababa. I wasn't surprised that my father had been lying to the family. Adey didn't question my version of things. What a relief. Some sanctuary at last.

Later that evening, Aunt Almaz came to visit with her husband. I greeted her politely at the door. Her suspended smile transformed into gritted resentment. "What are you doing here?" she growled.

"Aunt Almaz, please. I'm not here to cause any trouble," I tried to reassure her, with little impact.

"I sent you to live with your father. Don't you understand? Adey cannot take care of you!" she shrieked.

"I know. I'm looking for my mother," I said. "I need Adey's help."

"Just go! Get back to your father's place. Stop disturbing the family, you good-for-nothing ingrate!"

---

4. Spiced tea. (Amharic).

I'd never intended to be a nuisance or cause problems—for anyone. I knew my presence was a burden, but where else could I turn? Finding my mother *had* to be the solution.

"Almaz! Tewodros is not disturbing me and he cannot go back to his father. He has just explained the awful time he's had since leaving here." Adey spoke calmly, but firmly.

Aunt Almaz took measured breaths, realising that finding my mother was the quickest way to have me gone. After calming down, she said she'd help on the condition that I would not ask to live with Adey if my search failed.

My sweet grandmother secretly promised otherwise.

Swift to take up the cause, my aunt began enquiring into Bishkash's whereabouts. Mebrat had last heard that she was living in the township of Debre Marqos, in the west Gojjam region. Delighted with the news, Aunt Almaz informed me that I could leave immediately, though she had no address, only the district and hearsay that my stepfather was working in a pharmacy somewhere there.

Gojjam lies northwest of Addis Ababa, so I needed to return to the city and set out again from there. Like the mad meanderings in years past, my life was starting to resemble a game of Snakes and Ladders rather than a noble pursuit.

During this entire time, Solomon still had no idea I'd left the mission in Gurage. I asked Adey and Aunt Almaz not to tell him about my visit to Asmara. I knew he would be angry and (just like his sister) accuse me of causing trouble. Now that I had Padre Roberto's support, I didn't need anything from Solomon. There was no point in telling him of my plans.

Did you guess that my aunt called him directly? She expected him to pay for my return airfare. I can't imagine how *that* conversation went, only that their shouting would have made the telephone unnecessary. The end result? Within days, my ticket was booked: flight to Addis, bus from there to West Gojjam.

Before my departure, Aunt Almaz asked that I interrupt my

journey to get another letter from the Gurage mission (because I just love traipsing around the countryside collecting pieces of paper). Determined to move me along, *she* had paid for my ticket and needed to prove my student status to claim a refund. She instructed me to take the letter to Asmerom's wife, Meseret, who worked in quarantine at the Bole Airport (Addis Ababa). Aunt Meseret would forward the letter so that Almaz could reclaim the money.

Another stuffed suitcase and mixed farewells weighed me down as I was driven to the airport.

The familiarity of Asmara and all the (mostly) good memories anchored in me a sense of self. This clean, beautiful city still projected the aromas and pleasurable activities of people living well. The war for independence continued, but since the opposing Dergue were seen as the offenders, Eritreans remained optimistically defiant. At that stage, the war didn't undermine their spirits: it enhanced them.

Their success at overcoming harsh challenges mocked my chaos as each haphazard solution became a slippery slide into the next problem. I wanted to *live,* not just survive.

Compounding that, Adey and I were so comfortable in each other's company. She loved me—I'm sure of it. I wanted to stop the car and run back to her cosy embrace. Instead, with a fierce shove, I was thrust towards the rungs of the next ladder.

I saw Adey for the last time only months before completing this book. What a gracious lady. This time it was I who took her in my arms, though our reunion was bittersweet. Aunt Almaz's fierce gaze oversaw every moment, still looking for hints of my assumed wickedness.

Prior to leaving, I'd told Aunt Almaz that I would stay with Letense (one of my father's relatives) when I landed in Addis Ababa. But on arriving, I changed my mind and decided to stay at my favourite hostel in the city. My need for control inspired me to have some say over what I was doing. Surely, with small steps to independence, I could redefine myself beyond the limited vision of those around me.

As it turned out, this was a good decision, since I narrowly avoided another possible trap from which Solomon could banish me again.

The next day, with a spring in my step, I went to see Padre Roberto. I had missed his light-heartedness and genuine concern.

"Padre, I'm back!" I exclaimed, when I found him sitting in the church garden.

"My child." He waved for me to come closer. "Seems like Asmara was good for you!" he said, as he inspected my face. "No more baboon's bottom, eh?" He laughed. "Still, I guess that seeing you here means you were unable to find your mother, no?"

"No, Padre. But I'm told me she might be living in west Gojjam."

"Oh?"

"Yes. I'll take a bus there and try to find her."

"Good, Tewodros! Don't give up. Now—you'll have to excuse me since Mass is about to start." He rubbed my head and sent me on my way.

I left the church grounds feeling successful somehow, even though nothing had really happened. While I stood on the busy street, waiting to catch a minibus back to the hostel, I noticed a familiar-looking lady standing nearby. Could Aunt Almaz have slyly followed me to be sure I was out of her life? Wah! This woman was impeccably dressed, though her posture showed that she was very upset. As I looked away, trying to appear nonchalant, she swung towards me. Wide-eyed, I stared back, ready to defend myself against a red-clawed finger of accusation.

Then I realised that it was Aunt Ruta, one of my father's other sisters. She seemed to be waiting for a taxi. I'd never gotten along very well with her either, because she had a particularly close relationship with Solomon and always defended him during family discussions.

"Tewodros!" She recognised me. "What are you doing here?"

"Oh . . . well, I'm . . . staying here at the church and . . . now I'm just going out to meet some friends," I lied, not wanting to give her any details.

"You were meant to come to Letense's house last night."

"What do you mean?" The grapevine works fast.

"We were all expecting you there. Even your father. He's very angry with you." She pointed her finger at me. (Ah, there it was.)

"Oh, what a shame, Aunt. I had other important matters to attend to, you know." I tried to sound sophisticated and grown up, my stomach fluxing between nerves and suppressed anger. "You didn't need to go to any trouble for me."

"Go and visit your father, like a good son," she preached.

That did it. I seethed. A good son would have a good father who acknowledges him. So, Solomon was angry was he? Well, so was I. I was my own man now. I didn't need to be bullied by family expectations anymore.

"I can't. I'm so busy now. Why don't you say 'hello' to him for me?"

She gaped, silently opening and closing her mouth like a hyena with a bone stuck in its jaws. Just then, a minibus pulled up at the kerb. (There *is* a god!) With a tickle of victory, I jumped on board and waved goodbye from the window.

As the vehicle drove off, I thought how uncanny life could be. Through my chance meeting with Aunt Ruta, I felt that God was teaching me to trust my instincts, to follow the truth of my heart. This was great advice—if only I could tell the difference between instinct and curiosity. I didn't need life to keep smacking me in the face, and I'd certainly had enough of turning the other cheek.

Continuing my roundabout of errands, I returned to Bole Airport the following day. I didn't have the letter for Aunt Almaz's refund yet, because first I wanted to find Aunt Meseret and check that the arrangement suited her, before making the long trip back to Gurage. I had no memory of her, but she'd visited my mother in Asmara when I was a baby. That had to be a good sign, right?

"Aunt Meseret?" I approached the beautiful middle-aged woman.

"Yes?" she looked up. Her jet-black hair was pulled neatly back into a bun at the base of her head, perfectly framing her heart-shaped face.

"I'm Tewodros, Solomon's s-son," I said.

"Tewodros? It can't be! How big you've grown." She stepped out from behind the counter and kissed me on each cheek. "I remember this hair," she said, stroking me gently on the head. "I had never seen hair so soft on a baby!" She smiled at me. "I used to visit you and your mother in Eritrea, not long after you were born. But you probably don't remember that, do you?"

I shook my head.

Aunt Meseret was very interested to know what my life had been like. She and her husband, Asmerom, had little time for Solomon. She'd seen Bishkash struggle and said she often wondered what had become of me. Aunt Meseret listened intently and it wasn't long before her co-workers moved closer to hear what was going on. Soon, there was a mesmerised little group around the desk, interjecting with "oh" and "ah" (and the occasional curse) as Aunt Meseret filled in the blanks of our conversation.

"But don't worry, Tewodros. I will take you home and ask Asmerom's permission for you to stay with us," she said confidently.

Such kindness defied tradition. Asmerom was also a well-known and respected doctor. And they lived in Bole, a very elite area. Would they risk their reputation for me, the shame of the family? For all my manly projection, I had no real idea how to make my way in the world. Aunt Meseret's offer was the helping hand I needed. I couldn't turn it down.

Straightaway, she left work and drove me to her house in Bole, not far from the airport. Theirs was a large European-style home, surrounded by a high fence and patrolled by a personal security guard. It was every bit as grand as my father's house. Aunt Meseret needed to return to work so she introduced me to the maid, who was told to give me some food. Then, she was gone.

A few hours later Asmerom's car pulled into the driveway and the maid urged me to go outside and greet him. As I stood there, my knees almost gave way. A dark-skinned, balding man stepped out of the vehicle. My eyes tricked me into thinking it was my father. But this *had* to be Asmerom.

I introduced myself and explained how I had ended up on his doorstep. He invited me into the dining room to talk things over. He was kind and reassuring, and spoke to me as to an adult. (Deciding to "be a man" was working out pretty well.) Not long into our discussion, Aunt Meseret returned from work and explained to her husband that she'd be pleased for me to stay with them. He didn't hesitate in agreeing, and I was given their son's room to sleep in. He and I were about the same age and because of this arrangement, he was happy to sleep on the sofa. This family rearranged their lives—for *me*. It was too generous to comprehend.

Enthusiastic to help me feel settled, Aunt Meseret arranged for one of the neighbour's guards to escort me to the local school the very next day, but I was unable to enrol for the year, since classes had begun two months before. That night, Aunt Meseret suggested that I enrol in night school. I started Grade Seven not long after, and enjoyed the evening classes.

Considering these opportunities with my aunt and uncle, I decided to suspend my plans to find Bishkash. Besides, I needed to gather more information on her whereabouts before venturing off to find her.

Life was good with Asmerom and Meseret. They treated me well and provided for my basic needs. I tried to express my gratitude in all I did. I was polite and studious, working hard over my books and trying not to disrupt their lives any more than I had. Every day was a gift that left me amazed. I felt like I'd taken a leap of faith and landed on a soft welcoming safety net. It was all so unexpected. If this was what it felt like to be growing up, then I wanted to run headlong into the adult world.

Aunt Meseret encouraged me to set goals and embrace any opportunity to extend myself. "Tewodros, I've been thinking, and of course I'll need to discuss it with your uncle first, but maybe in the future you can go and study in England, just like my son did."

Was I dreaming this?

"Or maybe you could go to Scotland where my daughter is studying. How does that sound?" She beamed. I still wasn't sure where England was and I'd never heard of Scotland before moving into this house, but from her son's descriptions they seemed like very nice places. Oh, to sleep without fear and to wake with excitement. Aunt Meseret's optimism for my future was intoxicating.

But the iron fist of life was preparing another blow for me, cleverly disguised in a velvet glove. *When a fool is cursed, he thinks he is being praised.*[5] I was too much of a fool to realise that I was still a child, unable to withstand the onslaught when the grown-up world goes sour.

Aunt Meseret and Uncle Asmerom had already done so much for me that I wouldn't dream of asking for pocket money to buy non-essentials. I needed some stationery to send letters to my friends in Gurage. So I decided that the only thing I could do was to sell some of the Italian-made clothes Padre Roberto had given me.

At night school, I persuaded one of my classmates to buy a shirt. I was practically giving it away, so he got a bargain. My lack of funds seemed easily solved. But this simple trade would ultimately contribute to my downfall in my aunt and uncle's house.

The maid had disliked me from the outset. When I was around

5. Ethiopian proverb.

during the daytime, she seemed upset that she was no longer able to roam the house freely and do as she pleased, like she could when the rest of the family were out. For whatever reason, she tried to cause problems between my aunt and me. She often complained to Meseret that I was staying in my room all day and didn't talk to her. I kept the door closed, but she told my aunt that she'd noticed me with new stationery, sending letters *and* dismantling her son's toys.

On one particular weekend, Asmerom was away at his clinic in Nazret. He was dining at a restaurant and noticed that 50 *birr*[6] was missing from his wallet. At first, he assumed he must have left it at home, in the pocket of one of his other shirts. On returning, he mentioned it to his wife.

Aunt Meseret spoke to the maid and the gardener, who were both responsible for doing the laundry. She asked if they had washed the shirt in question. The washing was already done and no money was found, but *apparently* I'd been seen sneaking suspiciously away from the laundry. They didn't think much of it at the time, they said, but it would certainly explain why I looked so guarded.

In an instant, Aunt Meseret was pounding on my door and entering before I could respond. I could tell by her posture that something was wrong—really wrong.

"What are you doing?" she demanded.

"Studying."

She glanced down at the desk and noticed her son's old radio, dismantled. Damn my curiosity.

Since the Gurage mission, where I helped Father Dalloi connect electricity to various parts of the village, I was fascinated to know how such things worked. Of course, the best way to learn was to pull them apart (carefully—I was very methodical). I always reassembled them.

Despite my care, the jumble of wires and parts on the desk was hard evidence against me. The things in this room were her son's,

6. US$10 (approximately).

not mine. I never thought I was doing wrong because I always put them back together.

Gullible boy who thought to be a man.

"You rotten child!" she screamed. "How dare you do this to me, after all I've done for you." She paced the floor behind me. "You can't be trusted, you *leba*."[7]

"What?" How could a bunch of wires make me a thief?

"Yes. *LEBA!*" she shouted as if I hadn't heard the word well enough the first time. "That is what you are, aren't you?"

It was my turn to be open-mouthed in shock.

"Aren't you? You took the money from Asmerom's shirt pocket!"

"Money?"

"Don't mock me. Answer, yes or no. Did you take the MONEY?" She thrust her face at mine.

I sank down in silence, hoping she would go away.

Her fingers fluttered over her neatly pinned hair. "How could you do such a thing?"

"Aunt Meseret, there must be a mistake. I didn't—"

"Why did you do it?" she snapped. "Why did you take money from Uncle's pocket?"

"I never did." Tears of frustration and regret were damming up. Why had I bothered sacrificing my clothes to get some funds? That effort to show my hosts consideration was my undoing.

She noticed the envelopes and writing paper. "Where did you get those? How could you afford them?"

I couldn't tell her the truth. Selling clothes to pay for the stationery would be considered mischievous, something that a naughty boy would do. Yet if I'd asked for the money initially, they would have called me unappreciative to want such meaningless things. Either way, I would be judged as a bad character. A slap on both cheeks, it seemed.

"I bet you used to trick Almaz and your grandmother like this!"

7. Thief. (Amharic)

"What?"

"Almaz has been calling me."

Here we go.

"She warned me, you know. And, all the while, I've been defending you. But now you've proven she was right all along!"

Was this family conspiring against me? I panted in despair. "Please. Trust me. I—didn't—steal—any—money!"

"Almaz told me you used to steal money from your poor old grandmother just so you could play soccer. How could you do that to us?"

How could I—? Wait a second: how could *she* turn on *me* all of a sudden?

Aunt Meseret left abruptly, locking the door behind her—from the outside!

This made no sense. Life made no sense if it could lift a boy up and slap him down, over and over again. Had I "done unto others" something truly wicked, so that it was a free-for-all to "do unto me"? Oh, to be another boy in another time and place—and another family. I wouldn't have cared if they were poor as long as they loved me. I would have done anything for that.

For the next twenty-four hours, I went without food or water, locked inside the room. Aunt Meseret wouldn't open the door until the following evening when she returned home from work. Even then, she was still in a foul mood.

The door flew open.

"Take your bag of belongings outside *now*," she ordered.

I complied.

"Now open it and show me what's inside!"

As I crouched down to open the bag, she struck me across the back with her belt. I winced as much out of shame as pain. Aunt Meseret called to her son. He came outside and she said, "Look at what your cousin Tewodros has done! Look in your room and see what he has done to your things!" He stared as his mother

165

continued to beat me.

My bag contained photos, letters from friends, and things from Padre Roberto. They were my entire worldly possessions. I showed her everything, still trying to prove my innocence.

"Give them to me," she hissed, lunging forward, snatching the photos and letters. Triumphantly, she tore them up, throwing the tiny pieces at me. Her fury was indefatigable.

"Help me tear up his things." Aunt Meseret ordered the maid, who had coincidentally turned up. "Destroy everything!"

Paper is nothing, but the words and faces of friends adorn the heart with happiness. Now all were in tatters.

The betrayal stripped me. The humiliation gutted me. I fell into a heap and mourned the treasures I could never replace.

My belongings were no longer fit for use, but Aunt Meseret confiscated everything anyway, and I was locked in the room once more.

Hate is such a slight word compared to what I felt then.

A while later, Aunt Meseret opened the door and told me we were going to talk to the owner of the shop where I'd bought the stationery. She wanted to verify my story. We were accompanied by her sister and their security guard. On the way there, she tried to scare "the truth" out of me.

"You know, Tewodros, if you don't speak the truth you will be sent to jail where they will beat you," she threatened, "and electrocute you. I know the prison manager. I'll make sure that you are adequately punished."

Petrified as I was, I refused to tell her what she wanted to hear. I wasn't going to lie to her and when she realised that her threats weren't working, she tried another tactic. "You are such a smart boy. I wanted to send you to England, remember? But I can't send a dishonest boy. Just tell me and I'll reconsider. Isn't that what you want? Tewodros? Tell *me THE TRUTH!*"

I ignored her for the rest of the walk to the shop, which of course was closed when we arrived. Not to be deterred, Aunt Meseret, her sister and the guard all began banging loudly on the door until the owner eventually emerged. He opened the counter window and Aunt Meseret questioned him. "Do you remember this boy?" she asked, grabbing me by the scruff of the neck and pushing me in his direction. "Did he buy anything from you?"

I could feel her nails digging into the back of my neck.

He looked at me blankly. I told him when I'd last bought something from his shop. Aunt Meseret covered my mouth and ordered me to be silent. Like most of the shopkeepers around, this fellow was from Gurage, and I think she might have been worried I would start communicating with him in Guraginya.

Choosing his words carefully, he said, "*Maybe* he bought something from me, but I really can't remember."

"Think harder! Did he hand you any money recently? To buy stationery?"

"Like I said, I really can't remember." The old man scratched his head. "I have so many children buying from me every day."

Frustrated, Aunt Meseret led our cavalcade home where I was imprisoned once more. Later that night, she brought me some dinner. She'd managed to calm down. After I finished eating, she asked me to go outside and talk with her.

We stood on the front veranda. As we looked up at the brilliant night sky, Aunt Meseret pointed out a star which had some sacred meaning for her. Reverently, she swore to it that she would not tell Asmerom, nor would she punish me if I told her the truth. My reputation would be safe and she'd know some peace from all this.

As politely as I could, I explained that I was Christian. I could go to the priest and tell him any truth and he would forgive me—God would forgive me. It didn't mean anything to me to swear by a star, but I wasn't hiding anything either.

Again she asked me about the theft, so I swore to the stars *and* to God that I didn't take her money.

Silence.

We were both exhausted by the events of the past few days. I couldn't think beyond that moment, but it was no surprise when she informed me that I was no longer welcome in her house.

As swiftly as it had begun, my taste of the good life was over. I would have to leave early in the morning.

It was time for me to move on and find my mother.

I thanked Aunt Meseret for the positive things she'd done for me and for giving me the opportunity to live with them. I was polite, despite everything.

Returning to the room, I prepared for my departure the next day. Needing a good night's sleep more than ever, I tossed and turned and stared bleary-eyed out the window. I went over and over the events, but I couldn't resolve them. A blur of screaming faces whirled in my mind. In my mental exhaustion, they transformed into soccer balls, yelling at me that I would never score, that I couldn't reach for my dreams, that no one would ever love me. They bounced just out of reach, no matter how I kicked and chased. And they screamed and screamed at my pitiful efforts.

Morning came.

Wearily, I gathered the remnants of my belongings and waited by the locked door. Aunt Meseret released me into the hallway. With a curt "goodbye," she thrust a small amount of money at me and turned away. Outside, I took one last glimpse of that big beautiful house. I would never have come if I knew I'd be leaving on such a bad note.

The security guard took me to the bus station and located the bus bound for Debre Marqos, west Gojjam.

As the bus driver's assistant placed my bag on the rack, he introduced me to one of the other passengers. This was an old man who was headed for the same place and was familiar with the township. He agreed to help me find my mother and her husband's pharmacy, at our destination.

The landscape became a blur. The old man chattered on, recounting stories of his younger wilder years.

Eight hours later, we arrived. As the bus drove through the streets, I focused on every building, looking for pharmacies, looking at anyone who might resemble Bishkash.

It was already late in the afternoon, so we decided to stay in a hostel for the night and begin searching the following day. I had no address, no contact details and basically no idea where to begin, so I was grateful for the old man's assistance.

That night, I couldn't sleep. The hostel was situated next to a bar where the old man went to drink. The rickety old shack rattled with music well into the early hours of the morning, and I was constantly disturbed by bursts of laughter and commotion. It sounded so alive: people who had jobs, friends to meet, money to spend. Maybe not all of them were content, but they were connected in ways that gave them meaning.

I was a strange kid in a strange place on a strange quest. It was all so intangible.

The music thumped on as thoughts (and hopes) of Bishkash filled my head. Would she recognise me? Would *I* recognise *her*? Would she wipe away the pain of these years since that truck ride, and make me feel whole? Dreams of magical endings are all well and good, but then—you have to wake up.

We rose early, although the old man was a little worse for wear after his night out. Walking the few blocks to the shopping area, we went into every pharmacy in search of my mother or at least someone who might know her.

No luck.

Days quickly turned into a week and we had achieved nothing. Nobody had heard of Bishkash or her husband. The old man had been very supportive, but now it was time for him to leave.

The day before his departure, he introduced me to a half-Italian half-Eritrean guy who often came to play billiards at the hostel after work. He was a wealthy man known for his generosity. He quickly understood my predicament and told the old man not to worry because he'd take care of me—and he did. He paid for my accommodation, my meals and transport. Over the following days, this man kindly joined in my search.

Two intense weeks had passed. Despite having asked, looked, walked, enquired, and inspected the town high and low, I felt like I was under layers of deep shadow. Each hint that I might finally see my mother led me like a pinhole of light. Anticipation tightened in my chest until the next clue blacked out. Bishkash remained elusive, and I was left stumbling in the dark, no longer knowing which way to turn.

I had no cash to buy a return trip to Addis Ababa, so my helper asked his billiard companions to pitch in for the fare. Money pooled onto the worn green velvet table. It wasn't long before there was enough to buy a bus ticket back to the big city.

With no clear vision ahead, I felt reckless. What if I stayed here . . . with them? Maybe I could work in the bar or become my new guardian's helper to pay him back for all his kindness. I wouldn't be a stranger among strangers anymore. I would belong. I'd be connected.

But people are kind because they can be, in single moments. It's not an act of kindness to try to give meaning to another person's life: it's a huge responsibility. And strangers can't do that, no matter how good-hearted they are; that onus is on family.

I would have to keep searching.

I looked into each of their faces, thanking them. I took their money and their wishes for a safe journey and left to continue questing in shadow.

Was this return trip like climbing another ladder, or sliding dismally down a snake's back to old troubles? The year had passed and my (approximate) birthday was approaching. I would be another year older, and therefore more capable in the eyes of society, but I had no earthly possessions, no roof over my head and no idea how to find my mother.

Many happy returns? Well, many returns anyway. Now, blow out the candles and make a wish.

10

THOU SHALT NOT LIE

I pencilled my journeys onto a map. The lines spread up, down and side to side, each one stretching me a little thinner. They made as much sense of my life as a warped spider's web.

Along the way, I'd seen things—some terrible, some beautiful— and an awareness of others' suffering began to temper my thoughts. A new kind of hunger started to press its needs on my conscience. So far, I'd been chasing comfort for me. When I saw others suffering, I felt sad but separate. What could one lost boy do for one other, let alone countless others?

I believe that there are all kinds of courage. Some people are brave just to face another day. Others have the strength to change their lives completely. Sometimes, sadly, it takes a mountain of horrifying facts to rouse such determination.

The majestic Entoto Mountains look down over the sprawling city of Addis Ababa. The rolling foothills meet in gullies where steam rises from the mineral springs and small swift streams burble away into the expanding plains. Since its foundation in 1886, Addis has excited the vision of emperors, invaders, investors and, finally, travellers. For those who wish to prosper, it bubbles with opportunities.

If you go there now, you will see impressive buildings, historical sites and all the milling culture of a developing cosmopolitan city. The experience would be quite different if your visit coincided with the height of communist rule, in the mid-1980s.

Certainly there were exclusive areas where the well-to-do folk carried on with their lives, but there were also secret police periodically cruising the poorer streets looking for likely young men to "volunteer" for the war. The economy was overwhelmed. Jobs were scarce. Desperate people grasped at anything that would buffer them from the harsh truth of a land in crisis. Fear clung subtly amid the dust of the day and crept in with the chill of night.

The city hunched, limping forward instead of thriving.

Eighty-five percent of Ethiopia's population were challenged by poverty. Multitudes of these came to the city, having lost their farms through drought, relocation and war.

I was only one of many more homeless frightened people.

Two famines struck simultaneously and fiercely through 1984 and 1985. In the north, conflict between the Dergue government and the Tigrayan People's Liberation Front disrupted farming. Rain failure destroyed what was left of scant crops. In the south, more insurgence from the Oromo Liberation Front[1] caused similar loss. Compared to the famine of 1973, these two compounded into catastrophe. Over one million people died, while 5.8 million more were in need of relief.

Ethiopia, with her regal forefathers cast out, was caught in a tug-of-war between foreign-inspired fanatics and passionate rebels; all seemed to belittle the basic needs of the people. The country was like a motherless child looking for nurturing and identity, but being tossed and torn from one temporary caregiver to another.

None of this was evident on the surface, especially in the city.

---

1. The OLF was another rebel group that fought against the Dergue regime.

173

There was enough propaganda to keep people either confused or quiet.

Despite communism, the government didn't dominate everything. Religion was the food of the soul. Strong in religious traditions, our culture recognised official days for Christian and Muslim festivals. Such days were spiritual banquets for a population in search of comfort.

Minds were strained by fear or held together by faith. There was no middle ground. Overriding all this was the pursuit of money. People went to drastic lengths to buy their way out or at least to buy enough to live for one more day—because, particularly in a poor country, money is everything.

Like a failed knight errant I returned from my quest, heavy of heart and empty in pocket, back to the city of extremes. The bus brought me where it always had on every other trip: the terminal at Merkato. This was the centre point of my web of travels.

Merkato market is one of the largest in the world. Some might describe it as a place of wonders, where you can buy just about anything. But every step is assaulted by milling crowds, honking cars, harassing hawkers, pervasive pickpockets, predatory prostitutes, and abject beggars.

There was no sense of wonder here for me. I always came back to the stench of garbage, piss and people at their worst.

I stood there, chewing on an olive twig,[2] wondering which way to turn. I had struck out on my journey, believing that I could be my own man. The bitter truth—that I was nothing but a frightened boy (still)—made me gag more than the filth around me.

I coughed and spat out the twig. *Anywhere but here*, I thought and set off in the direction of a nearby hostel owned by a Gurage man. I'd stayed at his place occasionally, in transit from the mission, when I didn't want to see my father. The owner liked me because

---

2. Commonly used to clean teeth.

I could speak his mother tongue and I liked the hostel because it was cheap, convenient and painted a cheerful green. It conjured memories of the countryside.

As I rounded the corner, a tall lady bulging out of her blouse and short black skirt called to me. "Hey, sweetie, where you going?" (I must have looked like a man to some.) Her sickly smile revealed two silver teeth and some half-empty gums.

I ignored her and kept walking.

"Hey! I'm talking to you!" she bellowed. "You think you're too good to talk to me? *Ye shermouta leg!*"[3]

I started to run. I'd heard about these Merkato women and the horrible diseases they carried. Oh yes, someone had told me that they only had to look at you and you'd start to itch in places you shouldn't.

Ah, there was the hostel. I arrived, breathless, to find the owner sitting with his back to me, jigging away to some Gurage music that was blaring from the ghetto blaster on the counter. I had to throw a pen at him to get his attention. He spun around in surprise, but sighed when he caught sight of me. I'd been a regular customer, though my payments weren't reliable. Delivering my best smile, I hoped I could stay without charge. "Please, sir, I only need to stay a few days," I begged.

He shrugged me away. "You go stay at the mission in Gurage, eh?" He pointed flippantly, as if Gurage was just around the corner.

"*Ara!*[4] I left there to find my mother," I pleaded. "So, I need to stay in Addis until I get more information."

"Very well." He relented. "But you can't stay in the guest rooms because I can get money for those. You will have to stay in the workers' quarters," he thumbed behind him. "And you can only stay for a few days. I don't want you annoying them. They have to work, you understand?"

---

3. Son of a bitch! (Amharic)
4. Why! (Amharic)

I agreed and followed him to a back room. Two workers already rented the space, so there were no available beds. Gurage Man gestured at the floor. "There's your bed," he said.

When I looked at him in surprise, he scoffed, "You want it for free, no? You got nothing: you get nothing." He threw his hands in the air and left.

Over time, I would find out how prophetic his words were.

Market mayhem jostled me from sleep early the next day. A man was selling bananas just outside my window. He was shouting to an avocado seller up the road as they discussed the previous day's trade. I hadn't slept well anyway because of the unyielding dirt floor, despite my attempts to make a mattress out of my clothing.

I rose and dressed quickly, trying to smooth down my wrinkled outfit. I planned to visit Padre Roberto, hoping he could tell me what to do next. Stepping outside, I moved determinedly down the street, but the banana man caught my arm.

"Ah, you, boy—you want to buy a bunch of bananas? Take to your mum for breakfast, eh? Here, look. Good. Firm. I'll make a good price for you? Okay? Here—the best bunch—very cheap. What do you say, eh?"

My stomach growled. I hadn't had dinner the night before. I hadn't eaten since I left Debre Marqos. I clutched at the few remaining coins in my pocket, wondering how long they would last.

"Can I buy just one?" I asked.

"Aw—one isn't enough for a growing boy like you. C'mon—a whole bunch—good price."

I started to walk away.

"Okay, okay—one. We pick a nice big one. Here." He shoved a plump banana into my hand and waited for the money. Reluctant, yet grateful at the same time, I handed him one of my coins.

"Good boy. Good." He slapped me on the back, almost knocking the fruit from my hand. "You'll like it. You'll be back for more. See you again, eh?"

I thanked him and walked on, hearing the cries of the market bringing the streets to life. I was amazed (I still am) at how these people rise so early and come, often from far beyond the city limits, to shout all day trying to catch customers and sell their goods. Clutching the precious food in one hand and my last precious coins in the other, I walked on, anticipating Padre Roberto's warm smile.

Of course he was disappointed about my unsuccessful trip to Debre Marqos. Concerned about my financial situation, he asked me to come again in a few days to collect a package of money and clothes. It felt good to have someone to rely on.

I couldn't know how hard it was for him or how limited his resources were. Nor did I realise that the taint of my situation shadowed my every move. If the good doctor had done all he could for me and I had ended up on the streets, then I must deserve it: I must be bad. What could they do to change that? Could they even trust me? How many lies had I told to get in and out of trouble till now? Maybe I was just a lazy, trouble-making boy on the take. Either way, I'd be back asking for help. There was little Padre Roberto could do.

After a few days at the hostel, I was asked to move on. I became a suburban nomad for the second time in my life. This time, however, I was 15 and all alone. Instead of shifting from one relative's house to another, I was now shifting between the streets and houses of complete strangers.

It was even harder, knowing that my family were so close by. Aunt Meseret was living in her beautiful house, working at the airport where business people were coming and going from Europe and America. Doctor Solomon was driving through his private gates to work or home (but I did wonder who was doing his midnight beer runs now). I knew of the cafés in Piassa, the festivals, the cinema. Here was life, full of possibilities and comforts for those who knew no lack.

Poverty means failure. The poor are rejected in every way: beaten, cast out. Animals are tolerated more than the poor, though not by much. There is no love for them. Animals are only there to ease the workload of humans or to provide food. Otherwise they are a burden. People throw rocks at unwanted animals, cursing them and driving them off. That's the way of things: repel the unsightly, the unnecessary. Humanity doesn't come into it.

Guards are hired to stand at the front gate of a residence. They repel anyone seeking aid, including relatives. These men take pride in their position. They watch from the gatehouse, a tiny shed of coffin-like proportions, which is often also their residence. They do their job well, discouraging the day's good-for-nothing aspirants, knowing that, but for God's will, they would be begging in the street instead.

The fine line between having something and nothing delivers a chasm of difference in life quality. There is no denying that when you have nothing—you have *nothing!*

My mind wouldn't accept this. Remembering my knack for negotiation skills in earlier years, I knew I had to categorise the people of the street like those soccer gangs. Who banded together? With whom could I align? What could I trade to get help? Whom did I have to sidestep? This became an integral part of my survival strategy.

Then there was cold weather, thieves and stray dogs to contend with . . . and those slow-moving cars with sinister men, looking for boys like me whom no one would miss.

Death by combat or death by starvation—I was trying to leap beyond both. This was a new kind of dance and I had to step lively. *Move your neck according to the music.*[5]

I slept under buildings and awnings, in alleyways or anywhere I could lay down my blanket and avoid being disturbed. But no matter how carefully I chose a place, I was regularly spotlighted by the torches of security guards and shooed away. On one occasion, I was woken by a guard throwing rocks at me; animal that I was.

5. Ethiopian proverb.

Although I somehow managed to evade government detection, I was constantly aware of that threat and was suspicious of strangers approaching me in the street. I also steered away from other home-less people. I kept to myself and avoided areas where they seemed to gather, making a perfect target group for the authorities. By some miracle, I always left minutes before or arrived shortly after a round-up had occurred. When I think about it now, it's incredible that I avoided capture.

Stay afraid. Keep moving.

Above all of these fears, my biggest concern was having no food. I could survive without a bed, but I wouldn't make it without nour-ishment. At the same time, I couldn't bring myself to eat scraps from bins or discarded food from restaurants, no matter how hun-gry I was. Sometimes I would sleep just to avoid searching for a meal. Instead of begging, I learned of the cheapest places to eat and rationed the small coin collection given to me by Padre Rob-erto and other priests. Some days, I would eat with the priests at church. Most days, I was left to resolve things as best I could. Too many times life served me nothing—in abundance.

And yet, a strange thing happens when you have enough food— your focus is no longer driven by the need to survive—the ache in your belly is assuaged, but the hurt of all you have endured begins to surface. I don't know which is more painful: a starving body or a starving spirit.

There was no possibility for me to understand that the world was beautiful or to consider how I wanted to live in its beauty. I just wanted to live for one more night.

Homelessness devours the colour from your soul.

My world faded to shades of grey. The sun lost its warmth. *Is it day?* The stars didn't twinkle. *There's a sky?* All merged into a murky blur of running . . . running past other lives . . . running blind to keep from seeing what they had that I did not . . . running from the accusations of others and my own screams within. Just run and keep running, because to stop was to die.

With retrospective humility, I believe that you experience certain circumstances in life to prepare you for your future. When you are in the midst of life's challenges, it can feel like you are trying to hold back a tsunami with an umbrella. Having grown beyond that, I now have so much to give.

In those days of despair, I was yet to discover this truth.

My rush to survive ground to a halt, not from starvation, but from shock at what my life had become, as the madness of it stretched from days into weeks.

My heartbeat dropped from a steady pounding of disgust to a flickering pulse of despair. I would fade to nothing unless I could discipline my thoughts and regain my dignity.

Defiance came to the fore. I was in the street, but not of it. I couldn't bring myself to "dress down" (a huge advantage in the business of begging). I realised that I wasn't very good at being homeless: I worried too much about personal hygiene and I constantly resented my dire circumstances.

The Ethiopian man does not cry, so I would not cry. He is proud, so I chose to be proud. There must be strength and success in all he does. I would strive to succeed each day.

I woke up and focused my whole energy into that very day—finding food, staying safe, keeping warm, staying clean and well-dressed, and finding somewhere to sleep that night. This kept me going. It gave me spirit. The doom of tomorrow didn't exist. If I had to think about that as well, it would have been too much. The only thing I could endure was the present moment. To survive one more day was my triumph.

During this time, I came to experience the generosity and hospitality of the poorest of the poor.

I had observed others on the street begging for food and money, and while I'd asked the occasional passer-by for assistance, I never asked for shelter. I decided that I must. I really had nothing to lose. It was difficult, at first, to walk up to a complete stranger and ask if I could stay at his place. But it became easier, almost like second-nature, and I grew bolder in my approach. I didn't hesitate to ask *anyone*, and I was surprised to learn that it was often those with the least who were the most generous. Barely able to shelter and feed their own families, these humble people welcomed me into their small shacks for a night or two.

Material wealth has no real meaning. When you have nothing, you appreciate everything. Even the small moments make you feel rich. It's not things that give you meaning: it is the meaning you give to things that defines your life. That is real value. These kindhearted people taught me that.

There were times when nobody would take me in. Occasionally, I resorted to selling my Italian-made clothes for a few coins, enough to pay for space on the floor of a house-turned-hostel.

It happened one particular day that I'd sold all my clothes except those I was wearing, but that money was gone. I searched throughout the entire day and most of the evening for somewhere to sleep. I knew this night would be deathly cold. (Addis Ababa is set in mountain country, remember.) I became so desperate that I begged the local police to let me into one of their cells. They agreed, and it was the best sleep I had during the entire time I was homeless. For one night, there were no worries about the weather, security guards, the government, the thieves, or the dogs.

I grew even more resourceful. I went to the dormitories at the Black Lion University where my father was a lecturer. I told the students there that I was Doctor Solomon's son and that I'd just come from a mission and needed somewhere to stay for the night, until I met up with him. They were impressed and offered me a bed.

They knew Solomon as a good teacher: knowledgeable and patient. Occasionally, he played soccer with them. They described his sense of humour. I couldn't imagine any of that from the devil I knew.

The following morning, one of his students offered to take me to his rooms. I didn't want to face him but, out of curiosity, I wanted to see where he worked. The student introduced me to the guards who allowed me to enter the building.

A secretary gave me directions and soon I arrived at the door of my father's office. I peeked carefully around the corner, through the open door. He was sitting at a large wooden desk, scribbling on a notepad, completely unaware of me. I watched him for a few moments, then tiptoed past his door and glanced inside the next room. There, life-like dummies were arranged on tables, presumably where he taught anatomy.

I made my way out of the building, my footsteps in the hall echoing the hollow feeling in my heart. Here was my father mentoring young people. He probably would have cared for me more as one of his students than he did as his scorned offspring. It was strange to realise that.

His wish had come true: I *was* no one's son now.

Did I look for my mother during all this? Well, that was the original plan, but I didn't know how to go about it, nor did I have any resources to pursue it. The government had relocated so many people because of the famine. Perhaps that included her and her new family, or maybe she'd already fled the civil war.

The government's plan was to remove people from hazardous fighting or famine areas and gather them around water, schools, medical support and basics. However, these things weren't always in place for the incoming residents, which created more deprivation and problem areas. Compounding this, the moves occurred during planting and harvest times, further reducing food production.

There's been much speculation (not validated) over what was really going on. An underlying motivation for moving people away from the war zones could have been to stop the resistance forces from recruiting disillusioned civilians.

City life was separate from all the action and we were only ever told that we must unite against the common "enemy of the state." The civil war was heavily backed by the United States and the Soviet Union on varying fronts, keeping the government's focus elsewhere. This continued to cripple the local economy and hamper recovery.

By this time, Ethiopia had accepted her international public shame and welcomed the support of other nations. Funds and supplies poured in from official channels as well as the rock concerts, Band Aid and Live Aid. Sadly much of this never reached the victims; some was redistributed to armed forces; some never made it through the battle zones.

So where was my mother? Could she be dead? Was she starving or in a refugee camp somewhere? There was only so much I could contemplate. I had to focus on getting through my own challenges.

And they kept coming.

Sometimes I didn't want to suffer any more, so instead of praying to God for one more good day, I asked to die in my sleep: *just take me—I can't go on like this.* But when I woke up to a new day, my first thought was: I am *alive!*

Compared to some, I was lucky. Many of the impoverished around me suffered from various handicaps: leprosy, encroaching blindness, elephantiasis, or some crippling deformity—the stuff of nightmares. Others used poverty as a tool, dressing and acting poor and helpless, playing on the sympathies of strangers.

Early in the morning, people would arrive from the villages and city outskirts, carrying crippled children, not always their own. The children were left on the street to beg while the adults went their way, not collecting them again until nightfall. Some watched all day from a secluded spot while the child lied, begged and pretended to cry through the day in order to avoid a beating later. (I'm not sure those tears were faked.) People even borrowed babies, using them as props for syphoning off the kindness of others.

At the mission, we were taught, *Thou shalt not lie.* These children were forced to lie all day, inventing different versions of the same story: *my parents are dead . . . my mother is sick . . . I have to beg to feed my baby sister. . . .* All focus was on money. All motivation was from fear. They didn't know that they were alive, only that they were afraid of dying.

Some of the poor chose to join the army for food, clothes and some kind of stability. They had come so close to death already that dying in a war didn't matter in the long term, as long as there was food that night.

Given our strict religions and morals, I was also shocked to see that prostitution was thriving on the streets. These were uneducated men and women. They had no idea about sexual hygiene. AIDS and other diseases were rife. Awareness has only been raised in recent years.

Prostitution is an age-old profession, but sex slaves and beggars are not part of the intrinsic Ethiopian consciousness. We are descendants of warrior tribes, defiant and free. I've tried to understand how this strong culture could be frayed by something so alien to its honour.

Foreign cultures corrupt. Bountiful, virgin Africa was split among colonial empires until all she could do was keep selling herself. The Horn of Africa was strategically beneficial to the superpowers. The coastline offered convenient bases from which to observe Arabia and Egypt, or to set up trade routes to India, with easy access to the Suez Canal. Lying just behind coastal Eritrea, Ethiopia became the next vantage point for those who missed colonising the coastline of their choice.

The Italians brought Catholicism, pasta, cafés, and their European ways, which left an indelible mark on Eritrea. The communists brought guns and idealism. The Americans brought robust appetites for everyone else's pie. That's a lot of foreigners drinking, smoking and looking for a good time.

There is a tale of a classic Ethiopian philosopher, Skendes the Silent. As a 13-year-old boy, he was sent to study in the ancient cities of Athens and Berytus (now Beirut). Learning at the knees of great philosophers, he became a man and was ready to return home. In his travels, he'd heard men comment that all women were prostitutes, which deeply angered him. Having a refined mind, he decided to test the theory by attempting to seduce his own mother while in disguise, vowing silence if he succeeded.

You can guess the outcome by his title.

This is but a snippet of the tale and it should be said that he was most often called Skendes the Wise. His observations on life are expressed in the biography *The Life and Maxims of Skendes*, which notes his view that human life is afflicted by "miseries, death, folly, stupidity, anger, wrath, labor, fetidity, war, killing, slaying, abstention, and fear."

Having witnessed much of that already in my young life, I have to agree.

The modern world continues to woo Ethiopia for her coffee and cheap labour. For all its beauty, this land that could have been Eden is still finding her way.

Within my haphazard existence, I was trying to create some predictability by developing a routine. Saturday mornings were the highlight of my week. A small fee got me a shower at the public bathhouse, and use of a clean towel; though I wondered how many people it had swiped across before me, so I only dried my feet with it. Since this was also washing day, I used my clothes to dry my body. All the burdens of the week would be washed away and I'd feel decent, for a short time.

The lady at the local laundrette washed everything by hand. This luxury was short-lived once my clothes went missing. I can still remember rummaging through piles and piles of garments while the laundry owner looked on.

"They must be here!" I pleaded. "Why don't you remember me?"

"I don't recall you or your clothes," said the owner, shrugging her big round shoulders.

"I had a denim jacket . . . a pair of jeans . . . a t-shirt." I was grabbing at anything that resembled my clothing.

"Look, I already told you, okay? I don't have your things!" She dismissed me and walked out the back to attend to her screaming baby.

"But I brought them here yesterday!" I yelled after her.

I left the shop, straining to keep the last of my self-esteem. Since Aunt Meseret had destroyed my belongings, I only had whatever Padre Roberto could give me—well, what I hadn't sold. I knew that I could get more from him, much to my shame, but losing material items didn't upset me as much as losing my ability to trust others.

What *could* I put my faith in? As I bargained with God for one more day—and day after day unfolded with just enough to keep going—I thought: God *must* exist.

Throughout my trials to this point, the only consistency had come from the Church. This was not the same as traditional faith, in which people believed that He could do anything for them as long as they prayed. They would skip work to pray on a particular saint's day, but there's a saint for *every* day. They became complacent and unaccountable, not taking initiative for moving their lives forward.

This kind of belief can make people lazy. They can lose their spirit.

The Church rescued me from this. It became my education, my art, my music, my reading, and my human contact.

The church grounds functioned as the social hub of the local community. People gathered there to meet friends or pass time when they had nothing better to do. Without a permanent home, I spent more time at the church, attending Bible studies and talking with the priests. My favourite activity was singing in the choir, mainly because we could dress up in the freshly laundered blue robes with white sashes, but also because I was treated as an equal. We rehearsed two to three times a week and then sang at the various services over the weekend.

I prayed there. Sometimes, I slept there. The church doors were unlocked at 6 A.M. for the first Mass of the day, and if I hadn't found somewhere to sleep overnight, I would be the first one lining up. Physical warmth took priority over spiritual warmth.

I had many unanswered questions for God and could spend hours drifting in and out of sleep, asking Him for guidance. One of my favourite hymns from that time states: *If God doesn't permit it, it will not happen. Not even one hair will fall out of your head, without His permission.*[6] The idea amazed me—I mean, we Africans have so much hair! I supposed I could trust (for a bit longer) that things would work out.

Church was my retreat. The people were peaceful, non-political—like one big happy family.

Many of the people I knew from that time have since settled in America and Europe. It's as if this environment gave them the strength to believe in themselves and make a new life. I went to Mass to be among these people. I came out feeling so good. The peace of it lifted me . . . until I felt hungry again.

I began to make friends. Of course, I had to lie. I was leading a double life and couldn't risk their rejection if they found out I was just a beggar. Thank goodness people see your clothes and not your stomach, or my emptiness would have frightened them away.

In a crazy twist of circumstance, I *pretended* to be the my father's son.

Every day I made subtle adjustments to my story, keeping it believable, keeping myself acceptable. I let everyone assume that I was living with my father and attending school. It was tricky to steer clear of any topics that would cause me to inadvertently reveal more than I wished.

I tried to remain well-groomed. Padre Roberto's donated clothes helped me with this deception. I was careful not to reveal him as my source and visited him in the evenings, after everyone had returned home. I saw my ruse as inventiveness rather than lying.

6. Based on the Bible's New Testament, Luke12:7.

As well as singing, we played soccer and volleyball. The others often went for coffee and cake in Piassa, which I couldn't afford. I would have to make some excuse for not joining them. It was so important to belong to this group. Their lives were full of laughter and hope. Ah, some soul food at last.

With regard to the war, the young people wondered, "Why fight?" We disagreed with the government; we celebrated on the official days for Tewodros I, Johannes IV and the victory at Adwa.[7] Those days represented unity for our nation. We didn't understand the others fighting each other.

The only thing we really needed to fear was God—and God said no killing. You can't just drop your faith and go out to destroy each other.

We couldn't voice our confusion over the war. Anyone nearby might be a secret cadre[8] always on the lookout for dissent. It was rumoured that people who were suspected of even the mildest form of insurrection were taken in the night and fed to the hyenas. In the morning, all that remained were their gnawed bones and horrified eyeballs.

Through my involvement with the church group, I formed a close friendship with Hailu, who was a deacon there. Hailu was Orthodox Christian and came from a family heavily populated with priests. He had mastered the art of singing in *Ge'ez*[9] and had been lured across to the Catholic Church for special morning sermons. They even gave him a room on the church grounds.

He was only a year or two older than me, but he took his role very seriously and was well-regarded among the parishioners.

Apart from his commitments, Hailu was quite a character and the seriousness with which he approached his work would vanish as soon he his duties were completed.

7. The battle site where Ethiopia secured sovereignty from the Italians (1896).
8. Military personnel.
9. Ge'ez is the liturgical language of the Ethiopian Orthodox Church.

Occasionally, I visited him in his room, where he would share stories about the events that had taken place since we last met. He had such a funny way of describing things. We'd spend hours rolling around on the floor, laughing at the antics of others.

From the wealthier church-going families, I knew the children of rich businessmen, ambassadors, politicians, and doctors. (How about that?) They organised some of the best parties in Addis. There was an unwritten code that you had to be dressed in the latest gear—and the competition was fierce. On extremely rare occasions, I had enough money and fine clothes to attend.

Fashion at the time was stonewash denim overalls, American sneakers and (the most-envied item of clothing) the Michael Jackson red leather jacket. The slick John Travolta haircut from *Saturday Night Fever* was a hot favourite, and endless tubs of wax and grease were applied to get that smooth look on our wiry afro-hair. Breakdancing was cool and Coca Cola was the drink of choice—but only through a straw. MC Hammer, Bobby Brown, Whitney Houston, and Michael Jackson's latest hits blared from the crackly sound system and everyone tried to imitate their icons on the dance floor. We were heavily influenced by all things American.

The only people who knew the real Tewodros were Hailu and the priests. I never heard them lie to the parishioners about my circumstances. They managed to brush off any suspicions about me. But the truth is never permanently hushed.

One evening after choir practice, a few of us were in Hailu's room. He was explaining the procedure for burning incense during special ceremonies. It was placed in a bell-like container, which was carried around the church on a rod and swung backwards and forwards, spreading the sweet, heavy fragrance.

Talk of this bell reminded Dereje (one of the boys) of something he'd heard recently. "Someone is sleeping in the church bell tower!" he blurted out.

My face burned and I wished the earth would swallow me whole; of course he was talking about me. I'd made a secret deal with Padre Roberto to provide one of the church guards with a blanket and, in return, the guard would permit me to enter the church grounds at night and sleep in the old bell tower. This wasn't a regular occurrence, just a backup solution when I had nowhere else to go.

After Dereje's announcement, I learned that one of the boys from soccer training had seen me enter the tower one evening. He'd told almost everyone I knew, to my shame, but it didn't seem to matter as much as I thought it would. They accepted me—maybe because their younger generation weren't as inhibited by stern traditions, or maybe because they already knew me as a friend.

I could relax a little from the pressure of all those lies, but having been betrayed in the past, especially when I felt safe, I remained guarded against their judgement.

In hard times, when people help you, you can't help loving them. There's a tremendous sense of gratitude. They reach out to you. They give of themselves. You feel valued and recognised. You feel worth something.

With no ID, no job and no one to vouch for me, I had to rely on the priests' kindness. I used to keep a pocket book in which I wrote all the details of my benefactors:

Father Tesfaldete	*10 cents*	*Tuesday, 28/02*
Padre Roberto	*a shirt*	*Friday, 15/04*

Each small token was an ambassador of hope. The value to me was immeasurable. Nostalgic over those intense feelings of gratitude, I let these men become giants in my memory.

That understanding enriched my life more than any of the *things* they gave me.

In those dire times, Padre Roberto would get so frustrated, not so much with me as with the situation. There were so many in need. Once, when I asked for money, he waved his arms at the wall. "What do you want me to do, Tewodros? Do you want me to knock down this wall and sell it, brick by brick, to give you money?"

When he had no more to give, he just couldn't speak, so he wouldn't talk to me. Resenting that, not realising how hard it was for him, I would get frustrated. I would go to church and *not* speak to *him*. Then he would come up to me and lightly bump my shoulder. I'd turn away, and he'd bump the other one. Our eyes met—his: full of kindness; mine: seeking acceptance (despite my defiance)—and we melted into smiles.

All right, then, God. I've prayed, I've trusted, I've hoped, I've suffered. I've even begged. There's got to be more I can do to change my life. I mean, if You don't permit even one hair to fall out, how can you permit me to starve? Do you want me to suffer?

Wah! That made no sense to me at all.

People would occasionally trip on the sharp rocks in the street, sometimes injuring themselves quite badly. I realised that every day was a huge risk, but I could die from tripping over a stupid rock. What was the point? I might as well take bigger risks and see what God would permit and how far I could get.

Almost a year had passed since I'd left Aunt Meseret's house and I hadn't managed to find a solution. This couldn't be the only way: just accept and endure.

I wanted to roar my dissent. I would *not* lie down and timidly wait for life to find me or end me. I was ravenous: I wanted knowledge; I wanted answers; I wanted to pluck the stars from the sky to illuminate a new path, not just for me. I decided that one person can change many lives. This became my new faith and I looked for any signs that would show me the way.

A lion, mighty among beasts, retreats at nothing.[10]

---

10. From the wisdom of King Solomon, Proverbs 30:30.

11

DAMNED IF I DO, DAMNED IF I DON'T

There'd been no food for days. No shelter. No money. Nothing but the clothes on my back.

My roar fell to a whimper as I wandered the streets, delirious and dry retching. The last crumbling edges of my dignity were thinned to a shadow and I was falling into a short terminal future; starless and unlamented.

One last shuffle to the church. It takes me hours. A small boy walks beside me, offering his hand for balance. Is he the ghost of my past, visiting his own end? Has he come to put me to rest?

I pause, almost passing out. He points to show how close we are to the doors of salvation. As we reach the steps, my tiny angel runs back down the street. Are the devils chasing him, too? *Stay defiant,* I want to cry out, but there's no breath left.

I stumble inside and listen to the full silence that only a church can hold. There is no song left in life.

Time doesn't matter. I don't matter. Nothing . . . matters . . . anymore.

Father Desta saw me. He was Padre Roberto's superior. Gently, he guided me to a seat in the garden.

I couldn't tell him, or anyone, over and over that I needed help. I could barely speak.

Yet, he spoke passionately. "Tewodros, you're a smart boy. I know you! I know that your life will not be like this forever."

Something in his voice struck me. There he sat, robust and handsome. He was a man of God, devoid of doubt. What must that feel like?

He went on. "I know that God has good things in store for you. Just follow your heart and you will find your way through these difficult times." He leaned back and casually lit a cigarette. He was so self-assured.

I wanted to swap lives with him.

I realised that I'd never seen a starving priest. Ha—that was exactly what I needed.

"W—ell—" I had to clear my parched throat. "Well, *Abba*, it's good that you say so."

"What do you mean?" He blew a ring of smoke high into the air as he ran his fingers through his slicked-back hair. He'd studied at Harvard University. After spending several years overseas, he behaved more like a foreigner than *habesha*.[1]

"You said that I should follow my heart, no?"

He nodded cautiously.

"*Abba*, I want to be like you," I confided.

"Like me?" He seemed a little confused. "I don't think you want to be like me, my son."

"Yes. I do! I want to be a priest!"

"A priest? Are you sure?" He was very solemn.

"Uh-huh! I can sleep at the presbytery at night, get three daily meals. Oh, and pray, of course. All my problems would disappear and my head won't hurt anymore." I knew it was the perfect

---

1. Of Ethiopian/Eritrean descent. (Amharic/Tigrinya)

solution; I just had to convince him.

Father Desta smiled sympathetically. "Well Tewodros, like I said, you can do anything you want if you have faith in yourself. And even though I'm not so sure you understand what it means to become a priest, I'll write a letter of recommendation for you. You can take it to Nazret. Do you know Nazret?"

I nodded. "Oh yes, that's the place you send some of the young boys to study."

"*Ara!* You do pay attention, don't you?" He chuckled and patted my head.

That evening as I walked away with the letter in my hand, a soothed appetite and some coins for my next quest, my mood lifted radically. Now, I'm the first to admit that becoming a priest was not high on my list of life accomplishments, but what else could I do?

The very next day, I took a bus to the village of Nazret, which lay about two hours' drive south of Addis Ababa. At the seminary, I met Father Emanuel and proudly showed him the letter. He read it through, pausing occasionally to look at me, and then asked me to take a seat under the shade of a tree.

We sat silently for a moment before the priest sighed, "Tewodros, *clothes put on while running come off while running.*"[2]

He smiled at me warmly, but I was completely confused.

"A letter doesn't gain you entrance into the seminary," he continued, removing his glasses.

"But the letter is from Father Desta. I told him I wanted to become a priest and he gave me the letter," I interrupted.

"I understand, Tewodros, but Father Desta doesn't want to crush your spirit. He knows you are facing a tremendous struggle at the moment, but to become a priest takes years and years of commitment. You might say it's a struggle of a different kind." His eyes seemed to look straight into my heart, though not unkindly. "Don't

---

2. Ethiopian proverb. It can mean that if you try to do something without really thinking it through, all your efforts will unravel.

mistake that hollowness in your belly for holiness. I'm sorry, Tewodros, but I think you are destined for other things. It's best you return to Addis."

That was that.

On the afternoon bus back to the city, I replayed Father Emanuel's words in my head. His comments reminded me of a priest in Gurage, who thought I was ungodly. He constantly criticised me for failing to be a vessel of God. He'd nag, "Don't slouch, Tewodros. God needs to see the top of your head reaching to heaven." He'd criticise, "Tewodros, why do you eat so quickly? Are you worried the devil will take your food?"

I realised that Father Emanuel was right: how could I become a priest when I wasn't certain of what I believed? As confused as ever, I stepped down off the bus (in more ways than one) into the madness of Merkato.

Father Desta (bless him) pursued a solution, but his good intentions brought a disturbing outcome. Over the following days, he suggested talking to my father. Wah! Just because I couldn't become a priest didn't mean I wanted to dive back into hell!

I objected, fiercely. I remembered lying in the street being kicked and beaten, vowing never to ask for his help again. Ever!

"Young Tewodros!" Father Desta scolded. "You cannot continue as you are. *If you gladly stoop to the ground, don't be surprised when you get trampled.*[3] You must rise up by whatever means are available. Don't say you want help and then reject it."

Priests and their proverbs! Even if they were right, it still didn't give me anything tangible to go on with.

I was aware that I had to do *something* to change my circumstances. I agreed to see Solomon, on the condition that I would not have to live with him. I had to maintain some measure of control over this connection. (*You just keep telling yourself that, Teddy.*)

3. Ethiopian proverb.

Father Desta immediately dispatched my friend, Hailu, to the Black Lion Hospital. There, he met my father and invited him to come and discuss my future with the priests. Hailu later told me he had to visit several times before he even got to meet Solomon, but when he eventually found him in his office, he had quite an interesting time.

"You *know* that naughty boy?!" At the mention of my name, Solomon was instantly infuriated. "Do you know what he did to my children?" His voice querulous, he jumped up from behind his desk.

"What did he do? Tell me." Cheeky Hailu found the doctor's agitation entertaining, and egged him on.

"That scoundrel! He used to beat my children—like this!" he said, as he dramatically raised and dropped his elbow to demonstrate my supposed fighting style.

Hailu tried hard to keep a straight face. "Are you sure he did it like that? I thought he would do it more like this." And he threw punches into the air like a professional boxer.

"No, definitely like this!" my father provided a more exaggerated demonstration, much to Hailu's amusement. Despite Solomon's obvious dislike of me, Hailu managed to coerce him into meeting the priests.

I was standing outside the church when I saw Solomon and Saba arrive. Father Desta greeted them warmly and led them through one of the office doors. It was a long hour's wait until they departed (without speaking to me).

Father Desta called me in. "Your father is very remorseful for the way he treated you in the past."

"I don't believe that," I said angrily.

"Now, Tewodros, at the moment he's the only one who can change your life."

"But, *Abba*, he lies all the time. He lies as well as Satan!" I folded my arms to stop the quaking at having said such a thing to a priest.

"Young fellow! You can't talk about him like that. And, you know, you don't have to live with him."

My eyes widened in anticipation of what I *would* have to do.

Father Desta spoke louder and louder as he tried to convince me that this would work. "Doctor Solomon is a good man. He wants to give you a proper education. Isn't that wonderful? He's already enrolled you in a college where you can study to become an airplane technician!"

"He's tricked you, *Abba*. That's what he does. He's a devil-man!"

"Please. I told you before. No ill words about your great father. Do you know how many lives he's saved?"

"Do you know that he has destroyed mine?" I retaliated.

"Everyone makes mistakes, Tewodros. Forgive him. Move on." I sensed he was losing patience with me. "You have a brighter future, now. When Doctor Solomon collects you, I want you to forgive him, regardless of whatever happened in the past. More importantly: you must ask him to forgive you."

"Forgive ME?" I exploded.

"Yes. Calm down, please. We're all trying to find a solution for you and, as a good son, I think it's proper for you to respect him and ask for his forgiveness."

I stormed out of the office, slamming the door behind me.

A few days later, I was in choir practice when a young boy came with a message that Padre Roberto was looking for me. I followed him outside to the car park, only to halt when I saw my father's small Mazda.

Could I run away before they saw me?

Just then Padre Roberto looked up and waved. "Your father has come to take you to college," he beamed and beckoned me over. He was standing with Father Desta who was chatting amiably with Solomon. Like a poorly strung marionette, I tentatively moved closer.

"Tewodros," said Father Desta, "I think you have something to say? On your knees."

The guard who'd let me into the bell tower was standing nearby. He moved within earshot of our gathering, eager to hear more.

I stood, defiant.

"Get down on your knees!" the guard yelled. His sudden interference shocked me.

"It's okay," replied Solomon. "The boy doesn't need to apologise. It's best we forget all that, no?" he continued, his tone almost angelic.

I knew! I knew he was tricking them. Everyone was saying what a good man he was. Why couldn't they see?

In a swift (savage) gesture, he grabbed at me. In panic, I recoiled, but not fast enough. Firmly holding my squirming hand, he struggled to get me to the vehicle. Amazingly, his voice was still calm. "Tewodros, it's okay. I'm not going to hurt you." He smiled apologetically at the priests.

Father Desta glared disapprovingly at me. Kind Padre Roberto couldn't see that my gritted scowl was *not* a smile.

Solomon's hard fingers belied his soft tone. "I'm taking you to college to study. Didn't anyone tell you?"

Gripping both my shoulders now, he looked around. "I have an idea," he said. "Why don't you bring a friend to see where you are studying? He can report back to the priests to show that my intentions are good."

Still sceptical, I felt a little calmer knowing that a friend could come with us.

"You!" He pointed to Mesfen, one of the altar boys who was watching from the steps. "Come for a ride with us. You can come back and tell everyone how lucky Tewodros is," he commanded.

Mesfen nodded obediently and ran towards the car.

Just like that, we set off. No goodbyes. No packing to do. Just Mesfen looking excitedly out the window, Solomon driving intently forward, and me, wondering what had just happened.

It was a hot day. The temperature inside the car was like hellfire, so I wound down the window and stuck my head out. The breeze ceased when the car halted abruptly. We were in the parking lot of the soccer stadium, in the heart of the city.

As we got out of the car, my father pointed to a huge office building nearby. "You see that building over there?" he asked Mesfen, who nodded. "Well, that is where my son is going to study. Isn't it a nice place?"

Mesfen was clearly impressed and looked at me in awe.

"So, you can run back to the priests now and tell them that everything is all right. You've seen that Tewodros is in good hands," my father announced.

"Good luck, Tewodros!" Mesfen said, convinced upon seeing a building from a distance that my future was made. He skipped away.

I looked up at the building's shiny exterior. Just like my father: good looking on the outside, but not what he seemed. I knew this area. There was no college here. What was his real plan?

I followed Solomon through the entrance gates. What else could I do?

We climbed the stairs to the first floor and stepped into a foyer. He opened an office door and called out. A man emerged and acknowledged him in a friendly manner, though there was money in his hand after they'd exchanged a greeting.

"You need to wait with this man in his office until the driver arrives to take you to college," my father said, barely looking at me. Then he swiftly walked through the door and disappeared down the stairwell, without giving me a chance to respond or ask any questions.

My chest tightened. He'd told Mesfen that *this* building was the college. How could Solomon send that lie to the priests? Surely, he knew he would go straight to hell for that.

A driver did arrive sometime later, and the two men escorted me to a car.

I tried to convince myself that this time Solomon really was taking care of me. (When you are afraid and confused and have no control over your situation, you have to tell yourself something just to keep going.)

We all climbed in. After travelling for a short time, I noticed that we were heading out of the city. Fear gripped me as I gripped the door handle, wanting to flee. I tentatively asked about our direction and they kept reassuring me, "Of course it's out of city. How can you fly planes where there are tall buildings?"

The car eventually pulled up at a large set of gates. A man appeared holding a *machine gun.* (No, *no*, NO!) He recognised the car and waved us through. There were no airplanes in sight, only people with long unkempt hair and disillusioned faces, walking aimlessly around the overgrown grounds. There was a distinct absence of classrooms. The only buildings I could see were shabby and urgently in need of repair.

One of the men in the car turned to me and said, "You will stay here for now until college starts. When classes commence, we will transfer you across to the college campus."

My bewilderment kept me mute. Nobody was being truthful.

I looked at my surroundings. What kind of place was this? It certainly wasn't another mission. The main building inside the complex was L-shaped; it ran along the right side of the entrance and then across the back wall. The building's windows were either shattered or completely missing and there were small holes dotted along the walls. From my time in Shire, I recognised these immediately as bullet holes. (There's no mistaking that distinct round shape.) The sheets of iron that formed the roof were held down with bricks that looked like they were once part of the dilapidated building.

I was taken to my room in a building located on the left side of the entrance. This was the workers' quarters. I was to share with a driver whose job included collecting the staff each morning and bringing them to work, as well as running errands throughout the day.

The room was narrow with a dirt floor. The walls surrendered sad layers of peeling paint, revealing a large crack that descended from the ceiling, where it was evident that rivulets freely poured in when it rained. The two flimsy beds that were crammed under the crack should have been swapped with the tiny bathroom, which had clearly never known running water. The heavy heat of the day intensified the putrid smell emanating from the room. I hadn't eaten since the previous day, so I backed out. My stomach cramped in protest at the prospect of life in this hole.

As I swayed, hands on knees, thin saliva dribbling from my mouth, I realised that here was a forlorn salvation: I would have a (leaky) roof over my head and three meals a day.

Well, it was actually the same meal served over and over. Breakfast was *shai* and dry biscuits, while *shiro*[4] was served with spaghetti for lunch and dinner.

I was worn from starvation and wretchedness and, despite less than optimum conditions, I could recover some strength here. Renewing myself, I would go beyond this.

Of course, there was always the outside chance that Solomon would hold to his promise of an education, this time. *Are you thinking what I'm thinking?*

I spent my first few days sitting on the veranda, stunned at this turn of events. As a new resident, I was treated with caution, yet I was so curious about everyone's circumstances. They couldn't all have been hidden away in the desert by reckless fathers.

I noticed that there was a mixture of languages spoken in low murmurs. Though I tried asking questions in Tigrinya, Amharic or Guraginya, I was ignored or abruptly dismissed.

Each morning, I sat at the edge of the coffee ceremony (oh yes, nothing stops tradition) and slowly felt included enough to make

---

4. Spiced pea stew. Cheap and easy to make, it uses few ingredients. To a hungry boy, it tastes good but like anything when served in abundance, the appeal quickly fades. (Amharic)

some tentative friendships. Reem was a young woman who roasted the beans and served everyone their required three cups of the aromatic drink. One day, I decided to stay behind and chat with her while she was packing up. Most of the others had retreated to their rooms. I began in Tigrinya, "Reem, how long have you been here?"

She was swirling the coffee grounds from the pot and looked up at me as they splashed out onto the dirt where we were crouching. "I don't know," she said vaguely, "maybe six months."

"Six months? And why did you come here?"

"It wasn't my choice." She shrugged. "My family is from Tigray. Several years ago, the war became so bad there that we fled to Sudan. We've since been repatriated, but must wait here until our identities are confirmed—my husband, my children and me." She sighed. "So, now we are here indefinitely."

"But why did they bring you *here*?"

"You don't know where you are?" She seemed surprised.

"No, I don't. My father told me that he was sending me to college. I'm waiting here until next semester begins." Saying it aloud, I could hear how ridiculous it sounded.

Reem laughed and shook her head. "You've been misled. This is a detention camp. Why do you think we are not permitted to move freely—to walk out those gates?" She half-heartedly pointed in the direction of the guarded metal-grill entrance. "We can't even feed our children when they are hungry, unless it is meal time."

"So we are in prison?"

"Not prison, because we've done nothing wrong, but it's like prison. They call it 'rehabilitation'—a required process, before they then send us back to our homeland," she explained.

"I didn't know this kind of place was in Ethiopia." I waved away a fly, trying to wave away this new confusion.

"Nobody does. That's the problem. When the emperor's reign ceased, the new government converted this old hotel into a place of suspended existence. But the rest of the country has forgotten all about it and now we suffer, incognito."

"Is everybody here for the same reason?"

"Yes. Some surrendered themselves on the battlefield, others were captured during the fighting . . . and then there were people like me, who've been repatriated."

Ah, Solomon, you've outdone yourself. All your gracious bowing to the priests and public show of remorse and generosity. What a scam! You've effectively locked up your son and thrown away the key.

Such drastic action could only come from fear. And then it struck me: he was afraid of *me*. A spark of defiance flared within and, with it, the strength to fight back.

I confronted the manager of the complex to find out exactly why I was being held.

At first, he was reluctant to explain anything. But I pestered him relentlessly. After a couple of weeks he admitted that Solomon had sent me to the detention camp to correct my rebellious behaviour. There was no intention of sending me to any college. According to the manager, college was just a story to pacify the priests and gain my co-operation.

Speechless, I nurtured that defiance.

Quickly, I observed the daily operations of the place and understood whom to help and, more importantly, whom to impress. Within a month, the staff had warmed to me (evidently not the rebel they expected) and I was given special permission to leave the camp on a day-pass. Aware that I could be arrested if I didn't return, I had much to achieve in one day.

First stop was the church. Padre Roberto was giving a sermon when I arrived. I sat at the back of the congregation until the service had finished, and then waited for him by the rear door.

"Tewodros! How are you, my friend?" he exclaimed, expecting to hear good news from me.

"Padre." The tone of my voice spoke volumes and his smile fell. "My father didn't send me to college."

"What do you mean?" He sat down hard on the steps. "Mesfen returned from the ride with your father. He saw the college. He was so impressed."

"My father lied. You have to believe me." I sat beside him. "He sent me to a detention camp on the outskirts of town."

My good friend stroked his long beard and slowly shook his head.

"If you don't believe me, you can come and see for yourself. It's certainly not a college!"

"But— I'm truly shocked. Why would your father lie to us?"

"I told you and Father Desta. You can't trust Solomon!"

"I'm terribly sorry, Tewodros. We should have listened to you. We thought we were doing the right thing." He kept shaking his head.

"You have to get me out of there, Padre!" I said, not crying, definitely not crying.

"I'm not sure if we— Now that you're in that system, how can we— Oh! I'll talk to Father Desta. If there's *anything* we can do, I will get a message to you."

"Thank you." I shook his hand and left as there were other people hovering at a distance, waiting for their turn to speak with him.

It was comforting to be back in familiar territory. A few of my old friends were playing in the garden. I stopped to talk with them, letting them believe that I was studying at college. I was too embarrassed to say otherwise.

Given Padre Roberto's uncertainty, I decided to go "right to the top" to enlist help; not to God, but the only other person who held my life in limbo. Returning to the camp, I requested an interview with the director, whose office was in the city. Not only was she Eritrean (something I hoped would work in my favour), but as the wife of the Foreign Affairs minister, she had considerable influence.

Every day, I checked with the manager for a response. "Today?" I would ask, my tone changing from hopeful to frustrated to determined.

Finally, approval came. On another day-pass, I travelled to the city to meet the director.

She explained her involvement in my current situation. "Tewodros, your father is a friend of mine." *Great. I should just turn around and walk out.* "I did him a favour. You were misbehaving, and I agreed he should send you to the camp. It's that simple," she concluded matter-of-factly.

"Misbehaving? But I didn't even live with him."

"Well, he tells me that you were disturbing his family, causing such problems that he even considered killing himself." She sighed. "And we can't have that, can we?"

Truly, he was diabolical.

"If he dies, it will be your fault. Your guilt. Your scar, marking you for the rest of your life."

Whether she was another person Solomon had successfully duped or her ethnic ties made her sympathetic towards him (of course, he was Eritrean, too) I don't know. I was beyond amazed that, once again, his initial crime translated into blame on me. How did he keep getting away with it?

She continued, "You know, Tewodros, it's time you started to behave yourself or this will be your life: locked up for good. Once you're locked up, no one cares, you know. It's time you demonstrate *keber*[5] for your father and stop making his life difficult." She paused as her assistant entered the room, puffing on a cigarette. She waited for him to sit down before going on. "Doctor Solomon is a good man. He's doing his best to raise you, so you need to start cooperating." She looked across at her assistant and he nodded in agreement.

"It's time for your next appointment," he announced, and the director abruptly stood up and left the room.

Show *keber.* Over and over, I considered what that was supposed to mean, as I made my way back to camp. So, to keep the peace, I

---

5. Respect. (Amharic)

should lie and agree with everyone? Surely that's not respect—for anyone.

I returned to camp having resolved nothing.

After several months of living in this limbo, I was evicted. Without warning, I was called to the manager's office.

"Tell me, where is the jacket?" He thumped his fists on the table between us. "You stole it, didn't you—you *baallaga!*"[6]

A barrage of insults rained upon me until I could make myself heard. "I didn't steal anyone's jacket."

He sneered.

"You can check my room!" I protested, knowing I was innocent.

"You think you are so smart? But don't think I'm stupid. Of course it's not in your room because you already sold it!"

Oh, no!—I *had* sold a jacket to one of the guards, but it was *mine*. I hadn't stolen it. The manager continued his accusations. "Your roommate told me that his jacket is missing, and the guard told me he bought a jacket from you," he snarled.

When he mentioned these two men, I started to make sense of things. There was a woman at the camp whom both the driver and the guard fancied. The woman, however, took a liking to me and we'd become good friends; perhaps because of my youth she did not feel threatened by me. Over the previous weeks, both the men had grown increasingly hostile towards me and must have manipulated an opportunity for revenge.

"Yes, I sold—"

"Ah, so it was you."

"No. It was *my* jac—"

"Liar. I won't tolerate a *leba* in this place!" he screamed, rushing at me.

Before I knew it, I was skidding across the dirt outside, grazing me knees and nursing the bruise in my back where he'd kicked me.

---

6. Naughty child! (Amharic)

"Get your stuff and get out. Your father was right, you good-for-nothing!"

The next day, I was driven to the director's office. She was elsewhere. Her staff debated over my status and concluded that I should return to my father. I strongly protested, insisting that they set me free. I convinced them that I could manage on my own. Eventually, they gave in.

So, six months of camp life had come to an abrupt halt and I was on the streets once again. Living in that seclusion had not softened me, since it wasn't exactly the lap of luxury, but it had softened the memories of how hard it was to survive as a homeless boy. I thought I could easily manage to find one meal a day and somewhere to sleep each night—and that at some point, somehow, life would magically change.

I was dumb, trying to call for help; I was deaf, straining to hear an answer.

The kindness of strangers is a treasured thing but, like all treasures, it can be rare. Sometimes, after being rejected all day, I would simply lie down next to the road, snatching sleep (like a thief) when no one was looking.

Even though I faced hardship daily, I was never tempted to steal. I couldn't—wouldn't—reduce another person's life quality just to buffer my own. This world was so brutal, but nothing would induce me to contribute to its brutality.

At that stage, I must have looked dishevelled enough to deter anyone who might consider robbing me.

I didn't return to the church. Enlisting my father's help had been the priests' last resort, and led to *his* last resort to expel me. I was so ashamed—for everyone. I struggled on with intermittent solutions. The only things ever-present were the gnawing in my belly and the extremes of the weather.

More than frantic, I returned to the detention camp, begging the guards to let me in. Most times, they agreed. I'd ask one or another of the detainees if I could stay for the night. There was always someone who would let me share his space.

The randomness of days falling away left me with no clearer direction. What dreams I had of reuniting with my mother had come to a dead end, as there was no more information regarding her whereabouts. No magical solutions were emerging and I was weakening again.

Knowing that *sitting is being crippled*,[7] I visited the director's office regularly to ask for assistance. Maybe she would lock me up again. Maybe they would let me stay in detention until I reached adulthood. Then they might give me a job. Could I sit on the sidelines of my life for that long?

Queuing up outside her office each day, I realised that adulthood held no guarantees for security either. There was an interminable line of people seeking aid.

On one of these days, I started talking with an Eritrean lady, Asmhet. She told me that her husband had been murdered by ethnic guerrillas known as Afar *shifta*[8] and she alone was caring for their five children. She was desperate for any assistance the director could provide.

That day, as on so many other days, the office hours ended while our queue was still far from the door. With her assistant in tow, the director walked straight past the multitudes still waiting to see her.

Enough waiting! I decided to follow. As they approached the director's car, the assistant looked back at me and hissed, "Go away!" Then he blocked the path to prevent me from getting any closer.

Mute and overcome, I watched the director drive away from all the problems, and wished I could do the same.

"I don't think she could help you anyway." Asmhet had followed after me, and noticed my disappointment. "Why don't you come

---

7. Ethiopian proverb.
8. Rebel, outlaw or bandit. (Amharic).

and stay with me and the children? I don't have much to offer, but at least you'll have somewhere to sleep," she said.

A dewdrop in the desert couldn't have been more valued just then.

Asmhet lived in one of the poorest sections of the city, known as *Tal-ian-sefer*,[9] an area overrun by prostitutes, pick-pockets and thieves. Day or night, drunken people wandered the streets, yelling exple-tives to anyone who happened to cross their paths.

On arriving at her house, I noticed that Asmhet had converted the front area into a small liquor bar and I learned that this was the main source of income for her large family. Although I'd stayed at many different houses since leaving Gurage mission, Asmhet's house was undoubtedly the smallest. Defying cramped conditions, she often welcomed local kids, especially those having trouble with their own families.

On one of the first nights at her house, I went to bed alone but woke up beside three strangers. This became a regular occurrence.

The unpleasantness of sharing my bed was heightened when As-mhet's son crawled in with me after his own bunk had been taken over by an invasion of bodies. He preferred to lie with his head at the opposite end of the bed, putting his smelly feet in my face. The stench was so bad that I struggled to keep myself from dry retching.

I stayed with Asmhet's family for almost four months, though I often squabbled with the son over his smelly feet and her other children over their general lack of hygiene. Lack of food contrib-uted to the tension. I was still scouting for alternatives or begging on the streets. Most days in her house, the cupboards were empty. Even when there was food, I felt too guilty to eat any of it, since I wasn't paying any rent.

It must have been strange for her children to have me there. I was a complete stranger—older, possibly more educated (most

9. Italian-area. (Amharic)

209

likely, with those fussy cleaning habits, eh?) and not contributing anything to their upbringing.

The compounding strain flared when one of the older boys thought I was eyeing off his girlfriend. He left me reeling from bruised ribs and a bloody nose. If this was Life's way of inviting me to look further, I didn't need stronger encouragement.

It is said that when one door closes, another will open. After so many closed doors, I decided it was time to force open one of *my* choosing.

I finally choked down my pride and went to visit Padre Roberto.

He was still as generous (and sneaky) as ever, giving me clothes and pocket money whenever possible. If the other priests had known, he would have been in big trouble. One time, he'd piled a plate with food from the kitchen, but spilled it on the floor in his rush to avoid discovery. He heard Father Desta's steps approaching and hurried to hide the mess.

Dear caring Padre. I wasn't the only boy he helped. He must have made a special bargain with God to keep us alive since he risked the wrath of his superiors so often.

Even though I knew he was challenged, I pestered him to help me find somewhere proper to live. (I still harbour guilt over how I managed to persuade him.) Every day, I'd heard how God was watching over me. *Really, God? Then, watch this!*

I cornered Padre Roberto one evening after Mass and concocted a story that no priest would dare ignore.

"Padre, I need to tell you the truth about my living arrangements." My fear-filled heart was about to leap right through my shirt and give me away.

He raised his eyebrows and looked at me curiously.

"It's . . . well. . . . " I was working up the courage to lie to him.

"Tewodros, what has come over you? Is everything okay?" he asked.

"Yes . . . I mean, no. This is difficult for me to talk about, but . . . God wouldn't approve of the house where I'm staying." I swallowed, trying to squeeze out the next words. "It's a place of sin, Padre."

"I don't really follow what you are saying."

"It is a sinful place where . . . I'm forced to take part in . . . a boy like me shouldn't even know about such things." I'd never lied to a priest before. Would a lightning bolt strike me dead? After all, maybe God *was* watching me now.

Pausing mid-stroke of his beard, Padre gave me his unwavering attention. Nervously, I produced some porn photographs (from a magazine I'd found in a back alley of Merkato) and thrust them into his face for dramatic effect. "The women gave me these photos and want me to do the same." My cracked throat made me more convincing. "In return, I am given a place to sleep."

"Tewodros, are you sure?" he replied. The colour had drained from his face and he looked much older than he had just five minutes earlier.

I nodded robotically.

"Come with me, my child. We need to talk." He led me to a secluded area of the garden where he proceeded to give me a long lecture about the evils of the world.

"I know, Padre, that's why I've been begging you. I didn't want to have to tell you everything, but I felt that I had no choice."

"Very well, leave it with me and I will see if I can find somewhere for you to stay."

Within a few days, he introduced me to one of his Italian friends. Franco was a kind man, known as the Pied Piper of street kids from all around the city. I'd often seen him arriving at church, his small Fiat overloaded with stray children whom he'd picked up along the way.

Franco wore dark sunglasses, which drew attention to his big nose, and his suits hung loosely on his small frame, making him look skinnier than he really was. He arranged for me to stay at his house in Mekanesa, a sophisticated area close to the OAU[10] headquarters and various diplomatic offices. It was within walking distance of the church, so I could access my "family" with ease.

When I arrived at Franco's large house, I learned that one of his mistresses owned the other half, which she's won in a court battle. Both sections of the house had rooms set aside for boarders and guests, and I was allocated a room in the mistress's quarters. I shared this with one of her relatives and a relative of Franco's current wife.

Is life ever normal?

Franco offered me shelter, breakfast and a little pocket money each day, while I was expected to take care of my own lunch and dinner. The mistress operated her own business from home, selling food to the locals, and she often discounted the price for me.

What a difference. Life was still a struggle, but there was potential here to grow beyond circumstance. That little bit of security swelled my confidence as well as my belly. I started to accumulate a few possessions—small mementos that gave me a sense of worth.

I got along with one of my roommates, the mistress's cousin, though he soon left for Germany. He was replaced by a university student, whom I also liked. But I disliked the other roommate, Elias, from the moment I met him. He was rude, demanding and nosey. He did as he pleased because he was related to the owner.

I continued visiting Padre Roberto and attending church. During this time, I was pleased to learn that Father Habtemariam (a parish priest from the mission in Gurage) had moved to Addis Ababa. I decided to ask his advice on finding Bishkash.

Coincidentally, while staying with Asmhet, I'd met a man from Gojjam. I told him about my unsuccessful search for my mother in that region. He said I should have gone even further than Debre Marqos, to Bure. Some people had relocated there from the war.

10. Organisation of the African Unity.

She might be one of them.

On hearing this, Father Habtemariam suggested I contact my stepmother, Saba, to see if she could provide financial assistance. This would help with locating Bishkash, and give me some long-term security once I found her, since my mother would probably struggle to take care of me.

I'd never thought of approaching Saba independently of my father. She'd always been so kind. It was worth trying.

Two years had passed since we'd met. I went to the clinic where she worked as a nurse, nervous about her response. To my relief, she warmly welcomed me and we chatted for a while about what was going on in my life and why I had come to visit her. She was pleased that I wanted to live with my mother, because she knew I couldn't stay with her family, since Solomon still refused to accept me as his son.

As I was leaving she gave me some pocket money and I told her I would come back to update her on my progress. I went to see her several times after that and each time she gave me a small amount of money to help with the necessities.

I started to save towards my search for Bishkash. Scant clues renewed the quest. A flicker of hope was better than none.

There was a calm rhythm to my life that I naively thought would last. Following my routine, I went to Piassa one day to have my clothes laundered. Franco's wife had driven their son to the airport, leaving the maid home alone.

On my return, I noticed that someone had disturbed my belongings. The cupboard door was ajar. I'd slowly been gathering a collection of meaningful things after Aunt Meseret had destroyed my previous treasures. Now, the cupboard was empty. Everything (my Italian clothing, some special rosary beads from Bethlehem and other bits and pieces) had disappeared.

My things—my identity really—what could have happened to

them? Baffled, I went out onto the street to ask if the neighbours knew anything. Habte, a handicapped man staying with Franco, was talking with some others.

"Hey Habte! Do you know what happened to my belongings?" I asked.

Expectation can leave you breathless. Anticipation for a good answer readies you to sigh in relief, but you don't dare, because the answer could be bad.

Chest tense with hope, I waited for him to give me some logical explanation.

He looked at me suspiciously, "There was a robbery today and Franco's stereo has gone."

He looked at me more pointedly, almost accusingly. "I don't know anything about your belongings."

I didn't really hear him. My mind gathered in the memory of missing things, trying to comprehend this new loss. I looked up and noticed that the man standing next to Habte was wearing one of my shirts. No sigh of relief, but a shriek of accusation burst from me. "Hey, that's MY shirt!" I stormed at him.

"What shirt?" he responded with an air of arrogance.

"The shirt you're wearing, *durrayye!*"[11] I pushed him on the shoulder to show him I meant business. "It's mine. Give it back—now."

"Hey, relax. It's not your shirt, okay! It's mine, isn't that right?" he turned and asked Habte.

"That's right. The shirt is definitely his. He's been wearing it all day!" Habte snapped back. (When I met him recently, he admitted to tricking me that day.)

Quaking with rage, I stormed back to my room.

What did you expect, Teddy? To actually keep some nice things? Do you really think you deserve to have a good life? You keep running, thinking you're safe, but that curse keeps catching you. Foolish, foolish boy.

Later that evening, my roommate Elias returned home and I

11. Hooligan! (Amharic)

asked him if he knew what was going on.

"How dare you ask me? How should I know what was going on?" he hissed.

"I thought you might have heard. Looks like the house was robbed and some of our things were taken," I responded calmly, trying to avoid angering him.

"Yes, I know. Franco's stereo is missing." He walked over to me and breathed in my face. "Did you do it?"

"Are you crazy? Some of *my* things are missing, too!" I tried pushing him away, if only to escape his bad breath. He swung wild punches at me and our scuffle drew a small crowd. Then, he hurled a few final words of insult in my direction and stormed out.

Everyone followed after him. Swiftly, in a whirlwind of accusations, the crowd returned and announced they were taking me to the police station.

No one seemed to remember that I was a victim of the robbery, not its perpetrator.

How many times in my life had this happened? It was crushingly clear to me now that family weren't just the people who loved you; they protected you, defended you, looked out for you, made space for you, invested in you, and opened up opportunities for you. Never would a boy with a family be in this situation, nor be left alone to confront such an outcry. I was an easy target. Those wanting to deflect attention from themselves, for whatever reason, just had to point at me.

My escort clustered around me as we stepped out into the night.

The atmosphere was surreal.

Along the way, my accusers called to complete strangers, saying they'd captured a criminal; like I was some terrorist who threatened the very existence of the world. We caused quite a stir as we continued along the street. The neighbours were always looking for gossip and the procession swelled. Before too long, though, they decided it was too late to go to such bother for a mere scoundrel boy. There'd be plenty of time to sort it out the next day.

And that was it. Everyone went home.

So did I, as confounded as ever. Did I consider running away? Of course. Wouldn't you? But I was innocent. I would make my defiant stand. Truth had to be my protector in the absence of anything else.

Next morning, Franco's wife called me out of my room and I was confronted by two policemen. She explained that she had no choice but to involve the police *because of my dishonesty*. Apparently, some of the neighbours told her that, after she drove off the day before, I'd left the house, suspiciously carrying a bag.

"But that bag was full of my dirty clothes. I was doing my laundry," I protested.

"I'll believe the neighbours over a good-for-nothing kid like you," she said.

"But I have the receipt to prove it!" I said. I stood up to get it from my room, but was pushed back into the chair by one of the police officers. "Contact the laundrette and ask them if you don't believe me. I always go there. The lady there knows me!"

The wife turned to the police, exclaiming, "I want you to investigate the mistress's maid and this kid for their involvement in the robbery."

The maid and I were taken into another room. A new kind of terror ballooned in my belly.

The police began interrogating the maid. When she became hysterical, they shoved a wad of cloth in her mouth to stifle her screams. Then they pulled some rope from a bag, tied up her feet and began beating her soles with a baton (a common interrogation tactic). After a barrage of blows, they pulled the cloth from her mouth and demanded, "Who stole the stereo?"

Petrified, she remained silent.

"I said *who stole the stereo*? Was it this boy?" This time, the officer threatened with his baton.

Nodding vigorously, she looked away.

"Is that a 'yes'? Was it Tewodros?"

"Yes! Ye—es!" she sobbed. "I saw him leaving the house with a bag."

Wah! I should have run away after all. The thunder in my heart marked time with the officers' steps as they came towards me.

They stood over me, yet ignored me.

"There's no point in asking him to admit his guilt, eh?" said one.

"No," replied the other. "He's had plenty of time to tell everyone the truth. He's brought this upon himself."

They nodded in agreement, then looked down at me, a little too enthusiastically. The first one growled, "We're going to beat a confession out of you!"

At this point, my mind somehow detached from my body and I observed calmly as they shoved the cloth into my mouth, then tied and hoisted my feet into the air. One policeman stood behind me and held me down while the other pulled out his baton.

I don't think I screamed. I felt calm, like everything was in slow motion. I didn't register any physical pain, though the policeman kept belting me, and I was way beyond emotional pain since nothing made sense anymore. It didn't seem to matter if I tried, lied or cried—life could hit harder than any man with a big stick.

After about ten minutes, the officer wearied from his exertions, without extracting a single utterance of confession from me (not that I could speak with a mouth full of wadding). He and his partner untied my feet and went to talk to the wife.

The maid and I sat, not looking, not speaking, not knowing what would happen next.

Soon after, the policemen re-entered the room and told us we were going to the station for further investigation. We shuffled behind them along the same road of my infamous walk the night before. And—just like the previous night—the two officers suddenly told us to go back home. There was no point wasting their time on hearsay. They couldn't prove anything and they knew it. I returned to the house where my remaining belongings had been piled up outside.

The wife called from behind the door, "You must leave. The law didn't get you, but God will be your judge!"

"God will be your judge, too. Don't forget that!" I shouted back at her.

The university student hailed a taxi for me, and I headed for Piassa.

The next day was Sunday. Naturally, I sought refuge at the church. Padre Roberto was hearing confessions before morning service. I entered the confessional box and, against common practice, revealed my identity.

"Tewodros? What you doing here?" he whispered.

"Padre, I want you to know that no matter what you may hear, I swear in God's house that I did not steal the stereo."

"Stereo?"

"Yes, I didn't steal it, I promise," I said earnestly.

"That's good you didn't steal a stereo, Tewodros, but this confessional box is for telling God of sins you *have* committed." He seemed rather amused. His warmth soothed my troubled heart.

"I really need to talk with you, Padre. Can I see you after Mass?"

"Of course, my child, of course. Now, unless you've got some real sins, you'd better let someone else in here to save themselves, eh?"

After Mass, I explained what had happened. It was clear to both of us that, despite inadequate information, finding my mother was my last refuge. Padre Roberto put together a bundle of clothing and gave me some money towards the bus trip. I don't know if he was sad, relieved or as exasperated as I was, but it was a touching farewell.

Not an intrepid explorer yet no longer a starving kid, I set out again, nervously hoping that there'd be someone to greet me at the other end this time.

12

THE LAND OF MILK AND HONEY

Ethiopia's landscape is as diverse as her people. Her bounty ranges from mountains and plateaus to valleys, tropical forests, semi-deserts, rivers, and lakes.

The notorious famine-scarred regions lie to the south, east and north.

Gojjam is a fertile region in the west, abundant with crops and fruit trees and famous for its mouth-watering honey and delicious milk. Since agriculture is the spine of the country's economy both in produce and employment, the Gojjam region is crucial to the health of the nation.

This land of milk and honey had survived the worst of the famines, locust plagues, exorbitant price hikes, and livestock epidemics. Only the war managed to undermine its abundant potential.

Across the country, the Dergue regime assumed rights over farmers' livelihood and lands, knocking down their homes to make way for vast state crop divisions. Farmers often had to travel far to reach their fields. They were required to deliver quotas of grain and basic crops for redistribution in the urban and resettled areas. When income was insufficient, they were restricted from moving elsewhere to work as labourers. As fighting continued and increasing numbers became needy, the state farms collapsed and the government's dominance began to weaken.

Like a naïve tourist, eager to leave my troubles behind and arrive in a kind of paradise, I was poised to begin the two-day bus journey to reunite with my mother.

It had been eight long, dry summers since I'd seen her. I was now 16 in years but, in my mind, that confused boy on the back of the truck still had so many questions: Was she even alive? Would she know me? Had she missed me? Please let the answers be yes, yes, yes.

It was early morning. Lively Merkato greeted me with the usual cacophony.

I boarded the bus and sat next to a well-dressed middle-aged man, who introduced himself as Dawit. We spent the entire journey chatting pleasantly. (I don't think I had to lie too much, since I was leaving the deceitful world of Solomon behind.)

I'd been advised to recommence my search in Bure, a provincial settlement far beyond Debre Marqos, the scene of my previous disappointment. Coincidentally, Dawit had a friend who worked in Bure and (small village that it was) he thought his friend, Sereke, should know of my stepfather. He promised to introduce me as soon as we arrived.

On the first day of travel, we passed through a deep winding valley and then across a long bridge that spans the famous *Abay*,[1] known as the *gurorro*[2] of Gojjam. This marked our entrance into the Gojjam region.

After crossing the bridge and ascending the adjacent mountain, we saw the landscape open up into an expansive lush plateau.

---

1. Blue Nile River. (Amharic)
2. Throat (Amharic)

As we ascended the heights, I gained new appreciation for this land. I'd seen no sign of war or destitution since the outskirts of the city; just new horizons of raw beauty. Even so, elements of war were never far away. Along the road there was a *kella*[3] where the bus was brought to a halt, and searched.

Items of particular interest were weapons and contraband being transported from region to region by businessmen. Possession of weapons resulted in immediate arrest. Contraband was confiscated. This could be anything deemed incendiary or disrespectful to the regime.

Kella officers were feared by many, but they could be bribed. As they milled around the bus and carried out their search, Dawit explained to me that an officer who was open to bribes could be identified by his protruding stomach; an unmistakeable sign that he was well-fed.

After passing through Dejen city and Debre Marqos, we had to stop overnight in a settlement not too far from Bure.

So close now—I was too restless to sleep.

Making a pre-dawn start the next day, the bus lurched ponderously along a heavily potholed dirt track. Exasperated at the tardy pace, I wanted to balance the bus on my head and race through the fields of wheat and sugarcane in mere moments.

Sneaking up behind us, the sun picked out Bure peeping over intermittent hilltops ahead. It was still early, and the sleepy little village was just yawning awake when the bus finally rolled to a stop in the business precinct.

Dawit explained that there were two main areas of the village: *ilay* Bure, on top of the hill, and *itach* Bure, located at the foot of the hill, where we stood.

The village shops and mud houses were surrounded, almost hidden, by an abundance of dense shrubs and tropical trees, which thrived on Gojjam's fertile soil. The air felt clean, and birds were

---

3. Checkpoint. (Amharic)

making a pleasant breakfast ruckus all around. Here, nature and man appeared to coexist harmoniously, something I had definitely not seen in Addis. Not since Tigray had I been surrounded by lush countryside. I breathed deeply, feeling the promise of good things to come.

From the bus station, we headed for Sereke's home in *ilay* Bure. This rose beyond a secluded dirt track that wound uphill between the houses. It took about thirty minutes to reach the crest. We knocked on Sereke's door, a little puffed after such a hike.

"Dawit! How are you? What are you doing here?" A middle-aged man greeted us warmly and gestured for us to enter. He guided us into the dining room where breakfast had just been laid out. "Sit down, my friends. You're just in time to eat," he smiled.

"Thank you, Sereke, but we have already eaten," Dawit humbly replied.

"Please, I insist." Sereke pushed a plate of scrambled eggs towards us. "So, tell me, why am I blessed with your company?" he asked Dawit.

"Well, I met young Tewodros here on the bus from Addis Ababa. He's looking for his mother. It seems her husband works in a local pharmacy and I thought you may know of them."

As Dawit spoke, Sereke's wife entered the room with a fresh pot of piping hot *shai*.

"What is your mother's name, Tewodros?" Sereke asked me.

"Bishkash Kidane."

"Kidane?" he said, sipping his *shai*. "I know an Alem Kidane, but not a Bishkash."

"You do?"

"Yes. She's married to my friend Belachew," he replied casually, unaware that I'd been waiting to have this conversation for so, so long.

"That's her! Alem is her nickname!" (*She's alive! She's alive!*) I couldn't sit still.

Sereke's face lit up, happy that he would be able to reunite us. "I know Alem well. I work with her husband at the clinic."

"Clinic?" I faltered. "I was told that they owned a pharmacy."

"No, Belachew works with me at the local clinic. I'll take you there to see him, but first, let's finish breakfast."

Over the meal, Sereke quizzed me about my plans for the future and when I told him that I was hoping to stay in Bure with my mother, he tried to convince me otherwise.

"Bure is only a small village. Nothing much here for a young boy your age." His serious tone dampened my excitement. "Staying here would be of no benefit to your future and would only burden your mother. Surely your doctor father can care for you much better in the city."

"Well, I would prefer to live with my mother for a little while," I politely replied.

Dawit left after breakfast, and Sereke showed me to the clinic. When we arrived, Belachew had not yet started work, so Sereke left me to wait in his office. He returned with Belachew.

"Do you recognise this handsome young man?" Sereke asked Belachew, who was almost the same as I remembered him: short and stocky, with a neatly groomed moustache.

Belachew looked at me in utter astonishment, and the ends of his moustache curled up in a smile. "Tewodros?"

"How's my mother?" I asked.

"Her health hasn't been good, but now she is getting better—"

"Can I meet her?" I was too impatient for conversation.

"I'm sure she would love to see you, but perhaps I should call her first. It will be a shock, you know."

Local businesses usually had a telephone that the nearby residents could use. Belachew got a message to my mother by phoning a fuel station near their house. One of the staff ran to fetch her.

When she was brought to the phone and heard his news, she thought he must be joking. She couldn't believe I was able to find her, after all our separate misadventures. Belachew took a break from work and walked me to their house where Bishkash was nervously waiting.

Their home in *itach* Bure was tucked away behind the bus stop where I had arrived that morning. So ironic, that these last steps towards her mirrored the great circle I was now attempting to close.

As I entered the yard, it was clear that they were still living an impoverished life, even by Ethiopian standards. Their dilapidated mud house had piles of rocks placed around the base to shore up its foundations. The front door was made of a sheet of corrugated tin with cut-away holes to allow in light and airflow, but with no seclusion from the inquisitive gaze of passersby. The inside walls had been lined with newspaper; there was no running water; and Belachew told me that electricity was only available between 6pm and 9pm each night.

I stood on the threshold.

This was it. How did I look? How did *she* look? Would all my torment melt away as our eyes finally met? There'd been so much searching. Secretly, I wished *she* would have come to me. None of that mattered now. I'd found her. I was ready to give all I could to her and her new family, just to belong again.

We entered.

The greying shrunken woman who stood from the chair where she'd been resting looked much older than the 31 years she would have been at the time. But she was still my mother.

Nervous and polite, we exchanged greetings. Belachew returned to work without our notice. We were full, yet hollow, with no ability but to echo each other's fractured past.

She described how her family had fled the increasing violence and conflict on the streets of Tigray. They chose Belachew's homeland of Gojjam, hoping his family there might support them in making a fresh start. Bishkash and their two children, Habtamu and Mulu, had departed first while Belachew delayed for a few days to avoid suspicion. When she and the children arrived in Bure without him, family and friends initially feared the worst and believed that Belachew was dead. Despite my mother's assurances, she was constantly harassed to "tell the truth."

Isn't it amazing how others are so sure of what the truth is, based on nothing but their need to be right—or, at least, to make someone else wrong?

Everyone was relieved when Belachew arrived safely, a few days later. However, amid the stress of fleeing, he didn't obtain a *melqe-qiya*[4] from his former employer. This was a crucial document in ensuring his future employment. Without it, job placement was impossible.

Bishkash described the struggle for acceptance from Belachew's relatives because she was from another tribe. Although quite wealthy, most of them (with the exception of Belachew's eldest brother) refused to help, even though Belachew was unemployed.

The family endured this stress for two years. Two more children arrived—Hennock and Kidest—and Bishkash wore herself out selling homemade goods, just to keep the children alive. These products included *mesob, gabi, berbere*, and *shiro*.[5]

Meanwhile, Belachew pursued every possible solution, but failed with each attempt. Within the bureaucracy, they were statistics, not people. So they continued to suffer, all for the sake of a piece of paper. Finally, a relative in Addis Ababa was able to resolve the issue with the government and Belachew was given permission to commence work as a health officer.

Bishkash knew this would not suffice. Harking back to her childhood dreams and the encouragement she'd received from Grandma Zenebech, she was determined to pursue her education and attend university. While still in Tigray, she'd completed Year Twelve

---

4. An identification certificate. (Amharic)
5. Traditional hand-woven tables made from coloured straw, cotton shawls, red chilli powder, and chickpea powder. (Amharic)

with a score of 2.6, a remarkable result that guaranteed her a place at university. She still believed that education was the only way she could lift her family out of the vicious circle of poverty, and applied for a scholarship to a Russian university. (Ethiopia had close political ties with Russia at this time, so external studies were reasonably accessible.) After breezing through the entrance exam and interview phases, Bishkash was accepted. Elated with her achievement, she thought the future could only get better.

Regaining some control over her life, she decided it was best not to have any more children and went to the local clinic to discuss her options with the nurse. Bishkash wasn't a fan of contraceptive pills. The alternative was to have her tubes tied. Apparently, midway through the procedure, the nurse (working alone) was called away for some personal emergency. Bishkash was left on the operating table and almost bled to death.

On returning, the nurse was shocked at her patient's condition and transferred her to a regional hospital. By then, Bishkash had lost so much blood that the family was told to brace for her imminent death. Distressed by the news, their good friend, Sereke, had her sent to a hospital in Addis Ababa where she could receive better treatment.

I was stunned to hear this. In Addis? So close to me? And dying? If only I'd known. (She says, it is by the mercy of God that she is still walking the earth today.) Sadly, this unfortunate event cost Bishkash her dream of studying abroad.

I sat across from her as she shared these tales of woe, humbled by the trials that we'd independently endured.

I revealed the twists and turns my life had taken since she'd faded from my view, on that distant morning.

She nodded sullenly. "My son, from that day I've been trying to follow your movements. During your time with your grandmother in Asmara, family members occasionally visited and brought me news of you," she said. "I was so anxious when they said you'd been sent to live with Doctor Solomon. I prayed day and night that he wouldn't harm you." She paused to wipe a single tear from her cheek. "I worried so much that at times I couldn't sleep."

"You *know* that my life was very hard with Solomon?"

"I don't doubt it, my son. And when I heard you'd been sent to some horrible detention place, I went looking for you."

"You knew *that?*" Now, I was weeping. At last, I had some reassurance. All this time I wondered why she never came to claim me, why my letters got no response.

"Yes, I knew," she admitted. "But we couldn't find you. After that, we knew nothing. And here you are, in front of my eyes! Finally, I know peace." Her tears were freely flowing now. We sat in the comfort of that peace together, not able to voice our gratitude.

I still had one burning question—the first one that cleaved my heart, the last one that remained. I swallowed hard, looked her directly in the eyes and summoned the courage to ask, "Why did you send me away?"

Her response didn't console me. "My son, it was for the best. I didn't have any money. But your father did. I thought I was doing what was best . . . sending you to your father's family."

"But you knew what he was like."

"Yes, but I also knew of your grandmother's good heart and prayed that she would care for you."

"Well, she couldn't! Even if she'd wanted to. His family, his sisters, they wanted me gone—like I was rubbish—a stinking blot on their lives. I was just a kid, mother, a little kid." I couldn't hold back my rage at him, at them, at everything. "I'm so tired of this horrible life, of people telling me I'm nothing or that 'everything will work out'. For once, I want to feel safe! I want to stay here in Bure and live with you."

She dropped her gaze and slowly shook her head.

"Tewodros, that is not possible. I'm still struggling. I still have no money—and I have four children now."

That would be five, by my count, I thought.

"It's best you return to Addis. Bure is not for you. We have nothing for you. Besides, the government has been scouting for national service recruits. As a new face in the area, you will draw attention to yourself. They'll find you in no time."

My ears were hearing her words, but my mind was deaf to the logic. No one, not even the priests, had thought beyond this moment. I'd found her and I was meant to stay with her. *This* was all I had!

She continued. "This is a small village. All the young people are moving to the city. There's no future here. It's crazy to come from the city to the country. Don't you see that?" Her voice was steady now, though she seemed diminished under the weight of her own words.

"Mother, I have nowhere else to go. I am your son, your own flesh and blood. If I return to Addis, I—! I can't go back there. I can't sleep on the streets anymore. And starve. And beg. Besides the government would pick me up there, just as easily. Please. *Please,* let me stay with you."

"Well . . . you are here, now. I'll need to discuss it with Belachew, but I can't promise anything," she said quietly, our intimate connection closing off.

It wasn't the reception I'd hoped for, but it was something.

Life-changing decisions can be made on a shrug, not that I think my hosts were casual about accepting me. For want of an alternative, my tenuous welcome was extended indefinitely.

Over the following weeks I observed Bishkash's popularity among neighbours, which helped to balance the neglect from Belachew's relatives. People were drawn to her gentle nature and her devoted kindness.

I couldn't help but feel confused, though. She had protested my presence, saying she had nothing to give, but at every knock on the door, she would drop what she was doing and welcome the guests, treating them like royalty.

Each day without fail, visitors would come laden with fresh produce and snacks, providing a rich atmosphere in an otherwise deprived home. Coffee was always prepared. I marvelled that she had so many beans on hand, even with donations from friends.

Too soon, I was reminded of village mentality where everyone had an opinion, which was offered freely and often. Bishkash's visitors all agreed that Bure was not the best place for me, but opinions wouldn't put a roof over my head elsewhere, so I remained, despite the consensus.

Bishkash never said an unkind word to anyone, although she never went against an opinion either. It was as if the life had been sucked out of her and she did whatever was necessary to please others, with no sense of self any more.

This explained her detachment from me, but it didn't ease my frustration at being excluded. When no one was around she seemed powerless—quiet and slow—or she would suddenly yell at her children (all of us) without apparent provocation. The others accepted this as normal, but my experience (by now vast) had shown me that life *could* be dignified, polite and caring. I'm not really sure what the other children thought. Having no other options, we did what poor people do: we endured.

The reality of my new situation slowly came into focus: I was still begging, just in a different way.

I was bursting with impatience to take hold of life (rather than it having a hold over me).

More than ever, I wanted to study. I missed gaining knowledge and receiving that official stamp of approval. For years now, all I'd had to read was the Bible and religious material. I craved for more input. There were no libraries or resources in this tiny village, but there was a school. Resuming an education became my next priority.

One of Bishkash's special friends was a lady named Gete, the wife of a local politician. During one of her visits, my mother mentioned my desire to study. This lady had influence in the local school since her son, Melaku, attended. She suggested I go there and talk with someone about enrolling.

A couple of days later, Melaku (my elder by two years) escorted me to the school. Registrations had already closed, but the secretary advised me to explain things to the deputy director. On the way to his office, Melaku quietly told me that this man was known to accept bribes in return for favours. From my mother's stories, Melaku was a serious student from a good family. I doubt he would have resorted to bribery himself, but perhaps he thought I needed all the help I could get.

Little did he know, I had a secret weapon.

Melaku pointed to the deputy's office door, and I entered alone. "*Selam.* I've just moved from Addis to live with my mother and wish to start school," I said, as I squeaked awkwardly into the plastic chair directly across from him.

"What grade?"

"Nine," I replied (lied), and handed him a certificate to prove that I was eligible.

For the past two years, I *hadn't* been attending school. I knew I'd be needing documentation, so I had the certificate faked. If approved, this piece of paper would place me with my peers; without it, I'd have to suffer the jeers of being demoted to the juniors' class. Worse than that, the false document could mean real jail time, since manufacturing it was a criminal offence. I knew that life was a fine balance of risk and reward; my many crash landings didn't deter my desire to reach further still.

The deputy studied my prized possession, looked at me cautiously, and then asked me to wait outside. Melaku waited with me. Each passing minute seemed to confirm a sinister fate.

I was called back into the office. My clammy palms and shortness of breath did nothing to evoke innocence.

"Young man, where did you get this certificate?" he asked sternly.

"From my school in Addis," I answered, as confidently as I could.

"I don't think so. This is a falsified document." He eyes flicked from me to the paper to me again. "Someone made it for you?"

"No, sir. One of my friends bo—brought it. From school. I mean—the school sent it."

How pathetic was that? I might as well have said I found it in a box of cereal, or a space ship delivered it, or the fairies put it under my pillow.

Then Melaku's quiet suggestion popped into my head. "Sir, education is really important for me. I would love the chance to study." I glanced around to make sure no one was standing near the door, and lowered my voice. "I have a few *birr* for you if you do this favour for me." I had no idea how to bribe someone, but it was worth a try.

He looked me up and down then paused before reconsidering his position. "Perhaps I misunderstood then," he said. "Indeed, it seems that this certificate is exactly what we're looking for. Now—was it Grade Nine, you said?"

"That's right, sir." I could have crowed with relief.

"Fine. The director returns from vacation in two weeks. He'll check all new records to ensure proper documentation has been received and processed."

A wave of panic flattened my exuberance, but the deputy reassured me. "I doubt the director will see any problem with this by then. . . . " He leaned over his desk and whispered, "Uh . . . do you have the money with you today?"

My pockets jingled with the last of Padre Roberto's money. (He would be Saint Roberto for this miracle.) I nodded.

"Good. Wait outside the school fence until five o'clock. I'll meet you when I finish work. You understand?"

Back to crowing, then! I nodded and left.

I found Melaku, who'd been waiting patiently, and when I

explained that his advice had worked, he swung me about in a victory dance. He went home, leaving me to my secret rendezvous.

At 5pm precisely, I met the deputy and we walked some distance down the street, away from the school perimeter, for our little transaction. I remembered how my father slipped money to the guard when he was taking me to "college." I tried to do the same.

I gave the man 60 *birr*,[6] hoping it would be enough, but he said, "You can pay me the rest later."

The rest? I had no idea how I was going to gather more funds, for this or anything. Those two weeks of wondering were long.

On the appointed day, I lined up with a few others in similar circumstances. I could see the director peering through the window, surveying us one by one. All I wanted was an opportunity to study.

Please let him see my earnestness and not my forged document!

Finally, I made my way up to the counter. One of Melaku's teachers was there—he knew my situation, so I hoped he would offer some support.

The director questioned me about my enrolment information and I answered as briefly as possible. With the help of Melaku's teacher, I was accepted into Grade Nine and given a list of things I had to buy (oh, no) for school: uniform, booklets, pencils, etc.

Bishkash understood how important education was; surely she would help me get started.

As it turned out the deputy was transferred. At least I didn't have to find extra money for his bribe.

A few days later, the next chapter of my life commenced. At last, I no longer had to hunch against the onslaught of life. I could lift my gaze . . . I could dream again.

The classrooms were located behind the office building. They were contained in one long structure made of mud, with corrugated tin doors and windows. The tin on the windows could be swung back

---

6. US$13 (approximately).

to allow light and air inside during class time. The building was divided into several classrooms. Mine was located through the nearest door.

On the first day, each class was introduced to their monitor, a fellow student hand-picked to report back to the teacher on everyone's misbehaviour. At the end of the day, those named were punished.

Ah, the familiar swishes of the rubber hose. How it whistled and sliced the air relentlessly as students learned the errors of speaking rudely, being late, not knowing an answer, not understanding a question, losing a book, sitting the wrong way, or anything that even slightly interrupted the order of the day. (Why was I in such a hurry to get back to this?!)

Although I was never a miserable recipient of hose discipline, I was punished in other ways, equally painful.

My first lesson at this school was that a two-year lapse in one's education makes an enormous difference. I quickly fell behind everyone else. I struggled with my homework. Just to keep up, I started copying from students beside me. Panic perched on my shoulder throughout each day, keeping my palms moist and my eyes flicking to see if I'd been found out. The teachers soon uncovered my handicap, but they simply assumed I was lazy.

Not long after term commenced, I failed to complete an English assignment. The teacher (who seemed to take delight in picking on me) asked me a question from that homework. Unable to answer, I was sent outside and forced to crawl along the gravel until my knees bled. On another occasion, I had to kneel beside the teacher, facing away from the class, and remain there until lunchtime.

The other students talked of their futures, but only half-heartedly. War had always been the backdrop to our young lives, so nothing was certain and choices were few. The ultimate career was to be a World Series soccer player (yeah, right). Then, preferences ranked down from pilot to engineer to doctor. Nobody wanted to be a teacher, and I certainly didn't want to be a doctor.

I didn't know what I wanted "to be" except alive! But I knew that the difference between life and death was an education—a good one. I was determined to finish school and forge ahead to the next possibility. If you had no education, you had nothing. Even my father would have been dead, but for his training.

"Tewodros! What are you doing?"

"I . . . I was thinking how great life will be when I have a career, sir."

"On your knees, boy! And stare at that wall! There will be no thinking in my classroom!"

Each punishment built up hatred in me, making it harder and harder to concentrate, yet incurring more frequent reprimands. There wasn't even any joy in playing soccer during breaks.

Two years until I finish? Oh, God, just get me through this.

The eye of the leopard is on the goat, and the eye of the goat is on the leaf.[7]

With the teachers' eyes on me and my eye on that certificate, I just kept moving steadily (slowly) towards my goal.

Home life with my new family wasn't exactly as I'd hoped either. They were trying to save money to build their own house, so they were very tight-fisted, never spending one cent more than required for survival.

My mother and the maid (servants are a tradition, you know, and nothing breaks tradition—not even poverty) were responsible for the cooking, but there never seemed to be much food. The same dish was served up day-in day-out: *shiro* and *injera* (in other words— mush and sour bread). There were no vegetables, no meat and no variation. Most of the time, I went to school without breakfast.

So much for the land of milk and honey.

Whenever I complained, Bishkash said the food budget was

7. Ethiopian proverb.

fixed—it would have to be good enough.

"But, mother, I'll go blind just eating *shiro* every day!"

That wasn't just a hysterical outcry, not that I really thought I'd go blind, but I was undernourished already and soon became quite ill. In that mountainous region, nighttime temperatures plummeted. The room I'd been assigned was attached to the side of the house (more of a tiny annex than an architectural living space). Of course, I was very grateful for a roof over my head, but I'd expected substantial walls as well. The chill air crept in, invading silently, yet leaving me with a raucous enduring cough.

Some locals advised me to eat a raw egg mixed with honey every morning to get rid of the phlegm on my chest, while others suggested I take an early morning run before breakfast; neither of which seemed to work. I tried the remedies individually and in combination, but the congested cough hacked on. It would become a memento from Bure, for years ahead.

Life began to fall into a routine. I was comforted by its steady rhythm.

Saturdays were reserved for bathing—a favourite day, just like in Addis Ababa. A friend and I would head down to a nearby crystal clear stream. I'm sure Padre Roberto believed that cleanliness was next to godliness because he always made sure I had soap. My friend and I scrubbed each other's backs and watched the week's grime float away.

On a recent return trip, I learned that there is a bottled water factory on that exact location. Now, whenever I drink water in Ethiopia, I can't help thinking of two carefree boys splashing in the shallows.

After bathing, we dressed in clean clothes and strolled back into the village with the bold swagger of youth, ready for the next adventure. But, we were in Bure, so the nearest thing to excitement was watching the bus arrive from the big city. We were always sure to be in the vicinity of the bus stop by 10am.

Swallowing my pride, I had to admit that everyone was right: Bure was no place for me. I missed the hubbub of the city; living on the edge had a strange kind of excitement (when I wasn't falling off it, that is). I just didn't have a country mind. I would sit and watch the travellers, and sometimes strike up a conversation with them, just to get the feeling of the city. I longed for the day when I could be on that bus, heading back to the place where, hardships and all, I felt most at home.

Hailu, my friend from the Catholic church in Addis, and I exchanged letters frequently for my first year away. They were always so full of gossip and jokes, and I could feel the city buzz lifting off the pages. Hailu also passed on my messages to Padre Roberto. Even over such distance, their contact was a lifeline.

Having lived in several tribal regions around the country by now, I was fascinated by the different customs. In Bure, the locals' opinions covered every possible topic, and were usually approached from all social, religious and superstitious perspectives to be sure of appeasing everyone. Witches were common in this area, so there was as much superstitious advice as there was practical and, just in case nothing else worked, one prayed for the right outcome.

The fear of darkness was very real, and not just because of the wild beasts. There was talk of strange beings that were human by day and hyenas by night. Howls in the darkness reminded us that life was predatory and beyond our control. The notion of devils was intrinsic to interpreting the world and all things inexplicable. We huddled together and reassured each other with anything that would keep soul-stealers away.

Superstition was commonly used to justify positive aspects as well. If someone was smart, apparently he had "good medicine" in his head. People would pay witches to cast spells for intelligence, good health or good business. Little wonder, then, that my cough persisted when it must have been "a devil trying to catch my breath."

After a long year (mostly on my knees), I somehow managed to pass Grade Nine. Halfway to my goal! I decided to return to Addis Ababa as a celebration.

On arriving, I arranged lodging at the Gurage man's hostel in Piassa, and then went directly to the church to meet Padre Roberto. He was pleased to hear of the success in finding my mother and resuming school. Truly a sympathetic man, he was saddened to learn of her ongoing struggle and, to help ease the strain, he offered some clothing and shoes for her children.

Over the next two weeks, we met several times. It was wonderful to feel his welcome and know that I was no longer a burden to him. I also caught up with old friends, but I was embarrassed to be living in Bure, so I told them I was based in Bahr Dar, Ethiopia's second-largest city, about five hours drive from my actual home.

That wasn't stretching the truth too far, was it?

During my stay, I visited Father Habtemariam. Knowing me since mission days, he could appreciate what an achievement it was to pass my grade after missing several years of study. He suggested we visit my stepmother Saba, and tell her of my progress.

Father Habtemariam accompanied me to Solomon's house.

Saba greeted us at the door and showed us to the lounge room. I was relieved to learn that my father was away on business. Father Habtemariam explained the reason for our visit, telling Saba that I was going to need financial assistance during my final year of study. Saba agreed to send me money on a monthly basis through a bank transfer and asked me to forward Belachew's account details.

Father Habtemariam left me with Saba. We enjoyed our afternoon as I helped her in the garden. She always did her best to make me feel welcome, which was apparently unusual because I'd heard many troubling stories from friends about their difficult relationships with stepparents. Saba was lovely. It was my own blood father who was the problem and I often wondered how she could have ever married a scoundrel like him.

Visiting her recently, I reminisced about those strange times when everyone lived under Solomon's tyranny.

"You know, Saba, you really married the wrong man," I commented.

She looked at me quizzically.

"You should have married his older brother, Asmerom. He was a doctor, too, with a great reputation. And so kind. The two of you would have made a great match. Instead, he got Meseret and you got Solomon."

She laughed shyly at the thought of Meseret and Solomon together. What a house that would have been! Yet, as Solomon's widow now, she still respects his memory, even though he left his family in dire circumstances. It must be so sad and strange for them to have nothing, after all his success and bravado.

Gentle lady that she is, she gave me a splendid time that day I came asking for help. She took me to the taxi stand in the evening, and handed me enough money for food and the ride back to the hostel.

This time, the city felt bountiful.

I returned to Bure with a stronger focus, knowing that a better life was soon within my reach. In contrast, the domestic situation became increasingly strained and uncomfortable.

Bishkash saw that I was able to make changes in my life and shape my future. What she didn't see was the determination born out of desperation *and*, for all that, that nothing would have changed if it weren't for the generosity of others.

When she began expecting more and more from me, I realised that giving her the clothes from Padre Roberto was a mistake. Both Bishkash and Belachew now believed that I had easy access to clothes and money from people in Addis Ababa and assumed that

I would continue to provide the family with various items. I tried to explain that those clothes were a one-time-only donation and the only money I'd been given was to cover my transport costs.

They didn't believe me, and the home atmosphere became tense. I spent less time there and more time with friends. I only went home to sleep.

About two months had passed since I'd sent the bank details to Saba and I still hadn't received any money. I knew she was reliable, so I asked my mother and stepfather about it.

"Please check the bank account. I need the money to buy a new uniform!" I begged. I'd far outgrown my only uniform and couldn't force it onto my lanky body any longer.

Belachew said he had checked.

"And?"

Bishkash was always siding with him. "Tewodros, you don't even trust your own shadow," she quipped. "You must be patient!"

My patience wore out after another month passed, void of money. I realised I had to confront them.

Dinner was the only time we were together. As they sat across from me one evening, I announced, "I'm going to contact Saba and find out why she's not sending me the money."

Belachew's hand stopped midway to his mouth and Bishkash almost choked on a piece of *injera*.

My suspicions were confirmed. "Why are you taking my money?"

"Tewodros, I told you when you first arrived that we couldn't care for you. It's already hard enough—and now—feeding you and sending you to school . . . well, it's just too much." Her reply was feeble.

"That's why I asked Saba for help." I was appalled. "If you needed some money, why didn't you ask? What you did is stealing!"

They both sat silently, not knowing how to justify their actions, and then she said, "My son, we used the money to feed you and the children. Is that such a crime?"

I looked down at the meal in front of me: *shiro* and *injera*, the same food that we'd been eating since the day I arrived. "If it was used for food, why haven't the meals improved? Why is there no variety? No meat? Not even vegetables?"

"I don't think you understand. Do you know what a horrible life I've had, what a struggle it was to raise you?"

"Raise me? You sent me away when I was eight, and I would never have seen you again if *I* hadn't searched for *you*!"

"I think you're being very selfish," she claimed.

"I don't care what you think!" I shouted back. "I don't know any love from you. I don't feel it at all. You might tell me, but words are hollow. The life you gave me was just hollow."

She turned her eyes from me and rested against Belachew.

Enough! I ran out into the street. What could I do now? I was being robbed by my own mother. Angels and saints! How do I solve this? There was no salvation here. *The dog I bought bit me; the fire I kindled burned me.*[8] This incident marked a drastic change in my relationship with Bishkash. It was, in my mind, the final betrayal.

The end of the school year was fast approaching, so I decided to bide my time until graduation. By then, I could move out. In the meantime, I continued to distance myself from the family as much as possible.

Night life in Bure was fairly low key.

I'd meet up with some of the locals, in the evenings. We'd go to a bar, which was usually no more than a front room in some house. There was music and lively chatter. I quietly observed as bus drivers, businessmen and even some of my school teachers would drink too much, tell bad jokes and leave the bar in the company of a prostitute.

Most often, though, I would sit in a little café, sipping tea, and

8. Ethiopian proverb.

wonder over the craziness of the world. . . .

When had we stopped being a fierce people? Perhaps long-term fear had worn these people out. Perhaps the lack of noble leadership had left them feeling dazed. Instead of ferocious protests, everyone (who dared) whispered dissent, most often in the form of jokes.

There is one that tells of some ministers and the dictator, Mengistu, coming to Gojjam. Their progress is stopped by the flooding *Abay*, which had risen to cover the bridge. The only way to cross was to swim. The ministers were afraid, but Mengistu (who wished to appear fearless and defiant) walked to the bank and cried, "I am Mengistu. I will swim across!" Then, he jumped in.

The rushing water swept him along and he started to struggle. A farmer saw him floating by and rescued him. Once he arrived safely on land and caught his breath, Mengistu fiercely threatened the farmer, "Don't tell anyone you saved me! Or I'll have you shot."

"Oh, Colonel Mengistu," the farmer sighed. "Of course I won't tell, but not because I'm afraid of you. If anyone finds out that I saved your life, all the people of Ethiopia would want me dead!"

Not everybody was silent. There have been notable Ethiopian poets and thinkers: the voices of the people. They've written in protest at the fraying of our country. Some were arrested. Others went into exile. Yet, they continued to reinvigorate our spirits.

I suppose the rebel fighters felt that bullets were the only punctuation that would bring dictatorship to a full stop.

I sat with the hubbub of people around me and the hubbub of thoughts within, trying to see what my own struggles amounted to. Was a teenager capable of such deep pondering? Probably not, in so many words.

Only now, in retrospect, can I identify what drove me on. Like my namesake, I was defiant—yes, but I wasn't going to struggle for what I believed in, just to die! Looking around, I could see that tradition wasn't enough, religion wasn't enough, education wasn't enough, and certainly (for me) family wasn't enough. At that stage, the war was proving that not even rebellion was enough.

What made life *wonderful?* What was it that lifted people out of the mundane into greatness? What burned in my chest, searing my throat with every word of longing? Like a campaigning emperor, I wanted to expand my horizons.

We are not politically free if we are bound by crowd mentality; we are not spiritually free if we are condemned by beliefs that supposedly keep us safe. We are only truly free when we have made our own conscious choices.

Life is not fated: *it is choice.* Whatever kept calling me, I chose *that* as my purpose. Along the way, perhaps, I would be blessed enough to hear someone tell me, "I trust you. I believe in you."

Would life—could life be so fantastic? My heart roared a defiant *YES!*

How many cups of tea did it take to realise that? More than a few. It helped to fill the hours while I waited for the family to fall asleep. I couldn't face them anymore.

No one at home objected to my absence. But they made a clear statement that I was not one of the family when they began locking me out. One night, I returned from my late night musings and, instead of sneaking in quietly, I had to knock on my bedroom door. My stepbrother, Habtamu, opened it. As I stepped inside, he lay down—on my bed. From then on, I was forced to share a single bed with him. It wasn't his fault. I was just so stunned at the layers of betrayal that had insidiously crept into every aspect of my home life.

Tea, anyone?

13

FIRE AND BRIMSTONE

One afternoon, as I returned home from school, I caught the scent of *shai* and freshly baked *ambasha* wafting out onto the street. Moving closer, I could hear happy chatter inside the house. I recognised Bishkash's voice, but not the guest. As I entered, I saw a beautiful woman sitting, talking with my mother.

"Hello. You must be Tewodros. My name is Asfehet," she greeted me warmly. "I'm on my way home from a trip to Addis Ababa and thought I would see how your mother is feeling."

"I'm okay." Bishkash blushed.

"So, how do you know each other?" I enquired, interested in anyone who'd been to the city.

"Well, we both studied agriculture at Awasa University," she replied.

"Mother." I was amazed. "I didn't know you'd studied at university."

"Yes," she replied. "I tried. But on a field trip, I bled heavily again. My health failed and I had to quit."

"Your mother is a fighter, Tewodros," Asfehet exclaimed, and

Bishkash blushed again. "She's a smart woman. She recently passed an exam in Debre Marqos to work in the Finance Minister's department, but because she didn't have as much experience as some of the other women, she wasn't chosen."

"I didn't know that either." I felt like such a stranger.

"I don't know why I keep persisting. I think God is telling me I'm not destined to study. I should just accept the life of a peasant!" No hint of a fighter in her reply, I noticed.

Asfehet stayed until late that night. I walked her back to her hotel, where her boyfriend was waiting. Along the way, we talked about my situation and how I was struggling in Bure. She told me I could visit her any time I needed a change of atmosphere.

Keep expanding those horizons, Teddy.

I visited her several times in her village of Denina Atkashta (about a 90 minute drive from Bure) and it wasn't long before we became good friends. During one of my visits, she told me that her sisters and mother lived in the city, Bahr Dar. This was one place I'd longed to see, as it was famous for the Blue Nile Falls. Asfehet and I planned a trip there on my next visit.

We decided it was best to leave early, so I stayed the night at her place. At 6am, we were woken by the sound of a car horn. Asfehet (who worked for the agricultural department) had asked one of the government drivers to give us a lift to the highway. We'd overslept and he was impatient to get going.

While idling, he'd been listening to the radio and we noticed his concerned look as we settled in the car. He turned up the volume. We heard an announcement that Wereta and Hamusit (two towns near Bahr Dar) had been captured by TPLF/EPLF soldiers and the bigger city was their next target. The government couldn't afford to lose such a strategic point, meaning more battle would ensue and the danger would intensify.

The colour drained from Asfehet's face. With concern, she said, "Tewodros, I don't think today is a good day to go to Bahr Dar. Why don't we leave it for another time?"

"But there's always war in this country," I protested. "If we made our plans around the war, we'd never achieve anything!" She didn't seem convinced.

"I think we should just stay here," she said. "I can take you there when things settle down."

"Please, Asfehet, you know how they exaggerate on the news. I'm sure it'll be all right and, if it's not, we can turn around and come back, okay?" I was so eager to see Bahr Dar that I didn't want anything to stop me—not even a war.

The driver left us at a cluster of buildings beside the highway. We had no set plans for the next part of the journey and hoped to find someone travelling in the same direction. A local man pointed to a 4WD parked beside a restaurant and told us it was a government car, chauffeuring a banker. As we approached, we saw people gathered around car radios and exchanging worried whispers. Inside the restaurant, Asfehet recognised the banker. We greeted him and sat down at his table to order breakfast.

"So, are you going to Bahr Dar today?" asked Asfehet.

"I was planning to, but it seems there's a bit of commotion in the area," the banker replied.

"Well, would you mind taking us with you? I need to see my family." She smiled sweetly, putting her charms to good use.

"Are you sure you want to go there today?" he asked her.

"I'm a bit nervous about the whole thing, but my friend is keen." She nodded in my direction.

The banker slowly sipped his *shai*. "Well, okay then. Let's finish our breakfast and then we'll make a move," he said.

I'd been looking forward to seeing Bahr Dar, but the radio news enticed me even more. I wanted to see firsthand the point of this war that was supposedly for our own good.

After breakfast, we set off. The banker sat in the front passenger's seat and Asfehet and I were in the back. We were joined by an armed soldier dressed in civilian clothes, who was on his way to Bahr Dar to join the government troops. I hoped he could give us some more details, but he wasn't very talkative. We'd driven along the highway for several hours, enjoying the comfort of the Landcruiser, when we noticed cars, taxis and minibuses packed with passengers driving in the opposite direction at high speed. As we passed, they wildly waved their hands and signalled for us to change direction.

Noticing only civilian vehicles, we paid little attention but, on approaching Bahr Dar, we began to see soldiers. They were running towards us, gesturing for us to turn back. The traffic flowing out of the town was increasing and, within a few kilometres, we entered a scene of chaos and panic.

Asfehet whimpered.

Everywhere we looked, the surrounds were overrun with soldiers and tanks. Our military passenger leapt from the car and started running towards the centre of the battle. Asfehet was rocking back and forth in her seat, clutching her heart. Her eyes were wide, her breathing shallow, like she was awake in a nightmare. Despite the predominant flow of traffic out of the city, the driver decided to forge on. The banker seemed as curious as I was to witness the cause of this confusion.

Cautiously, we approached the outskirts of Bahr Dar. The banker noticed a couple of his colleagues on the street. When we pulled over, they advised us to make a swift retreat.

We weren't far from Asfehet's family home, so she and I decided to walk there. The car continued into the town. When we arrived at the house, Asfehet's mother and sisters were sitting out the front watching the passing tanks and soldiers. Asfehet's mother almost fainted when she saw her daughter walking towards her.

"Oh Lord! You shouldn't be here! How did you get here? Are you okay?"

Asfehet broke her silence. "Tewodros wanted to come. It's his fault!" I looked at her mother and smiled; not quite as charming as I'd hoped.

We spent the rest of the day and much of the night sitting outside the house, watching the tanks and soldiers crawl through the surrounding fields. Gunfire roared and flared from a distance. Waves of adrenaline surged through our bodies. If we slept at all it was in patches.

After our restless night, loud explosions accompanied the sunrise. More gunfire rattled as I peered outside. The military presence on the streets had dramatically increased. Soldiers were like ants racing up and down the roads and halting on every street corner. I ducked my head each time shots rattled, so close now. We were voluntary indoor prisoners for the remainder of that day.

I regretted my curiosity. I regretted it then and I still do today, with remorse that my insistence caused Asfehet such trauma. I had seriously underestimated the potential danger and was beginning to wonder if I'd signed our death warrants. The fear in the neighbourhood was substantial. Nobody knew how this would end.

As the sun set in a violent sky, we dared to venture out and ask the neighbours for some possible news. In the dim evening haze, we noticed that some of the passing soldiers were drenched (in water, not blood) from head to toe, and many were also covered in mud.

Three sodden soldiers approached. Exhausted and overwrought, they began talking to the elders. They asked for a change of clothes so they could avoid detection among the local civilians. The soldiers spoke very politely. It didn't seem like they were requesting life-saving help. They were so young. And so old at the same time.

This could have been me, I thought.

One of the neighbours (a devout Protestant) invited them into his house. He gave them clothing and offered to dispose of their uniforms. He made tea and fed them, and then he offered them some religious comfort (because he believed God would punish him if he let them leave without passing on the Word). In their

247

state, I'm guessing, any form of comfort was appreciated.

When they emerged, we asked the three soldiers how they got wet. One of them explained, "The northern rebels were advancing quickly. Our general feared that Bahr Dar was about to be captured, so he—he bombed the bridge." He couldn't go on.

"We were defending it," another continued. "Our friends were on it. We had no warning. The river just rose up, taking the bridge with it. Pieces of rock, wood—bodies. We were thrown into the water. We just kept swimming."

They were carrying machine guns and bombs which, much to the disgust of the elders, they gave the children to play with. I picked up one of the bombs and a soldier showed me how to detonate it. It was the first time I'd seen a live bomb up close. I held it fretfully, nervous that it might go off by accident.

We decided to hide the bombs and machine guns behind the house. If attacked, we thought we could defend ourselves. When the Protestant neighbour heard of this, he insisted that everything be returned to the army.

What were we thinking? That we could launch our own private war when the veterans were fleeing? Such is the madness of battle fear.

These soldiers were the first of many defectors. Like zombies, more and more stumbled past. Some looked dazed. Others were clearly angry. All were weary. I looked into their faces, wondering, *What is his story . . . and his . . . and his?* How could so many young people be so broken?

I was wrong to think that my people weren't fighters. But the contrast between passionately defending something you believe in and forced conscription by a government you don't respect starkly highlighted the fear and betrayal these young men expressed.

Among the opposition, the TPLF were fighting to overthrow the Dergue, and the EPLF were fighting for independence from Ethiopia; something they fiercely felt was theirs by right. For them, it was "freedom or death."

I could relate to that, but not so I would kill another for it.

We might come from different tribes, but we are Ethiopia. We are Eritrea. We all endure challenges and celebrate the successes. In that light, we are all people of the world, enduring the peaks and troughs of life. Does war stop the winter? Does it make sense to take the food out of one child's mouth to put it in another's? Can we continue to strike out because we've been struck, when a helping hand would build bridges rather than demolish them?

Battle sounds endured, but only sporadically now. The bridge bombing appeared to have been the climax of the confrontation. The TPLF/EPLF (rebels) lost that front, but they would only regroup and magnify their influence and power in other areas.

In all, we spent about four days in the precarious safety of Asfehet's family house. After that, the military presence subsided enough for people to slowly and cautiously venture out onto the streets. When it was safe enough to travel, Asfehet and I departed, relieved at surviving such an ordeal.

In the weeks following my return to Bure, I sensed a definite change in the atmosphere. Men of high standing in the community, such as teachers, were members of the socialist party. They had always been a familiar sight around town in their sky-blue uniforms, but now they carried rifles, ready for action.

Radio broadcasts (and gossip) told of the TPLF/EPLF advancing and capturing more land each day. Our armed citizens were undertaking training, in preparation for war. The tension was demoralising. I don't think there were enough superstitious spells or saints or traditions to give the people peace of mind. This was really happening—and it was happening now. The crazy thing was that it had been going on for more than two decades . . . just somewhere else.

The TPLF/EPLF were playing cat and mouse with the Dergue. They could have captured Bahr Dar and all the other villages, including Bure, but their strategy was to attack, replenish their supplies and retreat. Then, they'd wait for reinforcements to arrive before launching the next assault. It was a waiting game for everyone and nobody knew when or where the next attack would occur.

The Dergue, on the other hand, was struggling and Mengistu Haile Mariam was not a happy president. He couldn't understand how the TPLF/EPLF could start with just one gun and end up defeating his army, time and time again.

Towards the end of the year, Bishkash and Belachew finished building their house and we all moved in. Traditionally made of wood and mud, with a tin roof, it was a much better setup because it was big enough to cope with the large family.

I still had about three months until my Grade Ten finals, and I discussed my post-graduation plans with Bishkash. We both knew that I wasn't happy living in Bure and now, with war imminent, she advised me to move back to the city.

After living in the village for two years, I was almost 18 years old and ready for the change. My character was more suited to the city. I enjoyed the clamour, the constant movement and frenzy, talking with people, and accessing ways to improve my life; a sure contrast to the quiet remote village of Bure.

The undercurrent of big dreams that had filled my nights was swelling like the tide of fortune (let it be good). Always that voice beckoned me on. Could I leave this country, the only one I'd known, and find that grand adventure? The Italian priests had initially sparked my interest in the world with stories about Italy. I knew that several young people from their Church had been sent abroad to study. Getting overseas definitely appealed as the next goal. With no money or support, it seemed a ridiculous notion. But I'd tried everything else here. The world elsewhere had to have the answer.

Trust would have to build the wings that lifted me to freedom.

I passed Grade Ten (just) and, once the results were awarded, I bade the teachers farewell. My English teacher was particularly interested in knowing my future plans. He was a local man from the highly superstitious Amhara tribe.

When I told him I was moving back to Addis, he took my left hand and turned my palm towards the heavens. His fingers traced over the creases in my palm, from my wrist up to the base of my fingertips. He then raised one finger to his lips and considered his words before speaking. "Young Tewodros," he said gravely, "you see this long deep line here?" He pointed to my palm. "It tells me that you are going to have a long life." He smiled. "But it will not be without struggle. You will be challenged for many years to come, but in the end it will be worth it because you will find your peace." He rolled my fingers closed and tapped his hand firmly against my chest. "Good luck!" he said, and walked off.

I wasn't a superstitious person, but something about his tone made me inclined to believe him.

The day before my intended departure for Addis, I was packing the few things I owned. Padre Roberto had given me a blanket, which I'd lent to my siblings. Knowing how cold it was in the city at night, I went to fetch it.

Belachew saw me carrying it to my room. "What are you doing?" he asked, blocking my way.

"Packing my blanket. Why?"

"It's not your blanket. You gave it to the children. Go and put it back on their bed." he demanded.

"It is my blanket. I gave you and Bishkash the big blanket and *lent* this small one to the children. I will need it in Addis, so I'm taking it back," I retorted.

"You are so selfish! First you take the dressing gown you had given me, and now you want the blanket." Belachew was in a fighting mood and wasn't going to back down.

"Look, Belachew, I'm tired. I don't want to fight, okay? So, I'll give you a choice. Do you want to keep the large blanket or this small one?"

"No! We're keeping both of them!"

I tried to get past him, but he pushed me backwards. The whole family was watching now. My two stepsisters, Mulu and Kidest, started crying.

I moaned, "Just leave me alone, Belachew. Tomorrow, after I'm gone, you and your family will never have to see me again."

He pushed me a second time and we wrestled with the blanket. I couldn't believe his reaction. Mid-scuffle, his fists bunched up ready to punch me. I looked to my mother for help, but she just watched passively. The children kept screaming.

Dropping the blanket, I ran out the back door and onto the road with him bellowing in close pursuit, "I feed you, put shelter over your head and take care of you and this is how you return the favour?"

I'd known Belachew to be softly spoken and gentle by nature. I'd never seen this side of him. I ran up the road to a neighbour's house. She was the maid for one of my teachers. She sometimes came to my mother's house for coffee and I knew she liked me. She welcomed me in and calmed me down, allowing me to stay the night; my last in Bure.

I awoke early the next morning and waited until Belachew had gone to work before returning to the house to collect my belongings. I told Bishkash how upset I was, not only by Belachew, but by her lack of support. She stood there, holding Kidest closely. Not one word did she say in support of me. Her gaze was cold. We really were strangers, it seemed. I asked her to give me the blanket so I could leave in peace.

"Tewodros, I can't. I will have a problem with my husband if I allow you to take it," she said.

"What kind of mother are you?" I asked. "I've done *nothing* to hurt you and you treat me like a villain. One day, you might need me. You will come to me for help. What will you expect of me then? You can't treat me like this and think I am "the son" and should always show respect—no matter what. You treat me like nothing? Then that is what you are to me, too. There is nothing left."

I was panting as I entered my room, shattered that even in this last moment there was no peace. Stunned by betrayal and loneliness, it took me a moment to notice that all my belongings had disappeared. When I turned around, Bishkash was holding the blanket. Handing it to me, she mumbled, "The rest of your things are at the neighbour's."

I took the blanket from her and left. I didn't look back. The child in her arms was not me—it never had been.

After collecting my belongings, I walked into town. Once more, I was travelling away from my mother on the back of a truck, only this time it was of my choosing. Leaving my things with the driver, I confirmed our departure. There was time for one final walk around the village.

The milk of this country life had soured. The honey embittered my senses. *Was* I cursed? A worthless devil? After all, I had nothing to show for myself—not on anyone else's terms. Would my bright future be just a mirage in the wilderness?

Trust, Teddy. It's time to look forward now.

Blind with the pain of a wounded lion, I was no longer sure of the way ahead.

14

THE PAPER CHASE

For two days, the rattling bus crested hilltop after hilltop, bringing us ever nearer to the city.

My hardened heart ricocheted within. I'd seen what the simple life brings. Out in the villages, country people chose one thing, one life—but then, that was all they knew. Their minds didn't grow. It was too easy for a corrupt government to manipulate them. They had pride and they had fear, but they didn't have knowledge and it kept them poor.

I wasn't afraid of lack any more. I wasn't limited by my need for acceptance. I'd forged my own strength now. I was voracious to make Addis my city, to make my life my victory.

Back amid the city bustle, I checked into the Gurage-run hostel in Piassa. There was a new cook called Turunesh. She was a tall, friendly woman whose cheeks swelled like harvest fruit when she smiled. Friends from the start, we chatted in Guraginya, while I ate food at her discounted rate.

My primary focus was to find a permanent place of residence.

No more begging or starving for me. If I was to build a foundation for grand new days, I had to have a place I could call home. Just a clean, cheap room to rent would be enough. *Then* I felt I could achieve anything.

Every day I went looking, listening to the locals and meeting with street brokers, who could get you anything from tickets for the soccer stadium to cars to business contacts. Instead of running an office, brokers congregated in the local areas, usually under the shade of a tree, on a street corner or in front of particular buildings. There, they waited for business to come to them. The benefits were twofold: they had no overheads and, more importantly, they were able to maintain a constant street presence, keeping tabs on their prospects.

The next step in my plan for security was to get a job. I still had to be wary of army conscription but I thought that, with so many young men involved in the war, I could easily find work. Equipped with my Grade Ten school certificate, I almost felt smug about my imminent independence.

Employer after employer machined-gunned the same questions at me:

"Do you have a Year Twelve certificate?"

"Do you have a driver's licence?"

"Do you have any work experience?"

"Do you have any references?"

"Do you seriously think I will give you a job when you have none of these?"

Clearly, I'd have to accumulate more official papers (which would incur more costs) before I could leap into this grown-up world. So, every effort went into changing my circumstances. I didn't rest if there was something I could learn, ask, do, or practise.

Late one afternoon, after another full day of knockbacks, I went to the kitchen to chat with Turunesh. She was preparing *kitfo*,[1] and

---

1. Spicy minced beef (sometimes eaten raw), often served with cottage cheese. (Amharic)

looked up as I stuck my head around the corner. "Tewodros. How's it going?"

"Fine," I replied flatly. "I'm still looking for somewhere to live."

"If I hear of anywhere I'll let you know," she said, wiping her hands on a towel before handing me a glass of juice.

I took a sip and then saw Turunesh's bright face become sombre. "Tewodros, you had a visitor today."

Not a welcome visitor, I guessed.

"It's your mother," she said.

My mother?

"And she's renting a room here tonight. She's waiting for you upstairs."

My fresh liberation—invaded already! "Here? But I don't want to see her. I told you what she and my stepfather did."

"Yes, but she's your mother. You only have one. Please go and see her," Turunesh coaxed.

I stood with my arms folded.

"Please, Tewodros. At least find out why she has come to see you."

I walked away.

"She's in Room Twelve," Turunesh called after me.

Reluctantly, I dragged my feet to Room Twelve and knocked on the door. There was no answer. I knocked again, jiggled the handle and realised it wasn't locked. I quietly opened the door and peeked through the crack. Bishkash was lying on the bed with my stepsister, Kidest. She looked up and gestured for me to enter.

"How did you find me?" I asked, between gritted teeth.

"A relative told me you were here," she replied timidly.

"And why did you come?" I knew this visit would be more than just a greeting in passing.

"There is nothing I want from you. . . ," she faltered.

Was she remembering the harsh words of my departure from Gojjam?

She went on, ". . . except—you promised to take me to those priests."

Long before the argument over the blanket, I'd suggested that the priests might be able to assist her and the family. Given the tense nature of our farewell, I never thought she'd ask me to follow it through.

I bit back my anger, "Okay, but when I've done that, I don't want to see you again. Do you understand?"

She bowed her head and nodded.

"Tomorrow is Sunday, so I will take you to church then. Be ready by eleven o'clock." I left the room quickly, without waiting for a reply.

It wasn't out of some newfound maturity that I agreed to help her; it was out of fear. Although I didn't believe in the supernatural world, I'd never really tested it and wasn't ready to now. If I disrespected her wishes, someone might curse me. Her family . . . her neighbours . . . the whole village may well curse me. I decided it was best to follow through on my promise.

The next morning, I collected my charges and together we took a minibus to see Father Habtemariam. I had called him the night before, so he was expecting us. It's sad to say, but I felt embarrassed introducing my mother to the priest. He escorted us inside to one of the offices for a private meeting.

On hearing the reason for our visit, Father Habtemariam promised to discuss it with his colleagues, but he was unable to offer immediate assistance.

Next, we met with Padre Roberto. I was relieved to see that Mass had finished before we arrived. The large gathering of people outside the church allowed us to slip by unnoticed. I walked ahead of Bishkash, hoping no one would know she was with me.

Padre Roberto was already aware of her situation, so I only needed to update him. Like Father Habtemariam, he wanted time to talk with the others.

My mother's journey to the city had proved fruitless. Her eyes were blank with disappointment.

Wanting my obligation to end, I bought her a bus ticket back to Bure for the following morning. Ironically, we slept in, only aroused by an argument from the alley. I'd grown accustomed to waking up with such disturbances. They were mostly between prostitutes and their clients. They were always about money.

We raced the few blocks to Merkato bus terminal. As I dashed ahead, one thought filled my mind: She can't miss that bus!

At the terminal, I frantically searched for the westbound bus to Gojjam. It was already in motion and heading for the exit gates, right beside me. I jumped out in front of it and frantically waved my mother's ticket at the windscreen, signalling for the driver to stop.

I turned to urge her on. She was struggling in her long dress with Kidest on her hip. "Hurry up!" I cried, since they were still a few metres away.

The bus slowed down, but didn't halt. The driver's attendant jumped off as Bishkash came alongside the door. He helped me push them on from behind, and then leapt aboard after them as the doors swung shut. I could see Bishkash holding onto the rail through the bus window, struggling to keep her balance.

This time, I was the one left standing in the dust.

She didn't look back.

Through Turunesh's connections, I was able to move out of the hostel about two weeks later. Her friend, Belaynesh, lived alone in one of the better streets of Sebara Babur,[2] and she offered me her spare room for 60 *birr*[3] a month—a reasonable price for the area. I'd saved some money from selling clothes and felt excited to make this move.

Belaynesh reminded me of a well-worn handbag. She was a middle-aged woman with saggy pouches under her eyes, which she attempted to cover with heavy powder. Her leathery skin cracked the make-up, especially around her mouth when she smiled.

---

2. Translates to mean "broken train area."
3. US$13 (approximately).

Belaynesh had been married and divorced numerous times, and I'd been told that in her prime she was very beautiful, and quite wealthy. But life hadn't been kind to her, and now she spent most of her time gambling and drinking.

She ran her own bar from home. The front door doubled as the entrance to the business. My small room was to the left of the bar, and hers was to the right. Unlike her room, mine didn't have a door that opened directly onto the street, so I had to enter through the bar. Outside my room was the wash area and toilets, which her customers also used.

Three prostitutes worked there. The bar was only small, yet burst rowdily into life at night. I tried to stay out as late as possible most nights, partly because it was difficult to sleep with that noise, but mostly because the prostitutes would come into my room between jobs, wanting to talk about their sleazy customers.

Despite the regular disruption, I quickly settled in. I had my own single bed. Reflecting my philosophy for attaining quality, I bought new crisp white sheets, and I decorated the room with wallpaper I'd collected from the markets.

I knew education was the real key to a better life, so I was excited to be studying Grade Eleven at night school.

It felt good to pick up the city rhythm again. In my spare time, I enjoyed meeting friends or going to the church.

Just when I thought I'd seen enough shocking things in life, I looked up one night and there was Belaynesh in her nightgown, standing in my doorway. She said the prostitutes were using her room for business. Then, she crawled into my bed, wrapped her arms around me and called me her son. But her intentions held no motherly love.

As she fumbled for me in the dark, I pushed her away time and time again. "Please Belaynesh! If you need somewhere to sleep I don't mind, but stop touching me!" I begged.

"I'm just holding you. I'm not touching you. Don't worry my

son," she said calmly, and then continued running her hands over my body.

"Belaynesh, please. Don't!" But it seemed the more I pushed her away the more determined she became, and the tussle continued. I lay rigid, wanting to flee, but where would I go? This room was more than a convenient roof over my head: it represented my independence. I teetered on the edge of the bed, shrugging her off and pulling the sheets tighter. I spent the night wrapped like an Egyptian mummy. Needless to say, sleep was sporadic.

This occurred frequently!

The next morning she would inevitably ignore me, pretending nothing had happened. One day, I came home to find the wallpaper partially ripped. Of course it had to be Belaynesh. In a fury, I confronted her but she insisted it was one of the prostitutes.

Maybe this was God's cheeky way of punishing me for the time I lied to Padre Roberto about being forced to live with prostitutes.

Hailu was still residing at the church. He was as full of dreams for the future as I was, and we would walk in the nicer parts of the city, talking of our plans to travel. Given that most of the positive influences in his life had come from the Catholic Church, he was keen to visit Italy. I wanted to go everywhere, which really meant *anywhere* else.

The priests asked Hailu to run errands around the city or to nearby villages. He usually drove a church vehicle on such occasions. He often dropped by my place to see if I wanted to join him, but with all my late nights of study, staying out to avoid the noisy bar and then Belaynesh interfering with my sleep, I was still in bed and he'd have to wake me.

But there was another reason that I didn't rise until mid-afternoon. When Hailu quizzed me on my sleeping habits, to my shame I explained that I couldn't afford to eat more than one meal, so I tried to sleep through the other two. He hid his concern, not wanting to embarrass me further.

Whenever I was with Hailu, everything felt better. I don't know if he felt protective of me, but he certainly showed me that life could be fun.

Our expeditions were always refreshing and we tried to get the most out of any opportunity presented to us. One time, a priest asked Hailu to buy him a necklace with a crucifix on it. The priest told Hailu how much he expected to pay and gave him the money. We visited almost every shop with religious goods in the area and, eventually, we bargained hard with one dealer who had the best price. The priest got what he expected, and the money we saved paid for a bus trip to a part of Ethiopia we'd never seen before.

On one such excursion, we were returning to Addis when I saw Bishkash trying to board our bus. I was sitting in a window seat towards the front, and watched as she battled the crowd to get to the bus door. While I felt sad, I had no desire to help her. She kept struggling until the bus pulled away, leaving her behind.

What coincidence brought me there on that day, at that time? I felt like I was in another dimension, seeing what my life would have been had I not been determined to pursue a different path.

Belaynesh's intrusive behaviour was ripping through my resolve as well as my wallpaper. I knew how hard it was to find accommodation, so I didn't want to risk being tossed out on the street. I just kept trying to avoid her.

One evening, Turunesh stopped by. She was so incensed at her friend's behaviour that she offered for me to stay with her family until other arrangements could be made.

I didn't hesitate. That night, I left my tiny tarnished retreat and moved into her basic one-room house (it was literally a roof over four walls and nothing else), in an alley off the main road through Gedem-sefer.[4]

---

4. Translates to mean "monastery area," named so because it is near Saint George's cathedral.

Gedem-sefer was a particularly noisy area. I was woken up every morning by heavy traffic, especially the trucks that passed along the main road nearby. Their straining engines shook through the ground, vibrating the dirt floor on which I slept.

If it wasn't the trucks waking me, it was the neighbour's wretched rooster, which wandered into the house and started scratching the ground near my head. If the rooster didn't turn up, an ancient man on his blow-horn certainly did. He trumpeted his way around the area, informing the residents of local deaths that had occurred in the previous 24 hours. He passed by at sunrise every single morning without fail, blowing his horn, then shouting out the deceased's name and funeral details.

This strange little shelter was home to Turunesh, her two children and their alcoholic father, who drifted in and out of their lives as it suited him. I soon discovered that Turunesh's son was out of control. Although he didn't disturb me in the mornings like everything else in the place, he ran wild during the day and late into the night, despite his mother's best efforts to discipline him.

I bit my tongue each time I discovered that he'd rummaged through my belongings and taken things (one of my pet hates). In the missions, we were each given our own things and made responsible for them. I'd grown accustomed to "mine" being mine, and expected that no one else would touch my property without my consent. After having my possessions violated so many times before, I was constantly frustrated over this invasion of privacy.

I had to move out.

Over the following months, I moved from place to place trying to find somewhere more permanent to live. I became a familiar face to the local brokers, whose tips put me in plenty of temporary accommodation, but nowhere stable.

Eventually, I was recommended to an elderly lady who had a room to rent. She was a childless widow who lived in a small house in Ras Desta-sefer; a decent suburb. Her house was like most others I'd stayed in: a long rectangular shape, with the narrow end of the rectangle facing out onto the street. There was only one entrance that led into the small front room, from which there was a door leading to the rest of the house. Since this front room became mine, the old lady had to walk through it each time she arrived or left the house.

The kitchen was at the far end, but it was a shared space with the smelly drop toilet. On seeing the condition of it, I refused to prepare or eat any food there. The toilet was already full from years of use. As often as possible, I tried to get to public toilets, although they were just as bad. In emergencies, I was forced to use this one, but had to close my eyes and block my nose to keep from emptying my stomach as well as my bowels! Despite this, I finally found some peace with my own room, my own bed and no one around to disturb me.

I lived with the old lady for almost two years.

One day, while on some errands, I recognised the neighbourhood of Saba's brother, Robel. I think I surprised myself as much as him that I was able to remember his house. I'd only been there once, just before my father sent me to the Dese Mission.

I spent a couple of hours with Robel that afternoon. It was obvious that he had little time for Solomon. He'd seen firsthand how Saba suffered, and always hoped she would leave her husband for good. (She had already left him several times due to his violence and alcoholism, only to return.) Robel was so angry with Solomon for all the pain he'd caused. "He shouldn't be allowed to get away with it," he complained.

He informed me that, as well as teaching at the Black Lion Hospital, Solomon was working at a clinic with a man called Mengestabe, a highly respected medical technician. Since Mengestabe owned all the medical equipment, Solomon was forced to maintain a good working relationship with him. Robel suggested I introduce myself to Mengestabe and ask him to convince my father to help me out financially.

Why not? I thought. Robel's strong emotions over Solomon's wrong-doings made me feel justified in trying. I did deserve better. All my efforts had increased my confidence, and I didn't think he could hurt me anymore.

Early the next day, I went to the area of Addis called Mexico where the clinic was supposedly located. After walking the streets, I eventually found two large red iron gates displaying the name, Santa Petros Clinic. They were locked.

Some locals told me that the clinic opened at 2pm, but Doctor Solomon wasn't usually there before 4pm. I returned the following afternoon in time to speak with Mengestabe, before opening hours. I waited outside until a man came to open the gates. Thin, with a grey moustache, he looked about fifty years old and seemed to fit Robel's description.

"*Aboy*[5] Mengestabe?" I asked.

"Yes?" he replied, as he hunched over the lock, trying hastily to open the gates.

"My name is Tewodros. I am the eldest son of Doctor Solomon."

He paused and stood upright. "Doctor Solomon's . . . son? But I've never even heard of you." He looked at me, confused. "I know Mehari, Tinsae and Johannes, but I have never heard him speak of Tewodros."

"I'm sure he doesn't," I said simply.

Mengestabe invited me inside and asked me to clarify the mystery. He listened patiently, though he was somewhat daunted by Solomon's secret. He offered to talk with him about arranging some financial support.

Hopeful, yet cautious, I visited the clinic again a few days later. Mengestabe met me straightaway.

"Tewodros, I'm not really sure whom to believe." He was sitting by the receptionist's desk, tapping his pen on the table. "Your father's account is quite different to your own."

5. Mister. Polite greeting for an older gentleman. (Tigrinya)

Why was I not surprised?

"What did he tell you?" I asked. *This has to be good,* I thought.

"He told me you were a lazy unmotivated son, who had given his family nothing but trouble. He said you were not interested in studying or doing anything useful with your life."

"Mengestabe, my father is a very good liar."

"He is a good friend of mine and I know the family well. I'm sorry, but I'm not sure I can believe your version of events," he said.

"If you need confirmation of my story, I can arrange for the priests who took care of me in my younger years to come and testify to his bad behaviour," I said. "They can tell you that my father lied to them about sending me off to school when, in fact, he sent me to a detention camp, *and* they can tell you that he refused to pay for my education."

"Well, all right. Yes, I would like to meet these priests," he said.

Some days later, Padre Roberto and Father Tesfaldete (from Dese mission, now living in Addis) accompanied me to the clinic and confirmed my story. They did their best to point out my unfortunate experiences due to Solomon's manipulations.

Gradually, Mengestabe understood and vowed to make my father take responsibility. He promised to deduct 100 *birr*[6] a month from Solomon's salary. I could collect it from the secretary, Hanna, who also happened to be Mengestabe's niece.

During my few encounters with Hanna, I learned that she too had endured much hardship. We formed a special bond, sharing our stories and offering each other encouragement.

She relayed messages between her uncle and me, and strengthened his support and interest in my situation. She even suggested to Doctor Solomon that he should treat me well, since I was grown up now and might take action against him. I didn't know this at the time, but something must have worked because the new arrangement seemed hassle-free.

---

6. US$22 (approximately).

Not long after we'd become friends, I invited Hanna to visit my place. She was impressed that I'd set myself up so well with so little money.

Slowly, I was building a life of quality. I scrimped and saved to buy the next special or necessary item. Each possession had its place. The dignified little world I'd created in that room reflected my commitment to rise above circumstance.

Since Bure, my cough had sunk into bronchitis, making me quite ill. Hanna informed Mengestabe that I needed a doctor. He x-rayed my chest free of charge but, on examining the results, he insisted that I wait for a consultation with Doctor Solomon.

How would my father react when he saw *my* name on his patient list?

He arrived.

I was called into his office by one of the nurses. Hanna gave me a nod of encouragement. I entered, and sat down in the chair across from his desk.

Silently, he walked over to me and checked my pulse. (I wondered if he noticed my anxious heart pounding at twice the normal speed.) He examined my throat and then carried out a standard checkup.

As he worked, I looked at his large dark hands—the same hands that beat me as a child. My chest rattled as I gasped for air. I tried to block it all out.

He returned to his chair and handed me a prescription. I realised that this gesture terminated his attention, so I left the room. Not a single word was exchanged between us.

It was a great relief when the cough cleared up altogether.

But my peace of mind was rocked soon afterwards. Father Tesfaldete told me that Doctor Solomon was up to his old tricks. He was planning to send me away to an army cadet camp where I would be clothed and fed, and he would no longer have to pay me the 100 *birr* each month.

Now that I was healthy, I decided to increase my efforts to find work, and fully gain my independence from him. I couldn't risk falling victim to another wicked scheme from that man.

The priests who'd been devoted to me for so long were getting excited at my prospects. One day, Father Tesfaldete offered to pay for driving lessons. Of course, I agreed! A driver's licence would almost certainly get me employed. I marvelled at how each change for the better invited more. When you have nothing, you have *nothing*! But when fortune turns, good luck begins to flow.

It was every young man's dream in the city to get behind the wheel. Driving around in a flashy car, catching the attention of the girls . . . was that for me? Maybe! It would certainly give me more of the independence and freedom I craved.

Acquiring a driver's licence in Ethiopia is a three-step process.

Step One requires passing a written test. With the first instalment from Father Tesfaldete, I purchased the driving manual and studied road rules, day and night, making sure I knew the book, cover to cover. I passed the test with ease on my first attempt. Father Tesfaldete shared in my pride at this first accomplishment.

The second stage meant getting behind the wheel, at driving school. Students were only allowed to drive within the compound. Different obstacle courses tested our abilities at weaving the car through curves and around objects.

I was aware that, no matter how well I drove through the various courses, there was no way to pass without bribing the instructor. My main goal at this stage was just to learn how to avoid an accident. Whenever Father Tesfaldete gave me some money, I would go down to the driving school and take a lesson. Sometimes this was weekly; other times, lessons were a couple of weeks apart.

The car that I learned to drive in was a little Fiat, so tiny you could virtually put it in your back pocket. Not quite the flashy look I'd imagined.

Stage Three required driving in traffic, with a licenced driver. I had to hire an instructor and a car (this time a Volkswagen Beetle), and we entered the traffic flow around the soccer stadium.

By now, I was eager to complete the experience. As I'd anticipated, a bribe would secure my success. So, after just a couple of trips around the city, I slipped the instructor his "due" and the licence was mine.

In all, the process took about six months. Father Tesfaldete was very happy to see his contribution put some spin on my wheels of success.

When visiting Ethiopia last year, I had to renew my driver's licence. Renewal requires effectively negotiating the obstacle course from Stage Two. While I was driving, the instructor kept shouting conflicting directions at inappropriate times, to make me nervous (and to make me realise that he wasn't going to pass me without a bribe). Some things never change.

Since the battle in Bahr Dar and the bombing of the Nile Bridge, the guerrilla forces were winning more and more skirmishes against the government.

By early 1991, not long after I left Gojjam and returned to Addis Ababa, the EPLF and TPLF forces had defeated the Dergue and taken control of the Gojjam region. From there, they took control of the Welo and Oromo regions, thereby encircling Addis and placing the guerrilla forces in prime positions to pounce on the capital.

Tension in the capital mounted as tanks and armed soldiers became a common sight on the streets.

Although defeat seemed inevitable, Mengistu's addresses to the public became more dramatic. In what was to become his final address to the public, he brought the nation to a standstill with a television broadcast. It seemed the whole country was holding its breath. Everyone ceased work at midday and gathered to listen, not knowing what to expect. I was with friends in a Piassa café.

Mengistu presented himself in full military attire, wearing dark sunglasses and clutching a long sword. He gestured with the sword, fiercely and often. Did he think he was rallying us to action? He called us to fight to the very end. He expressed his disappointment in us. He loved us, he said, and wanted to pave our (his) way with gold. But if we would rather be ruled by these donkey shits, then we must be worthless, too. Impassioned with his own vision of righteousness, he implied that he might follow in the footsteps of his hero, Emperor Tewodros, and take his own life.

Several times throughout the speech, my friends and I turned to each other in amazement: would he really commit suicide on national television?

I knew the city was surrounded, and wondered how bad things could get. There was talk in the café that, if pushed, Mengistu might order an identification check on all residents of the city, whereby anyone of Eritrean or Tigrayan descent would be shot dead, on the spot. That made me the target of double crosshairs, since I was a direct descendent of both ethnic groups. There was nowhere to run. Each corner I turned might reveal a gun barrel pointed at me. I was as interested as everyone else in our country's fate, but I had to go carefully. *A mouse that wants to die goes to sniff the cat's nose.*[7]

Subsequently, in a final attempt to prevent the government's inevitable downfall, Mengistu rounded up 2000 young men from the city streets (including some of my friends) and sent them to fight in the northern region. In years gone by, two of my mother's brothers had been sent to fight in the war against Sudan; they were never seen or heard from again. How incredibly lucky I was to slip through these nets of capture once more.

Mengistu's desperate efforts were in vain. In May 1991, the EPLF and TPLF entered Asmara and Addis Ababa respectively. Mengistu fled with his family, first for Kenya, and then to Zimbabwe where

7. Ethiopian proverb.

President Robert Mugabe offered them protection. Mengistu remains there still.

The Ethiopian court has since passed a verdict, finding him guilty (*in absentia*) of genocide.[8] I doubt though that we will ever see justice for his crimes.

Strangely enough, I'd been fascinated by this man. I didn't admire him, but he was such a controlling figure in our lives. I had a photograph of him presenting my father with his university degree. I wondered how an uneducated person like Mengistu could become so powerful. If this stupid man had dominated a nation, then surely I could gain some power over my own life.

By early June, the EPLF were in charge of the northern province of Eritrea; aspirations for independence were still paramount. The TPLF controlled Ethiopia. They allied with other rebel groups, and collectively became known as the EPRDF[9] (the current governing party of Ethiopia).

Seizing control doesn't necessarily mean holding success. The TPLF leader, Meles Zenawi, learned the true state of country's finances. Ethiopia's fuel supplies were severely depleted. The treasury held only 96 million *birr*, and the country's foreign exchange had been plundered by the Dergue, leaving only 3.6 million *birr* behind.[10]

The TPLF/EPRDF were inspired by Marxism and Leninism. During the early 1990s, Western ideas of democracy and human rights were grafted onto their principles. This won instant favour in the West, where the Ethiopian and Eritrean victors were hailed as examples of Africa's new (and improved) leaders.

Time would tell.

I viewed the new government with as much trepidation as before. After all, I had only known life under the dictatorship of Mengistu and the Dergue.

---

8. "Profile: Mengistu Haile Mariam," *BBC News Online*, 12 December 2006.
9. Ethiopian Popular Revolutionary Democratic Front.
10. US$21,000,000 and US$800,000 (approximately)

At least there was peace. By ejecting Mengistu's regime, the country was released from his stranglehold. For the first time, people dared to hope for change.

In the midst of this, I too was primed to leap ahead. Just show me the way!

A friend from Church remarked how easy it had become to obtain an import/export licence under the new government. Could this be the exit pass I needed to leave Ethiopia?

The licences were issued by the Ministry of Commerce. The very next day, I stopped by its central office in the city to register my name. An old man sat behind a desk, with a large notebook in front of him. He displayed the pages of his notebook, revealing a never-ending waiting list of names. With an unsteady hand, he wrote mine all the way at the bottom. (Is anything ever easy?) I should check the front window daily, he said. Once my name appeared, I could make an application.

Day after day, I returned, tightly wound with anticipation. My mind played out future possibilities. I am not a patient person. I was exploding internally with too many ideas going nowhere.

Weeks passed.

When my name still did not appear, my church friend suggested an alternative approach. I should talk to one particular man at the Ministry of Commerce, who was known to be "very helpful"; by this I understood that he accepted bribes.

I didn't have enough money to bribe him. How could I get his attention? What would it take to get inside the system? Then, I hit on an idea. I would need to subtly become a familiar face to him so that when I approached him to discuss the licence, he would be open to it.

So, I started "bumping" into him at restaurants and paid for his meals (okay, maybe not so subtle). I even went to his ping-pong games and cheered him on (pathetic, I know—but I was desperate!).

Then, one evening after he finished work, I waited outside his office. By now, he knew who I was and he greeted me warmly. We went to a nearby restaurant where we were joined by the restaurant owner's daughter.

After the meal, the three of us moved on to a bar and had drinks. It was still early. I noticed that Mr. Helpful and our companion had taken a liking to each other. I paid for all their drinks and left them alone to enjoy the evening.

The next day I went to his office, hoping to talk about the licence.

"Tewodros, my friend. How are you?" he greeted me warmly.

"Fine. You?"

"Oh, I'm very well!" He winked at me. "So tell me, what can I do for you today?"

At last, a way forward.

He gave me a list of instructions. "You will need to get a document from the local council stating that you don't have any outstanding debts. I suggest you go to the countryside for this paper, because those regions get priority over city residents. What type of licence do you want?"

I stopped scribbling his instructions on a scrap of paper. "I want an import/export licence."

"Yes, but *what* do you want to import? You can have a licence for textiles, electronics, specialised equipment and machinery, foodstuffs. . . . " He looked up at the ceiling, trying to recall the various categories. "Choose just a couple for your application. Bring all those papers to this office. We'll check your bank balance and, if all is correct, your licence will be issued."

It sounded too simple.

While walking home, I considered import options. Maybe textiles and electronics were best. I'd observed trading in Merkato, and thought such goods might be the easiest to sell. I hadn't visited Dese since I'd left the mission, so I decided it was a suitably remote place to gather the documentation.

In Dese, I had to apply to the *kebele*[11] for relevant papers. Somehow I had to prove that I was a local. I asked for a letter of support from a business advisory association. Of course, I had to become a member with them and pay an annual fee.

The *kebele* subjected me to an interview, full of questions. I stumbled through most of these, filled out more papers, and was told processing would take a couple of days.

Triumphant, I returned to Addis and showed Mr. Helpful my documents of approval.

"Fine," he said, perusing the details. "Now you need to submit these to the office downstairs, along with your bank account details."

"Er, I might have a small problem with that," I admitted, hesitantly. "I don't have the required 10,000 *birr*[12] in my account."

He leaned forward and gestured for me to come closer. "That's easily solved. You only need to provide the officers with a copy, not the original." He lowered his voice further. "Photocopy the personal details page from your bank book and then find someone who has enough money in their account and photocopy their account-balance page."

"Are you sure?"

"Absolutely."

Amazing!

I left his office and went to a printing shop. While duplicating my details, I noticed the man next to me photocopying his account-balance page. He had the right amount of money so I asked if he could make an extra copy for me. He agreed and handed one over, which I included in my batch.

Back at the office, I delivered my documents, along with the 300 *birr*[13] application fee. *Deep breath . . . wish my hands would stop shaking. . . .*

---

11. Local council/government authority for the local area. (Amharic)
12. US$2000 (approximately).
13. US$65 (approximately).

The process had taken me across the country and back but, finally, it was done.

All my life I'd been waiting for such words to have meaning: finally, eventually, at last. And now they were my present! The licence was issued. I had a comfortable place to live. I was studying. And although I still relied on money from the priests (supplemented by the proceeds from the sale of Italian made clothes that Padre gave me), I no longer struggled through each day just focussing on my survival. I felt a sense of hope.

About to become a man of the world, I discussed my options with Padre Roberto and he felt that, given my personal situation and the uncertain political and economic future of the country, it was probably wise for me to establish a new life overseas. He agreed to help with the cost of a passport.

Ah—more forms. I didn't mind. Chasing paper made chasing dreams more tangible. I wasted no time in applying for a passport at Immigration. Unless you were rich or had the right connections, this item was almost unattainable.

When I handed my documents to the officer at the counter, I made sure that I included my newly obtained import/export licence. Ethiopian passports indicate a person's occupation on the details page. I'd been told that if the words "student" or "unemployed" appeared there, then the embassies would reject it outright. With the licence, I could write the word "merchant," giving a very different impression.

"Where is the document that shows you have no criminal record?" the officer asked after flicking through the papers. *Wah!* I didn't have this document yet. With so many papers to sift through, why did he notice its absence? I gave him a vague answer about having recently moved to Addis Ababa, and then changed the topic. It worked. He stamped my papers and told me to come back in one week to begin processing.

Through Hanna's contacts, I got my first job at a video shop in the city. I was about nineteen years old at the time and had been living in Addis for twelve months. As the store driver, I was given the keys to the owner's Karmann Ghia. It wasn't exactly James Bond material, but it was low set with beautiful curves.

My duties included delivering and collecting of films, as well as running errands. I learned how to edit video footage and a range of other film production skills. I especially liked going to the airport to collect parcels for the store owner and clear any issues with customs.

After fetching the delivery, I often stood in the arrival lounge and watched as people r3eturned from overseas. What exotic places had they seen? What delectable food had they tasted? What magical mementos were bursting from the suitcases they were dragging?

How different life became when I had money. I felt successful, but it was more than financial stability, more than a sense of responsibility and purpose—I felt *normal!*

I enjoyed doing normal things, like going to a café with friends for coffee, going to the movies or dancing in the evening. Compared to all I'd endured, this was like being a member of an exclusive club.

Now I had all the acceptable symbols of the good life: car (well, not exactly mine—but close enough!), shoes, clothes, and money. It was an expected part of social etiquette to take girls out for macchiato and cake. All these things felt comfortable, but still something was lacking. I considered the great love that might await me . . . someone who wanted more substance from life than merely what was expected or acceptable. Was this what I was missing? Perhaps.

I passed beggars on the street. *That used to be me.* The thought sickened me. I reached into my pockets for money, but from my new perspective I understood that it was impossible to help them by giving a few coins (which I did anyway). How many were there? How much could one give?

The more contrasts I experienced, the more I wondered how life could be so different from one side of the street to the other. Life is not about luck. It's not about being black or white. Hard times change you; it's true. Anyone who has endured great suffering will know this. But do we learn to move forward, even with a limp, or do we pull back from the pain, searching for safety? Feeling safe can mean remaining within a system that keeps you poor. That's not life, either.

Some people wake to breakfast and others to uncertainty—yet we are one world. Having lived on both sides, I recognised that overcoming poverty needs everyone's awareness. I wanted to use my experience to make a difference to others. I wasn't sure about the details, but it was certain that I would have to leave Ethiopia to find the way.

Feverishly, I gathered information about living overseas. Consulting relatives, I learned that my mother's cousin, Mebrat, had moved from Eritrea to Egypt and, by all reports, was faring well (better than she could ever do in Eritrea).

Not long after I learned this, my passport application was approved. I chose to follow in Mebrat's footsteps and go to Egypt: a magnet for adventurers since the days when Alexandria was the centre of the ancient trading world.

I visited Mengestabe at the clinic. Perhaps he could convince my father to help fund my plane ticket. Did Solomon reply, "Ah, my son, how impressive that you have dreams. How can I help?" Not quite. Apparently he thought I'd hatched a scheme to get my hands on more of his money.

After almost a month of negotiation, Mengestabe coerced my father to comprise. Solomon would supply my airfare on two conditions: that Mengestabe bought the round trip ticket (that way I couldn't exchange it for money later); and that I send the ticket back once I reached Egypt. In other words, my father was sending me out of Ethiopia and (he was hoping) out of his life forever.

I didn't care anymore. His less-than-kingly generosity reflected on him, not me. By whatever means, I would be free. I accepted.

Next, I lodged a business visa application at the Egyptian Embassy. Hoping to impress them with quantity, I took the letter from the Dese business association, the new business licence, the medical record from the Santa Petros Clinic, as well as my passport, and presented them all in a special folder I'd borrowed from Hailu.

I was almost too nervous to sit in my neatly pressed trousers and borrowed suit jacket. There were a few other applicants waiting for the Consular-General to return from lunch. I was second in line.

Not long after his return, I was called into his office. He was a middle-aged man with an upward-curling moustache that mocked his frown, which grew as he perused my application. Peering from behind dark glasses, he fired a 20-minute barrage of questions at me.

The receptionist sat beside him and translated, allowing me time to consider my responses to each question. When this concluded, I was sent to the waiting room. No decisions were delivered until all interviews were completed. I must have reinvented the meaning of "impatience" in multiple languages, including hand gestures.

Late afternoon, the receptionist emerged from the Consular-General's office and called all the visa applicants, one by one, to her desk. The applicant before me was rejected, so when my name was called, I approached haltingly.

"Do you have the money to pay for the visa?"

"Yes," I said, and fumbled while handing her the money.

"Good," she said, after counting it. "Come back this time next week to collect your passport and visa."

Do you cherish a moment when your life changed, grandly and forever? Can you comprehend what it feels like to be living in a vacuum and, suddenly, to breathe? Almost disbelieving it, I could only whisper, *I am free.* The taste of those words was like the nectar of life.

I had to share this. I had to tell someone else, just to be sure it was true. Padre Roberto would understand. I raced to the church to find him. He was standing under a tree, surrounded by a group of young children who were giggling and poking his globe-like belly. When he noticed me, he stepped away from the group to greet me. The children tailed him all the way and continued to joke with each other.

I blurted out the good news. He beamed with delight, and he scooped me into a clumsy bear hug.

"Hallelujah!" he shouted in my ear, and then released me before placing both hands firmly on my shoulders. "I've been waiting for more than five years to hear such a triumph from you and—oh, wonderful day—it has arrived!"

Hearing him say it back to me, I was struck dumb with elation.

"And I suppose you're going to want the usual going-away package?" he teased, and twirled his beard.

"Of course, Padre. Why change our tradition now?" I joked.

He threw his head back and laughed; warm rich tones resounding with all his goodness. Then, as he returned to the group of children, he said, "Drop by next week. I'll have something ready."

Over the following days, I tidied up any unfinished business before visiting Padre Roberto one last time to thank him for everything. What an excellent friend . . . the only person in my life who'd stood by me, no matter what. I couldn't voice the words that would finalise our contact. Instead, I shook my head and dusted some snuff powder from his beard. His eyes twinkled (perhaps with more than smiles, this time).

The night before flying to Egypt, I was meeting friends for one final farewell. On the way, I decided to thank Mengestabe and Hanna for their support.

When I arrived at the clinic, Mengestabe was at the reception desk and Solomon was in his office. Hanna was out, but had promised to meet me at the airport.

I did my best to thank Mengestabe. Without his support, none of this could have happened. Graciously, he reminded me that Solomon had made it possible, actually, and insisted I offer a proper parting. Solomon emerged (under protest) and, nudged by Mengestabe, he reached out and awkwardly shook my hand.

That was it. No words of encouragement. No words at all, in fact.

An uncomfortable silence fell over the room.

Just get me out of here! As I left the clinic that evening, I realised my father wouldn't change.

I never saw him again.

In Ethiopia, it is customary for someone travelling abroad to have a house party with family and friends, but since I didn't have a suitable place or adequate finances, my friends and I opted for a night out on the town.

We pooled our money for a grand celebration and ate, drank and danced until it felt like the soles of our shoes had worn away.

During the evening, a friend asked if he could use my import/export licence while I was in Egypt. I hadn't considered this before and wasn't sure if I wanted to give it up; it had been so difficult to get. Not wanting to upset him (and already drunk), I agreed. I promised to make the transfer at the courthouse, before my departure the next day.

Much worse for wear, I was awoken by this friend the next morning. I wasn't really clear on anything.

Egypt? *Yes.*

Flight? *Okay, I'm on time.*

Licence? *Transfer? What?!*

Dishevelled and queasy, I somehow managed to gather the necessary documents.

One espresso, two taxis, and a few vomiting bouts later, we arrived at the courthouse to find several queues of depressing length. I explained my predicament to an official. He scoffed at my poor time management and advised me to sort it out at the Ethiopian Embassy in Cairo, instead. My friend reluctantly agreed, and we sped back to the old lady's house to collect my luggage.

Now impossibly late, I made a mad dash into the house to grab my things. The old lady came to my door and said she'd been worried. I didn't have time to explain or treat her to the farewell she deserved. Her kindness had made such a difference to my life.

As the taxi drove perilously along the airport road, adrenalin flashed through me. It wasn't just the anxiety of catching that plane (*c'mon, driver*); I realised that I didn't know if or when I would ever return. I tried to take in the sights and sounds of all that rushed by. The images froze in sequence, behind my eyes.

Would thoughts of my homeland become filed away under hardships . . . or hope? Memory is said to soften the pain, so I chose hope.

I still do.

Inside the airport terminal, all of my close friends were waiting. I was so late that we snatched each others' goodbyes before I made my way to the counter. Hanna was crying. I couldn't look back. I didn't want her to see *my* tears.

The guards searched my carry-on luggage and patted me down to make sure I wasn't taking any more than the allowable US$50 in cash. In the departure lounge, I pondered the enormity of walking boldly into the unknown. It was a big risk—but then, that had become my style.

I boarded the airplane for my first international flight. Not long after take-off, the aroma of food filled the cabin. My hung-over senses cringed. My stomach churned. When the hostess came with the meal, I had to refuse. The ultimate irony: after all those years of starvation, food was now mine for the taking and I couldn't stomach the sight of it.

Doing things in style, Teddy? Hold that thought.

15

INSHA' ALLAH

Flying over the desert and into the ancient Egyptian city of Cairo, I was flying on the wings of hope. From the window, I watched the sun setting beyond the arid horizon and it seemed that my desolate past was disappearing with it.

City lights began to sparkle invitingly before me, reflecting the modern splendour of fantastically tall buildings, along perfectly aligned streets. In profound contrast, the regal pyramids presided over all commotion, piercing the dark with eons of greatness.

The sky seemed huge with possibility.

While gazing down on this land of promise, I clasped a set of rosary beads (a gift from Padre Roberto). I didn't clutch them in desperation, or launch prayer-filled requests to protect me from harm. No. I felt so certain of my good fortune, so liberated, that I thanked God for the opportunity to start a new life.

In Ethiopia, we say: *Anticipate the good so that you may enjoy it.* God willing, I did exactly that.

Debarkation went smoothly. Then there was the queue for the

God Willing. (Arabic)

Immigration desk. Back home, I'd heard numerous accounts of people being refused entry, even with a visa. It seemed nothing was guaranteed until the passport was stamped. At each approaching step, I reminded myself of all the good that awaited me.

I blanched a little at the close proximity of military personnel. The guard looked me over unflinchingly, and then adjusted the large gun slung over his shoulder. His eyes didn't waver. I received permission to enter the country, and stepped past him to the luggage area.

With bag in tow, I walked from the terminal into the crisp air. Outwardly, I expressed quiet confidence, as if I did this every day— Tewodros, international man of action. Inwardly, my heart was leaping a giddy dance of freedom.

Its wild rhythm reflected everything around me. I strode into a world that was chaotically alive. Taxi drivers beckoned travellers to ride with them. Distant horns sounded the traffic jazz. Lights flashed in a crazy night kaleidoscope. Movement, sound and sensation vibrated through me right down to the soles of my feet.

I had arrived.

Mebrat's 20-year-old son, Kiros, was supposed to meet me here. I hadn't seen him since childhood, so I couldn't remember exactly what he looked like. I only hoped he would be able to identify me.

A short time later, I noticed three Eritreans standing near the taxis. As I approached, one of them called my name. It was Kiros. He and two roommates, Jacob and Werku, had formed a casual greeting party since they were also expecting Abiy, another Ethiopian who was supposed to be on the same flight. Within minutes, he joined us and we all piled into a taxi and headed for his home.

Like seasoned travellers instead of excited young men, we negotiated what I thought was a generous fare. In return, the driver carelessly puffed cigarette smoke through the cab, jerked gears in sync with the Arabian music that crackled from the speakers, and vigorously vented his frustration on all who crossed his path.

From the back seat, I watched the scenery fly by as we zigzagged across traffic, swerving and ducking between everything from Mercedes to mopeds. This "magic carpet" ride gave me a taste of the city I would discover in daylight.

Nothing makes a foreigner feel more welcome than a home custom. At Abiy's apartment, we were invited for coffee. Later, he gave me two pieces of advice for surviving in Egypt.

Survive? I thought. *No, no. I was going to thrive,* until he said, "Firstly—get a girlfriend. If you aren't rich, my friend, it's the only way."

It sounded like he was speaking from experience.

"Women from the Horn are in high demand as cleaners and babysitters and have a good reputation," he explained. "But for African men, it's a different story." He looked across at Jacob, then Kiros and Werku. "I am right, no?"

They all nodded in agreement.

My exultant mood wavered. I couldn't comprehend why there was no work for men in this country . . . that the only way to cope was by relying on women. Even in Ethiopia—the poorest of countries—I had managed without resorting to that.

"Secondly, you must register with Egyptian Immigration within seven days of arrival to acquire a one-month visa. You can decide between a visa for another country and a student visa. Maybe consider studying Egyptian Arabic because getting a visa for another country is a whole world of hassle."

Apparently, you had to make an application, pay a fee, present correct documentation (not so terrible, considering I'd just done all that), and expect a three-month processing period that could extend to one, even two years. Of course, that meant overstaying the initial visa, which incurred severe consequences; a risk only dared by those who had no other options. (Okay, that's not so good.)

Abiy explained that most Africans fled to Egypt, using Cairo as a base until they could secure a visa elsewhere. Fortunately, many countries such as America, Australia and Canada were accepting Ethiopian refugees who had escaped the civil war.

"You are half-Eritrean, no?" he asked. "You might present the United Nations with a strong case for refugee status. It is difficult, though. A friend in a similar situation was rejected. What you need is a relative overseas who can sponsor you. Is there anyone?"

"No," I replied.

"No one who can even send you money to help?"

"No," I echoed dejectedly. "There is no one."

The fragility of my circumstances carved me up in tiny, stinging cuts.

Abiy went on. "Well, whether you get a girlfriend or not, I suggest you go to Church because they can help you with money, clothing, food, and so forth until you get yourself sorted. It's much like Ethiopia."

Even if I'd been deaf, his last comment would have invaded my consciousness like a thief, stealing away the last remaining glimmer of the dream day that had been.

Abiy turned to Jacob. "Make sure you take him to Church next Sunday."

Jacob nodded. I sat.

At least, I was relieved to hear that the Church was active in Egypt, a predominantly Muslim country. But I would still be dependent and limited and poor.

Advice, like bittersweet coffee, is best in small doses. Concluding both, we took a taxi on to Kiros's apartment. He lived on the seventh floor. As there was no lift in the building, we had to carry my bag up all those flights of stairs. It was the one time I was relieved that I didn't have many possessions.

I was looking forward to seeing his apartment, but had unrealistically high expectations of what might lie behind the door. I imagined that housing in foreign countries would resemble what I'd seen on television at the local coffee shop in Ethiopia. I envisaged large rooms with high ceilings, a wood fireplace and bedrooms that opened out on to verandas or balconies. It never crossed my mind that it would be anything other than that.

When Kiros opened the door, I gulped on seeing a small room in need of a good clean. We entered, greeted an elderly lady who was sitting on the sofa, and then I was shown to the room I would share with Kiros.

"This is your bed," he said quietly, noticing my disappointment. "It's actually my mother Mebrat's bed. She works and lives with an Egyptian family during the week and only sleeps here on the weekend."

I nodded, trying to express some appreciation.

"There are six other people living here with us," he continued. "I know it's small, but most of them are working women just like my mother. So, the apartment is empty for most of the week."

I put my bag down and looked around. Posters of saints adorned walls of peeling cream paint, and a large crucifix hung above the bed that was to be mine.

"There's a balcony out that door if you want some air." Kiros pointed in the direction of some soiled cream curtains that fluttered before an open doorway.

I stepped onto the balcony which, like me, was hanging in darkness.

Kiros pointed over my shoulder. "Ethiopia is that way!" he said, proudly.

"Ethiopia?" The name made me shiver.

"*Aow!*"[1]

Even here, it reached out to take hold of me, this country that disowned me, yet owned me still. I took a deep breath and gazed up at the stars. Dizzy from height or weariness or shock, I can't say, but I had to close my eyes against this new turmoil.

1. Yes! (Amharic)

My thoughts jerked with Aunt Meseret's screaming face as she destroyed my few possessions. This was ripped away and replaced with my drunken father trying to convince me that my "real father" was off somewhere, fighting a war in the mountains. An image of my mother crowded into this seismic slideshow. I saw her balancing Kidest on her hip, desperately clinging to the rail in the bus.

Like snarling beasts making their last protests, everything I was trying to escape still snatched at chunks of me. I realised that I could never live in Ethiopia for any long period again.

I opened my eyes and looked at the stars, letting each one rekindle the spark of hope I had lost earlier that day. The sky *was* huge with possibility—and so was I. I had a bed. I had help. I had one month to find a solution.

"Tewodros? Are you hungry?" Kiros interrupted my thoughts.

"No, I'm tired. I think I'll go to bed."

"*Eshie,*[2] good night," he said, and closed the door behind him.

As dawn stretched, Muslim prayers projected through speakers across the city, startling me awake. Rubbing my eyes, I tried to process the strange room. Then I remembered there was a new city to discover, and leapt up. I stepped onto the balcony. All the sparkle of night had faded to reveal a cluttered assembly of shabby unfinished dilapidated buildings.

Incomprehensible amounts of discarded furniture and construction materials were piled on various rooftops. Others served as elevated stables to animals, giving real meaning to the phrase "stinking to high heaven." This incongruous mix of progress and peasantry left me speechless, but I didn't let the initial shock sway my determination. I knew one thing: *Little by little, an egg will walk.*[3] Surely, I would find my way through this labyrinth.

Within a few days, Kiros and I set out on that all-important trip

---

2. Okay. (Amharic)
3. Ethiopian proverb.

to Egyptian Immigration for my one-month visa. We were walking along the main road to the nearest bus stop. When the bus approached, it began to slow down, but I realised it wasn't going to stop. Kiros was already running alongside the bus, signalling for me to follow. He lined himself up with the door, jumped on and made space for my landing. Recklessly trying to keep up, I attempted a similar leap, but slipped. Kiros managed to grab my hand and pull me aboard.

So, I thought, *the egg must learn to run as well.*

At Immigration, my passport was stamped with the one-month visa. Within me, a faint ticking began the countdown: I only had four weeks to ensure my future.

On the first Sunday after my arrival, Jacob took me to attend Mass in a hall of St Joseph's in Zamalek.[4] This had become the primary gathering place for the Eritrean community. Jacob explained that there were three pillars of support in Cairo: the Church, the United Nations and the local Ethiopian/Eritrean community.

The Church helped new arrivals who had fled poverty, civil war and other hardships. It bolstered those who were rejected by the UN, as well as those who were still waiting for answers from the UN or any of the foreign embassies.

Until recently, the UN had offered hope to many Ethiopians and Eritreans. But statistics had changed (on paper, at least) since the downfall of the Dergue regime. Officially, outsiders had to acknowledge the "democratic" EPRDF (Ethiopia) and EPLF (Eritrea) governments, which meant the particulars for claiming refugee status were no longer extreme.

Ethiopians and Eritreans who had come to Cairo decades earlier, and even up until the year before my arrival, were swiftly granted refugee status and sent to Western countries. These people had gone on to re-establish their lives abroad, and many were able to

---

4. An island in the Nile, between downtown Cairo and Giza.

study at university and enjoy successful careers.

Now, applicants like me were not considered to be in desperate peril, so our requests for help went to the bottom of the list. Who would have thought that the difference of a few months could rob us of a brighter future?

Filling the gap between the Church and the UN was the African community itself. Jacob explained that after Mass each Sunday, a traditional lunch was prepared at someone's house and all were invited to attend. It was a time when people came together to share whatever contacts, money, clothing, and ideas they had to help their compatriots. I was relieved to hear of all the goodwill that people offered, despite their own troubled circumstances.

That day, our place had been designated as the meeting venue and we returned to an apartment full of people. The women had arrived from their week's work away, and some of the neighbours also came in for lunch. Amid conversation and laughter, the warmth of togetherness overflowed from room to room.

In every culture, in every house, there is something about smells and sounds that suggests "home." They bring a subliminal comfort that cannot be named, yet it pervades the consciousness and settles the soul. The delicious aroma of coffee and the exotic spices used in our traditional curries wafted my way. Feeling connected, I began to relax and enjoy it all.

I glanced around to see if I could recognise Aunt Mebrat. After skimming over several faces, I saw her sitting on the floor before the coffee ceremony. I made my way through the crowd to a small space next to her, and sat down.

She didn't greet me with the kindness that melts time and distance between relatives, but with tight-lipped kisses and diverted eyes. We chatted briefly about my flight and my first few days in Cairo, and then our conversation faltered.

After a few seconds of uncomfortable silence, Mebrat explained why she was upset. "Tewodros, you knew you were coming to meet me here in Egypt, yes?" Her eyes burned into me.

"Of course. I wouldn't have come if you weren't here," I replied.

"Tell me, then, why didn't you visit my sister, Ababa, and bring the parcel she'd prepared for me?"

"Parcel? I didn't know about—"

"She worked hard to prepare spices and *injera* for me, and we were expecting you to bring it." She shook her head in disappointment.

"But—"

"Your Aunt Ababa was shocked that you left without seeing her." She started to flick at her chipped desert-orange nail polish.

"I did visit Aunt Ababa and told her of my plans. I didn't realise she was expecting to see me again and I certainly didn't know she'd prepared a package for you," I said.

"But that is our culture, Tewodros. You should know that."

"I *don't* know that. I've never travelled before."

"But people shouldn't have to tell you. You should do it automatically."

Mebrat huffed accusingly, "So what are you doing here, anyway?"

"I still have to decide. Maybe I will study, or try to go to another country," I replied flatly.

"I think it's best you go home. Egypt is a hard country. Ethiopia is best for you," she said.

"*Ethiopia* is a hard country for me," I retorted.

"But you must go back there. Enjoy a short holiday here, but then go back."

"Mebrat, you know my situation—people like me have two choices: to be a homeless beggar or to become a soldier and fight in wars I don't believe in. Besides, the war might seem over, but nobody knows how the pieces will fall." I felt foolish, explaining what she already knew.

"I don't think your life here will be any better," she decreed, and abruptly returned to the gossip of the other women.

"Mebrat," I protested, "I've tried *everything* else."

She waved her hand in the air to signal the end of the conversation.

The atmosphere, for me at least, had become decidedly icy. I escaped onto the balcony.

Werku had overheard the conversation and followed me out. Gently, slowly, he offered me solace. "Tewodros, some people have been here a long time and have nothing but negative words to offer. It's not their fault. It's more a reflection on their own shattered hopes and dreams, but you need to know: nothing is impossible here. People in situations very similar to yours leave this country every day, for lands far away where they can have a better life."

His words soothed me, though not enough to dissolve my despair.

"It's just so hard," I protested, "to think I've left behind a life of never-ending difficulties, only to find similar challenges here. Doesn't God want us to do more than merely survive?"

"Tewodros, God gave you work on Saturday, knowing Sunday would bring rest.[5] It *is* a hard road, but with persistence and a little bit of luck, I believe we can achieve any dream." He reached out to shake my hand, then pulled me in for a hug instead.

"Thanks, Werku." I drew strength from his words.

As I lay in bed that night, I focused on Werku's advice. For as long as I could remember, I'd believed the very same thing: that life was good. Clinging to this, I focused on the only certainty I had—to move resolutely towards real freedom (not just escape). I realised I might have to overstay my Egyptian visa. This was no whimsical decision since the risk of arrest and detention loomed large. Egyptian prisons were the proverbial house of horrors, leaking stories of torture and inhuman conditions.

Success seems to result from a crazy combination of steady trust

---

5. Adaptation of an Egyptian proverb, meaning have faith and you will reap the benefits.

and wild risks. But balancing fear with faith requires continual practise. No matter how much I worked at it, I always felt like a beginner.

Little by little. . . .

Over the following weeks, I made new friends outside the apartment, in particular with an Ethiopian man called Ahmed. As a Muslim, he seemed comfortable with Egyptian life. He had a slew of beneficial contacts, and all the ins and outs of Cairo were like second nature to him.

Watching him operate reminded me of my own street-savvy days in Ethiopia. Old skills, new rules. All right, then—I *would* find my way.

Ahmed was a great source of information regarding work and immigration issues, as well as anything to do with cultural or local matters. I went out with him on Sundays instead of staying at Kiros's apartment, where I had to see Mebrat and the other women.

I liked Ahmed immediately. In our first meeting, he looked me up and down and said, "You must be a Type Two."

"Excuse me?" Was he implying that I had some kind of disease?

"Yes, a Type Two, for sure."

"And that is?"

"Well, you're a city boy from Addis?"

"Yes."

"And you know how to survive by networking?"

"I've had to do that in the past."

"And you're smart enough to get by on nothing. Right?"

I didn't want to admit it, but he'd just summed up my life.

Ahmed jostled my shoulder playfully. "Don't worry. Type Two is a good thing. There's worse than that."

"So how many types are there?" Now that I knew I wasn't being rejected, this system of his intrigued me.

"There are four. Type One are the refugees with family overseas, who send money regularly. They're reasonably confident about leaving Egypt soon—once the family sponsorship application has been approved. They don't need to worry about work and have the highest standard of living for a refugee," he quipped.

"And Type Three?"

He paused. "Type Three are those who have the hardest life here in Egypt. They arrive on foot, through a third country like Sudan. The journey takes several months. Many die along the way. Others are caught on the border and deported straight back home." He lowered his head. "There are cases where, once deported, they turn around and walk the entire journey again. Some people have done it three times . . . four . . . one guy did it nine times."

"Nine?"

"I know—it's incredible. I guess what they're running from is even worse. And when they do get here, they have absolutely no money and must depend heavily on the Church for support." He stopped and cleared his throat. "Finally, you've got Type Four. These people have been in Egypt the longest—they are the smallest group here. They arrived during the time of the Dergue regime and for whatever reason haven't left yet. Most of them have secured financial support from the United Nations and some are even studying at university. Type Fours do okay, but they're often frustrated in Egypt and seek ways of obtaining visas abroad," he concluded.

"So, what makes you think I am Type Two?" I was interested to hear his reasoning. "I could be a Type Three—or even a Type One."

"Well, you could be. But I doubt it!" He smiled. "There are two main reasons. Firstly, look at your clothes." He waved his hands up and down.

I looked at my t-shirt, jeans and then down to my boots, all gifts from Padre Roberto. "I don't understand," I said.

"You're wearing Italian-made clothes!" he replied.

"How do you know?"

"The tag is showing on your shirt," he laughed. "I instantly ruled you out of Type Three when I noticed. Then, when we started talking, you asked me about my job and indicated that you were interested in working. So, it was obvious you weren't Type One."

After this initial conversation, Ahmed and I continued to socialise and became good friends. I could rely on him, and looked forward to any advice he had to offer.

Gradually, I gained confidence in my ability to survive in Egypt and (tick, tick, tick)—I let my visa expire.

Throughout history, there has been tension between Ethiopia and Egypt because of the Nile River. Its source lies in the Ethiopian highlands, yet Egypt has been the major benefactor of its bounty. Political clashes between the two nations prompted periodic threats from the south to cut off the water, forcing Egypt into humble, yet resentful compliance. Now that we were in need, retribution was served up to us daily.

With their own unemployment problems, Egyptians had no place for an invasion of poor hopefuls.

Egypt was not without its own internal problems. There was general concern over terrorist groups that were attacking popular tourist areas. Like my illegally residing friends, I wondered if I'd jumped from the frying pan into the fire, as we lived in constant fear of discovery, arrest and police brutality. We kept a low profile, while avidly pursuing opportunities to move on . . . from the fire into some Canadian snow, perhaps? Or onto a cool Australian beach?

Overall, conditions in Egypt were very different from anything I'd previously experienced. Desert winters contrasted dramatically with heavy humid summers. The city hummed all day in a cacophony of people, engines, livestock, and the strange overriding magic of amplified prayers.

The Egyptians were volatile, but not violent. They openly

expressed their frustration with the weather, the traffic, each other, and life. Coming from a culture that lacked such public demonstrations, I was quite confronted. But I could see that it was probably a healthy non-threatening way to resolve any misunderstandings, and it certainly contributed to the lively street life.

The flurry of new impressions continued to lift my hopes. One of the first notable conveniences was the sealed roads. The asphalt streets were luxury compared to the gravelled dusty roads of Ethiopia where you literally carried the toils of a journey as pebbles in your shoes, with puffs of powdery dirt invading your clothes and caking your teeth.

Not everything was an improvement on my homeland. Despite a reasonably modern infrastructure, Cairo had no planned drainage system. Since it rarely rained, perhaps nobody anticipated the need for it. Over the three years I was there, I can only remember it raining once. The rain caught up particles of city grime and delivered such a murky deluge that the streets became rivers which even pharaohs would have feared.

The chaos of this place wove a spell on me, despite my fears, and I fell in love with its fast-paced boisterousness that expressed life in broad bright strokes.

During my first six months in Cairo, I continued to live with Kiros and, together with our other roommates, we shared the cost of food and all other expenses (although the employed women usually paid extra), making daily life very affordable for all of us.

Sadly, the rift between me and Mebrat hadn't completely healed. So, when five of my female friends asked if I would like to move in with them, I couldn't say 'yes' quickly enough. Besides, it was an offer that no right-thinking young man could refuse.

To me, this wasn't the same as living off a girlfriend, as I'd first been advised. Yes, they would provide me with accommodation and meals, but in return I would look out for them, as an unchaperoned life in Egypt could be difficult.

I'd never been in the position of care provider before—well, except for my calf, Taytu, but I was sure that caring for people was completely different. Still, I was somewhat daunted at the prospect. My new responsibilities weren't overly difficult though, because all the women stayed with their employers during the week, so it was only on weekends that I had to focus on them.

On those days, the apartment transformed from reclusive to festive. We invited friends over for meals and parties. We were all overstaying our visas, but in good company we shrugged off our concerns and indulged in feeling free and playful.

Monday mornings chased the women back to work. All week, I pursued exit strategies, visiting the foreign embassies repeatedly to apply for visas. I was actually awarded a tourist visa for Cuba, but it expired before I could raise money for the airfare. Still, I was learning the procedures, and success in one area should lead to success in another—shouldn't it?

Over the following twelve months, the women and I relocated time and time again, with adjustments to our group at each turn. We had problems with landlords or differences between the women, until eventually I was the only one left. I got by though, sleeping on one or another friend's sofa while trying to resolve my transient state.

Not keen to go solo again, I was elated to hear that my friend Hanna (from my father's clinic in Ethiopia) was moving to Egypt. I started looking for an apartment for us to share. I had a fairly good grasp of the language now, and I knew which areas and conditions had a reasonable standard and the best access to transport.

Still unemployed, I tried to initiate ways to make money until I could secure a visa for another country. With entrepreneurial flair, I planned a profitable event that would lift the spirits of my fellow migrants: a boat party on the Nile. A friend and I printed tickets, organised the evening's details and spread the word in the right circles. We invested what little money we had on the whole venture. But no one turned up. Everyone was too worried that a party would attract attention (and police).

To us, Egypt seemed to be a land of spies where everyone was very loyal to their own and quite ready to turn you in or take some sort of advantage. Taxi drivers would start chatting in Arabic (they really like to talk) and if you couldn't answer they would drive the long way, or charge whatever fare they wanted, since most of them don't even turn on the meter. If you refused to pay the extra tariff, they would haggle, or even chase after you.

One night, some friends and I were returning home from an outing. The taxi driver took such a detour that even he was lost. We were cruising the streets, trying to get our bearings, and ended up driving into a military base to ask for directions. No doubt, if the taxi driver had bothered to look, he would have wondered where his black passengers had gone and who were these white men, sitting wide-eyed and rigid.

When a black man turns pale, something is definitely not right.

An officer stopped us and asked what we were doing in a restricted area. We each had to give our names. But when it was Dereje's[6] turn, he couldn't speak. His mouth opened and closed like a gasping fish's. He fumbled for his identification card and read his name, syllable by syllable. We all cracked up laughing—even the officer, who sent us on our way. After that, every time we introduced Dereje to someone, we told him to get out his ID, just to be sure he got his name right.

Can you imagine being so panicked on a daily basis that you can't even say your name? I still laugh when I think of that night, but I wonder if it was our spontaneous laughter that saved us from a harsher experience.

Everything was risky: coming to Egypt, seeking asylum, looking

6. I knew Dereje from the Addis Ababa church group.

for work, avoiding police. If I was to manage at all, being a risk-taker had to be the key ingredient.

Hanna sent word that she would arrive sooner than expected. I was lucky enough to secure a place for the two of us in Yaguza, an area close to the Nile and within walking distance of Mebrat's place.

Feeling organised, I went to the airport. I was so excited to see Hanna again. Her friendship gave me such stability and comfort.

After a long wait, I was beginning to wonder if she'd had a problem with Immigration. At last, I spotted her waiting with two other young women. I rushed up to her and we swapped enthusiastic hugs. Almost two years of separation vanished in a heartbeat.

"Tewodros, I missed you!" She stepped back and smiled at me.

"Me too, Hanna. You're—" I choked back tears.

"Like family? Of course we are," she beamed. "Now, let's find my friends' lift and then we can really talk."

We all waited outside the terminal for some time, without recognising anyone who might be looking for the girls. So, I described the pleasant apartment and explained the budget benefits of sharing. They looked from Hanna to me to each other. Within seconds, it was agreed.

The three women were impressed with their new apartment. It was reasonably modern, spacious and very clean (I really can't have it any other way). After they sorted through their bags and settled in, we spent the evening in traditional style: sharing good food and drink.

The following week another girl, Sarah, joined our group, raising the tally of tenants to five. With our living arrangements settled, the new arrivals needed to work, so I contacted Ahmed to ask for his help.

He worked as a broker for wealthy Egyptian families. They employed Ethiopian and Eritrean women to take care of their children, cook, clean, and be at their beck and call—24 hours a day, five to six (and for a few, seven) days a week.

Since the women were new arrivals in a foreign country, it took from two weeks to one month for them to find suitable work. Without someone guiding them, they were susceptible to misuse by the wrong kind of employer or broker. Over the next month, each of my flatmates found a job with a suitable family.

Throughout my time in Egypt, I often heard the women complain about their employers, but it wasn't until my housemates shared their experiences with me that I realised how difficult it was. Although their work circumstances varied, they were experiencing much of the same trouble. As in any kind of occupation, they were answerable to their employers—usually the "madam" of the household. The language barrier frequently led to communication breakdowns, and left the women vulnerable and easily exploited.

With only limited language skills, the refugee women could not state their preferred job. They had to settle for anything and everything, and do it all for less pay. They weren't paid by the hour, but by the month, amounting to no more than US$100–200. Their relatives back in Ethiopia were hopeful of receiving perhaps half of that to relieve their poverty. This meant that the girls were not likely to turn down work, no matter how demanding (or degrading). Sometimes they were deprived of food or sleep, or refused permission to leave the house. They could even be denied a day off to recuperate. Such conditions were barely short of slavery.

I remained unemployed, despite all efforts. Gradually, I developed the skills and network of a broker, finding good positions for newly arrived girls and helping to resolve any difficulties. I understood the importance of my role and worked hard at presenting myself well. Dealing directly with employers, I secretly reviewed them for *their* worthiness while they thought they were assessing mine. I chose the best possible match for my girls' requirements and abilities and made sure both parties were aware of their responsibilities to each other. My first priority was the girls' safety, my second was the employer's satisfaction and my third was the recommendation I would receive to their friends, allowing me to find further work for the other girls I represented.

There was an Egyptian man named Lebnar, who acted as an agent, particularly seeking out Ethiopian and Eritrean girls. His multilingual skills made him the perfect mediator, but he was only interested in getting his finder's fee. He didn't care if he placed the girls in difficult conditions. He knew we were all so desperate for the work and in fear of arrest that we would not and could not complain.

If that was his only fault it would have been almost bearable, but his underlying intentions were more sinister. He would collect the new prospect on his motorbike, saying he was taking her to meet an employer. Stopping at his place for coffee first, he would drug the girl, have sex with her, take photos and later blackmail her. The personal and cultural shame for his victims was mortifying. Sometimes, they just packed up and went back to a life of poverty, feeling raped by the world, not just by one man. Watching them go from hope to heartache within a few weeks, I despaired for them.

As proud Ethiopian men, my friends and I felt powerless to protect our women. There was nothing we could do except warn the girls to stay away from him.

One girl was quite independent and determined not to follow the path of others into subservience, but to launch herself into the world on her terms. One day when I was out, she asked Lebnar for a lift to a job interview. I arrived home, wondering where she was. Later, when she told me what she'd done, I couldn't believe it. What had happened? Was she safe? He knew my address now, so were we safe?

She soon moved on, but Lebnar turned up one day looking for her. We had a stand-off. I was yelling at him to leave and never come back. He was yelling that he could turn us in at any time, and to stop roaring like some upstart lion in his country. Even though I felt more like a squawking chicken, my bluff must have worked because he didn't return.

Listening to my housemates, I was further disturbed to learn that a few even complained of sexual and physical abuse. Despite changing households on several occasions, the problem seemed to be inherent. The women were kept on tenterhooks, knowing they were working without permission from immigration. A disgruntled employer might go to extremes and announce that her maid had HIV, which meant immediate deportation. Any wrong move could produce an immigration officer at the front door.

The insidious threat of AIDS was raging across the African continent, compounding the war losses and sprouting new fear in minds already strained from too much hardship. There was ignorance and superstition surrounding disease in general and, since this condition was still such an unknown quantity worldwide, many didn't know they had contracted it.

Those who dared dream of a life elsewhere, and had been awarded a visa, were often devastated in the final process when the compulsory medical examination revealed HIV/AIDS. Asylum seekers diagnosed in Egypt were immediately deported, all hope torn from them. Everyone dreaded the disease. At the slightest hint of it (true or not), people were shunned. When it seemed life could not be harder, they suddenly faced slow certain death.

After living with us for just over a month, Hanna's two friends were able to contact the relatives who'd failed to meet them at the airport. The girls decided to move in with them. Subsequently, the rent became too expensive for the three of us. We soon found five others who were interested in sharing. Most of them had lived together previously, so the transition was relatively easy.

If *the egg had learned to walk,* and even run, the next lesson was to jump because we entered a series of abode changes that would leave an Olympic hurdle team breathless. For various reasons, we kept moving from place to place. We paid rent promptly, yet each landlord moved us on. Packing became an economical art, though the fear lining our luggage was a persistent stowaway.

This not-very-merry-go-round continued for some time. Even though home life wasn't very settled, Sarah and Hanna were working full time and supporting me in return for taking care of professional and day-to-day matters, but my life had become dominated by keeping a roof over our heads and not much more.

Within the Eritrean/Ethiopian community, all of us would have been glad for a different existence, for an opportunity to escape this ground-in hardship and embrace life where striving actually delivered quality results.

Weekly, we would gather to hear of anyone who had won the "visa lottery." There were regular success stories of someone immigrating to America, Australia, Canada or other more liberal countries. This kept us optimistic. Someone had changed his or her fortune. Who would have that chance next week? With this common goal we felt unified, even more so than back home. Ever hopeful, we huddled together on our ship of dreams, each supporting and protecting the others till an appropriate port called one of us to its shore.

For each departing triumph, we would stage a farewell party in someone's home with a discreet send-off at the airport, cautious to avoid the alternative exit method of arrest and deportation.

Amid goodbyes, there would be promises of sponsorship from that week's land of destiny. And, in fact, over the three years I was in Egypt, many returned to collect their families from the homeland, bringing us tales of a life beyond this.

In an effort to recapture my focus, I decided to study. I heard that the local Protestant Church had linked up with an English school, and was offering free lessons to anyone interested—and I was definitely interested, for a couple of reasons.

Since I wasn't planning to live in Egypt for the rest of my life, I thought English would be essential for succeeding in another country. Then there was the immediate benefit of communicating more easily with Hanna and Sarah's employers, as most of the wealthy Egyptians were fluent in English. Under Ahmed's guidance, my brokering was going well, but my incomplete Arabic limited discussions. I realised that learning English would be a good business strategy.

When I arrived at the church, I found some friends standing around a poster. Everyone was eager to sign up. We all went to the registration area and lodged our names. Details of the class location and times were passed out and, by the following week, I was studying once more.

Up until this point, the only English I remembered was from long ago, when Bishkash would teach me body part names and other simple words. Later, in my high school years, English was a compulsory subject, although I'd forgotten most of it.

The school was called the International Language Institute (ILI), where teachers-in-training honed their classroom skills. After four months of studying, I was able to build sentences, hold conversations and verbalise my thoughts in this new tongue. It gave me a great sense of achievement, something I hadn't experienced since my Morals and Ethics class with Sister Jimma in Gurage.

My class was relatively small, with only about ten students from diverse backgrounds and nationalities. I became friends with a Japanese girl named Satoko, who often brought her latest techno-toys to class.

I'd always been curious about gadgets, but after getting into trouble with Aunt Meseret I tried to keep away from other people's things. Still, insatiable curiosity is always poised for opportunity and when Satoko offered me the use of her camera for an upcoming excursion, I reached out with both hands.

I'd never used a camera before. After a brief demonstration of all its functions, she handed it over. This was the first time that anyone had ever trusted me with anything of value. Later, she even bought a camera for me as a gift.

Viewing the world through a lens, I was able to capture some of the ephemeral magic around me. This historical capital stood sentinel to the march of time; the statues silently endured while civilizations had fallen to dust only to burst forth in new ways. Having grown up through civil war, I knew existence was fleeting and fragile. Destiny could change between the beats of the heart.

Since that first excursion, I have paused the rush of time on people and places, assembling a grand collection of life's brightest and humblest facets. This was clearly the point when my emerging passion for storytelling through images became tangible for the first time. Through my pictures, I have invited others to look out at the world—and find themselves.

Accompanying the Eritrean Church group, or friends, I went on fantastic tours of discovery. We visited Mt Sinai, the Suez Canal, and other historical places. How grand it all was! With each discovery, I understood that I truly was a part of something bigger than the reduced, shadowy beginnings of my life.

I especially loved evening excursions to the pyramids. Under the mesmerising starlight, I could almost hear the whispers of kings and queens. I knew the ancients believed in weighing the heart of a man at his end of days. If it weighed more than a feather, he was doomed to the Underworld. All this beauty put wings on my heart. No more dark days for me. *Oh yes, great ones, I am ready to fly.*

My friendship with Satoko initially remained in the classroom, where we helped one another with lessons. Then, as everyone grew more familiar, we were often invited to other students' apartments, to parties and occasional sightseeing. Our contact continued even after my four months of free study came to an end.

Keen to continue with English, I found another course at the local British Council, although the lessons weren't free. Nevertheless, I gathered all the information about costs and class times. With Hanna's financial help, I was able to enrol and subsequently graduate through three advancing levels.

This school was more like an entertainment centre. The British teachers delivered fun interactive lessons, encouraged us through easy-to-follow textbooks, and gave us other language contact like watching "Mr Bean" videos.

I enjoyed spending time at school even when I didn't have classes. The teachers were so generous and positive. When they departed on their own adventures, they sent postcards that whetted my appetite for the bigger brighter world.

It was late 1995: decision time.

During my three years in Egypt, the EPLF continued their push for Eritrean independence from Ethiopia. In April 1993, a referendum was held. There had been violent student protests at Addis Ababa's university in the preceding months. Despite this, the voting went smoothly, with an astounding majority in favour of becoming separate. Eritrea gained independence one month later, on the second anniversary of the removal of the Dergue regime.

While these two countries initially maintained close relations, Ethiopia and Eritrea's civility soon soured over a border dispute. I had kept up to date with events. Even though I was glad to be away from all that, I couldn't remain in Egypt either.

Throughout this time, I had diligently changed my circumstances. People respected me, relied on me for support and advice. That was an achievement in itself, certainly. Some people might feel it was enough to have friends, a home and a reasonably meaningful job. But not for me. Surely, it wasn't wrong to strive for more. I wanted a whole world more!

Even though I was grateful, none of my small achievements were going to carry me into the future. And despite numerous applications, I hadn't secured a visa for any foreign country except Cuba.

Hanna's application for a Turkish visa was successful though and she was making final preparations to leave. Her ultimate destination was Greece, since she preferred to settle in a Christian country, but she planned to get there through Turkey.

It is a crooked path that leads to freedom.

Then two things suddenly brought my far horizons within reach. I'd kept in touch with Satoko after her return to Japan. Out of the blue, she surprised me with an offer to send the Japanese Embassy an official invitation for me. This should secure a visa and allow me to visit her in Japan.

At about the same time, I discovered I had a cousin in Australia who was prepared to sponsor me if I applied for a humanitarian visa. My cousin knew of the hardship in Egypt and advised me to travel to Japan and apply at the Australian Embassy there. He thought there would be fewer applications and probably (hopefully) faster processing times. But there was one catch: I would have to start the process from Ethiopia.

Was Japan the best option? It felt like a huge gamble to travel to another country, with yet another language, and begin all over again.

Sometimes, no matter how much thinking is done, fate decides. I applied to Caritas[7] to help finance a flight back to Ethiopia. If my application failed, I would remain in Egypt. If my application was successful, I'd hop to Ethiopia, skip to Japan and jump to Australia. *Insha'Allah.*

Just the thought of returning to Ethiopia brought those biting beasts back in my belly. Would curses of the past catch and keep me this time? Would I have to resort to charity—again? (Well, never from

---

7. An international NGO supported by the Catholic Church.

my father.) What would Padre Roberto think when I turned up?

Remembering the dust, the Dergue and the despair, I faltered. Surely the new government was better than the Dergue, but there was still tension on the streets and this new emerging conflict with Eritrea.

I wondered if any of my friends had reached for something more in life. I hoped so. I was a little embarrassed to be returning with nothing of real consequence. I tried to push all that aside. I was Tewodros: the man with a plan, and the plan was sure to work (this time).

The day of departure came quickly, and my housemates held a farewell party a few hours before I was to leave. I'd never realised how many friends I'd made in Egypt until that night when they all arrived on our doorstep. The turnout overwhelmed me and I had to reassure myself that I was making the right decision.

I'd booked a late-night flight. As the time approached, everyone walked me downstairs. Some of my housemates were crying as I hailed a taxi and jumped in. I wound down the window and gave them one final wave goodbye—which I could say in four different languages—but no words could complete such a farewell. The taxi drove me away from them, down the dark narrow street.

The journey to the airport felt nostalgic. I remembered my arrival into that land. The wild rhythm I'd first encountered had become the familiar beat to which I'd danced. The prayers from the turrets had rung through my days and the kaleidoscope of night lights had kept the spark of my dreams ablaze.

Overcoming all the challenges along the way, I had certainly embraced what was good. Little by little, a tentative step of hope had become a leap of triumph. Yet, what now loomed ahead seemed more like a gauntlet to be run. But I wasn't a frightened kid anymore. I had experience, some money and links to the world beyond. With such confidence, my exodus felt complete.

In Egypt, they say, "*It is written.*" And if somehow you manage to change your fate, they say, "*That too is written.*" So . . . let the words be kind.

Grandfather Fekadu Reda standing proudly in his police uniform. *(Asmara, Eritrea)*

Solomon, the man who made life hell for Bishkash and me. *(Ethiopia)*

My visit with Adey Selas on the way to Japan. *(Asmara, Eritrea)*

Great-grandmother,
Zenebech, on the right,
with her sister on the left.
(Ethiopia)

My mother, Bishkash, early in her pregnancy, hiding her belly behind her cousin Egegayhu. *(Mekele, Ethiopia)*

Relatives standing before the Kiorkes church, built by Zenebech's father for the local villagers, in memory of his ancestors. (*Adi Kemaleh, Ethiopia*)

Me, at about age 3. (Shire, Ethiopia)

Brinesh with her two daughters, her brother and her maid on
either side, and me, squatting front right, next to a cousin.
(Shire, Ethiopia)

The hospital wall, on the right, where I witnessed the execution of three men. *(Shire, Ethiopia)*

I'm on the right, in front, with Bisrat's family; not long before I start living with my Adey. *(Asmara, Eritrea)*

Solomon receiving his doctorate from Colonel Mengistu Haile Mariam.
This photo made me realise that being a doctor or the leader of a
country doesn't necessarily make you a good person.
(Addis Ababa, Ethiopia)

With the Gurage mission staff and classmates. I'm in front, second from
the right. *(Gurage, Ethiopia)*

With Padre Roberto, Hailu (left of Padre) and the church boys. I'm in the dark shirt, crouching in the centre. *(Addis Ababa, Ethiopia)*

Meeting with friends. I'm second from the left, beside Satoko. *(Cairo, Egypt)*

Nishi Nihon Immigration Centre, where I lost three years of my life. It looks like a hotel from the outside, but inside it's a different world. *(Osaka, Japan)*

Here, I'm standing in front of Nishi Nihon Immigration Centre on one of my monthly visits to renew my temporary visa. *(Osaka, Japan)*

Dressed for my cleaning duties, I'm standing at the stairs to Shelter House. *(Sakai, Japan)*

Sato granted me one year's rent-free use of this house. *(Osaka, Japan)*

I was pleased to talk to community groups in Japan about my experiences in detention and Africa. *(Osaka, Japan)*

I was often invited to schools to talk with the children about my experiences. *(Osaka, Japan)*

Anita and I (on the left) in a bar with Daniel and one of his friends.
(Kyoto, Japan)

Anita and I at our engagement party in Japan, before she left for Australia.
(Osaka, Japan)

Occasionally, I got permission to leave Osaka city, and enjoyed catching up with friends. Here we are at the annual O-bon celebrations.
(Shikoku Island, Japan)

After my second release from detention, I visited Mario and his lovely family. This was the last time I saw them.
(Osaka, Japan)

My new Australian family welcomed Bishkash. *(Brisbane, Australia)*

My sister-in-law, Megan, and I on a family holiday not long after I arrived in Australia.
(Sydney, Australia)

Once I settled in Australia, Anita and I sponsored Bishkash to visit us as. She had always wanted to travel abroad, but never had the opportunity.
(Gold Coast, Australia)

I recently went back to Japan to see friends and research some points for this book. Despite everything, it was good to go back there, though strange to visit as an Australian citizen without visa issues. *(Sakai, Japan)*

In 2010, I paid my grandmother, Alganesh, a surprise visit in Tigray, northern Ethiopia. She was working out in the field when I arrived and was shocked to see me standing in front of her. *(Tigray, Ethiopia).*

In 2007, I returned to Ethiopia for the millennium celebrations. On this memorable trip, I travelled throughout the country, researching family history. This shows the Fascilidas Palace of Gondar, the region of both my parents' ancestors. *(Gondar, Ethiopia)*

Anita and I at the beach, not far from where we live. *(Gold Coast, Australia)*

16

GATHERING GHOSTS

When you decide to leave a place, it means more than geographical relocation. Something within you departs, too. Ties are broken that can never be rejoined. If you do return, you bring along all of your latest discoveries. And you'll find that the old views will never look the same, whether you wish them to or not.

Inevitably, people move on. They grow up. Or grow old. Or become strangers without even changing their address.

Was I a stranger now? Better yet, had I grown up enough and moved beyond my past circumstances sufficiently to be accepted on my own terms? I know my plans were set to travel far from all of this, but do we ever completely resolve the desire for family bonds?

I wanted to believe that hearts were not bound by borders or distance or time. I wanted to rediscover all those who still lived in *my* heart, and see that I had never left theirs. With such trepidation, I stepped off the plane.

I was struck by the stillness, and the scarcity of people. I checked my ticket. This *was* Bole International Airport, wasn't it? In Addis

Ababa? I'd become so used to the hustle and bustle of life in Cairo that I felt like an outsider in a strangely familiar place. I took in this quiet new perspective. Nothing had changed, but me. And that meant everything would be different.

I'd arranged to stay with a friend whose income came from trading goods. Through his contacts, I saw yet another side of life. Even when socialising, these businessmen were always focused on money and assets. It seemed so suffocating and predictable. I *definitely* wasn't meant to be there.

While official channels delayed pinpointing my next departure, I was dependent on others. Bureaucracy ran on its own time and each day beat out the waiting game. Constantly hovering to leap forward, I watched as another day passed. And another. And another.

I met up with old friends, although many of them were lost to me. Some were living overseas, but others were still trapped in the same life as three years before. I wanted to throw everyone high up out of the dust, and say, *Look—look what your life might be.* But perhaps their vision was already shut down out of habit.

I was undecided about visiting relatives. Would I ever be free of the residual anger from their rejection? Despite my misgivings, I thought it was important to wish them well and show them that this "son of the devil" was not doomed simply because others had deemed it so. I was proud of myself and my achievements. After all, I was alive and thriving—they hadn't expected that.

As soon as I looked into their faces, the past became meaningless. I did not feel triumphant for myself, only sad for them. People are generally the result of their culture, and none of them had been prepared for the terror that had torn it all away.

They were shocked to see me, not really knowing how to connect the boy they remembered to the man I'd become. Their opinion of me (past or present) didn't matter, and I knew it never would again.

There was one visit that loomed large in my expectation. *Please, let this remain precious,* I wished, as I made my own private pilgrimage back to the Holy Saviour Church to see Padre Roberto.

He was like a giant in my life. Because of him, the child in me had reached out for more than charity. What victory could I demonstrate? What adventures could I relate? What wisdom could I share that even he would prize as a worthy gift? Since my dreams were still in incubation, I approached him with tentative steps.

As soon as I saw his familiar old face, the face of reassurance and comfort, nothing else mattered.

During one of my visits to the church, I asked a gathering of people about my friend, Hailu.

"*Wehee!*" one woman exclaimed, and put her hands up to her cheeks. "Hailu returned from Italy where he was studying, and now he has bought a house!" she said, almost as if she couldn't believe it herself.

"You know, he is rich now and money has changed him," someone else sniggered.

"What's that saying—*a person who has too much will do useless things*[1]—that's Hailu," a third person added.

I was confused to hear such negative comments. That didn't sound at all like the smart witty affable Hailu I'd known. It was hard to accept that he could be changed so easily by money.

Not long after learning all of this, I was sitting outside the church with some former friends of Hailu when one of them pointed to a passing car, and shouted, "Look, there's Hailu!" She, too, was disparaging about him.

When I saw him pull up down the road, I decided to go and see for myself. "Hailu!" I called to him, as he was emerging from the car.

He barely seemed to recognise me. He quickly shook my hand, then turned and walked away.

---

1. Ethiopian proverb.

When I related this incident to one of our friends, he told me I must have misunderstood. He and Hailu maintained good contact and he thought everyone was being unfair in their judgements. I told him I'd witnessed Hailu's behaviour with my own eyes and had no doubt that he was different now. As I complained, I couldn't know this mutual friend intended to tell Hailu exactly what I'd said.

About a month later, I was walking down the street when I heard someone tooting a car horn. I glanced in the direction of the noise. It was Hailu. He stopped the car where I was standing.

He chatted casually, laughing and making jokes. Despite still feeling hurt by his coldness a month before, I couldn't help but smile.

"What are you waiting for?" he teased. "Get in the car before I leave you!"

"You know, you are crazy? One minute you act like you don't know me and the next it's like old times," I said, as I climbed into the passenger's seat.

The old Hailu had returned. It was good to resume our friendship. Perhaps he realised how aloof he'd been. Perhaps those others gossiping were jealous of his good fortune. Either way, his company gladdened me, not his wealth. He always turned life into an adventure. I admired his spirit and gentle nature, and to this day he remains one of my good friends.

Meeting everyone gave me some kind of closure, as if my next intrepid quest had been waiting for me to finish here.

Not long afterwards, I received word from Satoko that things were in order. At the Japanese Embassy in Addis Ababa, I confirmed that her official invitation had arrived. Finally, I was able to make preparations for my next international departure. The embassy official informed me of the prerequisites for a visa: a return ticket, a valid passport and an exit visa from Ethiopia.

After years of daily practice, I started to feel like an undercover superhero: *DocuMan*—faster than the local post; more powerful than a receptionist's "No"; able to accumulate towers of forms, bound in triplicate.

Given that so many applicants were denied entry to developed countries, I was surprised by the speedy approval of my Japanese visa. As I booked the return flight, I inwardly laughed. This wasn't happening to a friend. It wasn't just a dream. This really *was* me.

I decided to visit Adey Selas in Eritrea, before leaving. We hadn't met for a long time and I didn't know if or when I would ever have the opportunity again. First travelling by road to Asmara, I could start my migration from there. Besides being cheaper, it gave me the chance to view the countryside, gathering rich images that will always fill me with the beauty of Africa.

A country might suffer war, but it still has mountains and valleys. Villages, set cosily into the hillside, coloured the landscape. People worked in the fields, reclaiming the dignity of daily life. Plantations swelled with the promise of new harvest. Now that hope replaced despair, there was a sense of vibrancy that had been lacking for so long.

The border between Ethiopia and Eritrea had reopened since the Dergue regime was ousted, and traffic could now flow between the two countries reasonably freely, as long as the traveller showed an identification card. I was surprised at the amount of traffic on the roads, especially since the greater percentage of it was heading north to Eritrea. People on the bus joked that Ethiopia would soon disappear.

In gaining independence, Eritrea was expected to be the "Singapore" of Africa: modern and affluent, with links to the international community (in a good way). The latest government encouraged Eritreans living "next door" to return home. This they did in droves. Not that they had problems with Ethiopia; they just loved their country.

When the bus pulled into the terminal, I anticipated getting reacquainted with the city. Asmara had evolved, and recovery from so many years of war was evident. It was cleaner than I remembered.

Flowers lined the streets, and new buildings were in various stages of completion.

Most of the passengers stayed at a hostel just across the road from the terminal. Despite the improvements, there was no shower or running water in the hostel (the war had prioritised politics over personal hygiene). We had to pay for water from a hair salon, downstairs.

After settling in, I went looking for my grandmother. My ambitious heart was primed for a fulfilling reunion.

I took a taxi to the house where I'd lived with her as a child. A stranger answered my knock on the door. When I asked to see my grandmother, he told me she no longer lived there.

"Is she okay? Is she still alive?" I asked anxiously. If the answer was "yes," then I knew I would find her. I had never considered life without her. She was such a fountain of goodness.

He nodded. Of course, she was still alive.

I walked up the road to another neighbour's house. Aunt Ruta and her daughter were living there. That surprised me almost as much as their warm welcome. Ruta and my father were particularly close. Her treatment of me as a child had reflected his attitude. We hadn't met since our chance encounter outside the church in Addis. Now, I asked her how I could contact Adey. She explained that, because my grandmother's house had been sold due to a family dispute, she was living with Aunt Almaz.

Aunt Ruta escorted me to Adey's new residence. We stopped on the way to buy her presents of groceries and green coffee beans. I was disappointed not to be seeing Adey alone, not to have those moments to ourselves. But with each step closer, nothing mattered except seeing her bright eyes, and feeling her warm soft hands holding mine.

When we arrived, I could hardly believe how well she looked; so strong in herself, like life could never take away her truth or her worth. I understood why I was always so drawn to her.

Words were not needed. I simply held her close.

She was still very active, going to Church every morning, and was generally in good health. She'd been to America several times to see her two children, Abel and Elsa, who often sent her money.

Aunt Almaz, on the other hand, had aged considerably. When I was younger, I remembered her overpowering perfume, neatly groomed hair and blood red nail polish. But now, her face was marked with stress lines, and her clothes were unflattering and looked worn.

While everyone bustled into domestic activity, I wondered, *Are these people my family? Is she really my aunt?* All my life I'd tried to convince myself of that. I remember forcing my mind to believe they were blood relatives. But I never felt any connection, except to Adey.

I had been staying with Aunt Almaz and Adey for several days when we were alerted of an imminent visit from Aunt Meseret. I'd met her several times since she accused me of stealing her husband's money, but she still refused to believe my story, no matter how often I declared my innocence. I wasn't sure how she would react this time.

Surprisingly, Aunt Meseret seemed happy to see me, as if we'd never had a problem in the past. I was friendly towards her, though found it interesting when she dropped hints about how much she loved Japanese pearls. Did she think I'd forgotten her betrayal? And perhaps, now that I had a little money, I wouldn't hesitate to make her happy? Is that all family was to her?

On the morning of my departure, I woke to the sound of raised voices coming from the living room. I went out to see several distressed visitors hushing and talking over each other at the same time.

"What's going on?" I asked. Their faces all turned to me at once. Then, the terrible news came pouring out.

"Meseret's husband, Doctor Asmerom, is dead," cried one of the ladies.

"Heart attack!" exclaimed another. "How can we tell Meseret?"

"Tell me what?" Aunt Meseret asked. She too had heard the

commotion and emerged from the bedroom.

"Meseret, your husband is sick," one woman said, but her voice was shaking uncontrollably.

"You are lying," Aunt Meseret snapped back. "Tell me what it is!" she demanded. Clearly, she sensed her husband was worse than sick.

"It's better you come with us, back to Ethiopia, to see him." One of them stepped forward and put her hand out to Meseret.

"I—said—tell me why you are here! *What has happened to him?*" Her face was covered in bright red blotches, and her eyes were bulging.

"Take a seat, Meseret." Two of the women guided her to the sofa. "Asmerom is . . . he's . . . we're afraid he has passed away."

Aunt Meseret fell back into the chair, screaming.

"We're so sorry, so sorry," the women echoed each other, trying to comfort her pain.

I grieved to hear the news, but I didn't know what to say. Asmerom had been so supportive of me, in so many ways. Now, as I piece all these stories together, I understand that he was a silent guardian over my early years, and of course he welcomed me into his home. In real terms, his generosity probably saved my life right from the start.

I didn't realise I was quietly crying. My only awareness was of Aunt Meseret struggling with this profound loss.

Strangely enough, when death divides people, grief connects them. Its wordless power overflows, dissolving all barriers of language, age or prejudice. We, who had never been a united family, tentatively reached out to each other across the abyss that such loss creates. Ironically, in a few hours, we would disperse again as each stepped towards a life that would differ from all that had been before.

Together, we went to the airport. There, our separateness claimed us. I would fly to Egypt and beyond. Aunt Meseret would return to

Ethiopia. I looked across the passenger lounge and saw her, crippled in her distress, being physically supported by relatives.

I knew I should appreciate every moment, that I was lucky, that I was finally flying to those long dreamed-of horizons. Instead, I felt hollow. This loss of Asmerom was a powerful farewell.

I knew nothing of Japan. *What was written for me there?*

I placed the headphones in my ears and peered out the window at the barren landscape surrounding the tarmac. The parched earth had cracked under the merciless sun. Dry wind flurried around the plane. It all looked so dead.

I turned up the volume to drown out the lingering echoes of Aunt Meseret's torn cries. Let Ethiopia and all its grief fall behind. As John Lennon's song "Imagine"' swelled through the headset, I closed my eyes and *imagined* . . . life abroad . . . better, brighter . . . that I would find inner peace . . . and a place I could finally call home.

But, like the El Nino that was brewing in the eastern Pacific, turbulent times lay ahead.

BOOK TWO

FAR HORIZONS

It is a crooked path that leads to freedom.

17

CAPTURE

Narita Airport, Tokyo. A child stands alone, looking nervously into the faces of the milling crowd, waiting for someone to claim him.

That can't be right—I'm almost 26 years old. But my heart fluttered like one hundred butterflies in this foreign uncertainty, making me feel like a lost child.

How could I identify my friend, Satoko, among all of these sleek-haired people? What if I couldn't? The last time we'd met was in Cairo, just before her return to Japan. That was about two years ago. As I was the only lanky afro-topped dark-skinned man in sight, the chances of her recognising me seemed much more promising.

I put down my suitcase and admired the impressive interior of the modern building. I've always valued sophisticated design: everything from ancient pyramids to technical innovation. This place was awesome in the grandest sense of the word. I was a long way from Africa.

Twenty minutes later, a small doll-like figure pressed towards me.

I could see it was Satoko. She halted abruptly and burst into a fit of apologies (in English, thank goodness).

We took the subway to her home suburb, not far from Chiba University. This was the beginning of many first-time experiences. I'd never ridden a subway train before. How smoothly it glided along rails and through tunnels. We ascended from the earth's depths to the cityscape where I caught glimpses of Tokyo at ground level.

Clusters of trees, kissed all over with delicate pink flowers, decorated the surrounds. Satoko called them *sakura* or cherry blossoms. Apparently, I'd just missed the peak of Spring's full bloom, but stunning patches of colour still burst forth in places, providing relief to the otherwise drab scenery.

Knowing that mastering life depends a lot on where you focus, I chose to see each fresh impression (even the dismal ones) as a flagstone on the bright new road of my future. Like a vivacious child, I wanted to look there—and there—and there.

We caught a taxi for the final leg of our trip. On the way, Satoko explained that she lived in a "mansion." *Impressive*, I thought, assuming she'd used the English word. We stopped in front of a large grey building, and my first lesson in Japanese presented itself.

The cities of my past had included dusty streets, and crowded buildings (with goats on the rooftops). I pondered the tall stately structure before me. Did Japan have such a high standard of living that each building was like a miniature palace?

"This is your house?"

"Yes. I live on the second floor," Satoko replied and paid the taxi driver.

"The second floor? The building is not yours?"

"No, of course not!" Satoko laughed and helped drag my bag to the stairs.

When she opened the door to her place, it didn't take me long to realise that "mansion" did *not* mean "large house," as I had learned in English class: *manshon* was the Japanese word for "apartment."

Although in most other languages, an area of this size would be more accurately described as a shoe box.

In the initial few days after arriving, I concentrated on preparing an application for the Australian Embassy, hoping to be accepted on humanitarian grounds as a refugee. A paper chase always seemed to become a bureaucratic maze in any country, but with my recent run of good fortune, I was confident a positive reply was imminent.

Even though Satoko had officially invited me, I don't think she had any idea of the complications that typically ensue. Perhaps she thought all I needed was to arrive, get my passport stamped and move on. Always with patience in my back pocket, I knew otherwise.

It rapidly became clear that I was awash with cultural overload, and needed some structure while I sat out "the visa shuffle." This high standard of living was costly. The language was daunting. I didn't have an African community to seek out for support. The prominently different beliefs and social customs made me wonder what I'd been learning all those years in Church.

Flagstone impressions? Yes.

A smooth way forward? That remained to be seen.

Satoko knew I had limited funds, so she contacted her friend José for some advice. Although he was Peruvian, José lived in a seaside village south of Tokyo. His mother was married to a Japanese man, so he'd been living there for years. He invited me to meet the local factory boss and apply for work.

Looking on a map, Satoko pointed out the village of Matsuzaka. It was located on Honshuu, the main island of Japan, with Isle Bay to the east and the Daikou mountain ranges to the west.

Sounds idyllic, I thought.

I don't like to be idle so the prospect of a job, after years of frustrating unemployment in Egypt, seemed like the perfect interim solution until I had a reply about my application. Besides, I needed money (the eternal motivator).

Even though I only knew a few people in Tokyo, every one advised strongly against leaving the city. There, in the cosmopolitan landscape, I was one of many foreigners and therefore less conspicuous. Going to a tiny seaside village, not knowing the language, was their idea of kamikaze madness.

Determined to maintain my independence, and trusting this would be a short-term beneficial experience, I didn't listen.

Risk and faith.

I learned that taking a risk is not always a solution; that when people advise you, it's good to stop and think—not always push and push until you move the mountain. Sometimes pushing hard will bring the mountain down upon you. From under the rubble, you can wonder, *What was that advice again?*

I gladly accepted José's offer and passed on the factory address to the embassy. So, before I'd begun to absorb the cosmopolitan city life, I was headed for the village of Matsuzaka in south-west rural Japan.

José collected me from the bus terminal and later that afternoon his uncle took me to the factory. Attempting to persuade the boss that I would be a good worker, he pointed to various parts of my body and squeezed my upper arms to show that I was a fit strong young man—perfect for factory work (I felt more like a donkey for sale at the markets).

After some moments of consideration, the boss agreed to hire me. It was explained that I could start the next day.

But the deal was not yet complete. José's uncle asked the boss for an advance on my salary to tide me over. The boss agreed and handed me some notes. I thought it was a nice gesture until we left, and the uncle asked me to hand it over as commission for getting me the job.

Early the next morning when I arrived, the boss took me upstairs to the dormitory where I was to share a small room with two other workers—one Japanese, the other Chinese. There were two more rooms, occupied by a couple of women from Peru. Each bed had its own cubicle with a curtain that could be pulled around for privacy, similar to those in hospitals. It was also clean. (A good sign, don't you think?) I stowed my belongings, and followed the boss back downstairs to my duties.

The factory was divided into several small sections, each responsible for a specific task and overseen by a team leader. I admired the workers' efficiency as they carried out their duties, though I noticed that the team leaders' primary responsibility was to tell them to work faster, move faster, walk faster, cut faster, pack faster, or do whatever they were doing—faster.

The local employees weren't overly friendly, unless one spoke Japanese. Having a black man in their company seemed to unsettle them, but I guess their worldly experience hadn't gone beyond this remote coastline.

My job was smelly and dirty. In this section, we had to soak frozen fish in a tub of water to defrost, in preparation for cutting. Our rubber gloves were more for grip than insulation. I plunged my hands repeatedly into the Arctic temperatures to retrieve each thawed fish.

Sharp knives make hazardous companions for numb hands. Within a few days, I'd seen some of my co-workers suffer nasty wounds; nor did I remain unscathed. One day, blood spurted like a fountain from my glove. Without me realising it, a cutting machine had sliced my index finger right to the bone.

How do you say *OW!* in Japanese?

I had obviously not inherited my father's medical resilience, because I fainted. I was rushed to hospital where the doctor lashed the bits together with a needle and thread, giving me The Matsuzaka Scar. . . . That sounds impressive, but (like a bad memory) it has faded over time.

Village life was uneventful. In my free time, I visited José and his family (and checked the mail) or borrowed a bicycle from the boss and cruised past rice paddies, taking in the peaceful landscape (then, checked the mail).

A few times, I rode around to the local car yards for some materialistic daydreaming. For me, a car was the classic symbol of freedom—you could go anywhere, anytime. I looked at the cars and secretly planned which one would be mine one day. I collected pamphlets on any that took my fancy, and even those that didn't. I hoarded them, much like I used to hoard rosary beads as a child.

I enjoyed practising my limited Japanese with the salesmen and sometimes I let them think I was a serious businessman. I remember one day in particular when, after quite a long discussion about cars, the salesman walked me outside onto the street and almost split his sides laughing when he saw me jump on a bicycle and ride away.

On the second Sunday evening of this rural rhythm, I was returning to the dormitory when I noticed a police car parked across the road from the factory. It was empty. Unlike my insides, which instantly filled with fear. I went to tell the boss what I'd seen. He assured me it was nothing unusual.

The next day was May 26, my thirteenth day of employment—a day that plays over and over in my mind. It started out like any other. The sun was shining brightly, though a co-worker warned me that heavy clouds of the rainy season were fast approaching, which would raise the temperature and make us sweat like baboons; perhaps a sign of what else was coming.

I wonder at the coincidence that "gloom" rhymes with "doom."

We'd been busily working for about an hour when ten darkly dressed men, equipped with radios and headsets, barged into the factory. A wave of panic swept across the floor when we saw that they were rounding up foreigners. Three of these short stocky men-in-black were heading in my direction. As far as I knew, my Japanese visa was still valid, yet my heart thumped in time with their heavy steps: *doom-doom-doom*. Not knowing what else to do, I remained still and let fate take its course. They grabbed my arms and led me upstairs to the office where four other foreign employees were already waiting.

Once there, they handcuffed us, rummaged through paperwork and checked time cards while questioning the factory boss. Through sign language, the odd English word and very basic Japanese, we tried to answer the questions asked of us. After taking down notes, the officers wanted us to show them to the dormitory and present our passports for verification. I approached my cubicle, retrieved my passport and handed it to the officer hovering behind me.

My visa was legal; *however*, I didn't have permission to work. I showed the officer my papers and explained to him (in English) that I had applied to the Australian Embassy in Tokyo for a humanitarian visa, and that working was simply a temporary means to sustain myself in the meantime.

Some of the other foreign workers were also pleading their situations, but the officers ignored everything except their own strict protocol. They were cold, distant and abrupt as they methodically moved throughout the dormitory, collecting and organising any relevant data. They reminded me of the machines in the factory.

José and his family, along with another Peruvian couple, were legally able to work and therefore released. The rest of us, about six in all, were ordered to pack our belongings.

No one knew where this was leading. Looking at the other workers, I could tell they were scared. Some broke down and started crying; others became angry and upset. Like the fish I worked with, I felt cold all over. My chest ached. I struggled to swallow. It was all I could do to remain standing and just breathe.

We were herded downstairs into a van where we fretfully waited while the officers went in search of others who were not at work that day. The interior of the van could hold about 24 people. With so many spaces yet to fill, I guessed we'd be in there for a while.

I thought of my mailbox. There'd be no chance to check that today.

The brooding clouds bore down on us with muggy conditions. There were curtains covering the windows so we couldn't see out but, more importantly, nobody could see in. If we dared to glance though a crack between the curtains, we were reprimanded by the guarding officers.

Before too long, the others returned with a very distressed Peruvian woman. She was an illegal worker. The officers had coincidentally discovered and captured two Filipino men who lived in her apartment building, also overstaying their visas. One of them had bloodied knees. The officers had fired gunshots into the air to scare him and he had run in fear, falling as he tried to escape.

The van drove to two more factories during the course of the day and several more foreigners were loaded in with us. While we waited for the raids to be completed, some officers climbed onboard and tried to ask us questions in Japanese. Many of us had great difficulty understanding them, so they eventually gave up and asked us to sign the papers they were handing out. The papers were written in Japanese with only very basic instructions in English.

I hesitated. Glancing around the van, I noticed everybody doing as they were told. So, I too put pen to paper. What is it people say? "Always read the fine print!" (*Even if it's in Japanese.*)

By late afternoon, the van was full and we started driving to an unknown destination. Along the way, we stopped for a toilet break at a refreshment area. Large groups of Japanese tourists were stretching their legs. They fell silent as we were marched passed them. Parents grabbed their children's hands and dragged them away to a safe distance. Others huddled into tense groups, staring or ignoring us. Neither felt good.

I entered a cubicle and crumpled into a heap, nursing my pounding head and choking back nausea. The shock of the day finally hit me. Fear turned to anger, anger to regret, regret to despair. I simply didn't understand why the world seemed to be shiny and full of hope in one moment, and transform into an incomprehensible devouring monster the next. I hated myself, my life and every fragment of my being. After a few minutes, the officer who had escorted me to the toilet began banging loudly on the door, signalling that it was time to return. Taking a deep breath, I opened the door and dragged my heavy limbs back to the van.

Late that night, some twelve hours after the nightmare had begun, we arrived at our destination—the Nagoya Immigration Detention Centre—where we were ordered off the van and separated into two groups, according to sex. Throughout the whole ordeal, the officers hovered around us, like wolves circling their prey, yapping "*Haiyaku!*"[1]

Again, we were handed papers to sign, and when I requested a translation, one officer replied, "This is Japanese law and you are criminal!"

We were marched upstairs. Our money, jewellery and belongings were confiscated and we were assigned to occupied cells. A Chinese man and the two Filipinos from the fish factory were placed in with me. There were ten cells along the corridor; numbers one to eight were for men, while nine and ten were reserved for women. The cells were about the size of an average bedroom, in which they detained up to seven people at a time. Each cell comprised one steel door, no windows, no furniture, and a Japanese-style toilet basin in one corner. It was dark, cramped and very noisy due to the thin walls.

Sitting down on the *tatami*,[2] we acquainted ourselves with the other detainees, who were playing cards on the floor. Few could speak comprehensible English, so communication was slow as we tried to translate. They explained that people were in detention for a variety of reasons including expired visas, illegal entry, and transit between prison and deportation.

1. Hurry up! (Japanese)
2. Japanese floor covering: straw-like mats.

I was the only one claiming refugee status.

I found a spare *tatami* to lie on later that night and considered the day's events. Despite the initial stress, I thought all would be resolved once the proper channels were pursued. I had been falsely treated like a criminal before, first by Aunt Meseret and later by the Italian's wife who thought I'd stolen his stereo. In this country of democracy and freedom, I didn't know the rules but I expected certain rights were without question. Surely, all this handcuffing and rough treatment was just fancy dress. I reassured myself that once they confirmed my application process with the Australian Embassy, I would be released to continue awaiting approval.

Looking back now, I realise I had no understanding of the harshness of the Japanese system.

These storm clouds were about to wash away any sign of a road ahead, and they would rain down on me for far too long.

On my first day as a detainee, I awoke to a curt voice shouting names in the corridor. I sat up and listened as the footsteps came closer and the voice grew louder. Two guards swung open our heavy metal door to reveal an officer standing stiffly, holding a folder and pen. He called out our names while one guard stood at the door and the other entered our cell to search our belongings. When everyone had answered to his name and the cell check was complete, the door was slammed shut and they continued along the corridor.

A few minutes later, an old lady's face appeared at a small slot in the cell door. Her crinkled features were soon replaced by a tray holding a small piece of bread and some milk for each of us. After passing these through the slot, she too disappeared.

This was to be the morning ritual.

Following breakfast, a Japanese-speaking cellmate helped me ask if I could contact the Australian Embassy, but the guard on duty told me it was pointless because I would be going home shortly. When asking another guard, I was told I had no right to use the telephone. This must have been a standard answer, since he couldn't have known my particular circumstances.

The rest of the morning was spent talking with cellmates, mainly trying to figure out exactly where in Nagoya we were and what the area was like outside the building. Two of the men had been living in Nagoya and had a pretty good idea about our location and our surroundings. I closed my eyes and imagined walking freely in the streets they described. That sense of space kept me calm.

Other than that, I watched the officers move people around the detention centre for the various stages of processing. I was amazed to see how busy it was; there was rarely a quiet moment.

The following morning, I was fingerprinted. Later, a strange-looking officer came to our cell, clutching some forms. His thick bushy eyebrows squished together in a mono-brow as he read out something in Japanese. I had no idea what he was talking about and a cellmate translated for me.

In simple English, he described the details of my arrest and the relevant Articles from Japanese law. He asked if all the facts were correct. When I responded, "Yes," I was told to sign the form. I asked the officer if I could have an interpreter to better under-stand what was going on. He refused. After a heated discussion, I relented and signed.

How many forms had I signed by then? None of it was getting me closer to a resolution, a telephone or release.

Satoko had been in contact with the factory boss and learned of my arrest. She tried phoning Nagoya detention, but thought it best to let things (me) alone. Her initial part in this play of circum-stance had been that letter of invitation. She probably felt there was nothing more she could do. Japanese generally are not like Westerners; they don't want to get involved or disturb the main-stream flow of things.

Each day, anxiety heated my belly, first as a small flame, but soon to be a roaring blaze.

Days after I was detained, an officer came for me. He spoke Japanese and I struggled to understand what he was saying. Once again with help from my cellmates, I learned that my arrest processing was complete: my baggage had been organised, I had been fingerprinted and photographed, my former employer had delivered my salary and, as I had already signed a deportation order, I only needed to arrange a ticket home.

Wah! I had never knowingly signed a deportation order! I rapidly tried explaining, but the officer cut me off. I threatened to call the UN, but of course no phone calls were allowed. He ordered me to retrieve the return ticket from my luggage in the storage room. After examining the ticket, the officers decided to have it altered so that I could fly out from the closer Kansai International Airport, rather than my scheduled departure point of Tokyo.

Going back to Africa had never been part of my plans. Every dream, every effort, every endeavour had been towards finding a better life elsewhere. Being forced to return cracked open all the fears of poverty and war and destitution that I had locked away (forever, I thought). The fire of resentment at having no control over my life became an inferno. So, this was to be my next round of disappointment? Bring it on. I would go back to square one and find another way forward.

That would have kept me focused—if I'd known the departure date. But they never told me. With every other paper signed and stamped, that was the one detail they let slip away and, as coming events would unfold, a large chunk of my life with it.

Exactly one week after my arrest, I was transferred along with several others to the Nishi-Nihon Immigration Centre located on the outskirts of Osaka, in preparation for my deportation. It was raining heavily when we arrived and although the van windows were covered with black curtains, we could see a huge modern complex through the front windscreen. A large number of officers were standing under umbrellas waiting for the van to halt.

Capture

We were led off the bus by ropes tied tightly around our waists, chaffing our skin. Men and women were separated and taken one by one into a small room. When it was my turn, I entered, then hesitated when I saw a latex-gloved officer waiting. The door slammed shut, and he ordered me to strip.

My mouth felt like I'd swallowed the Sahara Desert. He tapped his pen repeatedly against his notepad. I removed my clothes; *all* of them. He walked over and began checking me with his rubber-tipped fingers. I closed my eyes as humiliation prickled over me. He poked and prodded, making notes on his pad of any scars and markings. I turned around for him to meticulously inspect each and every part of my body. The degrading ordeal was over in just a few minutes. I was allowed to dress and move back out into the hall.

The next officer in the processing line checked my identification and belongings. Once my identification was confirmed, I was moved along to a female officer who handed me a blanket, a cup, a spoon, and a pair of plastic slippers. Then I was directed to yet another officer who was standing in front of a basket. He asked me to deposit the items received from the female officer, along with any necessities from my bag that I would need in my cell. No jewellery, expensive items, shoes, dangerous objects (razors, nail scissors, sense of humour, etc.), nor more than a handful of clothes were permitted inside the cell.

The men's cells were located on the second floor; women were on the third. Our floor was divided into two sections, A-side and B-side. There were nine cells along A-side, eleven along B-side, and the two sides were separated by the officer's control and monitoring rooms, with two large halls (one for each side) used for interviewing and checking bags.

I was sent to cell A6, about midway along A-side. The cell was much larger than the one in Nagoya, about double the size of a typical Western bedroom. I found the only available mat; of course, nobody else wanted it as it was at the back, right next to the putrid toilet. The toilet had a door, but the stench still wafted out as the other detainees went to and fro. Next to the toilet was a raised shelf with a television. There was a small washbasin on the back wall. Some overhead cubicle shelving pretended at personalised storage space. In the centre of the cell were two rectangular tables where we could eat.

I settled onto my *tatami* and surveyed the surroundings. There were 10 other men in the room and they appeared to be from all different corners of the world. I spoke to an Iranian man who was sitting directly opposite. Thankfully, he could speak English. As I explained my circumstances, he was surprised to learn that I'd been caught after only 13 days of work. He'd met people in detention who had been working illegally for numerous years before being caught. How was it that my lottery ticket stated: *wins bad luck—every time?*

Later that afternoon, I was granted permission to call the Australian Embassy. At last, I might get someone to sort this out. After filling out a telephone application form, I purchased a phone card, was escorted to a telephone in the guards' office and dialed the number.

The officer took the hand-piece from me and spoke to the secretary of the migration department. She asked the officer to write her a letter outlining the details of my arrest. The officer hung up, without even giving me the chance to speak to her. I'd been warned of imminent deportation. Despite my grave disappointment over the turn of events, surely I would not have to endure this situation for much longer.

Traditional beliefs in Japan acknowledge the ancestors. There is no belief in God.

Previously, any benefit to my life had come through the Church, so I associated goodness with those who believed in God. I grew up bowing to God and anything to do with God. I bowed in church. I bowed to the priests. I showed reverence to something that was greater than the conditions of my life. I surrendered myself to a belief system that promised hope where I had none.

When I arrived in Japan, I leapt at new challenges, confident that God was wishing me well. I respectfully tried to observe local custom. *Entering the village, obey the village.*[3] Noting that people bowed, I bowed too.

In relation to all I had learned as a child, who were these people really? Were they representatives of God on earth? Was there something sacred about them that required my obeisance? No. They were everyday people, living everyday lives. They didn't even believe in God, so why was I bowing?

Each small thing that conflicted with all I had believed in so far planted more doubts in my mind. How could I communicate with someone who didn't seem to be connected with something sacred, at least as I understood it? What was to become of me in this land of strange customs?

Up until then, my impressions of Japan had only come from a small factory (mostly populated by foreigners) and two detention centres (mostly populated by foreigners). The rapidity with which my glowing future vanished was stunning. Opposing this, the intensity of my frustration flared from knowing so little else of this country—no language, no solid contacts, no understanding of the culture or acceptable forms of communication.

I watched the way guards interacted respectfully with their superiors, only to turn on us as though we were asking to be dehumanised. We must promptly answer "*Hai*"[4] whenever addressed; we must call them "sir"; we must make no mistakes when answering any questions or we'd be abused for our incompetence; every request must be in writing on the correct forms; the only explanation for anything (when things didn't work, when requests were denied, when we were forced to change cells) was: "It is the rule!"

---

3. Japanese proverb.
4. Yes. (Japanese)

American films often portray military discipline by showing an officer who barks orders that the cadet soldiers strive to fulfil. If he yells, "Jump!" they respond with, "How High, Sir?!" Someone told me of a parody in which the officer yells, "Shit!" and the cadets yell back in unison, "How Many And What Colour, Sir?!"[5]

That's what detention life felt like—that not even going to the toilet was in our control.

From every official, the first comment was always: *"Why did you come to Japan?"* It was asked defensively, as if they were offended that I'd chosen their country. They were not looking at what circumstances I had come from, nor did they consider what contributions I might make. They only saw me as an intruder.

For a black person, going to a white country was like going to heaven. Everything white was perceived as greater in some way. In

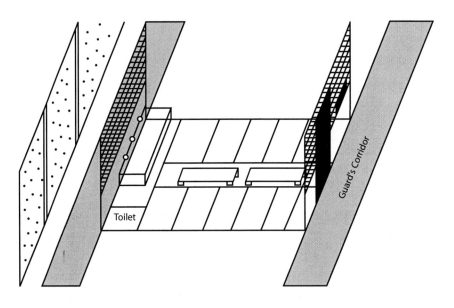

Typical Cell Layout at
Nishi-Nihon Immigration Centre

---

5. An approximation of the original.

Men's Floor Layout at Nishi-Nihon Immigration Centre

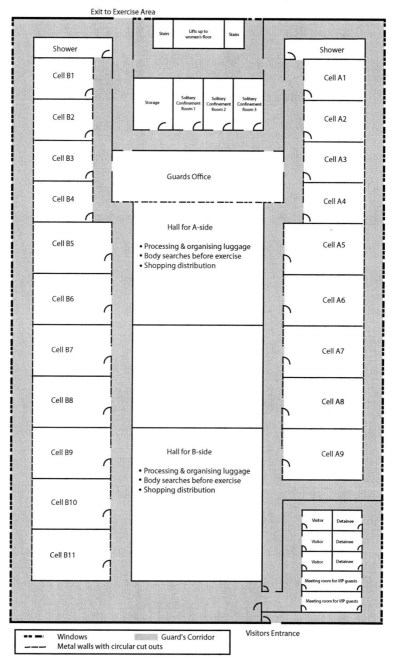

Ethiopia, the nuns always wore white clothes, the priests I knew drove white cars; the saints in pictures glowed white; and of course, Jesus was portrayed as a white man. The Ethiopian air is so dry, and the sun would blaze down, darkening the skin even more. As children, if we saw someone who looked pale, we thought, for sure they were rich. Dark, dirty and thin were signs of poverty and hardship.

My dream of escape and freedom led me to a white country. What a shock to find poverty and rejection of another kind.

18

NO HEAR, NO SEE, NO SPEAK

Routine had given me strength in the past. When I survived on the streets, habitual activities provided the framework on which I could hang my scant life. I revelled in them. For brief moments, I was in control.

My current situation was strangely reversed. I had compulsory shelter, compulsory food, compulsory (intrusive) recognition—yet I was still anonymous, still lost and still unwanted.

I was too raw with shock to consider the frightening prospect of maintaining sanity if this incarceration went from indefinite to interminable. Although I was no longer in control, I focused on what might give me strength.

It soon became apparent that daily life in detention was going to be predictable, as we adhered to a strict timetable. The schedule at Nishi-Nihon Immigration Centre went like this:

Refers to the Three Wise Monkeys from a 17th-century Japanese carving; pictorially, they represent the proverb: hear no evil, see no evil, speak no evil.

07:00 A.M. Wake up. Clean cells and detention corridors.

07:30 A.M. Breakfast. Milk (200mls), one slice of bread.

08:40 A.M. Roll call. Personal belongings searched.

11:30 A.M. Lunch. Small piece of fish, bowl of rice, *miso* soup.[1]

04:20 P.M. Dinner. Small piece of fish (or chicken), bowl of rice, *miso* soup.

05:00 P.M. Roll call.

10:00 P.M. Lights out.

As much as I hated the routine that the timetable brought, it provided me with a strange kind of stability, and the only guarantee in an otherwise largely unpredictable and uncertain environment.

It was unpredictable because fights could erupt between detainees without warning; cellmates could be deported without notice; new ones could arrive at any time of the day or night, always with the infernal clanging of that steel door. It was uncertain because nobody knew how long they would be detained; if they would be deported or released; or what the future held.

So, despite the monotony, the daily schedule anchored us during the rough seas we each were travelling.

There were two types of authoritative figures: officers and guards. They all wore similar navy-blue uniforms and military-style hats, but the officers were distinguishable by a badge of stars on their chests; the greater the number of stars, the higher the officer was ranked.

Our futures were held in sway by officers with their notepads and pens who, by merely stamping their *hanko*,[2] could enhance or reduce the quality of our existence. They held interrogations; controlled our application outcomes; decided on suitable punishments for "unruly" detainees; and prepared deportation (e.g., by

1. Soup based on fermented soybean, rice or barley. (Japanese)
2. Name stamp, used in place of a signature. (Japanese)

issuing plane tickets, visas and documentation to leave Japan).

The guards, walking the corridors with their torches and batons, were responsible for maintaining order, escorting detainees around the centre, supervising visitations and carrying out any jobs assigned to them by the officers.

Power was removed from us entirely. Whether we made a telephone call or took a shower, exercised or received mail, it was all decided for us and often at the whim of the officer or guard's mood.

There was a loudspeaker in the ceiling. From the early hours, it blared out instructions to wake up, clean up, eat up, or shut up. It was easy to see that all this "encouragement" to do things in an upward direction meant we were starting from the lowest point. Every part of the day was announced (just to be sure we wouldn't miss any of the highlights). You can imagine that my language skills improved with such repetitive drill—on certain words anyway.

Cleaning duties were forced on whomever was closest to the door. There was no point in making a roster since people were always leaving or arriving. With the toilet in the opposite corner, we either huddled around the tables or pretended to sleep. *Clang.* The steel door grated open to reveal the guards. "Whose turn today?" they barked, and thrust a broom at the nearest "volunteer."

The menu left pretty much everything to be desired; monotonous dishes that were at once thin and oily, with a slightly off aroma. Occasionally, I tried to trade mine for some noodles or biscuits, but no one was interested in second helpings of such cuisine (except the Chinese), so I'd skip a meal instead, hoping hunger would induce desire.

Appetite could also be curbed since the flimsy plastic spoons often broke in our attempts to gouge mouthfuls from the clumped rice. We had to repeatedly request a new spoon or just dig in with our fingers.

The daily search was demeaning. Although I'd been searched

on entry and, since then, always confined with every action fully exposed, the guards would ransack my things as though I had mysteriously smuggled in contraband. (Maybe they were looking for my private stash of dignity.)

We were denied any mental stimulation from newspapers or contact with the outside world. Conversely, the "luxury" of television was broadcast from 7 A.M. to 9:30 P.M. We had no control over the channels or volume. It beamed slanted visions of reality into our disenchantment, sharpening our senses to all we were missing.

General viewing included game shows, karaoke and soap operas—great for expanding vocabulary—but the prime irony was the Japanese obsession with culinary delights. Food programs were broadcast incessantly, from morning till night. Always, we saw delicious ingredients, or someone tasting them and describing the flavours and sensations. *Bon appétit, cellmates!*

Occasionally, there would be a film, but the guards thought nothing of randomly changing channels to interrupt our viewing. Even in a tiny cell, we grew confident within our known rights and would complain loudly about the mini injustice of not knowing who caught the bad guys and who got to kiss the girl; such was our cultural diversion. The guards would claim that someone in another cell had requested the change. It didn't require the Wisdom of Solomon to see through that.

Some cellmates were unfazed by the constant interruptions, choosing instead to play poker. They were overtly vocal in the extremes of winning and losing, cutting through all other activities like fireworks in a match factory.

The cells were designed in such a way that we could be seen at all times. Guards patrolled the hallways every three minutes, peering in through the head-high and waist-high porthole grills on either side.

Small luxuries were prized. The in-house supply store sold basic commodities like tea and packet soup. Within the cells, there was a kettle, so tea-making became quite a ceremony (though in no way Japanese). There was an ironic balance in this humble act of civility when we asked each other, "Tea?" and replied, "Thank you," as if we were anywhere but locked up. The kettle cord had to be handed over at night, along with the cigarette lighter and the pack of cards. No midnight parties for us.

The pen presented another limitation. Among all of us, there was only one. It hung from a string beside the bars. Of course, we weren't allowed to pass it around, in case someone used it as a weapon (or opened a vein out of desperation), but this made the inconvenience a feature frustration. People needed to sign various papers, lodge certain forms, and fill out applications. For those of us who wrote letters, it became a contortionist act. This circus ceased in the evening when the guards retrieved the pen, and began again the next morning upon its return.

Pursuing every avenue for help, I wrote to the Red Cross, the United Nations and whatever organisation might provide a solution. I sent a few letters back to Africa, but I never told them of my situation. Just as I had kept my street life a secret out of pride, I couldn't relate yet another grim tale. I was also writing a diary to keep track of time. So, for me, the pen was a connection to life beyond this. The detainees and I often haggled over such an essential tool.

With cramped, noisy conditions and routine interruptions, space and time seemed to warp any sense away. Not all of us were criminals. Some had come from dire situations, trusting in the goodness of the world to extend some portion of comfort and hope. We were not lazy or parasites, but ready to adapt wherever required, and to offer the best of ourselves.

The deportation process was confounding. We were all anticipating imminent expulsion from Japan, but continued appealing for every other option in the meantime. We were expected to pay our way out, but those with no money were harangued to find some. We

343

were made as uncomfortable as possible so that, of our own choosing, we would prefer to face whatever dire consequences awaited in our home countries rather than endure confinement any longer.

It felt insane. There was no tolerance there. Adding to the already crowded, uncomfortable, oppressive atmosphere, the guards regularly upbraided us.

I will never forget one named Kojima, who delighted in taunting us. Each time he passed my cell he would shout, "Go home, face the war and die like a man. You are nothing but a coward."

They treated us so callously (not all of them, but most), pumped up in their own self-importance of uniforms and power play. Marching up and down, they seemed like nasty wind-up toys never deviating from their programmed opinions and movements. Perhaps the schedule was just as important to keep them sharp as it was to keep us suppressed.

When no one hears your cry for help—instead you are told what to say and when to say it . . . when you cannot see the sky—instead, day and night are decided for you with the flick of a switch . . . when you cannot hear anything but degradation, which finally pervades even your thoughts . . . are you still human?

The conditions were conducive to illness and infections. Smoking was permitted inside the cells, but there was no ventilation system or windows to allow in fresh air—the only air-conditioning was controlled by the officers and set at temperatures designed to make our lives as uncomfortable as possible.

As a non-smoker, I struggled with every toxic exhalation around me. There was always someone lighting up and puffing away, the Chinese being the worst. Whatever gets you through the day, I suppose.

During the day, the cells were warm and stuffy. At night, the temperature dropped sharply. We didn't have beds, so we slept on the floor. Each detainee was allotted one *tatami*, a blanket and a pillow. My bones ached every night from that hard floor and the chilly air-conditioning.

Hell itself couldn't be better planned.

We were also prevented from forming strong bonds with each other. This was achieved through regular cell rotations. Random detainees were selected each time and moved to different cells. This was unsettling because we were constantly forced to deal with new people.

Mornings tended to pass quicker. At other times of day, the feelings of frustration and confinement pierced my resolve, sharper and deeper with each passing second. Minutes felt like hours, especially in the long stretch between lunch and dinner, and then again between dinner and lights out, as there was little of value to occupy our minds.

Nighttime was the worst. I dreaded the silence and darkness, which echoed another kind of blackness within me. My whole world had become four cell walls. I could name them: Loneliness, Bleakness, Sorrow, Emptiness.

I tried to conjure a starry sky, a broad horizon, a feeling of dreams pulling me forward. But all was void.

Oh to renew the dream that a lion has dreamed till the wilderness cried aloud.[3]

My heart reached for Africa, for the familiarity of a struggle I knew how to endure. Even then, to be a lion in the wilderness seemed better than being a lion in a cage.

As I strained to cope with physical confinement, my thoughts went back and forth, back and forth, mentally pacing behind the bars that kept me from a life of worth. With each passing day, I became increasingly restless and frustrated.

Help: a tiny word that conveys a significant message.

---

3. WB Yeats, Irish poet (1862-1942).

Of course, it must be filed, duplicated, passed on according to protocol, coded via Articles and jurisdictions, evaluated for degree of expedience—and placed in a queue.

The first time I was granted permission to call the Australian Embassy personally, a guard stood so close behind me that I could feel his breath on my neck. I spoke to the secretary of the Migration department about the status of my application. She asked me to be patient, as it could take (a long) time.

The receiver clicked, then hummed. *You have been disconnected.* Tell me about it!

With the whole world reduced to one cell, outside seemed like the Promised Land. I concentrated my survival instincts on that. If I could take just one step there. . . .

Outdoor exercise was rostered twice a week for 30 minutes, but I can clearly remember weeks passing, and sometimes more than a month, without my being let outside. "Bad weather" was often the excuse.

When we were fortunate enough to be released from our cages, we were given a couple of soccer balls. We played barefoot because we weren't allowed to access our shoes from the luggage room. The games were often rough, since everyone vented their pent-up frustrations. What had given me joy and release as a child now became individuals jostling defiantly for a modicum of control over this tiny annex of their existence. Consequently, many of us returned to the cell with some kind of foot injury.

During an exercise session one day, when cells from both A and B sides were combined, I started talking with Bashir, a Sudanese detainee. He told me about an organisation called Amnesty International. They were helping him with his refugee application. I took mental notes of everything he said but, still in the back of my mind, I was hopeful that Australia would soon accept me and I wouldn't have to worry about any other applications.

After exercising, we filed back into the building and dropped our dirty clothes into a communal wash basket. Although our clothes were washed for us, we had to purchase our own washing powder.

From there, we were herded into the showers, which were only permitted twice a week for 10 minutes, after exercise. The water in the showers was scorching hot, too hot to immerse my entire body in. While others seemed to adjust to the temperature over time, I had to stand to the side and splash the water onto myself.

Clothing came from our own luggage, but if things wore out, there were some donations from visitors.

Basic necessities were available at highly inflated prices from the internal shop. The purchase of specific items was arranged through a request form. If we needed anything, we had to access our money. To access our money, we had to fill out a request form. The officers made sure there was always enough cash left to buy the deportation ticket home. We had to make do with what was left. Even though they were handling our money, the guards were very honest, and I never worried that they might steal.

A few days after I met Bashir, a guard delivered a note from him containing useful contact details, and I made my first attempt to request help from Amnesty International. I spoke to Ms Toyoda. She described Amnesty's aims and limitations, but mentioned that they tried to discuss and promote critical cases with the Ministry of Justice (responsible for Immigration). Ms Toyoda requested a letter, outlining my background and current situation. She promised to keep in touch.

Irregular exercise, lack of hygiene and a poor diet sapped our energy, making our bodies weaker. Most of us were young, fit and healthy prior to our arrest, but after only a few weeks inside detention, we had deteriorated into weak shadows of our former selves.

I still had a gash on my leg from an injury at the fish factory. This became infected about a month after I was detained. Initially,

I tried to keep it clean, but when it progressively worsened I informed an officer. I'd heard there was a doctor's clinic in the detention centre and requested to be taken there. Several days after I lodged the request, three guards came to the cell and summoned the patients, including me.

"Solomon Fekadu!" I hated hearing my father's name, but I was tired of trying to explain to everyone that the naming systems differed between Ethiopia and Japan. Most people simply found "Tewodros" too difficult to pronounce and they soon reverted to calling me "Solomon." A fine legacy for an unwanted son.

The clinic was a white barren room with an examination bed in one corner and a small trolley containing a few items of basic medical provisions. In the centre of this small room was a desk. Behind it sat a short middle-aged man with glasses.

He was dressed in a long white coat so I assumed he was the doctor, although I was never introduced to him or given his name. His skin was so white it looked translucent. It gave him a ghostly aura.

He looked up from the pile of papers on his desk as I sat down on a three-legged stool. My aching bones would not settle comfortably. He scrutinised me, then approached, the coat dwarfing his already small frame.

There was a nurse perched on a stool in the corner. She motionlessly observed as the doctor glanced briefly at the wound on my leg. He glided back to his desk, turned to the nurse and asked, "*Tsugi wa dare?*"[4]

Was it over already? I looked at the nurse, hoping she would intervene. She stood, took a tube of ointment from the cabinet drawer and handed it to one of the guards. Another one hoisted me to my feet by the scruff of the neck and escorted me back to the cell. I wasn't allowed to keep the ointment with me. Instead, I was told that the guard would administer it as required.

By late August, I'd been in detention for about three months. In

4. Who's next? (Japanese)

that time, more serious health problems emerged. I was taking a shower one day when I noticed yellowish pus oozing from my right ear. Initially, I thought it must be water still inside my ear from the previous shower. I hoped so, anyway. Over the following days, I woke to find puss smeared on my pillow—it appeared to be getting worse.

As the guards walked passed my cell each morning, I showed them the pus-stained pillowcase. They blanched a little, but I still had to beg them for a doctor's form. This went on for days. Only when they got tired of hearing me call out did they finally cooperate.

I took my puss-stained pillowcase to the next doctor's appointment, determined not to leave without a proper examination. It was disgusting to look at but, as my Japanese vocabulary was quite limited, I didn't know how else to communicate my problem. Neither the doctor nor the nurse flinched as I held it up, so I put it on the desk in front of them where it drew barely an eye flick of interest.

I pointed to my right ear and gestured that something was coming out. The doctor stood, came over to where I was sitting, then bent and squinted at my ear. Distressed by his carelessness, I asked him to re-examine me with the proper equipment, but his reply was, "No ear."

He handed the guard a tube of cream (it must have been a cure-all) and gave him instructions for application. I asked the doctor when I should come back. He replied in broken English, "No come, just ask medicine," and with that I was ushered back to my cell.

Two weeks after this appointment, I awoke in the middle of the night with horrific pain. I screamed into my pillow, trying to muffle the sound from my cellmates. In the morning, I pleaded with the guards for another doctor's appointment.

Again, it took several days for my application to be approved. When I met the doctor, I asked for a referral to an outside hospital

349

because the detention doctor was, by his own admission, "no ear." He muttered into his notepad, "Okay."

Before anything else could happen, the guards shouted, "Finish," signalling that my time was up.

The doctor's response confused me. Did he mean "Okay, I will submit your request" or "Okay, I heard what you have to say, now get the hell out of here."?

One week passed.

I arranged another visit. The doctor wasn't happy to see me. With wild gestures, I demonstrated the excruciating ear pain I was still experiencing, and added sufficient cringing to signify a stomach-ache. He reached over the desk and pressed his hand onto my abdomen, then made a note and signalled that my time was up. His disinterest in my health was as corrupt as the pus in my ear.

"What about my ear?" I demanded.

"NO EAR!" he shouted back at me.

I jumped to my feet and slammed my fists down on his desk, shouting, "You have to help me! This pain is making me crazy!"

By then, I'd been in detention for nearly five months. The pain in my ear cut through all else: sleep, appetite, even cohesive thought. My rage couldn't be contained.

The doctor appeared unruffled. I was tempted to reach out and shake him by the neck to see if he really was flesh and blood. The guards thrust me back down onto the stool and I started to tremble.

A moan built from my hollow belly and poured out of me in molten frustration. The guards jostled me into silence.

My mind continued to shriek: *Ane sebb eye.*[5] *Ine sew negn.*[6] I am a human being!

The doctor spoke. "Foreigners here go home soon. Not my problem. But I ask boss. If boss say okay, then you go to doctor outside."

A promise of relief, at last. As the tension poured away, my legs

---

5. I am a human being. (Tigrinya)
6. I am a human being. (Amharic)

felt so rubbery that I almost couldn't walk. I returned to my cell. With deep, calming breaths, I told myself, *Pain is only in the mind. In the mind.*

Anticipation propelled me forward. I barely endured weeks of acute discomfort only to learn that the boss had denied the request.

Not just the doctors, but the guards in detention centres have a huge responsibility for the well-being of their charges. In an ideal world, the nature of these responsibilities would require staff to have good communication skills, empathy for the challenges these people are enduring, patience, integrity, and the ability to offer dignity despite the bureaucratic restrictions of the situation.

But in an ideal world, there would be no detention.

These were jobs no one wanted, assigned to people unqualified for anything else. For that reason, if no other, the situation was a recipe for disaster.

In Japan, the people accepted, obeyed and lived by the system. From what I'd seen, that society believed in rules and things. Always, I had believed in myself and life.

But it was slipping from me. If I no longer saw a bright road ahead, then I would have to find at least the first step or I would be lost forever.

Among the occasional donations to the centre, I sought out any books that could feed my mind. One particular book kept me occupied: the Bible.

I considered God's influence on man; how we endure much because of beliefs. Then I considered man's influence on God; how we justify inaction or allow certain conditions, expecting God to change things for us.

In detention, where there was no Christian belief, the Japanese had all the power. I knew that God would not intercede for me.

One of my cellmates smirked as I leafed through psalms and prophets.

"What are you doing, 'Solomon'?"

"I'm trying to understand Heaven and Hell."

"You don't need a book to tell you. *This* is Hell."

Well, he was partly right: detention seemed void of goodness.

I came to understand that the Japanese worshipped work. Perhaps the shame of losing WWII had pressed them into this kind of manic dedication. Perhaps it had always been an intrinsic part of their culture. Industry was a virtue. National pride was the rod that drove it on. Later, I learned that they even overlooked illegal workers if their economy was prospering. When they needed to swell the employment ranks, you worked. When the economy weakened, you got arrested.

My life had been such a patchwork of extremes. The more perspective I gained, the more I could see that the experience was not just about me.

When one person hurts another, it is sad; when the laws of a country hurt many who are already struggling, it is tragic.

There was so much hatred around me. The guards weren't evil, but their hate-filled treatment of us lacked all dignity (even for them).

Wisdom tells me we should hate the system, not the people. If the system creates fear and lack and loathing, we cannot love. When we cannot love, we cannot really live.

My life had been reduced to the least that was humanly possible, but I had to rise above it. I wanted to shatter the bars, shouting what I'd learned. I knew I *must* find a way out of there.

Herodotus, a Greek philosopher, said: *Lion with endurable heart, suffer the unendurable.*[7] He must have seen me coming.

Autumn had arrived in Japan. Just as the cherry blossom season was celebrated, so too was the turning of the leaves. I knew this, even though I was in detention, because footage of the changing colours was shown extensively on the television in our cell. The

7. Herodotus (c. 484-424 BCE).

guards seemed fascinated, almost proud of the brilliant shades of foliage, and often paused by the cell door to catch a glimpse of the broadcast.

The turning of the leaves was not the only thing presenting a change in colour but, unlike the leaves, *this* change was of little interest to the guards. The pus oozing from my ear had turned from yellowish-green to dark brownish-blood. Adding to the disgust was a putrid smell. And worst of all, pain had become my enduring state of consciousness.

Some days I lay on the floor screaming, unable to control myself. I rocked back and forth with my arms wrapped around my head, as another eon of agony routed my will. The guards would walk by, glance and then quickly walk on. The silence and darkness of the night was the worst. It seemed that when the lights went out, the pain intensified. The balance between my mental resilience and physical suffering swung dramatically to the latter. I could no longer master my other senses. All was defined by pain, leaving me with vague thoughts and the horror in my ear.

During this trying time, some Indonesian detainees moved into my cell. They had arrived in Japan by boat, undergoing quite an ordeal. When the boat entered Japanese waters, it was moored a few hundred metres offshore. From there, the trip organiser ordered them to swim to the main island so that he could evade detection.

Once on land, they spent their nights sleeping on the beach, after scouring the shoreline for food, eating whatever snacks the beach-goers had left behind. It wasn't long before some locals became suspicious and reported them to the police. They were arrested, interrogated and sent to the detention facility where, like the rest of us, they now awaited deportation.

These new cellmates were concerned about my ear. The guards' indifference to my pain offended them, and they suggested I go on a hunger strike—surely someone would take notice.

I was familiar with starvation from my time on the streets of

Addis. It was a daunting prospect to put myself in that state again—voluntarily. Life was trying enough without one deliberately making it worse. But I'd tried everything else. Food was the only thing over which I had any control.

It was mid-October when I stopped eating. I also decided from the outset that I would not consume any liquid, including water, to hasten the effect.

The first strike day went by. Free of envy, I watched the others eating their meals. On the second day, I felt slightly weaker and had to reassure myself that I was doing the right thing. By day three, I had lost considerable strength. My empty belly seemed to amplify the pain in my ear. I spent much of that day curled in a foetal position, trying to block out the pain that was *everywhere*. I was hanging on merely by primal instinct, and vaguely remember snapping like a wounded animal at anyone who ventured near.

My cellmates' requests to get me help were repeatedly ignored. The guards assumed it wouldn't be long before my stomach would win out over my head and I would eat. If only they knew that "defiance" was my middle name.

From the fourth day onwards, I slipped in and out of consciousness. I remember my mouth becoming so parched that the skin around it began cracking and peeling. Once, I woke up as one of the Indonesians was pouring water into my mouth. At other times, I could hear my cellmates screaming for the guards to come and help. I later learned that when detainees in other cells heard about my hunger strike, they too, demanded action.

By the sixth day without sustenance, I could no longer lift my limbs and had become incoherent. The guards entered the cell and began prodding my prone form. As if they were characters in a crazy silent movie, they tripped over each other to call for the boss. The boss came running and called for the nurse. The nurse dashed in and called for the doctor. After a little more shaking and poking, he called for a stretcher. I was jounced a few metres down the corridor to a single cell. This was across from the guards' office where they could watch over me.

The detention centre staff referred to these isolated spaces as "protection cells" for monitoring "special needs," but we knew it was really solitary confinement, for punishment. Detainees were sent there whenever they caused a disturbance. That might include a distressed detainee who'd been denied permission to make an important telephone call; someone who vented his frustration by cursing or putting up a fight when manhandled by the guards; or a detainee who'd done something as simple as attempting to change the channel or alter the volume on the television set.

We were forced to remain in solitary until we showed remorse and asked the officers for forgiveness. Therefore, depending on a detainee's determination and strength, he might remain in there for a couple of days or more than a month.

The most horrifying aspect was the lack of witnesses once you were behind that door. There was frequent talk of detainees who were deported under suspicious circumstances directly from the protection cell, to keep the beatings undetected.

These cells were as wide as about three *tatami*, with wooden floors and walls. Electricity and taps were controlled by the guards. We couldn't turn the lights on or off, but had to contend with living in darkness or battling to sleep under an intrusive glare. Thirst remained unquenched, and the stench from the Japanese-style toilet that remained unflushed was constant. There were surveillance cameras fixed in the ceiling and peepholes in the door.

I can't recall the first twenty-four hours in there. I was jolted into consciousness with a drip in my arm and a sharp pain shooting into my head when I tried to sit up. I fell back to the floor, overwhelmed that it had not just been a nightmare: this was still my reality. Seeing me stir, a guard entered and ordered me not to pull the same stunt again.

Later, they brought solid foods, but I couldn't stomach anything. Another guard had been watching me from the office window. He entered the cell, stared down at me, and then nudged the food tray closer with his foot. In my blurred vision, his body swayed in all directions. I felt several sharp kicks in the stomach, as he shouted, "*Tabete!*"[8]

Could I have a side order of compassion with that?

We were never given the names of any employees who worked at the detention centre, so we assigned them nicknames according to an obvious physical or personality trait. There was "Ashi ga nagai Sensei" (the guard with the long legs), "Se ga migikai Sensei" (the short guard) and "Urusai Sensei" (the loud-mouthed guard), to name a few. We had given the guards' supervisor the nickname "Hige Sensei," referring to his distinctive moustache.

Hige Sensei was one of my favourite officers and was very popular with the other detainees. He never spoke rudely or treated anyone with disrespect. He acted like an intermediary; the negotiator between Immigration and the detainees. When Hige Sensei heard what had happened, he visited me on several occasions. He always took the time to listen and often conveyed my distress to the other staff.

On one particular visit, he was accompanied by an officer who had alerted the Australian Embassy that I was sick. He explained that the embassy wasn't prepared to speed up the process. The two officers encouraged me to eat and become strong once again because, with no hint of a response, I would probably be in detention a while longer.

The Australian Embassy didn't seem to care if I died. The only concern from Japanese Immigration was that I would be less of a hassle for them if I could be kept alive.

I had to be strong, mentally and physically, to be able to fight the

---

8. Eat! (Japanese)

system. I remembered the words of my English teacher in Bure, "You will be challenged for many years to come, but in the end it will be worth it because you will find your peace." I promised myself that, once I regained my strength, I would contact Amnesty and other relevant organisations *every day* until someone took up my cause.

In mid-November, while I was still in solitary, a young guard approached the cell door. He didn't look much older than 15, but I figured he'd have to be a least 20. He shouted through the door that I had visitors. I scrambled upright. The rush of emotions was as dizzying as my fragility.

Under the young guard's escort, I stumbled towards the visitor's room. It was bare except for a single chair on my side of a glass panel. I sat down and peered through the glass at two Japanese: a young man with a noticeably receding hairline and a young woman with oversized reading glasses. They introduced themselves as Mr. Shiho and Ms Toyoda from Amnesty International. I smiled wide with relief.

Ms. Toyoda's eyes narrowed as she peered at my sunken face and glazed bloodshot eyes, and then down to the injection marks in my arm. Mr. Shiho showed the same concern—alternating between horror and disbelief.

I described my general experience inside the centre and what had led to the past few weeks' events. Both Ms Toyoda and Mr. Shiho stiffened as my story became more incredible by the minute.

After half an hour, the guard announced that time was up and I must return to my cell. Ms Toyoda said she would talk with the head of detention. She promised to contact me as soon as she had any news. They stood and waved as I shuffled back to the cell. Such a pleasant gesture felt surreal in those stark surroundings.

Mr. Shiho continued to visit me over the following months. He was gravely concerned and wanted to help, not just as a member of Amnesty, but as a Japanese citizen and a friend. Those visits were emotionally bolstering. More than that, they reclaimed me to the world of decent people and respectful interaction.

I'd been so dehumanised by the constant berating of the guards that I had started to think they must be right, that I was a worthless coward who deserved to die. But when I met Mr. Shiho, and even Ms Toyoda, I was reminded that not everyone in Japan was my enemy.

By mid-December, my appetite improved. The guards noticed my progress and transferred me into cell B1; the "home" of my exercise companion, Bashir.

To date, they had kept people of the same nationalities or the same language as far apart as possible. This strategy worked for the most part, except for the Chinese, whose numbers dominated the limited cells. So I was surprised, yet relieved, that at last I could ease the trying conditions a little in the company of a fellow African.

Bashir smiled broadly when I entered his cell. He had very dark skin and bright white teeth, so it was like a light turning on when he smiled. "*Oh, Salam wa allekum!*"[9] He stood and welcomed me warmly.

Cell B1 was located just across the corridor from the protection cells. It was smaller than the others, and I noticed only five other occupants. I settled my belongings on the spare *tatami*, next to Bashir. He was already preparing tea. The companionship of a friend helped me to tolerate my constant passenger: pain.

Bashir and I maintained regular contact with Amnesty International. Whenever the guards permitted, I called Ms Toyoda. She was looking at options available to me and advised me to apply for refugee status in Japan, even though the sixty-day window had long passed.

The sixty-day rule states that anyone seeking refugee status in Japan must do so within sixty days of arrival, but Ms Toyoda was

9. Peace be upon you! (Arabic)

convinced that I should apply as a back-up plan, for two reasons: first, it was a prerequisite for Amnesty support; and second, she'd been in contact with the Australian Embassy and was doubtful of a decision in my favour. She also agreed to engage a volunteer lawyer who could help me with these various applications.

Ha—a Japanese *DocuMan.* It was about time I had a superhero in my life.

Christmas was fast approaching.

A woman named Kaeda Mori had telephoned the centre and wanted me to return her call. Had Ms Toyoda found me a lawyer already?

First thing next morning, I applied to make a phone call. Kaeda Mori's request was logged, so immediate approval was given.

"Solomon Fekadu?" she haltingly repeated, when I introduced myself.

"Yes," I cringed.

I was relieved when she continued in English, "My name is Kaeda Mori. Ms Toyoda advised me of your situation. I'm from Tamatsu-kuri Church in Osaka."

"Thank you for calling me."

"That's fine, Solomon. My brother, Father Mori, is very active in the community. I'm the secretary for one of the programs run by the Church: the International Committee. We're sorry for your suffering and we hope to help you somehow."

A tsunami of comfort washed over me.

"I will come and visit you soon, okay?" Kaeda said.

"I would like that . . . very much."

"If for some reason I can't, I will send someone from our group. Do you speak Japanese, Solomon?"

"*Sukoshi,*[10] but I can't express myself very well."

My clumsy reply amused her. "Okay, I will send someone who can

10. A little. (Japanese)

speak English."

"Thank you—very much," I said, and hung up the telephone.

I returned to the cell feeling positive. It was encouraging to know that more people on the outside were becoming aware of my situation.

The New Year holiday period of one week increased difficulties inside detention because all the senior officers returned to their hometowns. They were the decision-makers, responsible for day-to-day management, so their departure put the centre in shutdown mode. This essentially resulted in no exercise, no showers, no visitors, no telephone calls, no shopping, and no movement within the centre.

We might as well have been invisible: no one heard us, no one saw us, no one spoke to us.

Shutdown meant there was absolutely nothing to do except sit and watch television, while channels were selected exclusively by the guards. The prolonged boredom raised the sensitivity levels of most detainees, and fights broke out over the smallest of things.

We pondered what we'd been through in the past year, and what we'd have to endure in 1998. I think most of us prayed that we wouldn't be sitting there at the end of the next year, going through the same motions.

Happy New Year, everybody (please, please, with the emphasis on "happy").

19

OUTSIDE INTERVENTION

The New Year did bring change—or was it more of the same, just in a different order?

Grey days faded into grey walls. Clear thoughts thinned into cloudy wisps. Nothing was defined any longer. I was not a black man in a white man's prison. We were all captives.

Anger became confusion became despair became utter hopelessness.

I wanted to scream, "I AM ALIVE! I AM DYING! I AM ALIVE!" but the words wrestled with one another before they could tumble out, till there was no energy to speak.

I shouldn't be fighting myself, I thought. I was named for defiance, wasn't I? Defiance is not anger: it's focus. I had to focus, had to keep going, keep reaching out. . . . Now that someone had heard my cry, there was a thread of hope.

An unexpected letter came from Satoko. My relief at a revived friendship quickly crashed. She wasn't writing to ask how I was or if I needed anything. She wanted money. Money? From me?

Years before, in Egypt, she'd given me a camera as a gift. Now she was asking me to pay for it—or give it back. I wasn't exactly snapping up photo opportunities in detention. Were her finances troubled so she was looking for any solution? Did she want to remove every connection with me? I didn't know what to say, so I didn't write back. Neither did she.

I'd thought I had at least the comfort of one friendship on the inside, but it was short-lived. Bashir smoked excessively. His constant habit caused tension between the two of us, although it wasn't the only source of conflict. He enjoyed playing cards with the Chinese, I didn't; he was friendly with the guards no matter how badly they treated us, I (rejecting indignity) wasn't; he accepted the course his life was taking, I couldn't. Bashir's world was simple: if he got his Marlboro, he was happy.

One day early in the New Year, I was half-asleep when I heard him asking to be moved to another cell. He got approval and was transferred almost as quickly as a cigarette burns out. I didn't blame him. It was the stress, not our natures, making it difficult to get along.

My first visitors of 1998 came 27 days into the year. Ms. Toyoda had invited them: Mr. Higuchi, and two other members of a group called "Asian Friends." This group mainly assisted Asian people with day-to-day life in Japan, but recently they were developing an interest in other foreigners and the conditions inside detention centres. Through later research, I viewed a message that Mr. Higuchi had sent to Amnesty regarding this visit:

> Solomon can't eat well and appears not to be mentally well either. . . . He looks thin and quite sick. . . . He said that he had been to see the doctor in detention, but didn't trust him and wants to see a doctor outside. . . .
>
> Mr. Higuchi, 28 January 1998

Outside Intervention

By mid-February, Ms. Toyoda visited again and introduced me to Mr. Tanaka, a lawyer who would subsequently handle my dealings with the Immigration centre. I'd never encountered a lawyer before, but I'd seen them in American movies as strong, fearless people whose presence alone commanded attention.

Mr. Tanaka's appearance shattered that image. He had baby-soft skin, small round eyes and a slight frame that would hardly get an intimidation rating. Observations aside, I was glad for any assistance and, over time, I appreciated his efforts as heroic.

I told him of the blood-coloured puss and that I could no longer hear through that ear. I asked for help in seeing a specialist.

Mr. Tanaka and Ms. Toyoda were eager to activate the official channels, so our meeting was cut short. That afternoon, they lodged an application on my behalf for an outside medical consultation. It was rejected.

Days fell together, sucked into a black hole of repetition.

There was little to do except read, watch television or talk to the other detainees. Looking back now, I can't explain how I filled my time. My supporters sometimes brought books, mainly for language skills and study, but there was only so much reading I could do. I watched as the others played cards, or I wrote letters when I had spare paper and access to the pen. Sometimes, the "writing queue" was days long.

Tearing out of a straightjacket of frustration, I'd rage at the guards until I exhausted myself. A strange inner calm would ensue, but only for a few days until the strangling sensation took over again. I really think I was on the edge of madness.

Alive . . . dying . . . alive. . . .

Towards the end of March, Ms. Toyoda sent me information about various visas for Japan. On page after incomprehensible page, one word kept jumping out—"alien"—a government term for non-Japanese. Foreigners in their country were Unwelcome

Foreign Objects. I felt like an eagle in a crane's nest, a jackal in a *tanuki's*[1] burrow, a hyena in a *kitsune's*[2] den. Wrong. Wrong. Wrong.

The more I stared at the papers, the less sense I could make of them. No one had openly discussed my options with me. Although I received regular visits from various organisations trying to assist me, I had poor understanding of what each group was doing. I guessed that little information was being fed to me because our conversations, letters and phone calls all came under scrutiny. They didn't want Immigration to know their plans, so they never elaborated during their visits.

Discontent and restless, I called Mr. Higuchi. He came at once.

Soon afterwards, I was relieved to learn that members from each group had decided to meet regularly and pool their resources. I began referring to them as my supporters. They included representatives from the Catholic Church, Amnesty International, and Asian Friends, and my lawyer, Mr. Tanaka. This coordinated approach meant that one of them would pass on my messages to the others.

Ms. Toyoda introduced me to a second lawyer, Mr. Narito. He would be dealing with my ear problem primarily, but would collaborate with Mr. Tanaka on gaining my refugee status, which was proving to be a jargon jungle.

Mr. Narito seemed to have a fresh outlook on life. He was relaxed and easygoing; quite different to Mr. Tanaka. I wasn't sure how well they'd work together as a team, but I was hoping that the knowledge and experience of one would complement the feisty attitude of the other.

Mr. Narito and Ms. Toyoda lodged another application for an ear specialist. Apprehensive about the approval, they decided to apply for my Provisional Release. This meant I could be bonded out to a guarantor. Of course, there were strict rules and regulations. Failure to abide by them would land me back in detention, forfeiting

1. Raccoon dog. (Japanese)
2. Fox. (Japanese)

the guarantor's money. My supporters remained hopeful that at least one of the two applications would be approved.

I didn't realise they'd made an application for Provisional Release until one week later when I was told it had been denied. No reason was given. However, Immigration would consider taking me to see an ear specialist if I paid for all associated medical costs.

When Kaeda Mori learned of this, she asked her brother, Father Mori, if one of the Church hospitals could treat me, without incurring medical expenses. He agreed, and Kaeda made the request official. But her suggestion was angrily rejected by Immigration. They would not surrender control over me, not even to a priest.

For all their love of order, the officials seemed determined to make this as complicated as possible. What were they gaining, really? Who sits on the other side of these paper-pushing desks and decides over the quality of another person's life? The intricacies of a strange game were unfolding, and I was the witless pawn.

Astonishingly, 315 days after I had first requested treatment for my ear infection, I was permitted to see a specialist at the Second Police Hospital. It was the first time in 402 days that I would leave detention. Emotions blitzed my body at the prospect.

My anticipation verged on delirium, as I imagined seeing the sky, and feeling the sun and fresh air. Yet, fear lurked beneath—I would be unenclosed, I would see people freely moving about their business and, after brief hours, I would have to return to detention.

Would I cope?

It was summer.

Until then, the four distinctive Japanese seasons had been filtered through contrary air-controlled discomfort. As I stepped outside, the warm sticky air enveloped my skin, tickling my nerve endings and spurring my senses back to life. Having emerged, raw with feeling, I was unprepared for the day's humiliation, such that would make begging on the streets of Addis seem like a picnic in the park.

Guarded by four officers, handcuffed, with a leash attached to my waist, I was dragged along the hospital corridors, on display for the public. An uncomfortable silence fell wherever I came into view: patients and medical staff stepped aside, averted eye contact and paused at a safe distance to watch me pass. With such a show, who could blame them?

We stopped in the waiting room. I was ordered to sit.

Seeing everyday people in their wonderfully mundane lives roused my memories. I was a boy dreaming of great things. I was a young man boarding a plane to adventure.

I tried to fill my mind with images of another place. In Egypt, I'd seen advertisements for Australian tourism, displaying stunning coastlines with the whitest sand. There I might lie on a towel under a kinder sun than any I'd yet known. The misty air rolling off the ocean would leave a thin film of salt on my skin. I'd taste it on my lips. And the sounds of those waves—huge white-capped beauties—they'd crash onto the shoreline and wash away my shame and frustration.

Australia wasn't the only place I "visited," nor was that the only time I went walkabout in my thoughts, but as I'd slowly been fading into a shadow, so had they.

Wake from the darkness, Tewodros. Wake up and dream.

Sometimes, I'd melt back to the lush northern highlands of Ethiopia, into Ge-ge Zenebech's soothing embrace. I even imagined myself in Italy, thanks to childhood stories from the priests at the mission. I could almost taste the cappuccino that I might sip while sitting in a winding alleyway of some ancient mountain-perched village.

Something dropped onto my lap, snapping me back into the nightmare. The guard sitting next to me had placed his hat over my handcuffed wrists to ease the evident fear of other patients.

Doctor Kawashima was the Ear-Nose-Throat (ENT) specialist assigned to examine me. She was a short stocky woman. She moved about me with great caution, especially as the four officers looming behind me seemed ready to pounce. It was a brief consultation, but the relief was immense as Doctor Kawashima cleaned and treated my ear and hastily prepared a prescription for antibiotic eardrops.

Stand up! Step outside! March!

I was escorted down the corridor to an exit that led outside to the minivan.

Halt!

The guards anxiously scanned the area to make sure they had a clear run to the van.

I stood unsteadily in my bonds, my gaze lifting into the deep, blue sky. Falling upwards, I might stretch the wings of my heart ...

March!

. . . And fly. . . .

Halt! Sit!

. . . Far away. . . .

As the pain in my ear diminished, I felt my spirit stir again, like a lion stretching, awake and hungry.

One week later, I was taken through the same process: same hospital, same humiliating manner, same public withdrawal. This time, I visited the Internal Medical department to have a stomach examination. I was escorted by five officers on this occasion; one handcuffed me and pulled the rope around my waist, two stood on each side and the others followed behind.

How I had increased as a threat, I had no idea. It might have been intimidation tactics, or perhaps it was protocol to add a guard for every excursion. At this rate, I might accumulate my own private army. I would have laughed if it weren't for the Nile flood of tears that I was straining to dam up.

Did anybody really consider what was going on? God knows (not that they'd check with Him).

In the examination room, the doctor tested my stomach, took

an x-ray and prescribed more medicine (which was given to the officers). I was ordered away without understanding what was wrong with me.

From there, we went to the ENT department where I went through a computerised hearing test. Doctor Kawashima determined that the hearing level in my right ear was significantly lower than average. She concluded that the loss of hearing was most likely caused by my current ear infection.

At the end of her explanation, I wanted to ask a few questions about the treatment. No sooner had I opened my mouth when I received a sharp thump on the head. The Passport Officer towered over me, gesturing for me to be silent.

I yelled at him not to touch me, to leave me alone. He pulled me up by the collar, but shouted at me to sit down and be silent. The other officers tensed. The consultation ended abruptly. I was escorted back to detention under resentful glares.

Untied, with handcuffs removed, I was put into an isolated room. The officers brought in an interpreter to relay their concern over my unruly conduct. They stressed that I must not shame them again.

I told them that if they were going to take away my right to speak at the hospital, then I wouldn't go next time. In exasperation, the officers ordered the guards to return me to my cell.

The next hospital appointment was two weeks later, towards the end of July.

When the day arrived, the Passport Officer ordered me out of the cell, but I ignored him. He shouted, "Hurry! You have to go!"

I continued reading. Eventually, he stormed off.

Later that day, other officers came to talk to me. They were unusually pleasant. One of my Chinese cellmates subtly signalled to me that one of the officers was hiding a video camera.

The officers attempted to coerce me into signing a form in Japanese. I couldn't read it, but guessed it stated that I rejected medical treatment at the hospital. I refused to sign, and then smiled at the camera. They shook their heads and retreated down the corridor.

Perhaps it was that darned Ethiopian pride getting in the way of my better judgement, or perhaps I really was plain crazy. With my strength returning, I'd decided to test my roar: I refused to attend any further appointments at the hospital.

Meanwhile, I was becoming increasingly anxious over my status. There'd been no word from the Australian Embassy. No interview. My telephone calls had been brushed aside.

I'd been in detention for more than a year and Kaeda was becoming concerned for my well-being. Actively seeking solutions, she had contacted an Australian priest, eliciting his support in dealing with the Australian Embassy.

This priest, Father Paul, wrote to the embassy expressing his alarm at my lengthy loss of liberty and noted that he would assist with any outstanding requirements to finalise my application. He faxed the letter: there was no reply.

Wishing to strengthen my case, Father Paul found a group in Brisbane that offered me sponsorship. He informed the embassy. He also met with the United Nations in Tokyo and learned that my refugee status with them was dependent on my application for refugee status in Japan.

No wonder the international refugee situation is challenging. If each country and each institution has its own rules, none of which would be easily available to the people most in need, the point of aid becomes lost in a labyrinth of legislation.

So: my ultimate goal was Australia. To influence that, I needed validation from the United Nations. To gain that, I needed refugee status in Japan. Visa vis-a-vis visa vis-a-vis visa. Simple, right?

The third component was something Ms. Toyoda had been proposing all along. When Father Paul explained the necessary process to my supporters, they agreed. So we filed with Japanese

Immigration, compiled the necessary documents for the United Nations and crossed our fingers for a result from Australia.

Then, the day after I refused to go to the hospital, I received a visitor from the United Nations. Mr. Choosin came to conduct an interview and accept my request for refugee recognition. We were given a spacious room and I was surprised when the guard left us to discuss our business in private.

The visitor's rooms, where I usually met my supporters, had glass windows that created a physical barrier between the detainees and the outside world. Conversations were conducted in the presence of a guard, who took notes to ensure that we didn't hatch any secret plans.

This was the first time in fourteen months that I'd been alone in a room without the hovering presence of a guard or an officer. It felt strange that I could actually reach out and shake my visitor's hand. I could speak freely, without fear of being reprimanded. I almost cried from the unexpected gift of positive human contact.

Mr. Choosin was from Thailand. Well-dressed in a grey suit, he was gentlemanly and compassionate all at once. I felt at ease straight away.

He informed me that the United Nations didn't have much power and, like Amnesty, acted as a monitoring body in Japan. Their role was to keep pressure on the government to abide by the Geneva Convention, to which Japan was a signatory member.

Japan had signed the agreement in 1951 and was therefore expected to accept refugees, but to date had shown little interest in adhering to the ruling. Throughout most of the 1990s Japan only accepted one or two refugees per year. According to a Japanese newspaper article,[3] the Ministry of Justice rationalised this low figure, stating:

There are few applicants to begin with because of the fact that, geographically, we are an island nation, and because we

3. "Questioning Japan's 'Closed Country' Policy on Refugees," by Yumi Isozaki.

have weak historical ties with refugees' origin countries. The rate at which we grant refugee status is in no way inferior to that of Western nations.

Mainichi Shimbun, 20 August 2002

Yet Australia, which has received criticism from the international society for detaining asylum seekers, had an approval rate of 93 percent while Japan had a meagre 3.8 percent for the same year.

Based on those statistics, Mr. Choosin believed Australia would accept me. Before he left, I handed him my application and confirmed that I'd already submitted my request for refugee status to the Japanese government.

One month later, in September, I met Mr. Woods from the Australian Embassy. As before, we were given the spacious private room. The guards were on their best behaviour; bowing respectfully, listening attentively and quickly responding to any of his requests.

Mr. Woods had an olive complexion, short dark hair, and a friendly smile. He didn't resemble the tall blue-eyed fair-haired sporty types I'd seen in advertisements. After slinging his suit jacket over the back of the chair he offered me a cigarette, which I declined. He chatted casually about the large number of foreigners in Japan, working illegally for years, and how unlucky I'd been to get caught so quickly.

More formally, he discussed the points in my application. He acknowledged that the situation in Ethiopia wasn't good and showed me some printed information he'd received about the rising tension between Ethiopia and Eritrea.

I had no idea of the recent developments there and was saddened to learn that while I'd been in detention a bombing had occurred at a school in Tigray. It killed 48 civilians, including numerous women and children. The Eritrean government had taken responsibility, but claimed it was a mistake and didn't investigate the incident. This provoked Ethiopia into armed confrontation.

I hoped Mr. Woods would consider these recent developments when making his final decision. Before leaving, he asked if I had any contact with the Ethiopian/Eritrean community in Australia, and offered to send me videos about these communities. He obviously thought detention was equipped with modern comforts.

I had waited fifteen months for this interview. With my future in his hands, I had expected something more profound.

Incredible. Another New Year had begun.

Detention was once again in shut-down mode. Two years had passed since I'd applied to the Australian Embassy and been detained. While much had happened, nothing had changed. I prayed that this year would bring freedom. I prayed that my life would make sense. Though I hadn't forgotten about Him, I wondered if God was offshore from this land of other shrines and temples. He certainly wasn't there to catch me when I fell under three major blows that came in rapid succession, early in 1999.

The first two were simultaneous. In late January, Mr. Choosin brought news from the Australian Embassy. My refugee application was unlikely to be accepted because I was in Japan—a country that is supposed to accept refugees—and this relinquished the Australian government of any responsibility towards me. Clang!

Mr. Choosin continued: the United Nations was unable to recognise me as a refugee. I asked for the reason. He could only shake his head saying that the decision had come from Geneva. Clang!

What once seemed straightforward had twisted into a crazy maze, spiralling back to the same dead end as each exit door slammed shut. Those pieces of paper were fundamental to my freedom. I'd reached out in every direction, trusting in ultimate justice. But *a bird hanging between two branches will get bitten on both wings.*[4] So it would seem.

---

4. Ethiopian proverb.

I am bitten to pieces.

What is left? No flight. No freedom. No future.

Rage bursts forth. Rage roars in my ears. Rage rips through my heart where I had made such a welcoming haven for love. So ready to give. To live. To prove my worth to everyone—anyone.

Scream, no sound.

Hold, but all is hollow.

Reach and reach for one touch, gentle in the darkness. . . .

Mr. Choosin's hand is resting gently on my shoulder. I look into his eyes. His compassion pours into me. It's not enough, but it is something. I gather myself and thank him for his time.

The pit of pain burns deep within.

Numbing myself, I return to my cell.

Driving the point hard home, a letter arrived from the Australian Embassy stating that my application had indeed been unsuccessful. In the "Other Comments" section, Mr. Woods had noted that because I "departed Ethiopia on a valid passport," there was no evidence of a threat to my safety. The embassy was aware of that fact from my first application made within days of landing in Japan, so why had it taken 637 days to make that decision?

I tried to contact Mr. Woods by telephone on numerous occasions, but was repeatedly told he was unavailable. I wrote instead, appealing the decision, but this went unanswered.

The third blow came soon after. The Ministry of Justice sent a letter stating that my refugee application for Japan had been rejected. Clang!

The reason for rejection was as follows:

Your application was submitted after the expiration of the period provided for in Article 61-2, Paragraph 2 of the Immigration-Control and Refugee-Recognition Act, and your statement for the reasons for delay of the application cannot be accepted, as it does not come under the circumstances to which the proviso to the same paragraph applies.

Ministry of Justice, 9 February 1999

To put it simply: I had applied outside the allowable sixty-day period. The frustrating part was that I was aware of that point, my supporters were aware and Japanese Immigration was aware from the outset. My extenuating circumstances had been detailed in the initial enquiry. So why make me go through the whole process: the waiting, the wondering and, finally, the rejection?

One after another, detainees came and went. Some passed through fleetingly. Others stayed long enough to tell me their stories, before vanishing to who-knew-where. My companions' faces became an endless parade of changing nationalities, and I was the keeper of their tales of woe. The guards, the routine and I were the only constants.

I had little money by then. My supporters brought certain necessities and, when deported, some of my cellmates left me their supplies of soap powder, food and shampoo.

My world had become so small that I was grateful for such "abundance."

By that stage, I was a record holder: longest residing detainee in Nishi-Nihon Immigration Centre. As you can imagine, there was no joy in learning that I'd been crowned king of detention endurance. It was neither something to be proud of nor something to aspire to. For me, it was a symbol of misery and utter loneliness.

My health was still far below any sense of well-being. My energy had lifted a little while I'd approached those thresholds of hope, but each closing door echoed in the hollow of my soul. I'd run out of coping strategies. Philosophy, defiance and detachment were broken threads that had only held me up for so long. Occasional insanity (never a conscious choice) seesawed with despair. Who was I now? What was I?

Links to reality frayed and dissolved. My thoughts were mere wisps. I was nothing . . . a lost ghost in someone else's strange dream. . . .

Ceaseless and unstoppable, a whisper came. And stayed. All else slipped away—all aspirations, all lesser goals. The whisper reminded me that life cannot be constricted by opinion, condition or enclosure. Life simply is.

Though a husk, I felt my heart still beating strong. I continued to put one foot in front of the other. The Japanese say: *Fall seven times and stand up eight.*[5] Life said: Stand up, Tewodros, and live.

So, I did.

My supporters had never dealt with someone in my situation before. In fact, except for Mr. Tanaka, none of them had ever attempted to help a detainee. I understood that must have presented a significant new challenge for them. Indeed, my predicament would have confounded even the most adept.

With a bad start to the year, my supporters decided to contact Mr. Suzuki, a lawyer in Tokyo. He had vast expertise in dealing with detainees and his advice was simple: "Don't give up! Keep pushing Immigration and eventually they will break."

During that time, the guards repeatedly rejected my telephone applications, cutting me off from my contacts. This denial struck me hard, since other people were allowed phone access.

Stand. Fall. Stand.

On one occasion after being continually rejected, I started yelling at the guard, demanding a reason why I was being blocked. I couldn't hold it together anymore. I lashed out in a hysterical frenzy, eventually collapsing onto the floor.

Fall. Stand. Fall.

---

5 Japanese proverb.

Despite the frustrations and uncertainty of my future, I felt that the chances of being deported from Japan were very slim. Since the arrest, my passport had expired, and civil war had erupted again between Ethiopia and Eritrea.

In 1998, after the bombing of the school in Tigray, the Ethiopian government began deporting anyone of full or part Eritrean descent, including my Eritrean father. It was a systematic, country-wide operation in which families were torn apart. The male head of the household was usually the first to be deported, the wife and children following within weeks (or sometimes months later).

The government claimed that the deportees had forfeited their citizenship by voting in Eritrea's independence referendum of 1993, and that they now posed a threat to national security. They were immediately stripped of their Ethiopian citizenship, without any legal consultation or appeal process in place.

In a radio announcement, Prime Minister Meles Zenawi claimed that he didn't need to justify the evictions. They could be carried out if "we don't like the colour of your eyes." Ethiopians residing in Eritrea began flowing back over the border to their homeland, in fear of reprisals.

I hadn't told anyone back there that I was in a detention centre. Calling from time to time, I learned that there were two rounds of Eritrean deportations. At the time, my father, my stepmother and their four children were still living in Addis Ababa, though they weren't targeted during the initial roundup. When the first collection of deportations ended, the family thought it was over.

Then in early July 1998, without warning, a second round of deportations began. People were abducted from their homes in the middle of the night. My father was taken during one of these raids. One morning at about 5 A.M., three armed soldiers escorted him from his house to the nearest police station. From there, he was taken to a processing point where they stripped him of Ethiopian citizenship and prepared his deportation to Eritrea.

I've asked people who knew about those events why Solomon would have been targeted, given that he held such an important position at the university hospital. Some say that because of his tribal links and his prominent official position, supporters of the Eritrean government may have sought him out. Perhaps they wanted his support—political or financial—and who knows, perhaps he agreed.

Doctor Solomon Fekadu Reda was imprisoned for two days in harsh conditions until the Ethiopian government had rounded up enough Eritreans to fill a bus, making the journey to the border worthwhile.

The deportees were deposited at temporary camps along the boundary between the two countries. The camps had been set up by the Eritrean government to cope with the mass influx of displaced persons.

I have read that the Eritrean government initially allocated 1500 *nakfa*[6] to each of the first 300 arrivals, to help them reestablish their lives. However, the government didn't anticipate that some 50,000 people would arrive on its doorstep within a few short months. Identity cards, six months of food rations and other basic items were handed out in an attempt to avert a humanitarian crisis.

In August 1998, my three step-brothers, Mehari, Tinsae and Johannes, escaped from Ethiopia to Kenya using Ethiopian identification. Luckily, Mehari also possessed an Eritrean identification card. That card proved that he and his brothers were Eritrean and in need of rescue. The Eritrean government went to Kenya and collected 600 Eritreans before the Ethiopian government (which was at the Kenyan airport) could capture those attempting escape. Anyone caught was imprisoned.

My stepmother and stepsister (Saba and Senait) were trapped in Addis, because Senait didn't have a passport and Saba's had been confiscated. Their lives became tumultuous. After tireless efforts,

6. US$200 (approximately).

they secured a 10-day *laissez-passer*,[7] and managed to return to Eritrea and reunite with the family.

When Saba and Senait arrived in Eritrea, they had absolutely nothing. Out of necessity, their possessions had been sold cheaply in haste to cover the cost of two air tickets. Other families in similar situations were forced to abandon their possessions, businesses and homes, with little prospect of ever recovering them.

This family's story is not exceptional. Many of the deportees had spent the majority of their lives in Ethiopia. They lived like any other Ethiopian citizen; they owned businesses, worked in government offices, possessed Ethiopian identity cards and passports, and even voted at the Ethiopian elections. No consideration was given to age, class or gender during the mass roundups. Everyone from doctors and lawyers to the rural farmers and elderly retirees was deported.

Moved by the plight of my people on both sides of that conflict, somehow I didn't feel as isolated in that distant land. I connected with their needs. Memories came crowding in—mountainsides in summer, music in the streets, people sharing coffee and organising their day. I empathised with their loss, having known abandonment myself. But what is one man's suffering to a nation's? Never, never would I have wished anyone to go through homelessness.

Strangely such news lifted the weight of blindness from me as I remembered my African roots. Who could I help? How could I help? I had to reach beyond the moment. Where earlier I had shuffled forward in darkness, I remembered again to seek the light; *for however long the night, the dawn will break.*[8]

I know it seems absurd to consider, but I realised how lucky I was. I could have died many times. But there I was. Alive. I could mark the turning points in my life by the moments when I went beyond

---

7. A one-way travel document issued by a national government.
8. African proverb.

my own dilemma—starving on the street, escaping war, surviving betrayal—and felt my heart reach for a better world than this, for everyone. A tiny beam of hope lit the recesses of my being and, as the rhythm of life grew stronger still, very slowly I crept forward.

Fall. Stand. And hope to dance.

One day, I found out by chance that I was not the only Ethiopian-Eritrean man being detained. An officer came to my cell with a letter and asked if the address on the envelope was correct. At first I was confused about why he would ask me, until I saw the writing. It was in English, but addressed to Addis Ababa. I assured him that the address was correct and asked if there was another Ethiopian locked up. He shrugged off my question with a quick, but stern, "No," and left me wondering.

Then a few weeks later, my Peruvian cellmate returned from a doctor's appointment and told me he'd seen another black man at the clinic. I questioned him further. His answers hinted that there might be another *habesha* on the inside.

Curiosity got the better of me. When the guard on duty passed our cell, I asked him, "Is there another Ethiopian man in here?"

"No, you are the only one!" he shouted back. He'd never tell me, even if there was.

Instead of asking again, I decided to write a letter (precious pen time) in my own native language of Amharic. When Hige Sensei passed my cell, I asked him as naturally as I could to give it to the other Ethiopian detainee. Usually, communication between detainees was only delivered if we knew each other's cell numbers. I expected a refusal, yet hoped my casual manner wouldn't give me away. Only pausing for a moment, he took the letter and promised to deliver it. A-ha!

I eagerly awaited a reply. Within hours, Hige Sensei returned, response in hand. He looked at me and jovially asked, "Do you know your countryman or were you just testing me?"

I could only smile as he handed me the letter. He nodded and left.

I retreated to my *tatami* and opened it with trembling hands. My penpal introduced himself as Berga, and wrote that he was suspicious of the source of my letter. So, I replied immediately and allayed his fears. From this time forward, we began communicating on a regular basis via these internal letter exchanges.

And the light within me grew a little brighter.

Over time, the guards wearied of being our delivery boys, and demanded a word-by-word translation, as well as a good reason why they should pass on the communication. Despite this, they rarely refused, although sometimes they would delay the exchange by a day.

Through these letters, I learned that Berga had been to Japan twice, but never beyond the airport. On his first visit, he was stopped at Narita airport in Tokyo, and taken for questioning. He was travelling on an Ethiopian passport and coming to Japan under the pretext of being a businessman, which the Immigration officers didn't believe for a moment. They put him on the next plane back to Ethiopia.

With the resurgence of civil war, he decided to leave again and ordered a new passport, but this time he paid an agency to process all the required forms for entering Japan.

Berga flew into Kansai International Airport and approached the Immigration booth. The officer questioned him, "Have you ever been to Japan before?" to which he replied, "No." The officer glared at him with his passport in hand as his eyes began to flick backwards and forwards between the passport photo and his face.

Berga hadn't changed his name (by then blacklisted) on the new passport. He continued to deny ever being in Japan until the officer presented him with proof. The officer then yelled, "YOU ARE A LIAR!" and a deportation order was issued.

Those letters channelled our pent-up frustration, so we didn't have to take it out on detainees around us. The exchange became a precious link of recognition and support, as one encouraged the other when he was down.

Time did what time does and life, as it was, went on.

Then one day we were informed that our cells needed renovating. All A-Side occupants (my side) were being transferred to B-Side. The officer in charge chose the members of each cell and, of course, Berga and I were kept separate. I was assigned a cell right next to his, but because they were in a straight line along the corridor, we couldn't see each other.

We quickly developed a strategy for talking: I would press my face to the grilled portholes and call loudly up the corridor, so that he could hear me. He would answer in the same way. We talked like that, in Amharic, for as long as those around us could tolerate it. Some days, they were more generous than others. Under the circumstances, I'm sure it added greatly to the maddening environment, but I'd been there for so long by then that this meaningful interaction was a lifeline I couldn't surrender.

Sometimes the officers teased me about bellowing up the corridor. Often, we were only silenced when the other detainees demanded that we shut up. There were also times when I didn't want to talk, but Berga did. He would call my name many times, but hear nothing. He worried about me on these days and he kept talking even if I didn't reply.

A voice in the darkness is a blanket for the heart.

In early April, Berga was led past my cell. He managed to tell me that the Eritrean Ambassador from China had come to see him.

Before I could get details, a guard approached and called out my name. "Solomon-san, *menkai!*" This was the signal that I had a visitor. Given Berga's recent news, I thought I too might get some much-needed attention. Butterfly wings in the belly.

The ambassador cut a regal figure in his crisp white shirt and neatly pressed suit. He was highly polished. Everything about him seemed to shine. From his face with its perfectly trimmed moustache down to his patent leather shoes, not a hair looked out of place. He introduced himself as Mr. Tewolde, the Eritrean Ambassador to China. I was struck instantly by his sincerity.

The ambassador knew of my father.[9] He reassured me that he'd met with Immigration officials to explain the current political problems between Ethiopia and Eritrea and the impact they were having on its citizens. He'd shown the officers statistics and diagrams to demonstrate the huge numbers of displaced persons, and that Eritrea was unable to cope with the influx of returning masses.

His explanation gave me some credibility with the detention staff, who could no longer doubt my home circumstances. So, I was safe—still locked up—but safe.

Two months after that, Berga started vomiting violently and was rushed to the in-house clinic. A young guard sent me along to assist Berga, who could barely speak.

As we entered the doctor's clinic, a stiff-standing triple-star officer glared at me and shouted, "Why are you here?"

The guard who'd chosen to bring me did nothing to explain my presence.

Berga was swooning. The officer was shouting. I was speechless (for once). And the guard quaked in his boots.

"Captain Three Star" continued to rant, straining the buttons on his uniform, proud veins of tension on his forehead. The doctor sat silently, perhaps wondering which of us would faint first. Then, as if someone had pressed a pause button, the room fell silent.

The doctor turned his attention to Berga, but as usual, without an examination, medicine was prescribed and we were shunted back to our cells. No explanation, no diagnosis—nothing.

The incident brought on a drastic change in Berga. At one point, I wondered whether the prescribed medicine had actually been a

---

9. This might seem incredible, but we Africans have large networks of contacts.

vial of poison, because he was suddenly filled with hatred. It oozed from him like the pus from my ear. Negativity and pessimism had invaded his body and seemed to take control of his once witty mind. He screamed every day and lost all perspective on life.

I recognised his despair in my own, but didn't know how to comfort him. A cripple cannot teach a cripple to dance.

His increasingly erratic behaviour would not be soothed, though I called and called. Saving him was so important, for both of us. As he withdrew further into darker places, my own emotional stability wavered.

Fall . . . fall . . . fall.

Early June. Inside, the icy tentacles of madness probed our minds for weak spots, not yet invaded. Berga's despair continued; my endurance was thinner than thin.

I could no longer discern reality from trauma from dreams. Was that a guard standing at the entrance to our cell? That wasn't my name he was calling, "Solomon. . . ? Solomon?" His shouting jarred me alert. "Solomon, room change! Prepare your belongings!"

I methodically gathered my few belongings and placed them in the plastic basket. Robotically, I walked to the door where three guards were waiting.

As I stepped out and turned towards the other cells, two guards grabbed me by the upper arms, spun me around and pointed me in the opposite direction. Panic struck as I was led towards the cells for solitary confinement.

What had I done wrong?

The officers kept me walking all the way to the elevator doors.

They are going to deport me! My heart plummeted to my heels. I'd held out—for what? To go from this madness to that chaos? I'd been confident this wasn't going to happen, especially after the ambassador's visit.

We stepped into the elevator and I was taken to the bottom

floor, to a room lined with guards and officers. One of the officers checked my luggage and then explained the papers on the table beside him—it was nothing like I expected.

"Under the jurisdiction ruling of probationary discharge, you are restricted to the direction of your supporters, with Father Mori (Kaeda's brother) as your guarantor."

I don't remember if he was speaking Japanese or English. I just stood there, dazed and uncomprehending. Then, it hit me: I was going to be released!

Another officer read out the conditions of my release: I must return to the Nishi-Nihon Immigration Centre each month to apply for a visa extension permit; I must not work; I must not leave the city boundaries of Osaka without Immigration's permission.

A starburst of energy rocketed up through me with dizzying intensity. I couldn't sign the papers quickly enough.

A guard assisting with my luggage whispered, "*Ganbatte,*[10] Solomon."

With the official business completed, I was escorted out to the public lobby where my supporters were chatting excitedly. I walked over to Kaeda and hugged her, then asked, "Why didn't you tell me?"

"Immigration insisted that we keep it a secret to avoid a disturbance on the inside," she replied. Then she introduced me to her brother, my new guarantor.

I clasped Father Mori's hand between both of mine and thanked him with all my rescued heart.

---

10. Do your best. (Japanese)

20

SUSPICIOUS MINDS

Light—it was everywhere. It had been 744 days since I'd felt the sun beating down on my skin. The road ahead glowed golden in the summer light as the car drove away from detention (away, away—this time that feeling was magic).

Like an intrepid team of rescuers, my supporters had unearthed me from the weight of bureaucracy. Their faces beamed with elation for their own achievement as much as my deliverance. The car hummed with excited chatter.

I slowly tuned out to bask in the surrealism of freedom. My body and thought processes crisscrossed every sensation at once, so that each part of me was pulsing to a different beat. I drew all that erratic energy back into my heart and glided on a cushion of gratitude, feeling whole for the first time in ages.

I was sad to leave the centre without saying goodbye to Berga, but I hoped that when he learned of my release he would gain strength and continue to fight for his own freedom. Deep down though, I worried how he would cope mentally, knowing that he was alone with no one by his side.

Kaeda and Father Mori drove me to their small (but very active) church in Sakai, a large industrial city in the Osaka prefecture. The place was to become my new home. The parishioners had kindly agreed that I could live in Shelter House on the church grounds, reserved for those seeking temporary accommodation. It was a two-storey building located at the rear of the church. The ground level included storage and parking space for the priests' cars. The small room upstairs was allocated to me.

The Church secretary, Noriko, opened the door for us and Father Mori helped get my luggage up the stairs. The room looked bigger inside than it was, because of the sparse furniture, but appeared to have all the basic essentials. Compared to my recent accommodation, it was a palace.

After getting a "royal" tour of the church grounds, I returned to my room alone to clear my head. It had been a strange day. I'd woken up in detention and would fall asleep in freedom. My release had always seemed like a mist in the distance, undefined and unreachable, and yet here I was. My incredulity faded by degrees as the sun slowly melted into the horizon. I decided it was time for a walk.

Night lights flickered on, mirroring the starry glimmer in the darkening sky. Men, suited in their greys, browns and blacks of ordered living, returned home from the city or slipped into small bars to be entertained by the young hostesses.

The ground beneath me became new territories of footloose thought and action. Walking, walking, blissful unhindered walking. Hours must have passed before I returned to my room. I lay in bed, exhausted by the day's events, but was unable to fall asleep. I didn't want the fresh feeling to slip away.

The room lightened with the rise of day. I showered and went downstairs where Father Mori was already waiting to drive me to his morning sermon. On the way, he asked if I had slept well.

"Oh, yes, Father. I feel like a newborn baby."

Well . . . the second part was true.

On the first Sunday at Sakai Church, Father Mori introduced me to the congregation. People lined up to talk with me and even invited me to their homes. After pleading for family acceptance most of my life, I found their kindness overwhelming. Still, it was difficult to process such concentrated attention. I barely had time to myself.

Out of politeness, I tried to assimilate the customs that were so strange to me, bowing not the least. Tall black man bows to shorter Japanese men and women. The lower the bow, the more humility one expressed. The key was for each person to have his or her head lower than the other, bowing further if this was not achieved in the initial bend. More hygienic than a handshake, but what a workout for me, having achieved celebrity status overnight.

I struggled with the basics of day to day living, including the language and practical things like currency and transport. Noriko offered me guidance by explaining timetables and ticket fares. She gave me a map so that I could find my way around or ask anyone for help by pointing to my destination. She also encouraged me in Japanese conversation.

Three days after my release, I attended the first of many meetings with my supporters. No one knew whom to thank for my successful release (there'd been so many layers to the process). It probably resulted from a combination of things: the reignited Ethiopian-Eritrean civil war, the ambassador's visit and Ms. Fukushima's intervention.

I hadn't heard of Ms. Fukushima before but, during the course of the first meeting, I learned that she was a politician with particular interest in discrimination against foreigners. She'd formally expressed concern over the length of time I'd been incarcerated and queried the rejection of my refugee status. Perhaps that finally swayed the decision in my favour.

I only gained information in bits and pieces, since everyone spoke so quickly and my language skills were nowhere near excellent (except in culinary adjectives).

Learning a new language is more than knowing words and their meanings. There are expressions, gestures and tones that all flavour the delivery. It's like being in a play where everyone knows the lines but you. Foreign names are equally challenging to absorb, unless you spend time with the people they identify.

The main characters in my particular drama were grouped into Church associates: Kaeda, Father Mori, Father Paul, Noriko; Amnesty International: Ms. Toyoda and Shiho; Asian Friends: Mr. Higuchi; the hospital doctor: Doctor Kawashima; and my lawyers: Mr. Tanaka and Mr. Narito. It was daunting to have so many people working towards resolving my situation, and to maintain a friendly, yet professional relationship with them all.

At one meeting, I learned that Ms. Toyoda was moving to Tokyo. Without her devoted efforts, I would have been swallowed up by the system. I smoothed out an African T-shirt from my luggage and presented it to her with as much grace as possible from someone who had nothing. She handed me a bunch of flowers, with congratulations on my liberty.

Ms. Toyoda's replacement from Amnesty was Ms. Fujii.

Then it was down to business. Having achieved my release and commiserated over the rejection of my refugee applications in both Australia and Japan, my friends turned the discussion to the potential for court-awarded compensation over my hearing loss, a point of particular interest to the lawyers.

The conservative opinion was simply to file for the cost of future operations required to restore my hearing. After further discussion, they agreed that the loss of human rights associated with my suffering was far more dramatic and therefore more likely to deliver a lucrative win.

I came away from the meeting assuming that every possibility for my ongoing freedom was being managed and in good hands. No follow-up action to my refugee status was discussed.

Even though I had been formally rejected by the United Nations, the organisation advised Immigration that I was not to be deported until Ethiopia's situation stabilised. Feeling safe for the time being, I took on research duties to support the compensation case. The details required were copious: medical reports, associated statements, research that justified our arguments. The list went on (and on and on).

I had to learn how to use a computer and quickly acquire all the skills of modern life. On top of that, my supporters expected me to be active in raising money to pay for lawyers, court fees and such expenses. At first, I was confounded how to manage that without breaking my release agreement, which prohibited work. More than that, they wanted me to stay close so that when they called, I would come. They gave me a mobile phone (expecting me to pay running costs) and summoned me to impromptu meetings, often quite late, or phoned whenever there was some detail to revise.

It was all Japanese to me!

I was acutely aware of my obligations to everyone around me. I couldn't agree to any activity that might jeopardise my liberty, but I was keen to show my appreciation, so I took on some acceptable caretaker duties at the church. Noriko instructed me on what and how to clean: three priests' offices and toilets, take out the rubbish, aid parishioners on site, team up to clean the chapel every Friday, and assist with Mass twice per week. Saturday was payday, and my reward for successful duties was ¥5,000.[1]

While working, I met various members of the congregation and the local community in general. Through these connections, I was introduced to Mr. and Mrs. Sato, a middle-aged couple in early retirement. Mr. Sato had inherited several investment properties,

1. US$67 (approximately).

which gave him financial independence. He spent his time managing them, collecting rent and pursuing his hobbies. His wife, Mrs. Sato, had an interest in all things international and conducted English conversation classes from home.

Mr. Sato treated me like a friend from the very first time we met. He invited me to attend his clay-sculpting class as a live model, in exchange for a few yen. (I was relieved to know it was only my head they wanted to sculpt.)

Over the following weeks, I was regularly welcomed into the Sato household and they soon claimed me as the son they never had. Formalities began to disappear and Mrs. Sato insisted I call her by her first name "Asuka," and her husband by his family name "Sato" (without the "mister").

I suppose Sato was what people call "new money." He'd been born and lived most of his life poor. The inheritance expanded his bank balance, but didn't include any sophisticated financial etiquette. He was a flamboyant spender, buying the latest gadgets, inviting out his friends from the gym and treating "the African" to some treats along the way. He would show me off to others with some self-importance, which I didn't think to question at the time.

There was some quaintness about Sato, too. He loved his garden and devotedly pottered about his plants, giving them detailed attention. Another of his hobbies was photography. It was exciting to find that I had an interest to share with him and we enjoyed discussions and activities that explored camera techniques.

In my ignorance of their culture, I initially saw Asuka as the perfect Japanese wife. She seemed competent in presenting everything well at home; she belonged to an active social group who often came to her place for afternoons of English conversation; and she took an interest in my background. She seemed content.

I was taken in by it all, feeling that at last there were people who really loved and understood me. They were concerned about my challenges at supporter meetings where, apart from language blocks, the various rules and conditions were never explained to me very well. So, Sato, Asuka and I would sit with all my papers, which Asuka translated, and discuss further options to ensure my future.

Third-world Foreigners' reputations in Japan were all negative, exacerbated by sensational media. It was only through my association with the Church that I became acceptable at all. So other Japanese people were amazed at Asuka and Sato's generosity. (It simply wasn't done.) The awed attention gave them the incentive to do even more for me. What I didn't realise was that it wasn't really for me—it was to impress everyone else.

The church congregation included quite a few nationalities. I made friends with some from the Philippines. They could relate to my situation and seemed more carefree than the Japanese.

Once a month, I had to return to detention to have my papers stamped, thus extending my freedom on a month-by-month basis. One of my supporters or new friends would drive me to the centre. While there, we always took basic supplies to Berga, Bashir and anyone I knew who was still on the inside.

These visits were a strong reminder that my freedom was tenuous. Since I had support, I was confident that I would never again have to endure such inhuman conditions. Urgently, I pursued my quest for the luxury of a normal life.

After one Sunday Mass, I heard that the keyboardist had been arrested for overstaying his visa. Jimmy, a Filipino, was being detained at the Nishi-Nihon Immigration Centre. A group of us drove out to visit him. While I was there, I wanted to see Berga.

On my previous visit, Bashir was gone. The officers refused to tell me where.

This day was like déjà vu. We filled out visitation forms to see Jimmy and Berga, but the officer told us that Berga was no longer there. We were given no further information.

After visiting Jimmy, I decided to call the Tokyo lawyer, Mr. Suzuki, to find out where his client had gone. Berga's disappearance was news to him as well.

About a week after he'd vanished, Berga called Sakai Church and left a message that he'd been deported to Bangkok. He called again two days later and told me what had happened. I asked Kaeda to listen, too. We recorded his voice with a portable tape machine as he recounted his tale.

On that fateful day, several officers came with a translator and took Berga to a downstairs cell. They told him it was time to return to Ethiopia, and presented forms for him to sign. Berga refused. Soon after, the cell door swung open and guards entered. They bound his hands and put a black sack over his head. Berga struggled, so they beat him and then injected him with something that caused unconsciousness.

When he awoke, hands and feet still tied, he found himself in a private room at the airport. His suitcase was by his side and several Immigration officials were on guard. He started screaming for help and was forced into silence. After continually pestering for a toilet break, he was allowed on the condition that he kept quiet. Inside the toilet, Berga started yelling again to get some—any—attention. They gave him another injection and he passed out once more.

When he woke next, he was onboard an airplane. In panic, Berga called to other passengers for help, but the officer guarding him apologised to them, explaining that his charge was "crazy."

Japan Airlines doesn't fly to Ethiopia but, from Thailand, Ethiopian Airlines flies direct into Addis Ababa. So Berga had been flown to Bangkok to be transferred onto one of those flights. After landing, he was carried on a stretcher by several officers to airport Immigration, only to have the Thai officials refuse his entry.

Next, the officers spoke with the Ethiopian Airlines manager, insisting that the deportee was the manager's responsibility. Even though Berga possessed an Ethiopian passport, his citizenship was

Eritrean. The manager explained that those two countries were at war (hell-o!) and he was therefore not willing to take charge of a passenger refusing to return home.

The kidnap caravan went back to the Thai Immigration officials. Arrangements were made for Berga to stay inside the airport. Left without money, he was forced to beg for food from other travellers. All his efforts towards refugee status had come to nothing.

His terrible story needed to be told. I contacted those who'd been supporting him in Japan to raise the alarm. One of these was an American university professor, Doctor Newport. This news distressed him because he feared that a letter he wrote may have led to Berga's deportation.

After visiting him in detention, Doctor Newport had written to Immigration asking them why Berga was not permitted some form of residency, even though he possessed a valid passport and sufficient financial stability. He didn't query Japan's general decisions to grant refugee status, but he questioned why Immigration had kept Berga in such appalling conditions for so long.

Doctor Newport explained that he'd had the letter translated into respectful Japanese to avoid any misunderstandings. Both the English and Japanese versions of the letter were mailed to Immigration and, according to Doctor Newport, there was nothing on the envelope indicating that it concerned Berga.

Shortly after the letter was sent, Berga disappeared.

A couple of weeks later, the letter was returned unopened and stamped "no longer at this address." Doctor Newport suspected that Immigration became nervous over questions about their activities and decided to get rid of the problem by getting rid of Berga.

Over time, I followed Berga's journey. Doctor Newport managed to arrange sponsorship for him into Malaysia and from there to America. Without that dedicated support, his story would have had a far more abrupt and despairing end.

Who could not be shocked at his experience? If we look, but do not see; if we see, but do not act; if we act, but can do little except satisfy bureaucracy—what are our eyes and hearts and hands for?

As time wore on, and the novelty of my presence wore off, I caught glimpses of harsh expectations behind the civility directed at me. I was too naïve to realise that a Good Samaritan can have a hidden agenda. I just kept moving towards the goal of finding my true home—and I knew it wasn't Japan.

That knowledge represented a fork in my road to freedom, where I travelled along one path and my supporters travelled along the other, though neither of us realised that we had become separated.

From my first contact with them, they knew that Australia was my goal, even though all the different applications had fallen through. Somehow they assumed I was so thankful for release that I was content to accept anything else. As patriots, they anticipated my unbound enthusiasm for becoming a local resident and devoting myself to everything Japanese.

Further misunderstanding arose from my assumption that Church in Japan was the same as in Ethiopia. To me, God was God. Kindness was kindness. How could there be a difference? Through the missions and the Church, I had received all the basic necessities and support. This never accrued a debt. Such a thing simply wasn't part of our culture. Even poor people shared the little they had, with no thought of repayment.

Not so in this land. As well as expecting my subservience and gratitude, every one of my supporters counted on being repaid for their efforts as soon as I had money.

None of this was ever discussed with me.

So, my past experience defined my actions while their expectations modified theirs. We blithely pursued our paths, never realising that the distance between was widening.

As soon as my practical obligations were completed, I ventured through the city. This didn't sit well with my benefactors. They demanded rather than inspired loyalty, revealing disingenuous concern. I was their trophy boy: when they pulled the strings I must pop into place.

My tenuous liberty was cloaked in another kind of imprisonment. There were no bars I could rail against, nor outright cruelty. I was confounded by saccharin patronising manipulation. And I couldn't help but resent it.

Rebellion rescued me. It reminded that I was more than this. Was there no one who could see that?

Coincidentally while on a visit to Immigration, I met Mr. Suzuki. When he asked about my refugee status, I told him that I had none (of course).

"Yes, but what is the progress of your case?" he wondered.

I looked at him, wide-eyed.

"You can't mean you have no court case opposing the decision?"

All I could tell him was the date I'd been rejected. Mr. Suzuki made a fast calculation, then flashed me a fierce look, "But you've only got a few days left to appeal!"

Why hadn't my supporters made this a priority (instead of focusing on the case that would win them money)? They had encountered Mr. Suzuki several times in the past, and his brashness had always unsettled them.

He snapped me into action. "Challenge them by any means," he said. "But do it now!"

The next meeting did not have a polite African sitting in the corner while everyone talked over his head. I leapt from my chair. "Why didn't you tell me I could appeal my refugee case?" I demanded. "Do you know the consequences if I miss this?"

"What do you mean?" Kaeda responded. "You don't know—"

"Exactly! I didn't know until Mr. Suzuki explained that any appeal will be void if it's not made by the end of this week."

"Why are you speaking with him?"

"I met him at detention. He told me in five minutes what you haven't been able to explain in months."

"We already have a lawyer—two lawyers. Mr. Tanaka is an honourable man. And Mr. Narito. You are nothing. They are everything and we are all learning from them."

Mr. Tanaka spoke up. "Solomon, please sit. Obviously there's a misunderstanding. We're here to help you."

I looked from him to the others and knew I had no choice but to trust them. Still, if I was the focal point of their efforts, then my opinion counted too. Before sitting, I spoke plainly. "If that's so, then please tell me my refugee appeal is ready to lodge, because anything else won't do."

After a bit of throat-clearing and paper-shuffling, they admitted to each other (though not to me) that there was much to prepare and then they launched a final barrage of questions at me to justify their efforts.

I had to find the confidence to keep telling them, "Yes, I want to live in Japan. Thank you for letting me clean the church. Of course, I am content to do what you think is best." It wasn't safe to say anything else. I felt my chin moving up and down . . . whatever it took to get out of there. I saw their heads nodding in approval, while suspicion flashed in their eyes.

Who was the puppet now?

Everything came together, though not without stress. I jumped through all their hoops, but was as baffled as ever about the official process.

One of my lawyers described each case in terms I might relate to. He told me the refugee case was like playing soccer (if only—that's actually something I'm good at): papers were passed and blocked, passed and blocked, until someone scored the winning goal. He described the ear damages case like poker: we held some good cards, but they might think we're bluffing. We should hold out for the best deal possible, though we might have to fold before pulling in a big win.

My appeal for refugee status was lodged with barely a sliver of time to spare. The lawyers played the game, waiting for the papers to be stamped and shuffled, stamped and shuffled, while I was primed for the ultimate penalty kick that would score.

But the odds were stacked against me from the start.

The courts demanded validation of my condition.

"Read the papers!" I wanted to shout. "There's a war going on."

Once more, I needed to accumulate a tower of paperwork on which to stand before anyone would take me seriously. Somehow I had to provide details of the civil war's development at different times in my life, witness statements of my hardship, and proof that I'd been displaced in my own country, as well as demonstrate what efforts I'd made to resolve this. Since I was just a starving kid for most of those events, I had no solid knowledge of the political background.

Now, so far away in time and distance, my main research tool was the Internet—which was in Japanese. As letters and papers from Africa slowly started to filter through, the Japanese court questioned them because the Ethiopian dates differed from the international Gregorian calendar by roughly seven years. What a mess!

Meanwhile, my ear case was progressing. The lawyers and I visited Doctor Kawashima (who had treated me during detention). She was very nervous that we were suing Immigration. Although she realised I hadn't received adequate treatment, she wouldn't admit this in court. One less high card in my hand.

Scrambling to pair up our facts, I was subjected to X-rays, an MRI and an ABR[2] test, none of which yielded conclusive results. We only found out much later that I really should have had an ultrasound scan to show soft tissue damage. Every doctor we spoke to was too scared to go up against the government, so we had to patch

2. Auditory Brainstem Response

together a convincing case with any scrap of evidence that remotely supported our argument.

The first day at court caused huge excitement. A foreigner is suing the Japanese government? A black man? A refugee? Headlines splashed across newsstands.[3] Journalists were haggling for details and snapping photos. One in particular, Mr. Masashi (a friend of Berga's lawyer), became interested in detention conditions. Over the coming months, he presented some daunting facts to the Japanese public through interviews with me and then others who found the courage to speak out. Sometime later, he even made a documentary exposing the shocking violation of human rights.

Aside from that, there was no grand inquisition. My lawyers and I assembled the appropriate papers for each step of "the match" or "the next hand" and, on an appointed day, we joined the queue at the courthouse. Shuffling slowly forward to the judge's desk, we finally met the defence lawyer. Papers were swapped and a new appointment (months from then) was decided. Hours of waiting . . . five minutes of swapping . . . months of my life ebbing away.

Asuka had travelled overseas and seemed to understand the difficulties of facing a foreigner. Because she could speak English, we slipped into long discussions about troubles, people and the world in general. Reassured that she and her husband were sympathetic, I retreated to their house for meals or to relax with a video on weekends.

Over time, Asuka slowly explained that she wasn't happy in her marriage and claimed that her husband treated her like his slave. In an independent conversation, Sato told me that he paid for a roof over her head and expected her to cook and be available for him. "It suits me," he said matter-of-factly.

---

3. *The Japan Times*, 21 October 1999.

Asuka started attending my official meetings. With the constant pressure on me to bring in money, she also suggested that I give some paid presentations to different community groups. She was very efficient in organising my speeches and contacts.

Within weeks of this conversation, I was presenting at schools, university and various colleges. People wanted to know of the conditions in detention, and about Africa. I enjoyed the interactions and the payment helped with court and associated costs. At last, I was gaining some control in my life.

Asuka was spending more time away from home and I grew concerned that Sato might be feeling neglected. But she told me that he was glad for her to be pursuing her own interests. However, this didn't fit at all with her admissions of discontent. What did I know? Maybe it was a cultural behaviour. Either way, it wasn't my place to interfere.

I returned to Shelter House late one night to find a letter stuck under my door. It was from Asuka.

Dear Solomon,

How is your feeling today? I miss you. I'm very uneasy about you. I heard you were back around 2 A.M. and I was surprised it. I guess you have a lot of things to discuss among you and your supporters. Today, also you had to meet your supporters and your lawyer. You stayed up all night on 12th. You are rather short of sleep these days. Beside you are worried about trial. You must lose sleep over it. Are you alright. . . ? I want to share your hardship. I will do what I can for you. It may be very difficult for you to overcome a difficult and it may take a long time for overcoming. I hope your hard work results in success. I wrote this in a hurry. My sentence is wrong. I hope that you can understand what I want to say. I love you xxxxx
With love, Asuka

I was so caught up with major commitments that I just put this aside. The Satos were so welcoming, and I assumed her feelings for me were motherly. After all, she referred to me as her "son," and even considered adopting me. I couldn't fathom her mixed message, so I went to bed that night and didn't think about it again.

Did I have Japanese nightmares? Did I still dream of something beyond all this—pure, powerful and enduring? I think I just dissolved into the nothingness of slumber, though sometimes it felt like waking up on a tightrope, stretched between all the commitments of a land that did not have my heart.

I tried to sink into the steady pulse of life around me, but living on a month-by-month permit beat down my day-by-day resilience.

My supporters weren't overly optimistic about the refugee appeal, but at the end of the day they could say, "Ah, well," and go about their own lives.

All the while, I lingered. Like a slow-motion pendulum, I swung between official waiting and private longing, the heavy rhythm seeming to slow with each pass. I wanted to climb the mountain of life and roar instead of feeling penned in by everyone else's rules. *It is better to be a lion for a day, than a sheep all your life.*[4]

Amid all this, I still suffered from recurring ear infections, even though I was receiving treatment. This lent credibility to the court dealings, but pain—searing, mind-stopping pain—is so humbling. I'm not proud to say that my inner roar diminished to a whimper. Nothing could compensate for that.

In the time since I had been released, Father Mori had also moved on with his life. He was ordained as Bishop of Osaka and had a new focus; he kept busy with his expanded obligations to the church.

Since Bishop Mori was still my guarantor, I sought his counsel. He was devoted to helping people and, for him, the best medium was

---

4. Elizabeth Kenny (1880–1952).

the Church. Wisely, he understood that my capabilities required different circumstances. My cleaning duties at the church were still an obligation, but he encouraged me to pursue every possible avenue that could lead to an independent life of quality, rather than waiting on decisions from those around me.

Strengthened by his advice, I spent even more time meeting people beyond my current contacts. That, in turn, caused problems at Shelter House. Parishioners wondered why they didn't see me around as often, and Noriko was conspicuously interested in my daily plans. Ever since my outspokenness at that meeting, Kaeda had been less caring and more interrogative.

The public furore over detention horrors was reaching a peak. The government was nervous over the exposé, as the world's attention started to swing towards those dark deeds. Headlines loomed large, describing guard misconduct and detainee suffering. The possibility for huge compensation cases threatened. If a government is afraid, you can be sure its cowering is felt at the most basic level of society.

One day, I needed to get away from everything and decided that if Immigration gave me permission, I would visit Tokyo. I could gather information about the war from the Ethiopian-Eritrean community there. At first, my supporters encouraged this trip, but then became agitated, worried that I was beyond their reach.

I explained my itinerary. I would only be away for a few days and they knew where I'd be and whom I'd be meeting.

Nuances of autumn red and gold paved the bus journey to Tokyo. I anticipated brighter days. Once there, I caught up with Mr. Suzuki, who wanted me to meet a journalist for more interviews, but I didn't have permission from my lawyers, so I declined.

While working my way through the list of agreed contacts, I received a phone call from Osaka, summoning my immediate return. Apparently, there was a doctor who could give important evidence for the ear case. When I explained that I still had research to complete, I was told I had no choice.

Dance, little puppet.

I returned to a surprisingly chilly reception. Ms. Fujii shunted me to the new doctor. His report favourably stated that prolonged use of the ointment, along with the rampant infection, could have killed the nerves in my ear. At last, we had some solid support.

At the next meeting, my friends all positioned themselves at one end of the table and stared stonily at me as I entered.

Somehow, among themselves, they had decided that I was preparing to fly the coop by liaising with "new supporters" in Tokyo. Threatened by this, they demanded, "You must choose. Choose us or go elsewhere."

Was I baffled? Yes! Did I feel betrayed? Of course! And yet they treated me as if I had betrayed them. But it was my life. If I wanted to look for every possible way to change my situation, that was my right.

"Of course, I choose you," I said. Their help had saved me from different kinds of death, yet here was a new variety. I sat at the opposite end of the table, seeing no longer a team of well-wishers but a council of fate.

They click-clacked their pens and flip-flapped their papers and pursed their lips with oh-so-charitable patience. "Now apologise for making us worry," they said. "We cannot continue the meeting until you say sorry." Then they turned to chat with each other, ignoring me completely.

Truly disconcerted, I didn't understand what I was apologising for.

The minutes dragged by. They prattled on among themselves, passing notes and laughing together. Occasionally, one would look up and call, "Say you're sorry! "

What is a word if its meaning is forced? Why didn't they see that once they forced me, I could no longer trust them? Where was their charity now?

Finally, I uttered the words they wanted to hear. Feeling more like a petulant child than a man in the lifelong pursuit of essential rights, I almost choked on their smugness.

Then, we got down to business as if nothing had happened.

They were excited about the latest evidence I'd brought in support of the ear case. It could mean a win and a substantial payout, a percentage of which they expected to keep for themselves. They reminded me that money, money and more money was needed for everything from stamps to court fees.

I couldn't do more than grunt an acknowledgement.

When the meeting ended, I wanted to explain my Tokyo trip to Mr. Tanaka, but Ms. Fujii interrupted and lectured me about secretive behaviour. After that, she resigned from my case. Her replacement, Mr. Ito, forbade me from contacting her again.

Four days later, a meeting was called to discuss the strategy for my refugee appeal. As part of the game plan, they believed there were only two options (if I wished to remain in Japan).

The first was to apply for *tokubetsu zairyo kyoka*,[5] which gave us a negotiation point for the refugee appeal. This meant I had to be 100 percent enthusiastic about living in Japan and seeing my future there. Some of the Eritrean community residing in Tokyo had received this visa on the proviso that they dropped their refugee appeals. For those with nowhere else to go, it was a great option. For the government, it provided a compensation-free solution.

The second alternative, according to my supporters, was to marry a Japanese woman. This would give me security and a visa. (Shades of Egypt stirred in my memory.) But I wasn't interested in marrying someone for the sake of bureaucracy. I had enough headaches (literally) without living in a loveless marriage. No matter how hard my life became, I would never compromise love.

I saw others who were desperate for a solution—any solution— choose Japanese brides. There seemed to be plenty of local girls

---

5. Special Permission for Residence. (Japanese)

willing to marry a foreigner. These matches weren't based on a profound bond. Some became parents and began integrating into the system, but after only a couple of years, these shallow connections often ended in divorce.

Neither of these suggestions were particularly enticing but, considering everything, I agreed with the first one.

In response to this decision, Mr. Ito faxed me a list of eligibility requirements for this type of visa. As a new team member, he had no knowledge of my history or my efforts to date. In order to qualify for *tokubetsu zairyo kyoka*, he stated I must demonstrate perfect oral and written Japanese. Then he scribbled:

> But you can't write Japanese, you didn't start to learn Japanese writing yet. You can't read Japanese papers. . . . We have no money, why we spend much money for you?? Tell us why! Are you saving money every week?
> Mr. Ito, 1 October 1999

Hai, sensei.[6] Whatever you say.

Christmas came and went. My life fell into the regularity of cleaning, attending meetings and chasing paperwork. Each month, I returned to the Immigration centre to extend my provisional release; each time, I hoped it would be the last and that I would soon know true liberation.

Early in the New Year, my ear infection flared up. Perhaps it was the winter chills that made it worse, or mabye I was becoming overwhelmed with the intensity of doing much, yet accomplishing little.

In the first official meeting of the New Year, Kaeda (who had taken over my sponsorship soon after her brother had become a bishop) conveyed a complaint from the parishioners. I'd outstayed

---

6. Yes, sir. (Japanese)

my welcome after six months in Shelter House. They wanted me gone by the end of February.

I was incredulous. I had nowhere else to go. So, this could even happen in a civilised country, eh? Well, I'd lived on the streets before, and the prospect of homelessness in Japan didn't scare me as much as they might hope.

Asuka was sympathetic and offered me a room in the Sato household. I didn't think it would be a good idea, as she had become quite overbearing. (There'd been more letters.)

Alternatively, she mentioned that her husband had a few vacant properties which might be suitable, even though they were slightly run down. I asked her to check with him first. Sato agreed and offered me a house for one year—rent-free! Ah, the softness of that velvet glove.

So Asuka and I cleaned the designated house, and Sato organised various tradesmen to resolve any maintenance issues. During one month, we transformed a dilapidated shack to basic, comfortable accommodation.

Although the attitude towards me had changed radically, I continued cleaning duties at the church. One day, early in February, I'd just finished work when Kaeda called me to her office. She'd found a cheap room to rent for ¥35,000[7] per month. When I explained that I'd already arranged alternative accommodation, a scowl flashed across her porcelain face.

Why did these people keep making life impossible and then get angry if I found ways to manage it? When I explained that I would be living in one of Sato's buildings, she flared up. At the time, I thought she resented my independence, expecting me to be beholden to her. Now, I realise that she knew the Satos would give me trouble. (If only she'd been clear.) Instead, she shouted, "You must get out of the Shelter House soon—even today!"

---

7. US$470 (approximately).

Ever since my trip to Tokyo, annoyance had festered beneath her polite demeanour and her words pierced like needles. I was tired of the tension that never seemed to dissolve between us. I calmly told her I would be moving out shortly, as promised, and walked off.

Space! My entire being craved space that was not controlled or monitored by another.

Once relocated, I quickly established a new life. Following the success of my initial speeches, I approached the local council to offer cultural exchange with different hobby groups, mostly frequented by housewives. I held introductory classes on my country's culture and foods. My reputation spread, and I became quite sought after.

Asuka made sure she was involved in everything I did. Her constant presence became increasingly suffocating.

I raced from supporter meetings to lawyers to presentations (with Asuka shadowing my every move). I noticed that Sato was calling her mobile phone more often. She would mumble that she was with a friend. Oh, no. Lying to her husband? About me? I'd been so busy pushing towards a solution that I didn't realise she'd become obsessed with me. Trying to create some distance, I told Asuka she no longer needed to attend meetings. But she showed up anyway.

Asuka's behaviour emerged as a seesaw pattern of compliance or intrusion. In one compliant stage, she offered to help with a fundraising dinner I was hosting. Cautiously, I accepted. All day long, we chopped and ground and sautéed, preparing for the next day's event.

I was so happy to cook some traditional African food and give my guests a more complete understanding of the real Teddy (well, they still called me Solomon).

Did I know that tongues were wagging? Had I a clue that others, particularly from the Church, assumed Asuka and I were having an affair? Not a flicker. Given the extremes of my situation, if someone had mentioned "stalker," I would have thought they meant hunting gazelles.

With all the preparations in order, Asuka and I returned to her home to have dinner with Sato.

From the moment we walked in, he grumbled like an irritated rhinoceros. At first unresponsive, he then rattled out a string of agitated questions about where we'd been, what party, how many people were coming, and what was really going on.

Asuka shrank tearfully into a corner.

I didn't know what lies she might have told him nor what I should say to calm the situation, since I expected he'd already drawn his own immovable conclusions.

He stood glaring at me, then at her, considering which way to charge. Finally he bellowed, "There will be no party tomorrow!"

Asuka began to whimper. I stepped in to explain, but he cut me off. "There will be no party tomorrow," he shouted a second time. "Now get out! Just get OUT!"

Of course, I left.

Forced to think things through, I realised that if Asuka had been lying to him then she'd been lying to me, too. Sato had obviously disapproved of her activities away from the house. Once he calmed down, I thought I could explain and everything would be all right.

Ah, Teddy . . . where's the village full of fixers when you need them?

Expecting that all would be well, I went out on an early errand for the party. Imagine my shock on returning to find that all the food—all of it—had been thrown in the bin. Sato had let himself in while I was absent and spitefully destroyed all our hard work. After so many years of starving, I hated seeing food go to waste.

What a smack down: iron fist, Japanese-style!

Impulsively, I marched over to the Sato household. In the doorway stood Asuka, shrunken and tear-worn. At the end of the hall,

Sato hovered, stiff and pale. Obviously, both had been through great pain since I'd last seen them. Calm descended upon me. There was nothing to be gained here except some kind of truce.

I asked Asuka to leave me alone with Sato. After a few moments of awkward silence, he apologised and explained that her lies had caused months of pent-up anxiety, which finally ruptured. This was more to do with them than me. For everyone's sakes, I must step out of their lives.

Even so, Asuka continued to call me and attend every meeting. She had a key to my house, and I would often return home to find things not quite as they'd been. She left letters on my table, gushing with emotion. I finally realised that this was clearly not normal.

Fed up with her constant interference, I decided to move out.

Asuka disapproved. She ranted on that I couldn't move out. Then abruptly, like a faulty current, her temper flicked off. No pressure. Do what is best. I should continue using Sato's house for meetings and presentations until the rent-free year was up.

Her proposal didn't make much sense: I didn't need two venues. Still, agreeing seemed like the easiest way to conclude things.

Lightening up, she offered to assist me in searching for a new apartment. Was there no escape?!

Within days of our talk and without my knowledge, she'd found an apartment, paid all the upfront expenses and bought me new appliances and furniture. Was she trying to make amends? What was I to do? The money was spent already.

The law suits were dragging on (and obviously, so was my time in Japan). I didn't think I'd be welcome sleeping on friends' couches for long and I needed a fixed address for Immigration. So, I accepted—but on my terms:

She didn't have a key.

"Of course, Solomon. This is your place."

She was not to visit or call.

"No, no. I respect your privacy."

She had to focus on resolving her issues with Sato.

"Yes, I really want to be happy in my marriage."

Whatever I said, she just kept nodding.

And she kept sneaking into the "meeting place" when I wasn't there. She even stole some of my personal items, only to mysteriously return them. I had to keep my diary hidden so she wouldn't turn up at meetings. To get around this, she contacted my supporters and kept tabs on me through them.

At one point, she asked me for a duplicate key to the new apartment so she could clean it. When I refused, she got mad and insisted that everything she did was because she cared for me. It was extremely unsettling.

Normally when you are afraid, it's obvious that you should run or defend yourself or take some kind of control. But how do you defend yourself from encroaching niceness?

Whether I denied it, laughed it off or ignored it, rumours of the affair never ceased. And Asuka's persistent behaviour didn't help. She constantly called, faxed, and arrived on my doorstep unannounced. There were even times when someone would knock, but the hallway was empty when I answered. It had to be her.

A friend of mine said Asuka reminded him of a fox. He explained by relating a Japanese fable about a conniving fox that appears as a woman. In this disguise, it goes about seducing men, showing them love, and then luring them into perilous situations that lead to disaster. Knowing what I know now, I couldn't agree more.

The extra stress caused sleepless nights. I decided to cut her out of my life completely. Arriving at meetings, I would scan the room to see if she was present. I ignored her calls and attempts to meet, but still cringed every time the phone rang.

I was relieved at one point when she went on an overseas trip. My only worries then were about gathering money (without getting caught for working without a permit), jumping from one court case to another (knowing that both were verging on impossible) and trying to remind myself that Japan was just a stopover (three years too long).

I never felt so foreign, so alien, as I did right then. This absurd mishmash of rules, expectations and restrictions was my life—my life!

He who digs too deep for a fish may come out with a serpent.[8] For all this hard work, I seemed to have unearthed a pit of snakes.

---

8. Ethiopian proverb.

21

AND THEN THERE WAS LIGHT

An Australian girl decided to go on an adventure. Just two weeks out of high school, Anita wasn't ready for university. Her heart must be in something to do it well. (When she commits, she excels.) Since she had studied Japanese at school, Japan seemed like an appealing destination. Anita's parents had always encouraged her to broaden her experience, so she chose a working holiday, starting with a hospitality position at the 1998 Winter Olympics in Nagano, Japan.

I was on a different kind of adventure. By then I'd been detained for several months; mine was relatively less broadening.

Instead of mingling with the international sports scene, Anita was employed at an exclusive hotel and restaurant situated near Numazu city, just south of Tokyo. The venue was once a cruise ship which, in its glory days, sailed the diamond crust of society around Europe. Now, permanently moored, it was a feature stopover for throngs of tourists.

Anita's hometown of Wagga Wagga was a long way from the bustling streets of Japan. She loved the change. As a young white female, she was treated very well. People were generous and polite. Everyone wanted to associate with her to practise speaking English. She felt more like a local tourist attraction than a staff member, and was expected to pose for photos with hotel guests and visitors.

The work was long on hours and short on pay, but Anita soaked up the culture and sharpened her language skills.

Coincidentally, the hotel staff included two other Australian girls—Hayley and Karina—who were employed around the same time as Anita. The three girls would meet up at the staff dormitory, and a firm friendship evolved.

In their spare time, the fun-loving trio would go shopping or seek out quaint restaurants that were tucked away from the regular tourist haunts. They enjoyed long walks by the bay, chatting with locals, and wandering on the whim of curiosity. Occasionally, they got lost and had to phone back to the dorm for rescue, or ask a local resident to drive them home.

Who wouldn't respond to their naïve adventurous smiles? This "Kewpie-chan"[1] stepped into a world of daily wonders, with friendly faces at every turn.

I was at the time desperately seeking treatment for my ear infection. The great trials of endurance still lay ahead and, apart from the limited broadcasts from the cell television, I had no concept of a positive Japanese atmosphere.

Anita wanted to explore more of the country. Her working visa was valid for 18 months, so there was plenty of time to look around.

After six months on the floating paradise, Karina returned to Australia, while Hayley moved on to Osaka. Anita ventured to the more remote Hakone for the summer.

This lush mountainous region is not far from the base of Mt Fuji. Since it is very popular with day-trippers from Tokyo, visitors flock there for its hot springs and golf courses, and exchange city air for

1. Anita's Japanese nickname, after the "Kewpie" doll.

the invigorating sulphur aroma from the volcanic activity.

It wasn't quite a luxury job. Anita was the only foreigner and had to keep up with the other employees. She found out what it was to work like the Japanese (and they work hard) and to talk like the Japanese (and they talk fast). Still a tourist attraction, though, she featured in endless guest photos.

I wonder if the cell television had broadcast summer tourist locations. Perhaps, if I'd looked up, I might have seen her, smiling, surrounded by city folk. If only I'd known her light would one day shine on me. If only. . . .

Anita's day started with early morning walks from the staff lodgings. The pristine surrounds hinted at mythical dragons and heroic legends as mist rose from the hot springs, shimmering against the mountain ranges and glistening on the road ahead. The contrast to rural Australia was vast.

As the tourist season waned, the resort prepared to close for winter. Anita wasn't sure where her travels would lead next until Hayley phoned from Osaka and invited her to come and teach English. This seemed easy enough.

So when the hotel closed, Anita headed south to Osaka and, after one week's intensive training in a prep course, she had the job. The Japanese were keen to learn. The workload was light and the atmosphere was always fun.

Sharing an apartment with Hayley and Christina (another Australian), Anita had low costs, and saved towards mini-trips elsewhere. She and Christina would drop in to the travel agent, who was by now familiar with their ambitions. "Where to this time, ladies?" he would ask.

Sometimes they were curious to visit a particular place such as Thailand or Nepal. Often though, they would close their eyes and drop a finger-point onto the map. "There," they'd say, delightedly, even before checking to see where "there" was.

The vibrant city excited their new cosmopolitan tastes. Anita and

Christina became best friends, sharing the same adventurous fun-loving outlook. They bought rollerblades and skated through the streets, by the river, even down stairs and through tunnels. A favourite destination on late night adventures was the 24-hour public baths.

At night, they started working in a local bar together. The job wasn't for money; they were just enjoying the nightlife and practising Japanese, often stretching the night into the next dawn (even if they had English classes to teach the next day).

The magical mystery tour continued to unfold as the girls would often help close the bar, and then set off in the early hours of the morning for the next discovery. If it wasn't on rollerblades, then they'd catch the first train heading somewhere yet to be explored. Breakfast in one region, lunch in another; they pursued fresh experiences with an appetite that only comes with freedom.

Evenings brought spicier flavours as they dined out, visited friends and went clubbing. They loved dancing. Friday and Saturday nights, the girls would dress up and head into town, returning only when the music in the club was finally turned off.

In that Land of Cherry Blossoms, bliss budded forth. Times were good—really good. Anita had money, she had friends and she was on the adventure of a lifetime . . . what could be better?

My supporters may have ruled my days, but night was my time to step into another world. Where could a young black foreigner disappear in Japan? I wasn't interested in small bars with attentive hostesses. I had no taste for alcohol or casual banter. Nightclubs seemed the obvious place to become anonymous. The effervescence of movement, light and music stripped away the grim haze that shrouded me. Just give me the beat!

Weekend was party time for Anita and Christina at their favourite night-club in the city. Taking a break from dancing, Anita pressed through the crowd, up to the bar and signalled for a beer. Behind her, someone was mumbling in frustration. She turned to make sure she hadn't offended anyone. "What's up?" she asked.

"I can't get through to order a drink."

"What do you want?"

"Just a beer."

She turned to the barman, waving "make that two," and was able to pass the stranger a beer on her way back to her friend.

Two weeks later. . . . That seems to be such a profound time period: too short when you don't want something to stop and too long when you're waiting for something to start.

I enter the club, feeling the rhythm pulse through me. The crush of bodies on the dance floor seems suspended between the beats as each movement spells out youth, vibrancy and release. I skirt the floor and climb the couple of steps to the mezzanine bar. It gives a great view of all that chaotic euphoria.

It was Anita's birthday. She happened to be out with the same friends, at the same club. Looking down at the dance floor from the raised bar, she noticed someone across the room. She sensed a light around him, something unique that defined him from others. Not realising she'd ever laid eyes on him before, she watched as he skirted the dance floor, climbed the stairs and came to stand right beside her.

I glanced to my left. A girl was tapping her beer glass to the rhythm. She sensed me staring at her and smiled back.

Five minutes later, we'd yelled introductions over the din. She didn't remember me, but I realised she was the one who'd bought me the beer a couple of weeks earlier.

Since everyone in Japan called me Solomon, I had introduced myself by that name, not realising I'd see her again. Unwittingly, I laid the first untruth in a subtle web that would tangle irrevocably over time.

Five hours later, we had danced, talked, laughed and, though the night had vanished, we weren't quite ready to say goodbye.

How can I impress this girl? I don't want to appear too forward. I don't know what she likes or dislikes. Maybe we can chat more over a meal.

"I'd like to meet you again. Have you ever tried African curry? I could cook for you," I offered.

She agreed. We exchanged phone numbers. And (floating on a cloud) I left.

For the next week, I was caught up in commitments. Out of the blue, Anita phoned. She was waiting at my train station, wondering if I was going to pick her up.

Wah! I never realised we'd arranged the particulars. I thought we'd arranged to arrange them. Later, as I came to know her, I understood that she was committed and loyal: what she says, she will do. Neither of us realised how this strength would save us both.

Quickly, to the station. My dream car was still in another dimension, so Prince Charming would have to arrive on a borrowed bicycle.

Way to go, Teddy—forget the girl, and then turn up late, on a pushbike—do I know how to impress the ladies?

She greets me as if we've always been friends.

I'm so nervous now. I'll feel better when I get to the cooking. She'll forget all this when she tastes my curry. I hope.

Anita is a breath of fresh air. I am fascinated to hear how she grew up in a country town with a loving family . . . school, friends, holidays . . . things most people take for granted. Her soft voice is full of sparkles as she describes the playfulness of her life. She stands on the edge of the world, candidly expecting the extraordinary.

But I—who am I really? Not a knight on a quest. Not a modern day adventurer. I'm not even a tourist.

She laughs over a memory from childhood. Every time I start

relaxing, flashes of tension jar me. What can I share in return? I can't tell her what's really happening to me. Who would believe such madness? I still don't.

As the evening progresses, her natural curiosity poses a few questions: Brothers and sisters? What's Ethiopia like? What kind of work do you do? Why Japan?

I want her to know the ideal me, the one who dreams and has passion for bigger things. Barely able to speak, I choke back the truth. I don't want to lie, but won't the facts drive her away? Life has taught me: NEVER tell the truth. So, I sit there, guarding my dark secrets with short deflective answers.

My commitments, intense as they were, preoccupied my time and thoughts. Yet, all that had to be kept separate from Anita. Her part in my life must be pure.

We would chat on the phone, attend occasional festivals, and get together with friends for dinner and dancing.

I especially enjoyed visiting Anita's Australian friends, Sharon and Steve. They lived on the 39th floor in a spacious apartment, with views over the city. Being expatriates they had imported a slice of their culture, putting a barbeque on the balcony, Vegemite in the pantry and Jenga on the coffee table. We would gather there with other friends, enjoying company and simple pleasures. My Jenga skills were somewhat lacking, but Steve was always ready to pour some Hunter Valley wine, saying, "Have another drink, Sol."

If this was a slice of paradise, how wonderful is the whole thing?

By then, media coverage had splashed stories, including mine, far and wide. Nervous that Anita's friends would realise their guest was the "infamous refugee," I remained softly spoken. Always, I feared losing Anita. My heart fluttered between delirium and terror. Perched halfway to heaven, it was far to fall.

I was jarred by periodic landings back into my world of lawyers, meetings and rehashed dismal details. I almost wanted to laugh at the contrast and cry at the frustration. For all their good intentions, they were still jerking my strings and putting words in my mouth.

Still, laugh, cry, laugh was a satisfying contrast to alive, dying, alive.

I had two secret worlds, really. I kept Anita safe from the frustrations of officialdom, and I was most careful to keep her a secret from them.

This wonderful girl had danced into my life on her carefree adventure and taught me to step to a new beat. She did not require pampering or conventional romance. Her insatiable curiosity brought us new richness every day. I couldn't define it. With her, everything simply flowed. Without her, everything was waiting to be filled.

This was a different horizon beckoning and, more than ever, I wanted to stretch beyond dismal days. Soon, I thought, I will stand tall.

Sometimes, Ani and I would stay in for the evening and watch a movie. At those times, I savoured every moment for its precious normality—choosing which film, settling down with popcorn—for me, it was unextraordinary bliss.

So—this was love.

My heart dared before I did. Without realising I'd taken the first step, I had already arrived. I grew into the comfort of Anita, the light and colour she brought, the generosity with which she shared herself. I watched her laugh with others, then turn to smile at me, and I felt like a privileged guest in her life.

Having never really known such connection before, I could never understand what it was, only that I longed for something that was beyond me, no matter how far I reached. There was that time, as a child, when I took my first Communion. It was thrilling to feel everyone's pride, to feel as though I'd taken one step closer to heaven. That exceptional day gave me the clue I was looking for.

One step closer? With Anita, I was there already.

Yet, what simply flowed and seemed natural to her required serious consideration from me. Anita would say, "Let's go" and expect to be off in an instant, but I couldn't. Once, she wanted to catch the bullet train to Tokyo. She phoned, hoping to whisk me away. Right then, I was in the middle of a lawyer's meeting. I had to be brief, decline and hang up. Such a trip was outside my probation bounds.

Sadness sneaks in through the back door of your heart, an unwanted visitor whose departure is usually much more dramatic than that first untended arrival. How unfair that I could speak out to the world, but not to the person I cared for most.

No matter how mysterious I seemed, this shiny girl kept coming back. Each day, this miracle dawned on me anew.

Of course, she noticed secretive phone calls. At odd times, I'd have to interrupt what we were doing and leave abruptly. Or I would agree to meet her somewhere, then not show up. Without the truth, she must have felt frustrated.

Once when we were catching a train, she said, "Try this ticket machine, Solomon."

I snapped. "My name isn't "Solomon." I hate that name. Don't ever call me that again. I am Tewodros!" I must have been so frustrated with everything. I didn't want to hurt her. What must she have thought? She let it go without comment and called me Tewodros—Teddy—from then on.

She's told me since that she wondered if I was some kind of secret agent, or worse—a terrorist! Too much imagination for a country girl, perhaps? Instead of worrying, she decided to trust me. So, there she was, this bright, beckoning girl.

How could I resolve all the subterfuge? I felt so inadequate.

When love ceases to be like two birds playing on the wind . . . when it becomes something that needs firm ground on which to stand—the heart searches deeper for those foundations.

Within all my covert operations, I could become distant and unsure. How could I live in the moment when I had friends behind bars? When I might face deportation? When a lonely housewife had terrorised me into a state of perpetual tension? My race of thoughts was a never-ending marathon, with freedom the ever-elusive goal.

Unfairly, I felt Anita was being childish at times, with all that carefree attitude and spontaneity. She didn't understand why I couldn't relax. I would lose patience. When each of us was convinced the other was wrong, our conflicting views thundered out.

It would have to stop. I had to tell her what was really going on. But when? How? The more you get involved with someone, the harder it is to explain a dilemma. No. It was my pain, my burden to solve. I would make peace with it. Then she would only see my courage and not be sullied by my past.

But the truth will out.

Anita had been able to extend her eighteen-month stay by continuing a further six months on a cultural visa, studying *Ikebana*. But after almost two years in Japan, she was no longer the holiday girl. She started thinking about Australia, about university, about going home. She felt it was time to commit to bigger things in life.

On a naïve level, I was confident to be part of that. I still hadn't told her of my other life in Japan, and that sickened me, but as she was leaving, was there any point of causing her distress? Surely, my issues would be resolved soon. The bureaucrats couldn't leave me hanging indefinitely. Could they?

Days of adventure turned to days of farewell. In a matter of weeks, Anita was returning to Australia. She was excited and, of course, I was happy for her. Ever hopeful, we were painting the broad strokes of our future. Mostly, our plans were open-ended: what if . . . and won't it be great when. . . .

In the middle of all this planning, we decided to have lunch in Kyoto with my friend Daniel. The meal was ordered. The day seemed perfect. Let this be a countdown to happiness. Then Daniel spoke words that were not his to tell.

"Anita," he began, "there's something you should know."

No, no, no, NO—not now—not like this! What was he thinking? I had once shared my doubts with him about informing Anita of my situation. He didn't agree; he thought I was being a coward. I expected that he understood I would tell her when I was ready. So far from home, I should have remembered: *confiding a secret to an unworthy person is like carrying grain in a bag with a hole in it.*[2] Not that Daniel was unworthy, but the hole—the hole that should have remained closed—burst apart.

His words cast an eclipsing shadow on the one place in my life that should have stayed bright, and Anita and I descended into interminable night.

She sat and listened, not really knowing what to think, as my refugee status, detention, legal battles, and all the disdainful details of my life in Japan were lined up like suspects for her to identify. As he spoke, every hint of a ruse, every clue of deception was confirmed. She closed down—not hearing me, not speaking, not looking at me.

What could I say in my defence? Sure, it was true, but not like that. Whatever I said after would be hollow in comparison. Any anger at Daniel paled as I was overcome with concern for Anita.

Some celebration.

Tears. Trauma. Truth.

For two weeks, we stood on each side of the chasm between our hearts and called across our grief and longing. How could I convince her that I wasn't a fraud? Where before I'd been loud, I was now silent; where I'd been reticent, those answers poured forth like

---

2. Ethiopian proverb.

the flood after a storm. I turned myself inside out; anything to show her that I'd been hiding nothing but my shame.

She pounded me with questions. "I want to know everything. Tell me every little thing," she demanded.

Piece by piece, I built the true picture of my world. She did not rest until she had it all. The sunshine girl raged against deceit. Her heart was so straight. By this, she lived.

Well, that's that, I thought. And now it will be good-bye.

We sat in tortured silence. I could see that she was wrestling with the tangle of truth. I wanted to turn my deaf ear, so that I wouldn't hear anything more. But her next three words saved my life.

"I believe you," she gasped. And then all her hesitation was gone. "I knew there was something you weren't telling me, but I wanted you to explain when you were ready."

Each soft word bound the wounds of my regret.

"And I am upset with you—but I don't blame you. Maybe I would've done the same thing in your situation." She looked up and smiled at me. "Who knows?"

Oh, happy man, who found peace at last.

This unifying moment redefined our hearts: the romantic dreamers became freedom fighters. Instead of a few pleasant weeks before her return to Australia, we launched into action, and (you could have guessed) it was paperwork that paved the way. We investigated fiancé and marriage visas, and considered contingency plans: Can we live here? In Australia? Thailand? Africa? Where can we have a life together?

Precious time raced by.

Rightly or wrongly, I hadn't informed my supporters of the relationship with Anita. As guarantor, Kaeda could make one phone call to Immigration and land me straight back in detention. Trying to counter the doubts incurred all around, I didn't want to lose either of them: my love on one side, my freedom on the other.

I was well-practised at compartmentalised truth, but I didn't realise that Anita wouldn't understand its importance. As part of our investigations into how we could be together, I gave her the phone number for the Australian group who were trying to sponsor me while I was in detention.

Always keen to support her daughter, Anita's mother, Sue, phoned the group for advice. And so began a chain of calls that fell like dominoes into the next passage of (dare I say it?) doom.

When Sue spoke to the group's representative, he recommended that she contact Father Paul in Japan directly, and passed on his number.

"Hello? Father Paul? My daughter wishes to bring her fiancé, Solomon, to Australia. We are looking at different visa options for him and trying to work out which one is best."

"Kaeda? This is Father Paul . . . what has he done?!"

"Solomon? This is Kaeda . . . what have you done?!"

"Ani? This is Teddy . . . what have you done?!"

"Mum? This is Anita . . . what have you done?!"

Out of a parent's good intentions, our plans collapsed like the Jenga tower we used to play. Father Paul had advised Anita's mother that I was not really suitable for her daughter, that I seemed charming but it would be best for everyone if she forgot me. Kaeda felt I had betrayed them all (again). Anita wondered, after all this, if I was just a charmer seeking a marriage of convenience.

Inwardly I fumed at having lost the vigilant grip on my situation.

Anita and I had only just struggled through the previous calamity. I didn't think there were any tears left, but we cried together for all the hurt and misunderstandings. She was so afraid, realising the worst possible outcome.

Her devotion rescued me. My determination inspired her. And her mother supported us both. Making our commitment an oasis to which we could always return, we dove back into the stormy sea of bureaucracy.

We decided that the best way forward was through a Prospective Spouse Visa in Australia. If granted, this would allow me to live there with Ani for nine months before marrying. I was nervous about reapplying to the Australian Embassy. They had already rejected my refugee application. What would they make of this?

Convincing the Australian Embassy that the second visa application was genuine required the proverbial cast of thousands: we delivered photos, letters, testimonials from friends, references from acquaintances, validation from Anita's family back in Australia that this relationship was enduring—every detail we could think of. Given my precarious Japanese connection, our hopes hinged on a welcome from the south.

It was mid-November. With only four days before Anita's flight home, I was granted permission to travel to Tokyo and together we delivered our treasured documents to the embassy.

On the day of lodgement, we got lost. Luckily, we made it just on time for our 11 A.M. interview. When our names were called, we could tell right away that the Japanese woman assigned to us was going to be uncooperative.

In between frequent glances at her watch, she flicked through our papers and barely answered our questions.

Feeling frustrated, Anita asked to speak to an Australian staff member, but was denied. How about her manager or supervisor? Permission was again denied. This lady was "in charge" and anything relating to our case was to be done through her. She was more interested in getting the fee for the application. Agitated, we resigned ourselves for the moment and handed over the required ¥70,000.[3] Within fifteen minutes, we were asked to leave.

Worn out, we headed back to Osaka.

---

3. US$950 (approximately).

Despite my track record with officialdom, I refused to be daunted. I had already planned a celebration. *It is better to travel hopefully than to arrive disenchanted.*[4]

An Ethiopian doctor named Werku, who resided in Japan, had become a great help to me. On this occasion, he was pleased to host a traditional Ethiopian party. Surrounded by friends, food and music, I surprised Ani with an engagement ring. The real Teddy stood humbly before her, not as a hopeful frightened boy running from his past but as a man who believed in the future, complete now that she would have me.

Departure always brings rounds of farewell. There was a flurry of parties and dinners, and chorus after chorus of goodbyes.

We were dining out with some girls from Canada, who casually asked of our plans. On hearing them, their forks clattered to the table.

"You're taking him to Australia?" one gasped.

"Australia? Isn't that, like, one of the most racist countries?" the other joined in.

"Yeah. They hate black people there!" the first exclaimed.

Their vivid descriptions went on. Great. Another delightful meal ruined, only this time it was my turn to be shocked. Was I going from one hell to another? Anita's eyes twinkled at me when she asked them, "So, how many times was it you've visited Australia?"

"Oh, no. We've never been there. But everyone knows how it is."

"I'd totally love to go, though. Apparently you've got great beaches. And what's with all those kangaroos hopping through the streets?"

Given their "expert" opinions, I stopped choking on my dessert and relaxed.

Ani and I rushed about preparing her belongings and boxing them to be sent to Australia. While packing away the symbols of her life

---

4. Ethiopian proverb.

in Japan—our life—the finality of her departure hit me. We visited each of our favourite haunts one last time, sealing what was already sacred.

Our time was up. Although it had been sunny in the morning, late afternoon winds chilled our misery, and rain blended with the tears on our cheeks.

As a child, I thought the beating in my chest was the vibration of a little man playing drums; not until studying science at school did I realise it was my heart. Even so: drum, heart, rhythm—they're all extensions of the pulse that connects life.

My chest thrummed intensely as I watched Ani fly away. That little drummer was already calling to her across time and space, waiting for her answering beat.

22

RUNNING THE GAUNTLET

I am running . . . reaching out to catch . . . something. But something chases me, too. The light ahead beckons. Swifter, I run. I struggle to escape but faster and faster I am pursued. My path is blocked. A dead end. And another. I must turn . . . and turn again. All the while, the light flickers away. Away. Away. The horror of that word.

I wake, still in a foreign land.

Without Anita, life in Japan became an intense race: I hurried to meetings; I sprinted to lawyers; I dashed to deliver presentations. And in between, I scurried away from Asuka whenever possible.

The one meeting I never made was at the Australian Embassy. Apparently, they had notified me of an interview by sending the fax to an incomplete number.

Cracks in my patience were starting to show, but what choice did I have? I had to jump and keep jumping through the hoops of formality, never certain if I would soar or crash.

Meekly, knowing what was at stake, I arrived at the rearranged

427

interview, early in January 2001. The Australian representative, Mr. Mitchell, had an old file on his desk (dated by more than two years). That first refugee application had come back to haunt me.

Where was my new file? I wondered. What about Anita and our relationship and everything we hoped to achieve—together?

It was clear that Mr. Mitchell had closed his mind before he opened his mouth. "So, Solomon, you've got another plan to get into Australia, eh?"

"Yes—I mean, no, sir. This is genuine."

"Oh—so, if this application is genuine, what was the last one?" he smirked at his secretary, Ms. Yamada.

His cynicism muted me.

"Well, you know, I need to establish your validity—this time."

Two years. Two years of my life were spent locked in a small room, suffering inhuman conditions while I waited for an answer from this office. My temper was surfacing.

Deep breaths, Teddy. Just get through this.

"Sir, I'm sure if you read our submission, you'll see that Anita and I have clearly displayed proof of the seriousness of our relationship and commitment to each other."

"When's her birthday?"

"I—uh—it's—it's in July, no June. We'd only just met then . . . and birthdays are not part of my African culture, so—"

"What kind of food does she like?"

"Pardon? She likes lots of food. I don't know what you mean."

"Someone close to her would know specific things about her. What kind of food does she like?"

"Spaghetti. I cook for her. She likes spaghetti."

"Too common. Everyone likes spaghetti. What kind of sauce?"

"Tomato sauce."

"Really? Are you sure?"

Was he laughing at me?

Enough. I stood to leave. I told him I had expected a serious discussion about my life and my future, not to be mocked. Mr. Mitchell assured me that this was serious. He asked me to sit down again, and launched into questions about my refugee status.

"I don't understand your line of questioning," I interrupted him. "I'm here because my fiancé and I are applying for a visa. If I told you all the troubles of my past, your day would end and still you wouldn't have heard the half of it. I am here now. This is my life now. Can we please focus on the purpose of today's interview?"

He listened while I described meeting Anita and how our relationship grew, that I never expected something so wonderful to happen to me. He asked no further questions, but handed me some standard papers for medical tests and police clearance. He said I could go ahead and have them processed, or wait until the embassy advised me to do so. The interview was over.

Two days later, Ms. Yamada exchanged notes with Mr. Mitchell stating that, while it would be appropriate to interview Anita in Australia, she didn't think it was worth the trouble; she assumed my intention to marry wasn't genuine.

To his credit, Mr. Mitchell thought such an interview could balance the perspective. He guessed that my unwillingness to answer in detail arose from my past mistrust of the embassy.[1]

When Anita met with Southport Immigration (Australia) in February, she spoke for over an hour about our relationship. The interviewing officer sent a thorough report to the Australian Embassy in Tokyo, which included these comments:

Ms. Carr impressed me with her knowledge of the applicant and the circumstances he now finds himself in. She appears to have fully considered all aspects of their relationship and

---

1. In later research, I was able to view his documents relating to my case, through the Freedom of Information Act.

seems to have her life in order for when he is to join her. . . . Ms. Carr came across as very sincere about her relationship with the applicant and seems to be very confident that the applicant feels the same way and is equally committed.

Southport Immigration officer, 8 March 2001

Was that a light twinkling in the distance? Keep running. . . .

Leaping to the left, the appeal for Japanese refugee status was gaining momentum (finally).

Sliding to the right, the accumulated documents supporting my ear case had been submitted to the court, in preparation for the trial. The government was trying to undermine the legitimacy of my case, implying that I had contracted an ear infection as a child.

My lawyers' argument was threefold: firstly, the initial diagnosis was incorrect; secondly, it was Immigration's responsibility to provide appropriate treatment, whether it was a re-occurring infection or not; and finally, my hearing ability had deteriorated since the infection inside detention and therefore the government should be held liable for the damage, regardless of when I acquired the infection.

The judge concluded that, due to the complexities of the case, I should obtain an unbiased diagnosis from an independent specialist.

Keep listening. . . .

I informed Mr. Tanaka of my relationship with Anita. He took the news well and said he wouldn't go against any private decisions I made. I reassured him of my commitment to my current goals in Japan, knowing I had to grasp hold of anything that could free me.

Every month, I made the required trip to Immigration. It felt like begging each time I waited for the stamp of approval on my provisional release form. I hated it.

My supporters held a tight rein on all my movements, grilling me about anything they thought seemed suspicious or that might somehow prove I was not worthy of their attention.

Their profile in the community had risen and they were now taking interest in more refugees (although no Africans). They seemed to be offering aid, but their compassion in public contrasted to their conceit behind closed doors. I was baffled.

The pressure to bring in money continued. I risked breaking my release agreement by getting a part-time job. My supporters approved because it meant I had ¥20,000[2] for the lawyers every time I got paid.

I urgently wanted to conclude everything. I needed results. I needed answers. Desperately running the gauntlet to freedom, with every turn a possible release—or disaster—I simply had to keep dodging. . . .

The one-year agreement for use of Sato's house was about to expire. I was living elsewhere, so I was glad to end this bizarre, terrorising connection. I invited both Asuka and Sato to dinner, as thanks for their previous support and generosity.

Tensely polite, we bade each other farewell.

It's over, I thought. At last, it's over.

Right, Teddy, keep dreaming. . . .

My peace came to a screeching halt when I received a phone call from their household. Doubting (yet hoping) it would only be Sato, I answered. Of course, Asuka's serious monotone voice pulsed into my only good ear. Without a greeting, she announced that she was sending me a fax, and then abruptly hung up.

What strange game had she concocted now?

I found her fax when I reached my apartment. Terse and to the point, she accused me of stealing money from her. Shaking with anger, I went to her house to confront her.

---

2. US$270 (approximately).

Sato answered the intercom. I told him I needed to talk with Asuka, urgently. He said she wasn't home. I wanted to come inside and wait for her. He refused, telling me he was busy. Not knowing what else to do, I left.

I heard nothing more. Thinking it was just another of her strange fantasies, I let it go. Days slipped by. She called again, wanting to meet. I needed to clear this once and for all, so I agreed.

We met at a coffee shop. Asuka mournfully told me her mother had died. (Sad for her, but that had nothing to do with the fax.)

"Why haven't you contacted me?" she burst out. "Why do you ignore me? I do things for you—to help you—don't you know I just want to help you?"

Carefully, methodically, I gave her an honest account of her behaviour and explained why I felt confused and threatened. I asked her about "the money" I was meant to have taken. She apologised— for the faxes, for the accusations, for everything. Her excuse was that she'd been venting anger and didn't mean any of it; she was just trying to get my attention. I explained that my life was very full and I needed to concentrate on resolving everything. She agreed to let me be, nodding all the while.

Was I surprised when she phoned the very next day to ask for another meeting? Actually, yes, because I really thought this time it was concluded.

My next court appearance for the refugee appeal was fast approaching. She resented me being pre-occupied. (Oh, don't mind me, Asuka. It's only my life I'm trying to salvage!) When she became petulant and—well, slightly hysterical—I invited her to attend. Perhaps if she understood the intensity of the demands on me, she'd leave me alone.

She did attend that day at court, along with most of my supporters and many other friends. I was relieved to see them sitting in the public gallery, and my lawyers appeared impressed by the turnout. Later, on the steps of the courthouse, Mr. Narito publicly thanked everyone for their contributions. They had worked hard collecting evidence, submitting documents and attending meetings and court hearings. Mr. Narito advised that there was nothing to do but wait. We had to be patient while the judges deliberated the case, which could take several weeks.

Asuka remained sullen amid the others' conversations. Why had she even come? I couldn't explain anymore, or rescue her, or deal with her rudeness to my friends. It felt so futile. I said goodbye. Her eyes barely met mine as she replied, and left.

Keep looking over your shoulder, Teddy. Keep looking. . . .

With the refugee appeal now under consideration by the court, my supporters refocused their energy on the ear case. (That's where the potential payout was, after all.) As requested by the judge, an appointment was arranged to see an independent ENT specialist by the name of Doctor Aoki.

Doctor Aoki was a very short man; so short that his head barely reached my chest when I stood next to him. After examining my ear, he expressed his embarrassment that a doctor in his country could give such poor treatment. He wondered how such an incompetent doctor still had a licence.

This news greatly lifted our spirits. He advised on different ways to deal with the court. It was all in Japanese and well above my understanding. I was only given sporadic translations, so I wasn't sure exactly what was discussed.

Our newfound confidence was shattered during my next court appearance. The judge produced a document he'd received from Doctor Gokumura, of Sakai Hospital, who had originally advised us not to sue for compensation. My lawyers' intently perused the paper. I knew it wasn't good. Mr. Narito kept wiping his sweaty hands. Mr. Tanaka dragged tense fingers across his pulsing temple, then bowed his head.

According to the document, Doctor Gokumura suggested the

damage to my hearing was probably (although he couldn't be sure) attributable to an infection during my childhood. This threw doubt on our side and strengthened Immigration's defence. They requested all documents from this doctor regarding my condition, shaking the only standing leg we had left.

But my supporters were defiant. (How about that?) It was difficult to prove either way. Besides, our argument was not "when" the infection initially occurred, but about "how" it was treated in detention. We returned to Doctor Aoki, who encouraged us to pursue justice. It was going to be a long winding road and we were still only at the beginning (even though we'd started years before).

In the great southern land, my dream girl was occupied with new responsibilities. Study and finances demanded her focus.

The Australian Embassy originally advised that processing normally took three months. Considering our unusual circumstances, this could extend to six. We remained hopeful.

Love from afar has a different language. We evolved a communication system of timely emails, phone calls and faxes, to diminish the distance. As direct people, we didn't feel limited in sharing our feelings; these were laced with frustration, but reassuring nevertheless.

Her previously normal life was now an obstacle course of political negotiations. Still she persisted in championing my cause. She arranged our wedding date; forwarded a letter of support from the priest who would marry us; chased Immigration and the embassy; and contacted Canberra and her local politician. She did all this— for me.

It seemed that *the whisper of a pretty girl might be heard further than the roar of a lion.*[3]

I had love. I had support. And, unexpectedly, I inherited a whole family of well-wishers. Once Anita's parents were convinced of her

---

3. Arabian proverb.

devotion, they generously welcomed me into their lives. Seeing their daughter's growing distress, they too urged the officials for closure.

To wish for one treasure and receive a chest full was a delight that the abandoned boy in me could not comprehend. With such gifts in my heart, it was easier to remain calm and respectful towards my Japanese support committee.

I stepped lightly through the rhythm of days, Anita's heartbeat keeping pace with mine. Surely, this paper shuffle would soon have me signed, sealed and delivered to Australia.

We fulfilled all their requirements; attending interviews, filling out more papers, answering more questions. We were honest and willing but, with my prior record, the embassy still treated me like an opportunist.

Finally, I received notice to proceed with the medical and police clearance, which had to be submitted within forty-nine days. (A positive answer must have been imminent.)

As if things weren't complicated enough, my passport had expired. I sent for the appropriate papers from Ethiopia, as well as police clearance confirming no criminal record from my time there.

No response.

The Australian Embassy contacted the Ethiopian Embassy in Tokyo to see if they could assist.

Still no reply.

Then they pursued connections in Nairobi, trying to get a message through within Africa.

Silence.

If the diplomats of two countries failed to communicate, what could we do? Desperate, Anita even contacted Interpol to see if they could assist.

My steps grew a little heavier as days of hope wrinkled into weeks of worry. The wedding date came and went. Anita arranged for another, with the requisite supporting letter from the priest.

Six months, the embassy had said. We crossed it off the calendar.

The paper shuffling continued.

Keep planning. . . .

In the middle of July, in the middle of more court proceedings, Anita arrived in Japan for a surprise visit. Well, I had asked her not to come, but she did anyway. I was feeling so battered from the continual blows of failure that I didn't have much to offer her personally. Insistent champion that she was, she arrived early, hoping to bring some light back into my life.

Without saying why, my friend Daniel asked me to meet him around 9 P.M., at the bar where Anita and I had first met.

I was late. Before I eventually arrived at 11 P.M., Anita's concern grew. When I snuck up behind her and gave her a big hug, it was she who was surprised, after all!

Was I a madman to ask her to stay away? Here she was in my arms: I could hold her, see her sunshine face. The rush of joy overwhelmed the past eight months of distance.

Brief moments of reunion could not interrupt the onslaught that owned me yet. Once more, dashing through days too complex to explain, I had to leave Anita waiting. She endured an intense week of embargoed love while I came and went, bruised but still standing.

And then she was gone. My heart, knocking at my ribs, raged against it all.

Reaching beyond available authority, I tracked down a friend of a friend in Kenya, who could arrange for the correct papers to be sent from Ethiopia. The snag was that he wanted US$1000 to make it happen. That blow was below the belt (the money belt, anyway). Somehow we scraped the funds together, wondering if it was a scam. Mercifully, the papers arrived, but once again, the divergent Ethiopian calendar complicated progress.

When I look back on my diary for this time, all I see are court dates, renewal dates, meetings, and the thin line of diplomacy along which I balanced to satisfy the people involved.

Exasperated, I spun away. Anita caught me every time, though I must have lashed out at her. I didn't mean to. It just boiled over. We see-sawed our way through the next few months. If I gave up, she would bolster me. When I was determined, she would regain strength. At times, we felt that nothing could stop us and, with the loyalty and confidence of her family cheering us on, our reward finally came.

Thirteen months after we first applied, I was awarded a Prospective Spouse visa allowing me Australian residency for a nine-month trial period. I received a letter from the Australian Embassy stating the details and, as my passport had expired, they would issue me a travel document.

I am alive. I am free. I am alive! What a different song to sing. My feelings were beyond explanation, but the gamut went something like this: relieved, obviously; excited to live with Anita; nervous because, till then, each time I'd started a "new life" I somehow wound up in trouble; and at peace because a safe and secure future had become my reality.

It would have been easy to simply fly away from all that was yet to be concluded in Japan. Out of respect for my supporters' efforts, and to be a man of moral substance, I wanted to see things through. I didn't want their experience with a refugee to cast a bad light on anyone else. I wanted peace and dignity on all sides.

Although Anita longed to have me with her (and safe), she was not one to decide for others. She felt I was courageous to stay. She respected how important it was to be true to myself.

A flurry of activity ensued.

Teddy,

I've found us a lovely apartment, five minutes from the beach.

I've ordered some great furniture (on credit).

I can't wait to see you.

It's so close now.

My Ani,

I have packed all my things, ready to fly to you.

My furniture is sold and I will move in with friends soon.

I can't wait to see you.

It's so close now.

It was time to inform people in Japan of my departure.

The first person I told was Asuka. I didn't want her to hear it from anyone else. Who knew how she might react? She calmly asked that I remember them well and to think of her as a mother.

Needing absolute closure, I decided to send a farewell fax to them as a couple, ensuring that Sato received the message as well. I didn't provide any departure details, only stating that I was leaving and thanking them for their generosity. Just before pressing "send," I hesitated. Relax, Teddy. It's the right thing to do. I pushed the little green button and continued with final preparations.

Next on the list were my supporters.

Mr. Tanaka was already aware of my Australian visa application, so I decided to approach him first. Though surprised at my success, he congratulated me and reaffirmed everyone's ultimate goal to see me in a safe free life. He suggested that I inform everyone else as soon as possible, since we had pending official business.

At the next court proceeding just a few days later, I was standing in the lift with my two lawyers when Mr. Tanaka spontaneously mentioned that I was leaving for Australia. He asked Mr. Narito to deal with it, as he was too busy.

Deal with what? I thought. Why would he advise me to tell the others, and then make it sound like I was sneaking away? After all that time, Japanese thinking was still a mystery to me.

Mr. Narito and I were left at the door. An awkward silence

prevailed. I apologised for not informing him first, but he congratulated me and assured me there was no ill will. On the front steps of the court, Mr. Narito invited Kaeda and another supporter, Mr. Ogawa, to coffee. We found a table at the local café. Mr. Narito, who still hadn't fully digested the news himself, explained that I had secured a visa for Australia.

I braced myself for a verbal battering, but they seemed pleased. I suspect that part of their reaction was realising they wouldn't have to deal with me for much longer.

Kaeda invited me to attend the cathedral's Christmas gathering that very night. There, I made a speech informing Bishop Mori and other church members of my good fortune. I expressed my appreciation for their good wishes. Humbly receiving their congratulations, I felt months of stress lift away.

I still had to apply for a monthly permit extension, ensuring that my presence in Japan was legal right up until my flight. To that date, 29 extensions had been issued. Had I really been running to get out of there for so long?

With the exit door from Japan burning brightly, the world was far less grim. My ticket was booked for 30 January 2002.

Give me wings!

Just after Christmas, I received a strange telephone call from Kaeda. Asuka had been in contact with her and was apparently very worried for my well-being. Kaeda asked that I contact Asuka immediately to put her mind at ease.

My stomach started to churn. Why would Asuka be worried? I was the happiest I'd been in a long time. My guess was that, while they'd been talking, Kaeda had disclosed my departure date and Asuka was in a panic to get hold of me one last time.

I called. Asuka's concern had nothing to do with my well-being; instead she commented that the fax I'd sent earlier was too brief, and her husband requested more details of my plans. Of course, she was really talking about herself; it was out of character for Sato to make such a request.

Can anyone reach out across time and stop me before I agreed to meet with her that day? Too late.

Sitting across the café table, while I touched on my plans, she nodded yet seemed jittery. Something wasn't right, but I couldn't quite pinpoint it. Her tears flowed freely when we parted company. I berated myself for thinking her handshake was more like a Judas kiss.

Three weeks to freedom. . . .

Early in the New Year, I attended a meeting at Mr. Tanaka's office to redefine my two court cases. I understood that my refugee appeal would be void, but I was still keen to pursue hearing loss compensation. Mr. Tanaka thought it would be too difficult to manage long distance.

Changing topics, he asked if it was true that I was running away to Australia without paying "the money" I owed Asuka. Although stunned, I calmly asked him who was spreading such a rumour. But he refused to answer.

Apparently, this is how it unfolded: after learning of my departure, Asuka contacted Mr. Kato, the journalist working with Mr. Suzuki. She started a lying campaign that suckered everyone. She rallied them against me, and my so-called supporters believed her, without an iota of evidence or the decency to ask me for the truth.

Still in ignorant bliss, I arrived at a meeting. It began with the usual greetings, including congratulations on my Australian visa. Then Mr. Tanaka started itemising outstanding costs that the supporters had incurred and asked that I pay ¥600,000 in lawyers' fees and ¥335,000 in court costs.[4] Kaeda then added that I owed the church ¥402,500 to cover medical expenses, and Mr. Ogawa wanted ¥30,000.[5]

As each person read out his or her list of accruing costs, Mr.

4. US$8,000 and US$4,500 respectively.
5. US$5,425 and US$400 respectively.

Tanaka busily typed away on his computer. He printed the document and handed it to me. My eyes scanned the page, but everything was written in Japanese. All I could recognise was the figure ¥1,367,500.[6] Seeing my confusion, Mr. Tanaka explained that this was a contract for me to sign.

I refused. I couldn't read it; it didn't appear to list any of my ongoing contributions; it completely ignored the fact that they had all volunteered to support me, possibly taking a percentage of the winnings should we succeed in court. Support? What did they think that meant?

I was sick with shock. Such betrayal—from all of them. I put the document on the table so that my shaking hands wouldn't reveal my terror. Who knew, with these people? They might interpret anything as a sign of guilt. *When spiders unite, they can tie down a lion.*[7]

Mr. Tanaka demanded, "Why won't you sign it?" I noticed that his hands were shaking, too, and his face was reddening. Mr. Narito looked uncomfortable with the situation and excused himself from the room.

"Why don't you sign?" Mr. Ogawa interjected. "Are you trying to run away? Asuka told us you are trying to run away with all of her money."

Each accusation escalated in pitch to a crescendo.

"Return the money NOW!" Mr. Ogawa raged. "RETURN THE MONEY—TO EVERYONE!" Then he grabbed me by the collar and started shaking me. He was pushing me around, slamming my head into the wall. "You are a robber and a liar," he breathed hotly in my face.

Fish. All I could think was fish. He'd eaten fish for lunch and the salty odour sent my senses reeling into a retrospective spiral all the way back to the arrest at the fish factory. My gut burned. My arms throbbed. My fury from all the injustices of this land powered through me, and I wrestled myself from his tight grip.

---

6. US$18,000 (approximately)
7. Ethiopian proverb.

"How do you know I am a robber and a liar? Have I ever cheated or lied to you?"

"Because Asuka told me so!" Saliva flew from his mouth, like an angry dog.

"How can you believe her word over mine? All of you, even Kaeda, thought she was strange when I first introduced you, but now you are siding with her. How can you do that?" I retaliated.

"Because she is Japanese!"

"And I am a foreigner, so you don't believe foreigners?"

"No. She is Japanese. I believe Japanese!"

"STOP IT! STOP FIGHTING!" Mr. Tanaka raised his voice above ours.

I turned away, telling Mr. Tanaka that I refused to be in the same room as Mr. Ogawa, and started to gather my belongings. Mr. Ogawa, outpacing me, snatched up his things and stormed from the room, never to return.

"Are you shunning Kaeda, as well?" Mr. Tanaka questioned me.

"She can stay if she wants," I replied.

Mr. Narito returned to an awkward silence, noting the room was one member less than when he'd stepped out.

Mr. Tanaka's tone was solemn, "Just tell us the truth. Did you take Asuka's money?"

It was almost as if they wanted me to be guilty. Did they prefer the word of a mad woman? They had witnessed firsthand how she'd forced herself into my life, how she constantly called me, and always insisted on paying for anything from coffee with my supporters to furniture for my apartment. They'd seen her become upset if I refused to accept, and how jealously she behaved if I ignored her.

Drained by the tumultuous meeting, we agreed to reconvene before my departure, giving everyone time to calm down. About a week later, I called Mr. Tanaka to arrange a second meeting. I reminded him of our prior agreement to split the potential winnings from the damages case, but he quickly changed the topic and never mentioned money again. Instead, he asked me about my Japanese visa which was about to expire.

Mr. Tanaka's concern seemed strange because he'd never previously taken an interest in my visits to Immigration. He asked that I let him know once I renewed it this final time. Then he mentioned that Asuka had asked him to mediate between us.

I declined. It was clear the woman could not be reasoned with and she could certainly not be trusted. I just wanted to get out of the country without further problems from her—or anyone. I did not sense his good will.

Countrymen hold together. Loyalty belongs within the circle. The real truth of that thundered down upon me: I was never going to win there.

All that time, all that effort towards justice, yet I could see that in such a culture no one went against the establishment, whether it was a foreigner against a neighbour or human rights against a government.

I'd been running for so long. The marathon was over. Just beyond the horizon, my new life waited. Keep believing, Teddy. Keep believing. . . .

23

WILDERNESS OF THE HEART

For my last two days in Japan, I was accommodated in a five-star hotel, with everything laid on. And it didn't cost me a cent.

Two Ethiopian athletes of international renown were in Osaka. In need of a translator, they contacted me. Quite the media pro by then, I fielded questions as cameras flashed, and enjoyed my celebrity status.

Secretly, my fingertips thrilled as they brushed over the plane ticket in my pocket.

The gala atmosphere inspired some of my friends to gather for a farewell party. Effervescent warm wishes and cold champagne bubbled freely.

In a break from the media, I checked my phone and saw a "missed call" message. Perhaps it was another well-wisher. I dialed for a quick chat.

Then, the Devil fell from the sky right into my lap.

"Yes, Solomon. This is the Australian Embassy. There has been a last-minute complication, and your visa has been suspended."

"No, I have it here in my travel document. I have my ticket. I fly out the day after tomorrow."

"If you pursue that course of action, you will be arrested at the airport or stopped on arrival in Australia. In that case, Japan will not accept you back. We will fax you the details. I can say no more." Beep—beep—beep—

All around me, people were talking, smiling and dancing. But I couldn't hear them. In a thick, numbing cloud of shock, I remained still. The swelling of my throat was not a scream or a cry; it was the words I would have to tell Anita, without understanding why.

Mechanically, I proceeded to translate. I mingled with the others. I faked joviality for their sakes. And I wondered over life's striving. Whether it was for excellence, dignity, fame, or wealth—if one phone call could destroy it, was there any meaning at all?

When I received the fax early that evening, my eyes raced over the pages until they fixed on the reasons for the suspension:

> Information was given by a third party that the holder's intention was to get married to an Australian citizen for the purpose of gaining entry and residence status in Australia and that there were plans to divorce after two years. . . . We have been notified by the relevant police authorities that he may have been involved in criminal conduct that is punishable by the law in Japan, which is yet to be substantiated with evidence and is subject to further consideration of cancellation.
>
> Australian Embassy, 25 January 2002

Strangely the scent of fox hung heavy in the air. I choked on it, unable to fathom the depths to which Asuka had sunk this time. *The tongue is but three inches long, yet it can kill a man six feet high.*[1]

I sat. Stood and paced. Sat, again. Icy fingers of fear ripped down within me. I must have reached for the phone ten times before I was finally able to dial Anita's number.

---

1. Japanese proverb.

She listened in silence. I uttered each word with dread. I hadn't informed her of the "Asuka Catastrophe" because I thought it was settled before we met. All sorted. No need to worry her with it. Was there?

But this news revived her past feelings of doubt, when I thought I was protecting her from the darker details of my life. She wondered if I'd made other plans, or found another girl. She tried to justify it for herself. "It's alright. I'll forgive you, Teddy. Just tell me the truth."

Ah, if only I knew. "Anita, believe me. I'm as confused as you. There must be some mistake. You know how things have gone crazy before. I have my bags ready to go to the airport. I'm supposed to get an Exit Visa from Immigration today, so that I can leave Japan. Now I'm not sure what they will do. I'll phone you when it's all okay."

She never got that call.

Equipped with my suitcase and hand luggage, I had a friend drive me to Immigration. Every month, I'd managed this detail without a reminder, but this time Kaeda called repeatedly, wanting to know if I had arrived yet. Every ring tone signalled "trap, trap, trap."

When we got there, I advised my friend that if someone came for my things, to give the hand luggage only. In the large case, I had packed keepsakes from Anita. I wouldn't have anyone pawing through those. I had another special collection in the small case: Asuka's letters. Instinct had guided me to keep them as evidence of her abnormal obsession and harassment. I couldn't wait to hand them over in my defence.

Instead of the usual stamping of forms at the front desk, I was escorted to an interview room, surrounded by four guards.

"You are under arrest. Sign here!" the officer barked, shoving a piece of paper at me.

"I'm not signing anything." I faked confidence. "I haven't done anything wrong."

"You lied to us. You are not living at your registered address."

Well, technically that was true, but I'd still been using that address for meetings—at Asuka's suggestion. More the fool, me.

"I'm going to Australia. I moved out because I'm leaving this country."

"You go nowhere. You are criminal. Now sign!"

"No! I shouldn't be here."

"You are thief. We detain you while we investigate."

How had Asuka arranged this? Whatever else, surely she didn't have influence over the Australian Embassy!

I found out later that she had quite an arsenal in her offence. First, she'd spun a damsel-in-distress tale to Mr. Suzuki, who advised her to contact Kaeda and Immigration about the "false address." Then, she told the police about the "stolen money." And finally, she presented all these "facts" to the Australian Embassy. Put together, that's some coup.

But had the embassy phoned Anita to verify anything—or even informed her as my sponsor? No. Had they asked for any proof of the accusations, or even validated the source? No.

I didn't understand how our tireless efforts could be voided by that one communication. Nor was I aware that some of my supporters had colluded with Asuka in the lead-up to that moment. They were gathering like a pack of hyenas, just beyond the light, waiting for my downfall. And peace be with you.

"Fine," I said to the officer. "If I have to stay, I have my things in the car."

He snapped at one of the guards, "Send someone to fetch them."

My friend faithfully handed over the small case only, and returned home to enact our contingency plan: Get help!

My personal belongings were confiscated, including the precious travel visa and plane ticket. Then I was taken to another room where my arrest was officially registered into the system. I knew the routine from there: handed over to detention; assigned the once-familiar cup, blanket, plastic spoon, and a pair of slippers; deposited in a cell with some Chinese.

The day after my arrest, I sent a letter to the Australian Embassy, firmly denying the allegations by the third party. It was challenging not to write "crazy psycho obsessive stalker who is out for vengeance and has tricked you all," but I carefully reinforced my innocence and eligibility for the visa. In the absence of substantiating evidence, I naively believed that the embassy would reinstate their approval.

It wasn't my deafness that stopped me from hearing a response. There was none.

Back in Australia, Anita panicked. Without my return call, she didn't know where I was or what was happening. She tried phoning any and every official body that might have explanations, to no avail. It was Australia Day[2] and no one was working. If anyone ever wanted to design a torture of endurance, that had to be it.

Once relocated, my first action was to submit a request to phone Anita. I had to speak to her, to reassure her that this was all a big mistake. When I finally did get through, I told her I was fine, that all was being handled, and that I would be out "next week." This became my mantra, every week, ad infinitum.

At the next possible opportunity, Anita phoned her local immigration office, as well as Mr. Mitchell in Japan, seeking answers. Until the Japanese police cleared me of charges, Mr. Mitchell said he had no choice but to suspend my visa.

I was yet to discover that detention had undergone some changes. I recognised a few of the same guards, who proudly showed off their promotions. They greeted me like some long lost hero. Of course, none of the current detainees knew that I'd once held the longest reign there. Nor did they know that mine was the first detainee's voice to be heard by the people of Japan. No national threat, but

---

2. Anniversary of the first British fleet arriving in Australia, 26 January 1788.

my outspokenness had certainly rattled the roots of the *sakura*.[3] Detainees still suffered, but now fared better in lockup with the revised system of regular exercise, improved hygiene, showers five times per week, and—get this—two pens per cell. I never imagined I would return to reap these benefits. It was a strange kind of victory, but a victory no less.

Other changes revealed themselves over time, but some things remained the same: Edible food? Barely. Sleeping on the floor? Where else? Abuse from guards, morning checks, smoking Chinese? There's no cell like home.

I connected with no one. Singular focus on my goal probably made me an island, but I had endured too much of detention before and could not fully comprehend facing it again. I built emotional walls outward against all else to defy the all-too-real walls that closed me in.

Through a series of phone calls and letters to the Australian Embassy, I learned of Asuka's malicious actions, as well as my supporters' preference that I stay in Japan to complete the court cases. Locking me up was a heck of a way to get my cooperation. Perhaps the potential for money was their prime motivation, after all.

I contacted the United Nations, whose secretary took note of my situation (whatever that meant). The Australian Embassy refused to do anything until the police investigated. The police hadn't contacted me yet, so I couldn't present the evidence in my defence. There seemed to be no legitimate reason for me being there, yet there I sat.

Despair did not descend. No longer did I rail at the heavens and wonder over my strange fate. I was void of questions. If logic, politics and politeness could devour each other, then I would strip away all that was civilised, all that aspired to anything. Raw beyond any sense, my one enduring thought was this: I am defiance.

---

3. The Japanese flowering cherry blossom tree. (Japanese)

"Visitor for Solomon!"

As always, I flinched at that name. Yet, expectant that my friends on the outside had begun a rescue, I stepped eagerly into the glass-divided room. Natsumi, a friend of Asuka's, stared back at me. I'd met her when presenting at a university where she was a lecturer. I hadn't seen her for some time, so I guessed her visit wasn't out of concern for me.

"Asuka is very upset," she said.

I didn't answer.

"She wants you to return her money."

Silence filled my mouth.

Natsumi launched an assault of insinuations, screeching at me as though her piercing voice could force those lies into my head.

I stood up and turned to the guard. "Take me back to my cell."

He remained unmoving, dazed by her continuing tirade.

"Hey!" I yelled. "Get me out of here." Just before exiting, I turned back. "Shame on you," I said simply. The words split the air like a sword of truth. The door closing after me drove it home.

On Valentine's Day, I was denied permission to call Anita. So: demeaning manipulation was still detention's modus operandi. Fine! Love to me was more than a day or a season. I would love beyond bars and walls and restraints. My heart, the last vestige of tranquillity, merged with and became the driving core of my rage.

All day, visitors were announced. The cell door clanged continually with traffic to and from that room. The halls buzzed with talk of a United Nations representative who was investigating each detainee's situation. As the day grew long, deafness seemed appealing. I had listened so hard for my name to be called that my ears ached with strain—an unappreciated irony.

"Visitor for Solomon!"

Steps of determination led me to the interview room (not the visitors' room—a good sign). A softly spoken young man introduced himself in fluent English as Mr. Ono. He was already standing to leave and he apologised for his lack of time, but wanted to acknowledge that he'd received my message.

"Well if catching your train is more important than my life, then you'd better go right now." My brittle tone got his attention.

He regained his seat, getting comfortable. His clear eyes looked at me without pretence. "Why don't you tell me all about it?" he invited.

By degrees, my voice lightened as I talked of Ani. I showed him a treasured photo that she'd sent with a letter, and let him read the precious pages that I'd carefully folded and unfolded countless times in the few days since I'd received them.

Incredulity stretched his features. "Why are you in here when you have a fiancé in Australia? Such a letter! You should be with her."

You don't say.

I told him about the fox. I'd been over and over the details in my mind, trying to comprehend how she wielded such power. The others were all reasonable intelligent people. What did Asuka have over them? Was it Sato's money? Did he have connections that could affect them? Maybe. But I really think the explanation was quite simple: she was mentally unstable and they were scared of her.

Mr. Ono sprang from his chair, clenching his fists and shaking his head. "Who is this woman? How can she take away your life like this? The Australian Embassy should never have acted without verifying the situation. This is blatantly wrong!"

Ah, wisdom, at last!

"I'll make a formal request that you are not to be deported because your country is still in turmoil. As I understand it, you cannot return to Ethiopia because your father is Eritrean. You cannot return to Eritrea because your mother is Ethiopian. Yes?"

"Right. That's the simple version."

"Well, I'm here to help. You can make a collect call to this number (he handed me a card) to have any necessary items delivered. I'll take your photo for my records (he snapped a quick Polaroid). Don't you worry, Solomon. I can't promise anything, but I'll do my best. If I could get you out by next week, I would."

Now, where had I heard that before?

Only the day after, the cell echoed with, "Visitor for Solomon!"

Excellent. Could Mr. Ono have moved mountains already? I walked down the hallway with new vitality. But when I entered the room, it was Asuka's sullen face I saw on the other side of the glass. It took all my strength to approach, restraining myself from smashing through the divider and squeezing all the poison from her.

Her head remained bent.

I waited.

Whatever tactic she'd planned, I made a final attempt to penetrate her conscience. "The issues you have with me, we can resolve. Lying to all these people—these officials—is only going to come back at you. I can prove my innocence. Then you will be the criminal. Don't you see that? Just withdraw your false claims and let me get on with my life. I won't seek retribution."

Her shoulders lifted almost imperceptibly. Without looking up, she said, "I want my money."

"What money? Even if you imagine I owe you money, do you think locking me up is the way to get it? Don't you realise that if I was in Australia, working, I'd be earning money? Whatever it is I'm supposed to have done, you picked the worst way to get it back."

Her eyes flicked up at me briefly. Her voice droned quietly, almost like a recording, "I want my money."

I thrust back, sending the chair scraping across the floor. Leaning into the glass, I grimaced, "You—are—crazy."

Immediately, when I returned to my cell, I composed a letter to Ani. I never told her about what was happening inside detention;

just that I loved her and would see her soon. A soothing balm as much for me as for her.

For a while, there was a stream of visitors.

I had begun to write this woeful tale in notebooks and on scraps of paper, seriously wondering if I would ever see freedom again. When friends came with simple presents and much encouragement, I smuggled my story to them. Page by page, I slid palm-sized pieces under the small gap below the glass, away from the predatory gaze of the guards. I also asked them to gather all my evidence and deliver it to Mr. Ono.

Asuka came again, but I refused to see her.

The lawyers, Mr. Tanaka and Mr. Narito, brought the latest news of the ear case. I asked them to reinstate my appeal for refugee status, since who knew what was going to happen with the Australian Embassy. I also informed them that I wanted to take legal action against the third party for wrongful imprisonment. Surprisingly, they were sympathetic and said they'd see what could be done.

The defiant approach was working. Despite my confinement, I felt strong.

Another visitor was a caring priest named Father Michael Angelo. We'd shared many conversations at the church. He came to express his loyalty and support. He knew I was innocent and had stated this clearly to everyone, including Asuka. In his gentle voice, he confirmed his friendship and urged me to remember my dreams. Then, he said a prayer of peace for me, before leaving.

I became ill.

In retrospect, I can see that it was probably caused by extreme anxiety. At the time, though, I thought it was food poisoning and hoped it would pass. When it didn't, my nausea doubled at the thought of detention's medical standards. Amazingly, I received swift attention upon request.

"What's wrong?" asked the doctor.

"I think I'm allergic to the fish and chicken in my meals," I replied.

"Okay. We'll change it," he concluded.

It was never that simple before. What delectables would they bring me instead?

The next meal arrived. Rather than provide an alternative to the cadaver content, they had simply removed it. What I saw was rice floating in a greasy broth that looked like it had already passed through someone's digestive tract.

I gagged back a bitter laugh, pondering the new, efficient request system. Loosely translated, it could easily mean, "I'm sick of this shit."—"No worries. Try this shit, instead."

Yummy.

The light of my life, Anita, had been indefatigable, sending the Australian Embassy emails and faxes, desperately trying to arrange for my release and have my visa reinstated.

The situation obviously went way beyond the usual conditions that got boxes ticked and papers stamped. Their response was repeatedly generic and brief.

It wasn't until March (two and a half months after my confinement) that the embassy requested further comments regarding these accusations:[4]

> The information given was that you were involved in setting up a business in Japan in partnership with a person, who had given you quite a sum of money to help you start the business. It was their understanding that this never happened and when you were asked to return the money to the person involved, you told the person that the money had been transferred to an overseas account and could not be withdrawn, unless either

4. See scan of original embassy letter on p. 517.

you or the person physically travelled to the country to withdraw. The person claims that the money has not been given back. Also the person made several requests on several occasions. The person also alleged that you stated you intended to go into a false marriage to obtain residence in Australia and divorce after a two-year period. The person also alleges you failed to correctly inform the Japanese Immigration bureau and your guarantor details regarding your place of residence and place of employment, which led the guarantor to withdraw their support. We have been able to contact your former guarantor who has confirmed that this allegation is correct.

Australian Embassy, 8 March 2002

I had forty-nine days to respond. I wrote a five-page letter to the embassy addressing each point of contention, as well as detailing my relationship with Asuka, my supporters and lawyers. The claims were elaborate and completely ridiculous, yet revealed that Kaeda was more involved in my arrest than she admitted to me. So, as I was driving to Immigration that day, she was already pulling the plug!

Forms, applications, secret diary, and beautiful pages from Anita: paper became my only proof of life.

My lawyers updated me on legal developments. They had been in touch with the Australian Embassy, which advised that they wouldn't discuss anything with them until they received a signed power of attorney from me. But—they wouldn't discuss anything with me either. Status quo, there.

"Asuka wants to take you to court, Solomon," Mr. Narito confided.

"Fine. If she wants to swear before a judge to tell the truth, and then tell lies, it will be her problem, not mine."

"But Anita must come to testify."

"Why? This has nothing to do with her."

"Maybe," he replied sceptically.

"It's absurd. She is a student and can't just drop everything because some crazy lady makes ridiculous allegations. Whatever you want to believe is up to you. But our love is sincere and time will prove that." Strength flowed from those words. All could not be lost. Not yet.

I changed the subject. "Anyway, what's the news on my ear case?"

"Well, we have been asked to investigate possible compensation laws between Ethiopia and Japan. This could take up to one year."

A year? At that rate, they'd better start planning my retirement pension as well. My mind frayed a little more at the thought of losing another year of my life to this.

"Your refugee case is still in limbo because of all this business. Everyone is waiting on the police report. If charges are dropped, Australia might reinstate your visa. If the refugee status is denied, we can appeal to a higher court. What do you want to do?"

Just get me out of here! I wanted to scream. "Appeal, of course," I said instead. "Appeal, and keep appealing." However long it takes.

Saturday night was my scheduled phone time with Ani. As the stress and frustration of each week congealed, she must have sat with dread beside the receiver, waiting to deliver the next series of deadends. "No, Teddy, it didn't work. I'm sorry."

Some Saturdays, they never gave me phoning permission. Would it be worse for her not to deliver bad tidings? Neither can have been easy.

Anita had motivated a miniature legion, contacting local politicians, human rights and Amnesty International representatives—anyone who could make a positive contribution to our cause. The best advice she was given: Keep at them. They will see it takes more time to manage putting you off than to stamp your papers. So, whereas before we had marked time through the drawn-out procedure, this time she upped the ante from fortnightly to weekly to daily enquiries, forcing them to respond. How she did this and kept up with her studies, I have no idea.

Sitting in the cell, time became void. I dreaded the mindless madness of tedium. Each weighty second ground towards the next. Hours carved through the day with the ponderous viciousness of a glacier, crushing all beneath it.

I wrote. The pages of my life were out there somewhere. Someone would know this story. If my life was to be words rather than actions, then let them flow.

The guard barked, "Parcel for Solomon."

Like flicking a switch, energy surged through me. Yes, I would have to watch while he opened it, checking for contraband. Yes, I would have to translate anything to be sure the message was legitimate. Did they think there was an escape hatch between the pages? Perhaps some underwear that made me invisible?

"Fine. All in order. Here's your package."

I retreated to my mat and held it carefully. Should I read the letter first? Should I look at this photo? What is this tiny figure? This time, Anita's mother, Sue, had sent me a small guardian angel (I still have it with me). Each delivery was like a spark of Christmas in the bleakness of winter. The winter was long, but the presents kept coming.

Sue could see the challenge her daughter had taken on. She knew that Anita was generous of spirit, but also level-headed. Although wanting to protect her own child from harm, she was always trusting of Anita's judgement and it was obvious where her commitment was directed. Based on her daughter's integrity, Sue poured uplifting messages my way. Simple things reminded me of normal life. On the phone, she would describe the renovations on her house. Always mindful not to send anything that would be confiscated, she wrote chatty letters and included a photo or some memento.

Threads of hope wove a safety net around me.

The power of a Western family's devotion kept the officials careful of my treatment. Someone was watching. Someone could validate my rights. Those small gestures of kindness from my new family landed with a big impact.

Sue told me later that she believed so strongly in what they were doing. "If we could get you to Australia, if we could see you together because you love each other—that would be wonderful. But, think of this, Teddy—no one knows how a relationship will go. After all this, we wouldn't want to see you part, but if you did—if you both tried life together and found in time that it wasn't going to work— you would still have your freedom. That is surely the greatest gift we could give you."

When others had helped me in the past, there was always a trade-off. I understand trade-offs from my home culture and all that bargaining with God. So often, people had offered to help me (not the least, Asuka) and then revealed another layer to their actions. My trust in human kindness had well and truly worn away the first letter, leaving rust instead.

Ani was beyond obligation. She never made bargains or false promises. She just said we will try and we will keep trying. Across the cultures, this honesty and respect penetrated my fears. I knew that I loved her, but hadn't understood until then that she would have crossed wastelands of despair to find me. Her message was unwavering: I will not abandon you.

In the Land Down Under,[5] she exposed underhanded dealings that hindered our case. Mr. Mitchell had written this to the Australian office: He could dump her on arrival and Australia in effect would be stuck with him. The receiving agent sided with him, and brushed Anita off.

Responses from other organisations trickled through. I was not Australian. We were not married. I was not applying to Australia as

5. Nickname for Australia.

a refugee. They had no choice but to wash their hands of me.

The situation was taking its toll. There'd been zero progress since the arrest and the immediate future looked just as hopeless, despite all our efforts.

Stressful thoughts crisscrossed without rest, carving deep tracks in my resilience. *Evil enters like a needle and spreads like an oak tree.*[6]

Maybe I'm not meant for this world. Everything proves it. My existence makes life hard for others. Always has. What is the point of that?

I couldn't stand the strain on Anita. Alone, I would deal with it—or not. But before she met me, her life was a happy adventure. This had to cease. No more hurt. Hurt no more. If there was nothing else I could do, then at least there was this: give her back her life. She had already done so much, sacrificed so much. I would always have that gift, but I couldn't take from her anymore. Time to let her be.

It is strange how, in moments of great stress, small details grab your attention. The phone felt warm in my hand. The cord jiggled in slow motion. I heard the familiar hum as my call echoed down the line.

The conversation was brief. I knew what I had to say.

Immediately after hanging up, I phoned Sue. I knew that Anita would need her comfort. It was the best I could do. No kind chat that night. No cheerful talk of weather and the garden. But I wonder if even wise King Solomon knew that a woman who asks the right questions is a powerful force.

"Teddy, is this really what you want?"

No.

"Do you think it's what Anita wants?"

No.

"If you were outside detention, wouldn't you think differently?"

YES!

---

6. Ethiopian proverb.

"I cannot tell you to decide one thing or another. Just follow your heart."

Only hollowness rolled from my mouth instead of words. I would have roared if I could, but at what? There was no more fire in me, so what did I have to offer Anita, anyway?

It was done now. I didn't need to think or feel anymore. She was safe.

24

TO HELL AND BACK

During my period of freedom between detentions, detention centre horrors were slowly exposed. The most notable of these seemed to come from Nishi-Nihon Immigration Centre.

Continued media coverage of the atrocities prompted action from both domestic and international NGOs[1] in protecting the rights of those detained. The United Nations increased its support. A number of church groups became sponsors. My former support-ers, headed by Kaeda, offered their services to other detainees. In fact, they made regular visits to everyone except me.

Politicians, too, were becoming more engaged due to public pressure. One parliament member, Renko Kitagawa (Social Demo-cratic Party), was particularly interested. He had researched con-ditions throughout the country and noted that the criticism of Japan's facilities was widespread. The Japan Times printed the fol-lowing quote on 20 April 2002:

The UN advised the Japanese government in 1998 to review

---

1. Non-government organisations.

its internment policy and bring it into line with the UN treaty. Non-compliance with the treaty means not following the law. However, there have been few changes. Japan's Immigration centres are not centres, but jails. The country has a long way to go to reach international standards.

Prime Minister Koizumi responded to the concerns, stating that detainees were treated fairly and in accordance with the provisions of the relevant Japanese laws.[2]

Overall, Japan's international esteem was plummeting with regard to these issues. A discontented government sought swift quiet solutions to outspoken devils like me.

One day during exercise, a Latino man began chatting with me. His name was Mario. While passing the ball, we quickly swapped stories. He was from Peru and had been in detention for eight months. With his Peruvian wife, he had three little girls, who were born in Japan. Overstaying his visa, he'd been apprehended working at a leather factory in Kobe. His appeal was currently in court. We got along well, and by the time exercise had ended, he asked me to transfer to his cell.

"As if they're going to let me change cells," I scoffed.

"But, *habibi*,"[3] he said. "Are you surrounded by smokers?"

"Yes."

"And you don't smoke, right? My cell is non-smoking, so you can apply for a transfer."

A bitter laugh cut my mouth. "It's that easy?" My heart was a void from all the discomfort I'd endured here previously. "Of course, I'll move," I continued. For a second, I almost felt lucky.

---

2. The International Convention about Citizenship and Political Rights of Article 7, Showa 54th, the Treaty for Torture, Inhumane Treatment and Punishment of Article 6, Heisei 11 and the Treaty for the Rights of Children of Article 2, Heisei 6th.

3 My friend. (Arabic). Mario had adopted this word from the Arabic speaking detainees.

It took me a couple of days to get the forms. I'd been busy with visitors and telephone calls. Each day, without fail, the shout would come from down the corridor, "*Habibi?* When you come my cell?" Eventually, I was welcomed (via the relevant official documents) into cell A5.

"Hey, *habibi*. Why you take so long?" Mario stood up to greet me. He was shorter than I remembered, but his colourful dialect was unforgettable. I laughed as he bear-hugged my waist.

There were only six other detainees in Mario's cell. I noticed how tidy it was compared to where I'd just been. Everyone had his own area neatly organised. The air, while not fresh, was cleaner and easier to breathe.

Mario had set up home in the right-hand corner, at the front of the cell. He had photos of his family tacked to the wall, and the shelf was stacked high with biscuits and snacks; courtesy of his wife. There was an empty area beside his, so I ensconced myself on the *tatami* and watched Mario go into entertainment mode, offering me tea and biscuits—the perfect host.

The surreal undulation of days rolled by.

Mario was so amiable and we grew close, constantly confiding in each other. During our discussions, he expressed tremendous anger over his treatment in Japan. He explained that Peru was the first Latin American country to accept Japanese immigrants back in the late 1800s. Many of these were farmers escaping poverty in rural Japan. They expected to make money in the coffee plantations before returning to their homeland. Yet, to this day, their descendents continue to live there. Even the former Peruvian Prime Minister was of Japanese descent. But here in Japan, Mario's own children were shunned in their country of birth.

Whenever the guards walked past, he shouted, "Hey you—you like a tape!"

I asked him what he meant by "tape."

"Click, click, click," he explained. "They just go 'round and 'round. They're programmed, no matter right or wrong. They don't think for themselves. Just keep clicking over, like a tape."

Of course, he was right.

Prior to my arrest, my regular visits to the Immigration centre included seeing an Ethiopian couple, Abebe and his wife Sailedingel. They'd been locked up for almost two years because their application for a refugee visa had been denied. I used to bring them supplies. Abebe was shocked the first time he saw me on his side of the bars. Whenever I passed his cell, his hand stretched through one of the grilled portholes, offering me a banana or a small packet of crackers.

At the time of their arrest, Sailedingel was pregnant. When the officials became aware of her condition, she was taken to hospital and the baby was aborted. The couple suffered from stress and constant ill health, but were told that the medical assistance they required was only available in Ethiopia. Much of their suffering made national news, though only their supporters, Immigration and I knew of the forced abortion.

Apart from Abebe and Sailedingel, I hadn't seen any other Africans inside detention. But just because I couldn't see them, it didn't mean they weren't there. Mario told me he'd seen guards beating an African man in cell A7 several months earlier, before my arrest. Desperate to know that he was all right or even still detained, I wrote a letter to be passed along.

The next day, one of the guards delivered a response from Samuel Dhaka, a Ugandan detainee. Through an exchange of letters, we became close friends without ever meeting. I learned that he'd arrived in Japan in 1997 and overstayed his three-month work visa.

He'd managed to avoid detection for several years, until one night when he had strange visions, and began pacing inside his small apartment. The landlord, who lived downstairs, heard the commotion and called the police to investigate. Samuel was arrested and immediately transferred to the detention centre.

Like that of so many others, Samuel's experience inside detention had been very traumatic. He was sexually assaulted by one of the guards while on his way to the shower. When he tried reporting the incident, the guards refused him permission to make any telephone calls.

Samuel started shouting in protest, but was beaten into silence before being hauled into a protection cell. Surveillance cameras captured the entire episode. (In general, the guards denied that such footage existed and conveniently remembered only when video evidence could be used in their favour.) Determined to hold them accountable for such abuse, Samuel had subpoenaed the tapes and was in the process of suing the Japanese government for damages.

I was further distraught to learn of the dramatic disappearance of another detainee. Somehow, Samuel had smuggled this story to a newspaper. Titled "Where could he be? Is he dead or alive?" the article described the possible suicide of a Vietnamese detainee. Late one night, Samuel witnessed a frenzy of action when the guards rushed to cell B3. Everyone seemed panicked. One of them held a video camera. Soon after, whirling sirens announced the arrival and subsequent swift departure of an ambulance.

For hours, two directors supervised rubber-gloved guards, who scurried like rats before a flood to contain the suspicious circumstances. They carted towels, took measurements and photographs, and refused to answer concerned detainees' questions. The next day, the room's entrance was sealed with a white sheet, blinding everyone to the night's surreptitious activity.

Another story received considerable media attention: a shocking incident involving a Chinese man who was bound in a blanket (or box—depending on the newspaper article) and put on an airplane to China. Thankfully, the pilot refused to take off, knowing one of his passengers was in such a state. The authorities were forced to return him to detention.

This smorgasbord of savagery assaulted our taste for life. In all ways, I was becoming thin.

Mario and I were the only permanent members in our cell. The others, mainly Chinese, usually stayed for a few short weeks before being deported. Most of them were criminals in transit from Japanese jails; incarcerated for murder, assault, drug dealings, and theft. The close atmosphere was decidedly scary.

When new detainees arrived, Mario and I quickly delivered a well-rehearsed speech on cell hygiene, noise, personal space and so on, and then kept mostly to ourselves.

One day, a new detainee came. He wasn't Chinese as we were expecting, but an Iranian who'd been arrested at Kansai International Airport. He was short, like Mario, and had dark wavy hair.

After listening to our cell rules, he introduced himself in Japanese, "*Watashi wa Tibashi desu.*"[4]

We learned that he couldn't speak English, except for a few catch phrases, so we conversed in Japanese. He was a curious character. Mario and I offered him tea and cookies, and then started asking about his experiences.

"So, you are from Iran?" I was first off the mark.

"Yes, I have a wife and a child back home, but I am Kurdish Iranian so—well, life is not good for me there. I try to find a better place. First Turkey—then Greece," his eyes rolled up to the ceiling and he pointed in the air as if it was a map, "then France and then Japan. When I arrived in Japan, I had trouble filling out the Immigration forms. You see, I can't read, write or speak English and I can't read Japanese. So, I only filled out my name, and approached the Immigration counter. When the officer asked where I was staying, I replied, 'hotel.' But then he wanted to know which hotel. I

---

4. My name is Tibashi. (Japanese)

couldn't think fast enough and he immediately became suspicious. 'Where are you from?' he asked. 'France,' I said pointing to my fake French passport, but he didn't believe me. That's when they took me to an office and called the French Embassy."

Wah! This couldn't be good, I thought.

"The officer handed me the telephone and someone on the other end started speaking French. I had no idea what they were saying, but the officers were all watching me intently. 'Enchanté . . . tout suite . . . arabesque . . . le banan. . . . C'est la vie!' I jumbled out a few French sounds, then tried to hang up the phone. An officer rescued the handpiece and asked the embassy staff what they thought. My fate was sealed."

Mario and I both rolled on the floor in hysterics as he animatedly told his story.

"When the officers uploaded my fingerprints onto the computer, they found that I'd been deported from Japan five years before."

"Really? You been here before?" Mario grew serious.

"Of course he has. He can speak Japanese better than us!" I replied.

Tibashi nodded and sipped his tea. "I had a machine that made telephone cards. It was good money, that's why I chose Japan when I had to flee my country. Just before I was arrested last time, I hid the machine under a bridge. Now I want to find it and start up business again."

"Where did you get such a machine?" I wanted to know.

"From the *yakuza*.[5] These days, life is all about the money. I don't hurt anybody, but—whatever it takes, I do it. That's the way of this world: money . . . or nothing."

It shocked me to hear someone reduce life to a transaction, but I knew from my own country that money was the great divider. Still shocked, after all I'd been through? Yes . . . still.

"That's your plan?" I asked.

"Absolutely," he replied confidently. "If I can find a way to stay

5. Mafia. (Japanese)

in this country, I'll do it. You have no idea what people are getting away with here: they travel in and out on fake passports, get involved in all kinds of deals, and then leave again before getting caught. For the Japanese, foreigners all look the same—well, you're black—but it's all salt and pepper to them."

No wonder the Japanese hated the rest of us.

"So," he continued. "What about you? What's your story?"

Mario took the lead and explained his circumstances. Then I concluded with mine. When I mentioned the word "refugee," Tibashi interrupted.

"Tell me what that word means: rafick-something? I've heard it at the Kansai detention centre from one Pakistani guy. When I told him I can't go back to my country, he said, 'Then you are rafick' and told me to call the United Nations."

"It's 're-fu-gee,' not 'rafick,' and it means you can't return to your country of birth for some reason—that your life is in danger if you go back."

"I have big problems in my country. Ha." His face lit up like he'd won a prize, "I am re-fu-gee!"

This was our first encounter with Tibashi and, over time, we learned that he was a very funny man. He continued to struggle with the word "refugee" and often asked me what that "r" word was again. He, too, became one of the long-term detainees.

The number of long-termers (held for more than a year) had increased notably, since my last incarceration. For those not claiming asylum like my friend Mario, reasons for wanting to stay in Japan varied considerably.

Mario had come to Japan hoping for a better life for his family, and was detained until his family's prospects were considered. Although he was locked away, his children were free to attend school and continue their education and normal lives, albeit without their father. If he had refused those conditions, all would face deportation and an unstable future elsewhere.

Others were arrested for criminal activities and expected deportation without a trial.

The number of short-term detainees (under twelve months) was much greater than the former group and mainly consisted of people from the Asian region, China in particular.

The Daily Yomiuri newspaper reported that there'd been an increase in crimes committed by Chinese nationals and consequently they became the focus of a police campaign. According to the article, the MPD (Metropolitan Police Department) had distributed pamphlets, warning Japanese residents of frequent burglaries. These pamphlets described a typical thief as a "thin man in his 20s or 30s" and "wearing a worn-out suit and dirty shoes." The campaign encouraged residents to "call 110 when you think you have seen a Chinese."

Following protests from human rights activists, the MPD was forced to withdraw the pamphlets.[6]

The furore expanded. The public profile of groups representing those on the inside was raised almost to celebrity status as they gave their opinions, expressed outrage and used the media to advantage.

Not infrequently, I saw Kaeda being interviewed on the cell television.

"That one," commented Mario, "she really does something for us."

Someone in the cell began screaming, "Noooooo!"

My throat raw with fury, I realised it was me. "Lying, false witch of a woman. She used my situation to become so important. She's nothing! She's—"

"Hey, hey, hey. Calm down, now, eh? You'll make yourself sick. Let's just change the channel." Mario reached for the remote.

The Iron Chef was sautéing squid. Ah, the luxuries of reformed cell life.

There we were: various kinds of salt and pepper, within grey

---

6. The Daily Yomiuri, "Foreigners stereotyped unfairly as criminals," 19 April 2002.

containers, shaken to the core of our humanity. This tasteless life ground on. My plastic cup runneth over.

"*Habibi.*" Mario looked hard at me. "You are strong. Second time for you. Only a strong person can climb that mountain, eh?"

"Nobody believes I will survive."

"And you? What do you believe?"

"I don't know anymore."

"You fight to live, good friend. Is there nothing you want to live for anymore?"

One thought filled my head. One answer echoed down this long dark tunnel. One constant never deserted me.

Mario saw the flicker of light in my eyes.

"Hold onto that, *habibi*. That is your life: not this!"

How could I have been so confused? There had been love—finally, wonderfully, miraculously—and I had let it go. *Like a fool who is thirsty in the midst of water,*[7] I had let my pain blind me to the cure I needed most.

It was June 11, Anita's birthday. The phone was in my hand. I cleared my throat, trying to think of just the right thing to say. "How-are-you-I'm-fine-how-are-you" wasn't quite the opener I wanted. "I'm sorry" seemed too cliché. Ring. Ring. Maybe she wasn't home. Ring. Ring. Maybe this was a stupid idea—

"Hello?"

"Ani . . . Ani. I—"

"Teddy? I've been waiting, hoping you'd call, but I know how stubborn you can be—Teddy—I can't believe it . . . hello? Are you there?"

Already, I felt soothed, though I still doubted my worthiness. Of all the things I could've said, I knew the truth was all that mattered.

"I need you, Ani. . . . I am lost without you."

7. Ethiopian proverb.

"I'm here," she said simply. "I'll always be here."

I am undone and remade.

Bubbly chatter filled the few minutes of allotted phone time as she described small wonderfully insignificant details of life in a distant universe of freedom. And, incessantly, she'd pursued avenues for my release, always against confronting conditions. Most recently, the official world had ground to a halt because—no doubt this was of momentous priority—Japan was busy hosting the World Cup Soccer.

The world is round and I am a ball. Kick me one more time.

But for Anita, I would never have bounced again.

Good news arrived for my compatriots. Abebe and his wife had been granted Provisional Release. On hearing this, Mario sagged a little.

"*Habibi?*" he asked. "Do you think we ever get out?"

"I did once already. Abebe is out. It happens."

"But I applied six times to be released. If they rejected the five previous ones, why be hopeful?"

"Mario—like you told me: we are strong. You're not a criminal. All you wanted was to give your family a better life. You can't give up."

Within a few days of that conversation, Mario was taken from our cell by the Provisional Release officer to hear the result of his pending application. As he was led away, I noticed his crossed fingers. Prayer or luck? I sat in silence and anticipated his return.

About twenty minutes later, he reappeared at the entrance to our cell. Tears streamed down his face. It looked like he was partially paralysed because he could barely walk. I helped him into the cell and sat him down, preparing myself for the worst.

"*Habibi*, I can't believe it," he blubbered.

"Don't worry, Mario, you will win eventually. Why don't you stop crying for a bit? It's not good for the guards to see you weak," I said.

"But, *habibi*," his red swollen eyes looked up at me, "I have been granted release!"

"What?" I jumped to my feet. "They're going to release you?" I swept him up into a hug of victory. His body convulsed in my arms. "That's wonderful! Do you know when you can go?"

"NOW!"

Tibashi was sitting across the cell, listening intently. I looked over at him and shouted, "Tibashi! Mario is leaving us!"

"*Omedetoo*,[8] Mario," he said flatly. He'd become close to us, particularly to Mario, and I guessed that he didn't want to lose his friend.

Nonetheless, Tibashi helped us pack Mario's belongings.

It felt festive when Mario presented us with his towers of crackers and dry foods. The photos of his family remained on the wall. "My family is your family, too," he said, pointing to the pictures. "People need people. We all need each other. You hold on to that, okay?"

I was going to miss him.

Tibashi and I remained, a shade greyer for his parting.

"C'mon, Tibashi, let's make some tea."

Tibashi returned to his mat, lay down and stared at the ceiling. That became his daily state. The fire in him had gone out.

Mid-July, five and a half months after I was arrested, the police arrived.

I was escorted into a room with four men, who announced themselves as Sakai Police. Without an interpreter, they rattled out bullet points of the investigation so far.

I interrupted them. "I'm sorry? I'm deaf in one ear due to maltreatment here, you know."

In consternation, they looked at each other.

I continued. "There's been an investigation? That's wonderful. What took you so long? And what could you possibly be investigating since you haven't spoken to me till now?"

---

8. Congratulations. (Japanese)

Ignoring me, they continued. "Investigation requires: that you do not leave the country (no worries there, mate); that you are not deported (I couldn't agree more); that you must sign acceptance of the charges for investigation to continue (hang on a second!)."

I wouldn't be intimidated. "Firstly," I stated, "I demand an interpreter. Secondly, I'm not a criminal. Thirdly, I'm not signing anything until you can prove the charges." Triumphantly, I flipped the system right back at them.

They gathered their papers and left.

My lawyers informed me that the next court date was imminent; this time for my ear case. Although they were still seeing things through, they seemed unenthusiastic and sounded tired whenever we spoke.

Immigration assumed that my previous translator, Doctor Werku, was biased because he was my friend, so they rejected his services. Instead, they engaged someone from Tokyo; an Eritrean woman called Lemlem. Through Eritrean friends, I'd heard of Lemlem. By all reports, she was useless. My lawyers shrugged. It was the court's decision.

Hoping to counter their complacency, I discussed the details with my friend, Endo. He and his wife, Megumi, visited often, always lifting my spirits. I got to know Endo through his wife Megumi whom I had met while giving a speech, not long before I landed in my second detention. They had travelled overseas where Endo had worked in various Japanese Embassies, including the one in Ethiopia.

Endo's assistance became invaluable during that time. With his work experience overseas, he knew the ins and outs of bureaucracy. He also knew how handicapped I was, as information was passed around me, but never explained to me. No wonder there was constant confusion between me and the lawyers.

The court had requested details about Ethiopian laws regarding compensation for foreigners but, to date, no one had followed up. In particular, the judge wanted to know if a Japanese person suffered a similar condition in comparable circumstances in Ethiopia, would the Ethiopian government award compensation? The court had been in contact with the Ethiopian Embassy in Tokyo, but it appeared they had no knowledge of such a law. So Endo arranged for one of his acquaintances in Ethiopia to research this information and send it to us. Almost immediately, Endo contacted me with this reply:

> The "International Convention of the Elimination of all Forms of Racial Discrimination," which Ethiopia has signed in 1976, defines the prohibition of segregation or discrimination in compensation. It says that you should be protected from any discriminatory act such that a government discriminates against you in compensating any damage or loss because of your nationality. Therefore, the government of Ethiopia should not discriminate against a Japanese national in compensating for any loss or damage caused by government staff.
>
> Extract from Endo's documents

In basic terms, Endo explained that the Japanese government had a "Reciprocity" clause. The clause stated that the Japanese government only compensated foreigners whose countries compensated Japanese nationals. The court and my lawyers were very grateful for Endo's contribution.

Additionally, after revising my court documents, Endo told me that while my lawyers had argued extensively regarding my ear case, it was not yet exhaustive. Further research revealed information that qualified the ABR test I'd taken:

> The ABR test provides information regarding auditory function and hearing sensitivity; however, it should never be used

as a substitute for a formal hearing evaluation, and results should be used in conjunction with behavioural audiometry whenever possible.

eMedicine Website

Endo suggested I take a different hearing test to prove, once and for all, that my right ear had diminished hearing. Ultimately, though, the outcome would rest on my lawyers' attitude and their willingness to see me win this case. Through Endo's help, things were becoming clearer.

My big day in court finally arrived on 17 July 2002. Mr. Narito met me in detention at 8 A.M. to brief me on the expected proceedings of the day. The detention doctor would testify in the afternoon, after me; Lemlem would be the interpreter—two key points that would work against me.

In a strange way, I was looking forward to attending court as I thought I would be taken out of the detention centre and be given a glimpse of the outside world again—if only for a short time.

However, on the morning of the event, I was told that the court was coming to me instead. (When they wanted to move mountains, they could, and all for such an insignificant mole as me.)

Just before 10 A.M., I was escorted downstairs, handcuffed, and transferred to two other guards. I was driven around to the rear entrance of a large meeting room, located behind the Immigration centre. The space had been converted into a temporary courtroom for the day's events. Some friends smiled at me from the public gallery as I was escorted to a seat beside my lawyers.

Three judges sat directly in front of us; an old man in the middle, with a younger woman on his right and a young man on his left. They announced the opening of the court, and I was asked to introduce myself.

Almost immediately, I knew that Lemlem was going to let me

down. Barely whispering my responses, she looked at me instead of the judges when she spoke. She made obvious grammatical mistakes, even for simple things. These small stumbles pre-empted huge lurches of incompetence, given the increasingly difficulty in terminology. As it worsened, I almost wished I was deaf in both ears.

Endo had prepared me for my testimonial. I tried to stress the key points and did my best whenever the question lent itself to such a response. Temper fraying, I yelled at Lemlem every time she faltered, "That's not what I said!" But the lawyer for Immigration would tell her she was doing a "splendid" job. Right—because this day was all about her. Two hours of bungling translation left no one the wiser.

In the afternoon, the detention doctor testified. He appeared nervous and vague, answering questions in a roundabout way.

The judges called proceedings to an end. The result? They'd let us know.

When it was over, I walked towards my friends to thank them for their support, but the guards grabbed me from behind. I was pulled away, handcuffed and returned to my cell.

Exhausted, I sat. A bowl of soup, now cold, had been placed on the table for me.

A guard shouted from one end of the hall, "Solomon, *menkai!*"[9]

Apparently, my lawyers wanted to see me again. I was just getting up when another two guards arrived from the other side, shouting "Solomon, *keisatsu*[10]!"

"Lawyers, you mean. I'm about to see my lawyers, not the police."

The two sets of guards looked at each other, then at me.

"No. You come police now!" said one on my left.

"No. He must see lawyers. This way," said the one on my right, who reached for me.

---

9. Interview. (Japanese)
10. Police. (Japanese)

The other two stepped in. "He must pack his things and come. He is under arrest."

No more discussion.

I asked to finish my food, please, before I saw anyone. Can you believe that I was begging for a chance to eat that stuff? They gave me five minutes.

Once their footsteps retreated, I gave the food to Tibashi and threw my things together. My hands were shaking as I gathered the papers where I'd been writing my story (and venting my anger). I knew I'd be severely punished if these were found. So, I began ripping them to pieces, shoving them down the toilet, frantically flushing and stuffing in more.

All those hours of crime-show television should have taught me that the pipe always blocks up.

Footsteps approached.

"Flush, damn it. Flush!" I hissed, flicking the lever convulsively. The door clanged open just as the gurgling outlet started to clear.

The guards took me to see Mr. Narito. He thought the trial had gone well, despite Lemlem's translations. He agreed that she was woeful, but reassured me that all the documentation had been submitted for the judges' review, so my case wasn't purely resting on the hearing (no pun intended). Mr. Narito didn't seem at all surprised when I informed him that the police were waiting for me. More subterfuge?

I excused myself from the room.

I was escorted downstairs to collect my bags from storage (previously delivered by friends); these included Asuka's letters. Six police officers entered the room. I was ordered to sit down, but refused. Two of them wrestled me into a chair and held me there. The short dumpy chief investigator, Mr. Yamamoto, stood opposite, keeping the table between us. A police photographer stepped forward and took a photo. The flash startled me. They showed me the warrant for my arrest. Then, meticulously, they sorted through my things; separating, bagging, making notes. One officer clacked handcuffs around my wrists. The last one bound a rope around my waist, before dragging me to the minibus outside.

Quite the circus, but where were the clowns?

An hour's journey brought us to the Sakai Police Station. I waited, late into the night, locked in a cell. Sporadically, a guard would appear at the grill and bark at me like a savage dog. And I was the one behind bars?

Without explanation, I was taken to the basement and thrust into another cell. It was so small and dark that I could barely see the outline of a body sleeping on the floor. There was no space to move. No longer able to stand under the weight of the day's events, I slid down the wall, trying to avoid the unkempt dirty form lying there. I put my head at the opposite end to his. No sooner had I gotten comfortable when I heard a raspy murmur, "What are you doing? Flip around!"

His abrasive tone scared me, but I carefully turned in the other direction, tensing away from his closely aligned face.

In the light of morning, I saw that my cellmate's body was tattooed all over and some of his teeth were missing. I was sharing a cell with a *yakuza* man.

"*Ohayo!*[11]" That voice was like razor blades on sandpaper.

"Good morning," I replied cautiously.

"It's not good for you to put your head at the other end. It's near the toilet. Bad for your health. Understand?" He spoke in Japanese.

"Yes, yes, I understand," I replied in the same language, at which he was overjoyed and launched into lively conversation.

It was strange sharing a cell with a Japanese man. In detention, I'd experienced an "us versus them" mentality (foreigners versus Japanese); now I was in a situation where "they" were part of "us."

11. Morning! (Japanese)

478

After chatting with him for a while I felt that, while there was still a similar mentality here, it was now "bad guys versus good guys" (criminals versus police) and, by default, I found that I was associated with the former.

Great.

He was curious about my situation. He kept asking questions and excitedly interrupting my story, making comments about the details. Finally, in chainsaw tones, he offered some advice. "You tell this woman you'll be sweet to her, give her whatever she wants. Then get the hell out of here, man, and take the next flight to Australia. Hey—give me her address—I'll pay her a visit, eh—ha, ha, haa!"

Those teeth, that face—enough to scare anybody. I was almost tempted to say yes.

"Thanks, anyway, but I have friends taking care of things for me."

Given my new confines, I fully contemplated the labels "robber" and "thief." I was without family, without father, without country. I was tired of being accused and labelled for things I simply hadn't done. I was tired of protecting myself, defending myself . . . I was even tired of being myself.

Yet, I was not without hope. Someone cared for me. My mind was clear. I would not be suppressed, bullied or belittled. If the Japanese police were hoping to coerce me into confessing, let them try. Fully, aggressively, I blinded myself to all else but the truth. I was deaf to threats and lies. Let the fools speak, for I would be mute but to profess my innocence.

On the first day at the police station, I was taken upstairs to a small room and questioned extensively in relation to Asuka's accusations. I described the events of the past two years, and I advised my interrogator to check my luggage for the letters expressing her "love" for me. He admitted that they'd viewed the letters already, and would question Asuka about them. Then he told me to confess.

Dum-de-dum.

The next day brought them no closer to their goal. Handcuffed and taken to court, I was thrust under the spotlight of the prosecutor's interrogative glare. He peered down at me, looking over the top of his small oval-shaped glasses while an interpreter translated the document before me. The police were seeking a ten-day extension to hold me. I was asked to sign the statement.

Naturally, I refused. I'd already given all the information to the police. There was nothing more to be gained by keeping me any longer.

The prosecutor made notes and I was escorted away. With or without a signature, the police held me for the next ten days.

Mr. Yamamoto questioned me nonstop from morning to night. "What's your name? Where are you from? Bla-bla-bla? Bla-bla-bla?"

He had no chance. I was well-practised at this officious nonsense.

Listening for answers, but getting none, there were times when he actually nodded off to sleep, before he'd jolt awake and start again.

Ten days passed.

We returned to court. The police hadn't secured a confession from me so the prosecutor showed me photos of different places around Osaka where Asuka had taken the police, fabricating various stories about me. Still, she failed to provide real evidence to support any of her allegations. It was bewildering to see the lengths to which this deluded woman had gone to bring me down. The prosecutor extended the warrant for another ten days.

The interviews continued, and so did my silence.

Yakuza-man watched me as I sat on the *tatami* in the cell. I could sense that he wasn't in a good mood, so I ignored him. We hadn't been getting along very well. He always had his hand in his pants and paced back and forth, singing and talking to himself. It made my stomach churn and I felt like our cell was full of his filth. I did my best to avoid physical contact with him.

My thoughts were shaken by his gruff voice. With no idea what he said, I shrugged my shoulders in response. Almost immediately, he flew to his feet and charged at me like a Sumo wrestler. I jumped to defence, alarmed at how serious this might get.

He halted abruptly and swung out with a clumsy karate kick. I grabbed him by the thigh and held him in that position (orphanage fighting skills, go!). He was hopping mad, madly hopping around on one leg, wriggling to break free, shouting at me, trying to throw a few punches with his grubby hands. After failing to make any palpable hits, he pulled us both to the floor.

On hearing all the shouting and cursing, the officers came running. They opened the grilled gate and dragged us apart. I was transferred to another cell. With more *yakuza!* Not that it really mattered because the very next afternoon, two guards came and told me I was being sent back to detention, without being charged. Asuka had failed to substantiate her claims against me and, without a confession from me, there was little more they could do.

What that meant in relation to everything else, I didn't dare anticipate. I was just relieved to get out of there. I waited by the gate, ready for the handcuff/rope routine. Instead, they took me upstairs to my bags. All the officers, including Mr. Yamamoto, had gathered in the room to say goodbye. They wished me well and actually waved as I left.

On the way, we passed by Cell One where *Yakuza*-man was sitting with his hands in his pants. He yelled out, "Good luck, Solomon-san!" as I walked by. I couldn't help but laugh. Strange, scary little bastard—there was a clown after all.

On the first day of August, I was escorted back to the now familiar detention centre and returned to the very same cell, although the officers emphasized that this was not the normal procedure. Apparently, Tibashi had kept my space and was awaiting my return.

I was shocked to see him slumped against the wall when I entered.

His eyes were clouded over and he appeared to have lost considerable weight in the three weeks of my absence. I put my bag down and went to him. "What's going on with you?" I nudged him gently in the ribs.

I watched his eyes redden as he rubbed his hands over his face and through his hair.

"I've had some problems since you left. I couldn't stand not knowing about my refugee application. Waiting. So long. I just wanted to end it all." He paused for a moment, his breath becoming ragged. "One day, I called one of the guards to the cell door and asked him to bring me some detergent to clean the toilet. He returned a few minutes later and handed me a small cup through the grill." Tibashi's tears brimmed, as he prepared to tell me more.

I shook my head. I knew exactly what he was going to say.

"As I took the cup, I told him to go and get his boss. The guard looked at me, confused, and I shouted, "Hurry up, go now! Bring your boss!" The guard realised I was going to do something crazy, so he ran off. When he returned with his supervisor, I started drinking the detergent."

There was often talk of suicide and the diverse ways it could be done in a cell. While several people had tried it with various degrees of success, I never thought Tibashi would be one of them.

"When I returned from hospital, I was sent to solitary confinement. I protested. And you know what those bastards did? They beat me black and blue!" He lifted his T-shirt to reveal the fading bands of several large bruises and abrasions on his back and stomach.

Speechless, I reached out to hug his shoulders.

"It's so good to have you back," he cried.

If only I could do more.

The next day, I called Mr. Mitchell (at the Australian Embassy) to inform him that the police investigation had concluded in my favour, so he could reconsider my visa on those grounds.

I felt reasonably confident that I could pick life up where I'd left it, back in January. With such buoyancy, I phoned Anita.

She'd been quite traumatised, having learned of my disappearance through a letter from Samuel. When she enquired, the officials (apparently) had no information on my whereabouts. It didn't make sense, given the meticulous documentation on everything short of scratching your arse. Someone had to know something! Only the day before my call, she received notice from the Australian Embassy that I was being held at a police station.

I gave her the good news.

"Do you think Mitchell will sort it out now?" she wondered.

"He has no choice. The reason for suspending the visa no longer exists. They passed it already. They just have to reinstate it."

"Are you okay, Teddy?"

"I am, actually. I really am okay, despite everything." (Must have been the better food in jail.)

The guard cut us off before we could say anymore.

In my absence, Samuel had been released. A man by the name of Mr. Hiroshi became his guarantor. I remembered Samuel speaking about Mr. Hiroshi on a number of occasions. He was a communist—"a fearless warrior" Samuel called him—because he wasn't afraid of Immigration or its rules, and had successfully negotiated the release of several Chinese detainees. He projected an image of power although he actually had no qualifications and no prior knowledge, only his current successes.

Mr. Hiroshi and Samuel started to visit me regularly and Mr. Hiroshi's interest in my case increased. He reminded me more of a praying mantis than a warrior because of his angular facial features and thin limbs. As a child, I'd watched praying mantises lash out when under threat; Mr. Hiroshi was no different. During visitations, if a guard dared interrupt to tell him the time was up, Mr.

Hiroshi would spin around and shout, "Shut up! Leave us to talk!" As rumours go, there was not one incident when the guards refused him.

On August 12, Mr. Narito came to visit me. He was unusually upbeat and energetic. He pointed out that now I'd been cleared of any wrongdoing, I should focus on my application with the Australian Embassy. He and Mr. Tanaka were prepared to take care of all communication with the embassy for the low low fee of ¥1,500,000![12]

Just prior to that meeting, Endo had informed my lawyers that he could cover any costs. Funny how their enthusiasm (and expenses) conveniently increased.

As it turned out, there wasn't much they could do, since my next mail brought unwelcome closure. I received a letter with the Australian Embassy logo on it. This is it, I thought. My hands were trembling as I opened the envelope. The last two paragraphs leapt off the page and bit me:

> Since writing to you in March, there has been a considerable delay in considering the various aspects of your situation and I understand that you were subsequently arrested, but then released. However, the person making the allegations has written to this office advising that she intends to take civil action against you, and reiterating the claims made. I am yet to be convinced that there is no foundation to the claims and on that basis I am not prepared to exercise my delegation to revoke the cancellation of your visa.
>
> Australian Embassy, Tokyo, 16 August 2002

By chance, Anita had emailed Mr. Mitchell on that very day, requesting an update. She only received an automated response stating that, as of 16 August 2002, Mr. Mitchell was no longer working

12. US$22,000 (approximately).

at the embassy. He'd made the decision on his last day in office, leaving us with no recourse. No name was given for his replacement. I also noted that the postage stamp on the envelope was 20 August—four days after he'd left.

I decided to call Mr. Mitchell's number and request attention from his substitute. Her name was Ms. Hogan. I asked for clarification of the letter I had just received. She told me she would look into it.

Her reply snapped up my last hope:

You have sought our advice and we contacted our central office to confirm, however, we are unable to revisit or reconsider a decision that has already been made by the delegate. If you wish to travel to Australia, you will need to make another visa application of which I can give no indication of the possible outcome.

Australian Embassy, Tokyo, 11 September 2002

Bewilderment came nowhere near describing how Anita and I felt. We were in worse circumstances than ever: I was in detention indefinitely; Ani was a university student in Australia, hence financially strained; I had no valid passport; and now, no visa.

Oh, old hyena, eat me without making excuses.[13]

Two kids against two governments. What had they gained? Their employees were paid. Their papers were stamped. The buck was passed. Whichever way you want to call it, we were in chains. For what? When I think how all that energy and time, from both sides, could have gone into something worthwhile . . . dedicated to something good. . . .

Well, that thought is so momentous I can't even finish it—can you?

After reigniting our goal, Ani and I braced ourselves for a new

---

13. Ethiopian proverb.

campaign. We decided to focus on getting me out of detention, because a visa for any country would be impossible while I was sitting behind bars.

The lawyers were continuing to appeal for refugee status in Japan, so that had to be one option. If I was going to escape detention, it would have to be via Provisional Release. I would need a guarantor, so I decided to approach Mr. Ono. Having a United Nations name on the application would hold positive sway and I'd heard that he was the guarantor for other detainees.

After considering his current commitments, Mr. Ono agreed. So, we put together the required documents.

The fearless warrior, Mr. Hiroshi, came to visit me every three or four days. During one of the visits in mid-October, I showed him the documents Mr. Ono and I had prepared. The pages seemed so few; I was worried it wasn't enough.

Mr. Hiroshi flicked through it, shaking his head, muttering disapproval. Then he looked up and sighed. "Why should they let you out, based on this? There's no strong reason here. It's too polite. You can't come across as a whiny boy. This has to have impact . . . serious argument for your freedom. Do you want to get out of here or not?"

He agreed to take it home and strengthen the argument for me. But with each of Mr. Hiroshi's subsequent visits, he uncovered a new setback from Immigration: why couldn't I lodge and process an Australian visa application while in detention? Was my relationship still legitimate? They must have a letter of confirmation from Anita. And finally, they believed my refugee appeal and my compensation court case were contradictory to an Australian visa application. They insisted that I cancel both lawsuits if I was to be considered for release at all.

I grew incensed over this last demand because it seemed that Immigration was trying to blackmail me into dropping my cases against them. I strongly contested all points, knowing that if I dropped these cases they could flip me off their shores in an instant. I asked Mr. Hiroshi what guaranteed my safety.

"They are not your enemy," he replied. "Asuka is. And you need to get out of here and show the Australian Embassy that she was wrong."

"But I don't trust them. What if this is just a game? What if I drop the cases and they don't release me? It could happen!" I shouted at him.

He told me calmly that he was not asking me to trust Immigration: he was asking me to put my faith in him.

How many times had I trusted before and been betrayed? I wanted so much to believe him. But I felt justified in being wary of everyone. Doubt had clipped my wings and Tewodros the Risk Taker had forgotten how to fly. I couldn't give Mr. Hiroshi an answer.

After talking it over with Anita, I reached a compromise. Mr. Hiroshi helped me express a short statement to Immigration. Although I really didn't want to drop either case, I relented and agreed to drop my refugee appeal after (and only after) I was released; Mr. Hiroshi would see to it that I followed through on this. The lawsuit for my ear case would remain open and my decision was non-negotiable.

On October 28, my application for Provisional Release was lodged. I breathed in and crossed my fingers. Luck or prayer? God's delivery service for prayers must have a delay because, before I could even exhale, I received word that the court had made its final decision: my ear case was dismissed. I'd lost my last bargaining chip.

Devastated, I immediately called Mr. Narito to get clarification. The judges had pretty much ignored all research, facts and valid arguments, citing instead the original and unsubstantiated suggestion that my hearing could have been poor already, before the infection.

With my Provisional Release application pending, my ear case lost and my refugee appeal in limbo, Mr. Tanaka wondered whether I still required his services. It was especially difficult to decide because of the long journey we'd made together. That road, rarely smooth, had ended nowhere. Yet, after all this, I couldn't justify him spending any more time on me.

What the hell was I to do?

25

MIRACLES DO HAPPEN

*C*hristmas was imminent. It was time to "deck the halls." Well, in detention it was time to renovate. All the cells on our side were emptied and when we were relocated to the women's section, Tibashi and I were separated. I had no desire to form any strong bond with new cellmates. Waiting every day (every moment) for word of my release, I kept occupied with writing, and dreaming of freedom.

Although I wasn't sure how this festival was celebrated in Australia, I imagined Anita sitting with her family around a table, an abundance of food before them, and much laughter while they swapped presents and enjoyed each other's company. This idyllic vision soothed me as I endured my third "festive" season behind bars.

'Tis the season to be jolly. . . .

Whether God, luck or Santa Claus worked individually or had united forces, I don't know, but I was granted Provisional Release on payment of bond, early in 2003.

Mr. Hiroshi collected me on January 17. I was already packed when the guard came (I'd been packed for weeks). I wished good fortune to everyone remaining, and gingerly stepped towards freedom once more. Like Orpheus leaving the Underworld,[1] I felt all the ghoulish past pursuing me, pulling me back; such talons are hard to remove.

The officer signing me out explained that my guarantor, Mr. Ono, had arranged for me to stay at a Salvation Army homeless shelter in Tokyo. Did I understand?

"Yes."

He gave me the address and told me that I must visit Immigration monthly in order to renew my visa—as I had done previously—until a decision had been made on my Australian visa. Was I aware of this?

"Yes."

He gave me a temporary copy of my release papers for movement in Osaka and noted that these would be reissued once I arrived in Tokyo. Was I ready to leave?

"Absolutely, yes!"

It was late afternoon. Instead of surging with energy and feeling myself expand into this new liberated state, I went gently, carefully, as if it was a fragile thing to be protected and cherished. In this moment, I am free . . . and in this . . . and in this. I savoured each one, still unbelieving that it would last.

Samuel invited me out for the evening, to celebrate. Good company restored my confidence in leaps and bounds, and by morning I was crowing freedom down the phone line to Anita. She'd been poised for the news, with a travel booking on hold, and told me she'd be in Japan two weeks from then.

I had two weeks to create a haven for us, two weeks to chase up

---

1. Greek mythological story of a man (Orpheus) who goes to the Underworld to rescue his wife's soul, at the risk of losing his own forever.

all the required documents and arrange the meetings that would smooth the way for a new application with the Australian Embassy. After a year of waiting, two weeks was way too long.

Mr. Hiroshi and I went to Osaka District Court to withdraw my refugee appeal, the agreed condition of my release. Pen poised, I thought of all the effort I was signing away. That final piece of paper was my last link with a future in Japan. That had only ever been an agreement of convenience, never my ambition. I knew that living the truth was my only salvation. Nervously, I looked at Mr. Hiroshi, who nodded approvingly at my scrawl on the dotted line.

Coincidentally, Samuel and his lawyers were at court that day, preparing for a media conference to announce his victory over Immigration for sexual and physical assault. The media had not yet arrived, so I found Samuel and congratulated him. It had been a difficult battle for him since Immigration denied the existence of the video footage showing Samuel's beating. After months of persistent arguing, the tapes were surrendered, thus revealing the incriminating evidence.

Samuel was elated with his victory, but not with the measly ¥230,000[2] compensation he received. Amid the hubbub of media activity, he stated his plan to broadcast the tapes on television for the Japanese public to expose the government's mistreatment of foreigners.

One dedicated supporter[3] praised both of us. "You are pioneers. Without your determination and courage to fight for your rights, the system would not change. What you've done opens the way for full justice and equality. Your victory represents a win for many more."

Truth: how sweet the sound!

We bade each other farewell, and the winter winds whisked me

2. US$3,100 (approximately).
3. Michael Fox, American associate professor at Hyogo College, dedicated to supporting detainees.

away on an overnight bus to Tokyo. Like an emperor returning after battle, I imagined that the teeming crowd, the cosmopolitan cavalcade of flashing lights and the avenues of towering skyscrapers were heralding my triumphant arrival.

Tucked away in the shabbier city quadrants, I found the address of my new accommodation. It was an old rundown building, several storeys high. Its appearance stood in stark contrast to the rest of the city, yet to me it was a mansion. Not the tiny *manshon* of my first Japanese host, Satoko, but a space unhindered by bars or guards. My kingdom could have been the size of a postage stamp and been as glorious.

It was the dead of winter and the shelter was absolutely freezing, especially at night. As I lay in bed after the lights had been switched off, my bones felt like icicles, freezing me from the inside out. Okay—a postage stamp with central heating, maybe.

Two weeks had almost passed. It was now two days until Anita's arrival. I couldn't have our reunion in such surrounds. I moved to a cheap *gaijin* house,[4] in preparation. Each couple or individual had their own room with communal use of a kitchen, lounge room and bathroom—austere in every sense, but affordable for those with kingly dreams.

Always in the past when meeting Anita, I'd been late. *Not today,* I thought. Up early and dressed in my best clothes, I was more than a little nervous, I have to say. She was arriving at Narita Airport. The train rattled along, my thoughts dancing to its rhythm as I imagined our first moments together. In my haste and excitement, I failed to recall that there were two international terminals, a considerable distance apart. I only remembered when there was an announcement on the train.

I decided to take a gamble and get off at the first terminal. By now, her plane should have landed.

---

4. Foreigner's house; budget accommodation. (Japanese)

Tall black man frantically running. . . .

Anita?

Dodging suitcase trolleys. . . .

Ani?

And other travellers reuniting. . . .

Where could she be?

Sweating now, I kept repeating the flight number, willing her to appear. The clock mocked my efforts and, finally, I asked a staff member for an explanation. Of course, I was in the wrong terminal!

Back at the train station, I waited an interminable 20 minutes for the next connection. Whereas before the clacking wheels fed my excitement, now they seemed to revolve in slow motion, grinding and screeching reluctantly to the next platform.

Magically, crowds parted to reveal Anita sitting on her suitcase. The screens, the signs, the din—all blurred into inconsequence under her smile.

How long could she stay? Two weeks, of course.

Now: to face officialdom once more. Given our past exhaustive efforts and subsequent disappointment, we even discussed forgetting Australia altogether and living in another country. Brief consideration showed we'd be no better off, so we steeled ourselves to launch a new campaign for the Land Down Under. We knew the requirements for a Prospective Spouse Visa, but what if we got married (right here and now!) in Japan?

We consulted a range of people including lawyers, Australian Embassy staff, priests, various other individuals and organisations, including local government requirements for marriage. It proved no great advantage and actually incurred more complications.

City Hall wanted certain documents, including a birth certificate which I didn't have. Even after their requirements were satisfied, our request could take several months to be approved. We didn't have several months. As Endo had once told me, the maximum time that Immigration would allow me to be free was around twelve months (and there was always the possibility I'd be arrested again before then).

Time—*wah!*—always my life was bound in time that wasn't my own.

Swiftly, we returned to our only option and compiled all that was necessary to submit a visa application. Within days, the embassy called us in for an interview.

Ms. Yamada was the case officer. She was surprised to see us again, having first met us when she was Mr. Mitchell's secretary. In separate sessions, we each described our ongoing relationship, attending to Ms. Yamada's invasive inquiries. I faltered when she brought up the Asuka incident, since I fully expected it had been resolved and shelved. I was concerned that it might prejudice her against us. The questions continued. Nothing was off limits or considered too personal. Some two or three hours later, she permitted me to leave.

I emerged to find Anita lying on a bench, dozing.

Like two mice in a maze, Ani and I ran for the entire time she was in Japan. Here—to that meeting; there—to get those papers copied; quickly make that phone call; hurriedly request that fax. Run for love. Run for freedom. And at every turn, write it all down because you never know how those walls might cave in.

Light reflected in two glasses of red wine. We sipped slowly, taking in each other's gesture and voice. Her eyes glistened. Ah, my sunshine girl. The new day would take her from me once more. Let me be the master of time for a few sweet hours. The dawn would not claim her yet.

We didn't have a contingency plan if the visa was rejected.

Back in Australia, Anita hired a migration lawyer to deal with all correspondence on our behalf; whatever it took to ensure our success. The lawyer was incredulous at what we'd been subjected to and was optimistic about the outcome this time.

Is there a place where one wakes, no longer dreaming of heaven but knowing it, with every sense? Till I find it, I walk the dark hellish night of waiting.

Did all go smoothly in those months (yes, months) of limbo? Would you be surprised if I said no? Let the gods of irony play their last pranks, their hollow laughter echoing down the shadows of my existence. I was no longer alone, cast out and unloved. That wilderness was but a dim memory as all my striving brought me to the brink of a new life.

If I could reach out to that forlorn little boy, full of longing, I would urge him to keep stretching his horizons. I'd tell him of light and hope and love. I'd remind him to be true, always true to his heart.

In early July 2003, a letter arrived from the Australian Embassy. I knew that it had to be *the* letter. Light burst forth as I unfolded the page. Trumpets sounded. Angels sang. Heaven opened its gates to usher me in: at last, Australia would have me.

Not until I stood on that red soil would I believe it. Too much had been certain before and become undone. Like an archaeologist gathering in all traces of my past, I visited friends who'd been storing my things. I (haltingly) approached all the appropriate official bodies to sign off on every last piece of paper that linked me to Japan. Each movement reclaimed my fragmented self.

And, as much as possible, I kept my movements secret from any vengeful foxes that might cast out one final desperate snare.

With the best of intentions, I wanted to visit detention and offer encouragement to my friends there, one last time. The wisdom of others prevailed, and I avoided the risk of being so close to those bars that seemed to have a magnetic pull on me.

Despite the fear, to this day, I regret that one unmade journey. I understand true happiness now: it is not gained in comforts or safety, but in being with those in need, sharing what beauty one has found. *Being happy is better than being king.*[5]

Not all contact was lost. Tibashi had been released. He, Samuel and I met on the evening before my departure. No one could really appreciate the special bond we have; no one who hadn't lived through the horrors of detention, that is. These are unique friendships, forged from solidarity in difficult times.

When morning broke, I no longer cared for anything Japanese. My heart and mind had flown before me. It was all I could do to get to the airport without bursting from anticipation. My flight was at five o'clock that afternoon and, for hours, I paced the floor of the departure lounge until the flight was called.

I boarded the plane, found my seat and watched as the hostesses busied themselves with settling the passengers. I glanced out the window and imagined that, during take-off, police cars might rush out onto the runway and bring the plane to a screeching halt. Dark-suited men would come on board, approach my seat and escort me away.

I looked down at my hands. They had stretched out to my mother, begged for food, been handcuffed. And through it all, they held to a dream. They were the hands of a man who had reached for freedom and now cradled it, with the triumph and humility of one who knows what it is to have it ripped away. (Those talons go deep.)

Dawn seemed to kiss the wingtip forever.

Touchdown was at seven o'clock in the morning on 12 July 2003. I made my way to the Immigration counter where I filled out the relevant forms and handed them to the officer, along with my travel document.

"Welcome to Australia," he said, as he handed everything back and signalled me through.

---

5. African proverb.

No worries, mate.

After collecting my luggage, I continued through customs and into the lobby where Anita, shining with love as ever, was eagerly waiting.

For a moment only, though it felt like an eternity, I couldn't move.

It's hard to tell someone what is in your heart. Love is a miracle. I cannot express it in words. I stand before her as myself. I am here—that is my expression of love. I choose to go through life with her, so every day is love. I do not have to say it, because I live it. I live it with her. How lucky I am to have this. It makes me feel bigger. Let me reach around the whole world and show everyone: *expect a miracle.*

I dropped my bags, and held her in my arms.

We exited the building where Anita told me to wait while she brought the car. I laughed when she pulled up in her little 4WD soft-top; it was the same model that Padre Roberto used to drive around in Addis. We loaded my bags, I concertina'd my long torso into the front seat, and we headed for the Gold Coast and a new world.

Finally, I had come home.

Now, I have done battle with all the lies and confusion of the past. This book is my sword of truth. At last, I can lay it to rest. It represents the honour of my ancestors, my defiance against poverty of the soul, and the dignity of those who have truly loved me.

Until lions have their historians, tales of the hunt shall always glorify the hunter.[6]

I have always been wild at heart. And because of that I have escaped the hunters of war and lack and fear.

The heart of a lion is within each of us—proud, determined and

---

6. African proverb.

loyal to the true meaning of life. It wills us to live, not just survive. It fills us with purpose to create something positive, though despair threatens to smother all else. In doing so, we connect with what is sacred, whether we express that through love, religion, tradition, or the drive to succeed.

With pride, I can pass on this tale as *my* blessing. These pages celebrate my life. Let it set you free to live yours.

Be bold!

Afterword

MY KIND OF HEAVEN

*A*nita and I married on the 4 October 2003. We had a simple civil ceremony at the Brisbane registry office, surrounded by Anita's immediate family and close friends.

The day symbolised a new beginning and a new journey that would be filled with the modern challenges that many young couples face: finances, future plans, practical priorities, and others yet unanticipated. You'd think with my bureaucratic accomplishments that I'd slip easily into the system, but my head shook over car and health insurances (which I'd never had), superannuation (of which I'd never heard!) and speed cameras (which I didn't comprehend—until the fines started rolling in!).

How often do little challenges overwhelm bigger dreams?

This relationship grew out of six wonderful months together, yet continued for two and a half years, oceans apart. Finally, Anita and I were sharing a small apartment, juggling study schedules, everyday challenges and a budget that was frequently upset by my enthusiastic driving. It required a massive readjustment for both of us, particularly after such an emotional time.

I also struggled with my newfound freedom. I'd longed for it all my life, but I found it difficult to adjust, difficult to sleep and difficult to remain still. I felt incredibly frustrated over those wasted years behind bars. I felt as though I was so far behind what I could have (should have) been. I hated that feeling. I had to catch up.

How could I go through so much and then just move on? How could I establish a life in Australia and reconcile myself with all I knew of the suffering in the world?

Would Anita understand that I was driven to continue fighting for human rights? That I couldn't rest while others suffered? Fear flooded me. *What if she doesn't? How could she, when it is out of her experience?* Some might say, "You go on then, you go and do what is so important, I cannot run in your footprints." Yet, there she is: not behind, but right beside me—running to keep up with my big steps. She may not always understand, but she keeps trying. How I love her for that.

I feel so blessed, though sometimes deep anger still rushes up from nowhere, like some forgotten storm not yet blown out. I cannot explain it. To go beyond pain is to carry a scar, but do you limp forward, or leap? I choose to leap, though sometimes I fall.

It's taken me some time to find my rhythm in Australia. I founded a not-for-profit organisation called African Communities Association Gold Coast Inc, not only to assist African arrivals new to the area but also to share our vibrant cultures with the local community through song, dance, customs, and food.

From my experience, I've learned the importance of community and the sense of empowerment that comes from belonging, which contrasts starkly with the isolation and despair of feeling that you don't belong. I wanted to create a united group of Africans who could support each other and then reach out and build bridges with our fellow Australians.

In 2007, I was granted Australian citizenship and applied for an Australian passport. I can't explain how relieved I was to receive both of these. I now feel like I belong somewhere. I have a place in this world. I can now also travel freely without being treated with suspicion. There are many countries in the world where, if you travel on an Ethiopian passport, you are required to apply for a visa, even if it is just a transit stopover within the airport. Being free of that worry makes such a difference.

Since my arrival in Australia, my health has slowly improved. Aside from a seizure caused by stress and lack of sleep, I have otherwise been well. I had an operation on my right ear to patch up the eardrum where the infection had eaten through, although my hearing has not improved and I may need further operations in future years.

Anita graduated from university at the end of 2005, with great results. I was very proud of her. It can't have been easy, considering everything else she'd been coping with while I was in detention.

To mark her graduation, we travelled for three months in Ethiopia and Egypt. I wanted to show her the places where I'd grown up, the places that held so many memories for me. She'd heard my stories and I wanted her to see it with her own eyes.

You can revisit a place, but you can never go back to the experiences. In order to move forward, I needed to talk with my mother. I wanted closure. I'd felt like a motherless child for a large part of my life and, after pushing her onto that rickety bus in Addis Ababa, I wanted to resolve those painful issues. I needed to see her again.

I'd already met up with my step-brothers and sisters. They escorted Bishkash to the house Anita and I were renting in Addis Ababa. Our first few meetings were strained. I had so much to say and there were so many things I wanted to hear from her: that I was loved, that she realised how much she'd hurt me and that she was sorry. I didn't get any of that and I struggled to find words to speak. The vast gap between us echoed with the silence of our tormented hearts. We needed a bridge.

Over the following days, slowly, slowly, we started to connect. Not deeply, but on trivial matters. Towards the end of our stay I felt we'd reached a point of comfort where I could talk to her—*really* talk. During our discussions, I was shocked to learn that Doctor Solomon had raped her, a fact I never knew till then, but which greatly supported my understanding of her emotional distance from me, and my father's resentment and annoyance at my presence. I confirmed my mother's story with relatives such as Egegayhu.

Going back to Ethiopia gave me some sense of peace. It was clear that I had made the right choice in finding something bigger, something better. My people were still deprived, despite recent economic developments and improved standards of living. It seemed that the poor were still poor and the gap between the "haves" and the "have-nots" was greater and more pronounced than ever. Many of my acquaintances hadn't expanded their options. Their lives had remained the same. It was just a different date.

This trip allowed Anita to become acquainted with some of the people who'd cared for me. We spent a considerable amount of time with my good friend, Hailu. He is now married with young children: a boy and a girl. When we met him, he was working with Padre Roberto at an adoption centre for Italian families.

We visited dear Padre Roberto, who was still at Holy Saviour Church. He was just as I remembered him, and his beard was still so long that it scratched his desk as he spoke.

We also met Father Desta, who was living down south, not far from the Gurage mission, one of my childhood residences. We travelled there to find him still as carefree as ever, even in his old age. He entertained us all afternoon with his humour and views on life.

Since our return to Australia from this trip, many things have happened.

In November 2006, I heard that Doctor Solomon had passed

away from a brain aneurism. I only found out by a chance phone call to his brother in America, whom I'd contacted while researching for this book. I hadn't seen my father since I left for Egypt in 1991. Nevertheless, I was shocked by the news. He'd been such a large character during my childhood that I never considered his mortality. I felt like he was always there, that not even a disease could take his life away. Yet, he was gone.

For many reasons, I was sad. Once again, I grieved for all those years lost between a father and son. I'd always dreamed of meeting him one day, man to man. It would have given me peace to show him that I'd risen above all that torment and thrived.

Early in 2007, I learned that Father Desta had also passed away. I felt blessed that God had given me one last chance to meet with him and thank him for his assistance when I was a child. On the tail of this news, I received another disheartening message: Padre Roberto had fled Ethiopia, a place he'd called home for so many years, the place where he wished to be buried. He was responsible for a government-owned house in the city where he placed young people in need. Apparently, some young men had cheated him. Without his knowledge, they sold the house. The government discovered this while doing a routine check and my beloved Padre Roberto was held accountable. How could someone take advantage of such a generous old man? I knew what it was to be desperate, but I was never a criminal. Padre Roberto fled to Italy and I doubt that he will ever return to Ethiopia for fear of arrest.

After my father's death, I started to think more about my mother. That bridge between us was not yet strong. We needed to bond through new shared experiences. It had always been her dream to see a foreign country. So I applied to sponsor her on a tourist visa. Anita and I paid a US$10,000 deposit for the term of her visit, which allowed her a three-month stay in Australia.

She came in December 2006. I realised how different our lives had become. She was like a wide-eyed child; everything was so new, like nothing she'd ever seen before. She was daunted by microwaves, lifts, remote controls . . . she even fell off the escalators in shopping centres, having never ridden one before. During the day there were outings and adventures of different sorts, and then at night we took time to talk and reconnect.

We now have an amicable relationship and I stay with her and Belachew on my trips back to Ethiopia.

My relationship with Belachew has also mended over time and we get along reasonably well now. My stepbrother Habtamu was fortunate enough to receive an American visa through a system of random selection in which registered individuals from around the world can receive a Green Card. He lives in America and is studying computer technology at university. My stepsister, Mulu, lives with Bishkash and Belachew in Addis Ababa, and works for the electricity company. Bishkash's other son, Hennock, is somewhere in Israel. After troubled teenage years in Ethiopia, he took off in search of a new life. Family members occasionally hear from him when he is in need of money. The youngest of the family, Kidest, graduated from high school recently and is studying nursing in Gonder, a northwest region.

I speak to Hanna from time to time. After travelling to Turkey, she became entangled in a destructive relationship and it took her years to finally receive refugee status in Canada for herself and her daughter.

Mengestabe lives in America so that he can be close to his children.

Mebrat and Kiros also have moved to America, but it took ten years. Some years after Asmerom's death, Aunt Meseret moved there as well, and is living with her son.

Saba's brother, Robel, lives in Switzerland. He no longer works for Ethiopian Airlines and, as far as I'm aware, he no longer drives an Opel.

Last I heard, Father Habtemariam and Father Tesfaldete were both in Italy receiving medical treatment.

As for Japan, I've had no contact with any of my supporters since coming to Australia.

The latest news from Berga was that he'd moved to America where he was accepted as a refugee after a long struggle across a number of countries. I managed to contact him recently and learned that he is married and driving taxis.

Mario and I kept up regular contact until he and his family vanished. I've only recently found out that his final appeal for residency in Japan was rejected. He is living in Peru and works as a tourist guide—for visiting Japanese, among others.

Anita was shocked when I announced recently that I wanted to stop over in Japan on one of my trips to Africa. I still had boxes of belongings there, stowed away with friends. I desperately wanted to go through them and retrieve old photos and information that would help me finish the book. Anita thought my name would be on an immigration blacklist somewhere and didn't want me to go. With my Australian passport in hand, I (still a risk-taker) felt confident that it would all go smoothly . . . and it did. I entered Japan without a hiccup and spent three weeks going through the things I'd left behind, and catching up with old friends and acquaintances.

The Japanese are interesting people, though I am yet to comprehend their ways. I was excited to return and desperately wanted to reconnect with those who'd helped during my second stint in detention, such as Endo and Mr. Ono (UN), as well as other friends like Takahashi and Professor Miyawaki. I tried contacting each of them before leaving Australia. Endo didn't return my emails and I was unable to contact him via phone. Mr. Ono no longer works at the United Nations; I have no idea where he is. I did manage to contact Takahashi by phone. Even though I offered to meet him in his local area, he declined, saying he was too busy to catch up.

It's interesting (and sad) how time separates people.

I had two successes, though: I met with Professor Miyawaki as well as Professor Michael Fox.

I didn't contact Asuka for obvious reasons.

While in Japan, I took my constant companion (my camera) everywhere. I visited the Nishi-Nihom Immigration Centre (at night!) to film from the outside. I also took footage of Sakai Church and Shelter House. Nobody was around, except a gardener.

It felt good to go back there without a worry. It felt strange, too. I wondered why my previous time in Japan couldn't have been as easy! Friends still living there tell me life is changing. Police stop them more regularly on the street, asking to see their Alien Registration card or passport, and the numbers of foreigners being deported or jailed appears to be on the rise. Since "9/11," fear of foreigners in Japan seems to have increased.

My experiences have taught me to trust myself and my instincts, no matter if doing this seems to make life harder. Thank God I did.

Eritrea, my country of birth, has also been one of my recent destinations. With ongoing conflict between Ethiopia and Eritrea, there are no direct flights between the two countries so I had to enter via Kenya. It was a very sad arrival. I have such vivid memories of the place from my childhood. It was so sophisticated, so beautiful. While much of its beauty is still intact, it feels unloved and uncared for; the harsh times of recent years have only frayed into neglect. Secret undercover officials roam the streets, people line up for bread in the mornings, and daily life is carried out under the watchful eye of the Communist government.

It feels unjust. The fascists were cast out of Eritrea twice. It was there that the triumphant defiance rose up against Mengistu's Communist regime in Ethiopia. Whereas Ethiopia was for a long time like a motherless child, Eritrea was like everyone's whore—so many foreign invasions using her to their own ends, then leaving her to the next.

Now, there is fear and still some defiance. There's been an inconsolable loss of lives to that long war for independence. The survivors dare not degrade the memory of those heroes by caving in now, even though hardship dusts down their days.

I know of a man who was walking along the street, complaining to his brother about the high price of sugar. Unbeknown to him an undercover police officer was close by and overheard his comments.

"Excuse me," said the police officer politely. He escorted the man away, leaving his brother standing in bewilderment.

No one heard from the man for days. Everyone feared the worst. When he finally returned home, they were full of questions over what happened.

"Oh, I was so scared," the man replied. "They took me to the interrogation room. Then they force-fed me sugar all this time! Can you believe it? The police officer asked if I was so worried about the price of sugar now, since there was plenty for me. Of course, I agreed with him. Anything to get out of there."

His friends were aghast. "That must have been terrible!"

"Are you kidding?" he interrupted. "Just imagine if I'd been complaining about the price of chillies!"

Even in trying times, there is laughter.

While in Eritrea, I caught up with Father Thomas (from the Gurage mission), who was now living in the village of Barantu, where he was born. He has become Bishop of Barantu. I made the long journey to see him and hoped that he would still have some of my childhood photos from the mission. He just waved his hands in the air and told me he had too many photos and it would take him a long time to go through and find ones that might be of me. After travelling such a long way, I was disappointed that he didn't at least look. Still, it was heartening to see him.

My only other hope for some childhood photos was with Father Simon, one of the Gurage mission priests who is now living in Eritrea. I sought him out, only to commiserate with him on the loss of his house to fire. All his possessions, including photographs he'd kept over the years, were ash.

This trip to Eritrea represented a reconnection through respect for all who'd suffered from Solomon's harm. There was my stepmother, Saba, still as warm and loving as ever. Although I only gave her very short notice of my arrival, she welcomed me into her home like a son.

My stepbrothers, Mehari and Tinsae, still live with her and they too treated me kindly during my visit. They were grateful that I made the effort to visit (it was risky for me to travel to Eritrea) and proudly introduced me to their friends and neighbours as their brother. We reminisced over our childhood and laughed as we recounted their mischievous adventures.

Saba then took me on a long bus ride to the mountains in Keren to see my youngest stepbrother, Johannes, who had been imprisoned by the government. The prison was off the beaten track, set deep in the mountain.

I cried when I saw him. He's been locked up for several years now, without trial; he has no idea when he will be released. His crime? Trying to flee Eritrea while being conscripted. The war was too much for him to bear.

On a happier note, my stepsister Senait worked for the government as a television news reader. Through her work, she met and married an American journalist and they are now living together in America.

While relationships with my stepmother and stepsiblings are good, the same cannot be said for my encounters with Solomon's brothers and sisters. Like so many times during my childhood, their interfering dominated during my Eritrean visit.

Wolf-lady Aunt Almaz and her sister, Ruta, were upset to learn that I was writing about the family. (Funny that—do you think they have something to fear?) I'd always told Aunt Almaz that one day I would write it all down, but I don't think she ever believed me. Now, upon seeing it come to fruition, she was very angry indeed.

I only wanted to gather further information into our ancestry and build a greater understanding of who my father really was and why he behaved so badly towards me, but instead his siblings took it as a personal attack on the family. Being proud Ertireans, they began making threats towards me in defence of their honour.

I was shocked, deeply shocked.

Aunt Elsa phoned from America threatening legal action, which didn't really upset me because I knew I was writing the truth and their reactions were validation of that fact.

I did start to worry, though, when Tinsae pulled me aside early one morning and told me to be careful because there was a very real chance that Aunt Elsa (whose husband has well-connected relatives in Eritrea) would have me arrested. Knowing the system in Eritrea, I would never see the light of day again . . . all those years of struggling for freedom would have been for nothing. Not even Australian citizenship could save me from that.

The meddling of my aunts made Tinsae question my intentions. Sometimes he would tell me, "So long as it's the truth, just write it." But then, at other times (after wolf-lady had whispered in his ear) he would say, "The past is the past. You should just forget it and move on."

But how can we forget something so painful? I felt we'd all benefit from confronting our past and discussing the memories of my father. How wrong I was. When Tinsae suggested one day that I was fabricating stories, a piece of my heart broke. I realised that he didn't understand, nor did he want to. I fear losing the relationships with Tinsae and my other stepsiblings by publishing this memoir, but I refuse to pretend that these things didn't happen. No one should live in a state of numbness.

While all these crazy threats were flying around me, I took time out to reflect. Strange as it was, each morning, I woke up in Doctor Solomon's house. His graduation photo with Mengistu was on the wall. I looked at it each day, trying to understand this man who made my life so hard. I considered the lives of my stepbrothers: full of fear, anger and instability. I used to envy them so much as a child, but now I wonder, if I'd grown up as part of their family, would I have turned out like them? Would I, too, have a bleak future?

After Solomon's deportation, he never regained the social status or affluence that he'd enjoyed in Ethiopia. His family had to accept a drastic downgrade in living circumstances, and upon his death he left them with no security.

I'm sad that my father's family are struggling now, but somehow I don't believe I would still be suffering with them, even if in the same circumstances. It's not that I think I am better or above them; I'm just different. I can't accept that whatever happens to us is God's will. I believe it's not completely in God's hands; we have the power to shape our own lives. It may take years and it may not be easy but, slowly, slowly, things will change.

After almost a month's visit, I was fortunate to escape Eritrea without arrest. My domineering aunts incited the others into bullying and threats. They only allowed me to leave Eritrea after demanding that I sign a document stating that I would not shame the family name in this book. If telling the truth brings shame, then it is not of my doing but of those who have behaved without integrity.

Only recently, Senait contacted me from America. Her tone was accusatory as she rescinded her support for my efforts to uncover the truth. She insinuated that I was lying and manipulating, using the family for my own gains, shunning them (the very conditions that I had endured!), and not caring that Adey Selas had just died.

This last news brought such a wave of sadness that I still feel swamped. Compounding that, I was rocked at Senait's complete turnabout. I felt we had such a good connection. I assumed that since she was a journalist, living in America, she would have broader views. But, despite my efforts to explain that my intentions were to release us from the infected resentment instigated by our father, her retaliation grew even more vicious.

I can only surmise that a certain aunt has stirred everyone against me. I am deeply saddened, of course, more so because they have rallied through fear and residual anger over Solomon's impoverished legacy. In all humility, I simply wanted to liberate them.

There are all kinds of prisons. Perhaps the imprisonment of the heart is the worst.

When a culture perpetrates destructive behaviour for the sake of protecting the father's name—no matter his conduct—that culture is corrupt. My situation is not unique. Allowing a corrupt culture to continue will bring harm to generation after generation. Children will suffer under the burden of their elders' lack of integrity.

Historically, Ethiopia was seen as an innovative African nation. Sadly, that quality was undermined by decades of fear, famine and failure. Generations have held feebly to their traditions because all potential for growth was ripped away.

Yet, the modern world invites new experiences. It presents new opportunities. There is much to be shared, if only we can step beyond our fear. My research reveals strong tribal connections between groups that now fight as enemies. We will never lose our great heritage, but surely it is better to find ways of celebrating it rather than using it as a weapon, needlessly beating each other.

I do not write my story to claim a personal victory. It is my heartfelt desire to speak for those who cannot. For all the wonderful aspects of my culture, there is much that needs to change. For all the goodness I now experience in Australia, there is unawareness here, too. We must liberate ourselves from ignorant, stubborn traditions that harm our children and limit our own abilities to thrive.

On each side of the ocean, within the core of each nation, within the heart of each person we can offer the best of ourselves. We can learn and grow together. We can liberate our children from hindered thinking so that they appreciate life and value each other. Each one can speak out. Every person can be a voice against suffering. With knowledge, with integrity, with wisdom, we can make the world a better place—for all.

I return to the Horn of Africa regularly to film short documentaries. In September 2007, I was in Ethiopia to record the millennium celebrations. This was a very symbolic celebration for me. While Ethiopia was welcoming the new millennium, I was closing that chapter of my African past. My life was elsewhere . . . in Australia, with my Ani. My heart now beats to a different, more contented rhythm because after all the searching, yearning and despair, I have finally found my kind of heaven.

Time Line

Ethiopian history incorporating Teddy's journey

971–931 BCE	Reign of King Solomon; he is visited by the Queen Makeda of Sheba (her kingdom included ancient Ethiopia and Eritrea).
950 –BCE (circa)	Menelik I (King Solomon and Queen Makeda's son) becomes the first Jewish emperor, builds the Aksumite Empire (also known as Abyssinia) and establishes the Solomonic Dynasty; massive obelisks are raised in northern Ethiopia announcing to the world the authority and power of the ruling families.
4th century CE	The kingdom converts to Christian Orthodox religion when one of the huge obelisks in Aksum collapses, signalling the end of paganism.
6th century CE	Prophet Mohammed's daughter and her successor flee persecution in Arabia and receive refuge in Ethiopia, peaceably establishing Islam among Abyssinians.
7th century CE	Islamic groups overtook the trade routes with Europe and Asia, causing decline of the excluded Axumite Empire.
10th century CE	Semi-legendary Gudit is said to have ruled as queen for forty years after killing the emperor. She laid waste to the countryside, destroying churches and monuments and isolating various provinces. A royal infant was smuggled to freedom and through him, the original lineage continued.
13th century CE	The Solomonic dynasty regained the

throne, uniting the provinces of Tigray (north), Amhara (central) and Shewa (south).

1490   The king of Portugal sent a letter to the emperor, acknowledging the importance of the kingdom as the eastern-most home of Christianity. Portuguese missions were established.

1507–1543   Under threat and subsequent invasion from Muslims, the emperor requested and received aid from Portugal. After conflicts were resolved, the Christian Orthodox emperor continued to acknowledge Islam as one of his country's religions.

1755–1855   The Age of Princes; Teddy's ancestor (Ras Tesfasion) breaks with tradition and distributes land to each child.

1855   Emperor Tewodros II unites the warring tribal chiefs and forms modern Ethiopia (which includes Eritrea).

1880s   Britain and Italy vie for power over the Horn of Africa; Italy claims the northern regions, including Eritrea.

1888–1892   The Great Famine claims almost one-third of the population.

1889–1913   Emperor Menelik II's rule. Teddy's great-grandmother's family lose their land to repossession by the emperor.

1889   Emperor Menelik II grants Italy the region that later becomes Eritrea in exchange for the right to import arms.

1896   Frustrated with Italy's attempts at expansion, Menelik defeats Italy in The Battle of Adwa; Italy withdraws to occupy Eritrea.

1911–1912   Tripoli war; Teddy's great-grandfather, Reda, is conscripted into the Italian army to fight in Libya,

	and is killed in action.
1911*	Reda's son Fekadu is born.
1914–1918	World War I.
1930	Emperor Haile Selassie's reign begins.
1936–1941	Second Italo-Abyssinian War.
1939–1945	World War II; Mussolini is defeated in his attempt to invade Ethiopia; Italians are ousted altogether.
1941	Eritrea under British administration.
1951	UN oversees a federation between Eritrea and Ethiopia.
1961–1991	Eritrean War of Independence; rebels begin protests against Imperial rule.
1962	Emperor Haile Selassie dissolves the federation and attempts to annex Eritrea; a bitter civil war ensues.
1970*	Fekadu dies of liver disease in Asmara, Eritrea.
1971	Teddy is born in Asmara, Eritrea.
1973	Large-scale famine grips northern Ethiopia; Emperor Haile Selassie's inadequate crisis management leads to the downfall of the Imperial government.
1974	Colonel Mengistu leads the Soviet-backed Dergue to overthrow Emperor Selassie and establishes communist rule in Ethiopia; civil war is ongoing as Eritrea continues to fight for independence.
1974	Bishkash and Teddy flee from Eritrea to Ethiopia
1974	Lucy, the oldest known bipedal skeleton, is discovered in Afar, northern Ethiopia.
1977–1978	The Red Terror genocide and the Ethiopian-Somali War.
1979	Teddy is sent to Eritrea to live with Adey Selas.
1982	Ethiopia-Somali border war.

* Approximate.

1982	Teddy is sent to live with his father Solomon.
1984–1985	Widespread famine in Ethiopia and Eritrea draws international attention.
1991	Colonel Mengistu's regime is toppled by the rebel alliance; he flees to Zimbabwe.
1991	Teddy moves to Egypt.
1993	Eritrean referendum for independence; 99% majority of voters in favour; Eritrea becomes independent.
1997	Teddy travels to Japan and applies as a refugee to the Australian Embassy.
1997–1999	Teddy is sent to detention after being caught working on a tourist visa.
1998–2000	Border dispute forces another Ethiopian–Eritrean War.
2000	Teddy meets Anita in Osaka.
2002–2003	Teddy is detained for the second time.
2003	Teddy moves to the Gold Coast, Australia; he marries Anita.
2005	Teddy and Anita travel to Ethiopia together for the first time.
2006	Colonel Mengistu is tried in absentia for genocide and sentenced to death; he remains in Zimbabwe protected by President Mugabe.
2006	Solomon passes away.
2006–2009	Ethiopian–Somalian war (ongoing).
2007	Teddy returns to Ethiopia for the millennium celebrations (the Ethiopian calendar dates differ from the international Gregorian calendar).
2007–2008	Ethiopian–Ogaden civil war.
2008	Teddy visits Solomon's family in Eritrea and Bishkash in Ethiopia.
2009	Adey Selas passes away.

AUSTRALIAN EMBASSY
TOKYO

Mr Tewodros Solomon Fekadu
c/o 4-402-1, Hamadera Motomachi,
Sakai city, Osaka 592-4383

Dear Mr Fekadu,

I refer to your letter which we received by fax on 01/02/2002 in response to our notice of cancellation dated 25/01/2002.

In order for us to make a decision as to whether there are grounds to revoke the cancellation, we would like to seek your further comments on the allegations made by third parties.

The information given was that you were involved in setting up a business in Japan in partnership with a person, who had given you quite a sum of money to help you start the business. It was their understanding that this never happened and when you were asked to return the money to the person involved, you told the person that the money had been transferred to an overseas account and could not be withdrawn unless either you or the person physically travelled to that country to request withdrawal. The person claims that the money has not been given back, although the person made requests on several occasions.

The person also alleged that you stated you intended to go into a false marriage to obtain residency in Australia and divorce after 2-year period. The person also alleges you failed to correctly inform the Japanese Immigration Bureau and your guarantor details regarding your place of residence and place of employment, which lead the guarantor to withdraw their support. We have been able to contact your former guarantor who has confirmed that this allegation is correct.

Please provide your comments in writing in regards to the above issues and any additional information you feel that the delegate ought to be aware of and take into account within 49 days from the date of this letter. If you do not respond by 26/04/2002, a decision on whether there are grounds to revoke cancellation of your visa will be made using information already held by the Department.

Yours sincerely,

Immigration
8 March 2002

Department of Immigration and Multicultural and Indigenous Affairs

2-1-14 Mita, Minato-ku, Tokyo 108-8361, Japan
Telephone: 03 5232 4111   Fax: 03 5232 4173

Family, Friends & Foes

Book One: The Quest

A

Abel	uncle; father's side
Afwerke	relative; mother's side
Alganesh	grandmother; mother's side
Almaz	aunt; father's side
Alula	childhood friend in Tigray
Asfehet	Bishkash's friend in Bure
Asmhet	Eritrean lady who accommodates Teddy

B

Belachew	stepfather (married to Bishkash)
Belaynesh	landlord in Addis Ababa
Bishkash	mother
Bisrat	cousin; mother's side
Brinesh	cousin; mother's side
Brother Mengestabe	head of Dese mission; Father Tesfaldete's replacement

D

Dereje	friend at Holy Saviour Church, Addis Ababa

E

Egegayhu	cousin; mother's side (Nigisti's sister)
Elias	tenant at Franco's house

519

| Elsa | aunt; father's side |
| Emanuel | Dese mission layperson |

F

Father Dalloi	Gurage school director; acquaintance of Solomon
Father Daniel	acquaintance of Solomon
Father Desta	Holy Saviour Church priest, Addis Ababa
Father Franco	Gurage school director; Father Dalloi's replacement
Father Habtemariam	Gurage parish priest
Father Tekle	Gurage priest; Father Dalloi's replacement
Father Tesfamariam	head of Gurage mission; Father Thomas's replacement
Father Tesfaldete	head of Dese mission; acquaintance of Solomon
Father Thomas	head of Gurage mission
Fekadu	grandfather; father's side
Franco	Padre Roberto's Italian friend

H

Habtamu	stepbrother; mother's side
Hanna	Mengestabe's niece and receptionist
Hailu	church deacon in Addis Aaba
Habte	tenant at Franco's house
Hennock	stepbrother; mother's side

J

| Johannes | stepbrother; father's side |

K

Kidest	stepsister; mother's side
Kiros	cousin; Mebrat's son

L

Lebnar	Egyptian agent

M

Mebrat	cousin; mother's side
Mehari	stepbrother; father's side
Melaku	friend in Bure
Meles	Solomon's friend
Mengestabe	medical technician; Solomon's business partner
Meseret	aunt; Asmerom's wife
Mesfen	friend at Holy Saviour Church, Addis Ababa
Mohammed	Gurage bully
Ms. Aida	Italian visitor to Gurage mission
Mulu	stepsister; mother's side

N

Nigisti	cousin; mother's side (Egegayhu's sister)

P

Padre Roberto	Italian priest at Holy Saviour Church, Addis Ababa

R

Ras Tesfasion	ancestor; father's side

Reda	great-grandfather; father's side
Reem	Tigrayan lady at detention camp
Robel	uncle; Saba's brother
Ruta	aunt; father's side

S

Saba	stepmother; married to Solomon
Satoko	Japanese friend
Sereke	friend of Bishkash and Belachew's in Bure
Selas	grandmother (Adey); mother's side
Senait	stepsister; father's side
Sereke	friend of Bishkash's, Bure
Sister Jimma	morals and ethics teacher, Gurage
Solomon	father

T

Tariku	uncle; Aunt Almaz's brother-in-law
Tebeka	Gurage friend
Tesfaye	Dese mission layperson
Tinsae	stepbrother; Solomon's son
Turunesh	Gurage hostel cook

W

Werku	roommate in Cairo, Egypt

Z

Zenebech	great-grandmother; mother's side

Book Two: Far Horizons

A

Asuka Sato   supporter

B

Bashir   Sudanese detainee
Berga   Ethiopian/Eritrean detainee

C

Christina   Anita's Australian friend

D

Daniel   Eritrean friend from Kyoto
Doctor Kawashima   ear-nose-throat specialist
Doctor Werku   Ethiopian national; Teddy's friend

F

Father Paul   Australian priest
Father Michael-Angelo   Spanish priest
Father Mori   guarantor; Kaeda's brother

H

Hayley   Anita's Australian friend
Hige Sensei   detention centre officer

J

Jose   Peruvian fish factory worker; friend of
                                Satoko's

K

Karina	Anita's Australian friend
Kaeda Mori	supporter and later Tewodros' guarantor
Kojima	detention centre officer

L

Lemlem	Eritrean translator from Tokyo

M

Mario	Peruvian detainee
Mr. Choosin	UN representative (1st detention stint)
Mr. Ito	Amnesty International staff
Mr. Masashi	journalist; acquaintance of Mr. Suzuki
Mr. Mitchell	first Secretary, Australian Embassy, Tokyo (for first visa application with Anita)
Mr. Narito	lawyer for ear case
Mr. Ogawa	supporter
Mr. Ono	UN representative (second detention stint)
Mr. Shiho	Amnesty International member
Mr. Suzuki	Tokyo human rights lawyer and advisor to supporters
Mr. Tanaka	lawyer for refugee case
Mr. Tewolde	Eritrean ambassador
Mr. Woods	principle migration officer, Australian Embassy, Tokyo (for refugee visa application)
Mr. Yamamoto	policeman
Mr. Yamamura	Communist supporter of detainees
Ms. Fujii	Amnesty International staff
Ms. Hogan	first secretary, Australian Embassy (Mr.

	Mitchell's replacement)
Ms. Toyoda	Amnesty International staff
Ms. Yamada	migration secretary, Australian Embassy, Tokyo

N

| Natsumi | Asuka's friend; university lecturer |
| Noriko | church secretary |

S

Samuel	Ugandan detainee
Sato	Asuka's husband
Sharon	Anita's Australian friend
Steve	Anita's Australian friend
Sue	Anita's mother

T

| Tibashi | Kurdish-Iranian detainee |

Proverbs

Throughout different ages and diverse cultures, many wise observations about life have emerged. Perusing a vast choice, I list below those that I felt reflected specific points in my journey, though not all have been included in the final manuscript. They are grouped alphabetically under their place of origin.

AFRICAN

Being happy is better than being king.

However long the night, the dawn will break.

Until lions have their historians, tales of the hunt shall always glorify the hunter.

ARABIAN

Death feared him for he had the heart of a lion.

The whisper of a pretty girl can be heard further than the roar of a lion.

EGYPTIAN

It is written. If you change your fate, that too is written.

ERITREAN

A home without a mother is a desert.

While the wound stays hidden, the cure will hide.

ETHIOPIAN

A bird hanging between two branches will get bitten on both wings.

A cat may go to a monastery, but she still remains a cat.

A fool is thirsty in the midst of water.

A man who is too modest goes hungry.

A mouse that wants to die goes to sniff the cat's nose.

Anticipate the good so that you may enjoy it.

A person who has too much will start to chew porridge.

Clothes put on while one is running come off while running.

Confiding a secret to an unworthy person is like carrying grain in a
     bag with a hole in it.

Evil enters like a needle and spreads like an oak tree.

He who digs too deep for a fish may come out with a serpent.

If relatives help each other, what evil can hurt them?

If you gladly stoop to the ground, don't be surprised if they trample
     over you.

It is better to be the cub of a live jackal than of a dead lion.

It is like using a spoon to get water from the Nile.

Little by little, an egg will walk.

Move your neck according to the music.

Oh, old hyena, eat me without making excuses.

One scoops with a scoop.

One who recovers from sickness soon forgets about God.

Pride is no substitute for a dinner.

Singing "Hallelujah" everywhere does not prove piety.

Sitting is being crippled.

The cow is only as good as the pasture in which it grazes.

The dog I bought bit me; the fire I kindled burned me.

The eye of the leopard is on the goat, and the eye of the goat is on
     the leaf.

The first camel in the train holds everyone up, but it is the last
     which gets the beating.

The sky is so close for him who sits.

The son of the Nile thirsts for water.

Unless you call out, who will open the door?

What one hopes for is always better than what one has.

When a fool is cursed, he thinks he is being praised.

When one is in love, a cliff becomes a meadow.

When spiders unite, they can tie down a lion.

Where there is no shame, there is no honour.

You cannot build a house for last year's summer.

JAPANESE

Entering the village, obey the village.

Fall seven times and stand up eight.

It is better to travel hopefully than to arrive disenchanted.

One kind word can warm three winter months.

Sit on a stone for three years.

The nail that sticks up gets hammered down.

The tongue is but three inches long, yet it can kill a man six feet high.

REFERENCES TO LIONS

A lion, mighty among beasts, retreats at nothing.

—From *The Wisdom of King Solomon*, Proverbs 30:30

Lion with endurable heart, suffer the unendurable.

—Herodotus, Greek philosopher, c. 484–424 BCE

It is better to be a lion for a day, than a sheep all your life.

—Elizabeth Kenny, Australian physical therapist, 1880–1952

Oh to renew the dream that a lion has dreamed till the wilderness cried aloud.

—WB Yeats, Irish poet, 1862–1942

Glossary

A

Abba (Amharic)	Father; shortened term of reverence for a priest
Abbata (Amharic)	Father; term of reverence for a priest
Aboy (Tigrinya)	Mister; polite greeting for an older gentleman
Aboykeshie (Tigrinya)	Father; term of reverence for a priest
Adey (Tigrinya)	term of endearment for grandmother
Agame (Tigrinya)	outsider; refers to a village in Tigray, but used to insult
Agante (Amharic)	devil
Ambasha (Tigrinya)	tasty spiced bread
Amhara (Amharic)	tribe from central Ethiopia
Amharic (Amharic)	the national language of Ethiopia
Anchi gered (Amharic)	"Hey maid"
Ane seb iye (Tigrinya)	"I am a human being"
Ante anjebegna (Amharic)	"You're are stuck-up"
Aow (Amharic)	"Yes"
Ara! (Amharic)	"Why!"; an exclamation of surprise
Argeman (Amharic)	tribal elder
Arif leg (Amharic)	a cool boy
Ata, baallaga (Tigrinya)	"You misbehaving child"

B

Baallaga (Amharic)	ill-mannered
Baqqa (Amharic)	be enough; that's all
Berbere (Amharic)	red chilli powder
Beles (Tigrinya)	cactus fruit

Ben venuto (Italian)	"Welcome"
Beso (Amharic)	wheat
Budha (Amharic)	evil spirit, thought to possess

C

Cadre (Italian)	military personnel
Carnivale (Italian)	Italian carnival
Cashi (Tigrinya)	coptic priest
Chat (Amharic)	mildly intoxicating chewable leaf; common in Ethiopia, but illegal in Eritrea

D

Doro wet (Amharic)	spicy chicken curry
Durrayye (Amharic)	hoodlum; hooligan

E

Ebd (Amharic)	crazy man
Ebna la-Hakim (Arabic)	Son of the Wise
Enste (Amharic)	false banana plant
Eshie (Amharic)	okay
Etan (Amharic, Tigrinya)	frankincense
Eway! Eway! (Tigrinya)	"Oh my Lord! Oh my Lord!"

G

Gabi (Amharic)	a handmade blanket-like cotton cloth used to wrap around the body
Gaijin (Japanese)	foreigner
Ganbatte (Japanese)	"good luck"
Geat (Tigrinya)	barley or wheat porridge, often served

	with butter and a spicy sauce
Ge'ez (Amharic)	Ethiopia's classical language
Guraginya (Amharic)	the local dialect of Gurageland, Ethiopia
Gurorro (Amharic)	throat

H

Habesha (Amharic)	of Ethiopian/Abyssinian descent
Habibi (Arabic)	"My friend"
Hai (Japanese)	"Yes"
Haiyaku! (Japanese)	"Hurry up!"
Hanko (Japanese)	name stamp, used in place of a signature

I

Ilay (Amharic)	upper
In bocca al lupo (Italian)	"Good luck"
Ine sew negn (Amharic)	"I am a human being'"
Injera (Amharic)	flat pancake-like bread made from teff
Insha'Allah (Arabic)	God willing
Itach (Amharic)	lower

J

Jebena (Amharic)	clay coffee pot

K

Kebale (Amharic)	local council/government authority/district
Kebra Nagast (Amharic)	Glory of Kings: the tome that records the history of the Solomonic dynasty
Keber (Amharic)	respect; honour

Keisatsu (Japanese)	police
Kella (Amharic)	checkpoint/toll station
Kitcha (Tigrinya):	thin bread made from wheat; a staple food in Eritrea
Kitfo (Amharic)	spicy minced beef dish
Kitsune (Japanese)	fox

L

Leba (Amharic)	thief
Leg (Amharic)	boy
Laissez-passer (French)	one-way travel document issued by a national government or an international treaty organisation.

M

Macchiato (Italian)	coffee beverage
Manshon (Japanese)	apartment
Meqseft (Amharic)	curse; calamity; catastrophe
Metab (Amharic)	small woven leather cross on a cord
Melqeqiya (Amharic)	identification certificate
Men ika? (Tigrinya)	"Who is it?"
Menkai (Japanese)	interview
Merigata (Amharic)	Head of God
Meskel (Amharic, Tigrinya)	Cross (religious festival)
Mesob (Amharic)	hourglass-shaped tables hand-woven from coloured straw
Miso (Japanese)	Japanese soup

N

Nakfa (Tigrinya)	Eritrean currency
Netela (Amharic)	a shawl-like piece of cloth, used to

wrap around the shoulders and over
the head

O

Ohayo (Japanese) "Good morning"

R

Ras (Amharic,Tigrinya) duke; chief; prince

S

Sakura (Japanese) Japanese cherry blossom
Selam alaykum! (Arabic) Peace be upon you!
Selam (Amharic,Tigrinya) hello
Seytan (Amharic,Tigrinya) devil, demon
Shifta (Amharic) rebel; outlaw; bandit
Shai (Amharic) spiced tea
Shiro (Amharic,Tigrinya) spiced chickpea stew
Suk beli! (Tigrinya) "Shut-up!"
Sukoshi (Japanese) a little
Suwa (Tigrinya) home-made barley beer

T

Tabot (Amharic,Tigrinya) replica of the Ark of the Covenant,
kept in the inner sanctuary of every
Orthodox church
Tabete (Japanese) eat
Tamot (Tigrinya) afternoon snack
Tanuki (Japanese) Japanese raccoon dog
Tatami (Japanese) straw-like flooring
Teff (Amharic) an Ethiopian grain
Testa (Tigrinya) head

Tigrinya (Tigrinya)	the national language of Eritrea
Tokubetsu zairyo kyoka (Japanese)	Special Permission for Residence
Tsugi wa dare? (Japanese)	"Who's next?"

V

Va bene? (Italian)	"Okay?"

Y

Yakuza (Japanese)	mafia
Ye shermouta leg (Amharic)	son of a bitch
Ye materrba leg (Amharic)	useless boy

Bibliography

Appiah, Kwame Anthony & Gates Jr, Henry Louis, *The Encyclopedia of the African and African American Experience,* Basic Citivas Books, New York, 1999.

Bilkuei, Cola, *Cola's Journey: From Sudanese child soldier to Australian refugee,* Macmillan, Sydney, Australia, 2008.

Browning, Valerie & Little, John, *Maalika: My life among the Afrar nomads of Africa,* Macmillan, Sydney, Australia, 2008.

Cunxin, Li, *Mao's Last Dancer,* Penguin, Australia, 2003.

De Waal, Alex, *Famine Crimes: Politics & the Disaster Relief Industry in Africa,* African Rights and the International African Institute, 1997.

Hamlin, Catherine & Little, John, *The Hospital by the River: A story of hope,* Macmillan, Sydney, Australia, 2001.

Hirsi Ali, Ayaan, *Infidel: My life,* Free Press, New York, 2007.

Henze, Paul B, *Layers of Time: a history of Ethiopia,* Palgrave, New York, 2000.

Mezlekia, Nega, *Notes from the Hyena's Belly,* Picador, New York, 2000.

Wiredu, Kwasi; Abraham, William E; Irele, Abiola & Menkiti, Ifeanyi, *A Companion to African Philosophy,* Wiley-Blackwell, Hoboken, NJ, 2004.

Acknowledgements

As a child I collected names, dates and pieces of information, and then later, I scrawled my experiences on paper in detention, but I never realised that writing a book would in itself be such a journey.

There are so many people who have helped me along the bumpy road that is life. Some have been mentioned in my memoirs, others have not, but all will be forever etched in my mind.

In particular, I would like to make special mention of the following people.

To my great-grandmother Zenebech, whose soft warm arms made me feel safe and loved as a child. To my grandmother, Adey Selas, for your compassion and understanding, and to my mother, Bishkash, for your strength and honesty. To Brinesh, my mother and I will be forever grateful that you took us in and cared for us like members of your family.

To Saba, you are truly lovely.

To my step-brothers and sisters. I was an outsider as a child, but thank you for embracing me into your families as we have matured. Thank you for your insight and assistance with information for my my book. In particular, Habtamu, for your assistance with researching our mother's family history—a difficult task in a culture where little is written down.

Dear Padre Roberto, words cannot express how much I appreciate your patience and unwavering generosity over the years. I would hate to think where I would be if it wasn't for you. Heartfelt thanks also to Father Tesfaldete, Father Thomas and Father Dalloi, Father Habtemariam, Sister Jimma, Sister Nevas, Sister Chilinya, Sister Hiwot, and Father Desta. Each of you reached out to me in my times of need. It has not been forgotten.

To Uncle Asmerom, Robel, Hailu, Hanna, Mengestabe, Sarah, Elsa, Alemsehaye. Thank you for making my life better in some way.

To my friends who endured the unendurable with me: Bashir, Berga, Mario, Tibashi, and Johannes; and those who supported us on the journey, in particular, Mr. Yamamura, Mr. Ono (UN), Ms. Arima (UN), Endo, Megumi, Takahashi, Miyawaki, Michael Fox, Rachel, Maravic, and Kuboi.

Thanks to my first group of supporters at Sakai and Tamatsukuri churches, my lawyers, and Amnesty International.

To those who have helped me here in Australia.

To Anita's family for their faith in Anita and their support while I was in detention in Japan and for their patience and encouragement in the writing of this book. To our late and great Uncle Leo, for helping Anita when I was stuck behind bars.

To George, for your company and encouragement over beers.

To our dear friend and word wizard, Sidhe Kin-Wilde. I couldn't have done it without you, your magic wand or your constant support. Thank you.

Author

Tewodros was born in Eritrea in 1971 and lived his childhood between relatives' houses and the streets of Ethiopia. He has since lived in five countries on three continents and is fluent in four languages (Amharic, Tigrinya, Japanese and English).

He arrived in Australia in 2003 and now resides on the Gold Coast with his wife, Anita, where he is an active member of the community. He founded the African Communities Association Gold Coast Inc. and was president for five years. The aim of the association is to share African traditions and heritage through performance, education and training programs, and festivals.

He also works with a number of community-based organisations, volunteering his time to assist with the resettlement of African refugees to the Gold Coast.

Tewodros' company, Moonface Entertainment, works on films and documentaries related to East Africa. He regularly returns to Africa to shoot footage for his projects.

ABOUT THE TYPE

This book was set in ITC New Baskerville, a typeface based on the types of John Baskerville (1706-1775), an accomplished printer from Birmingham, England. The excellent quality of his printing influenced such famous printers as Didot in France and Bodoni in Italy. Baskerville produced a masterpiece folio Bible for Cambridge University, and today, his types are considered to be fine representations of eighteenth century rationalism and neoclassicism. This ITC New Baskerville was designed by Matthew Carter and John Quaranda in 1978.

Designed by John Taylor-Convery
Composed at JTC Imagineering, Santa Maria,CA